FUGITIVE JUSTICE

FUGITIVE JUSTICE

Runaways, Rescuers, and Slavery on Trial

STEVEN LUBET

THE BELKNAP PRESS OF HARVARD UNIVERSITY PRESS

Cambridge, Massachusetts • London, England • 2010

Library of Congress Cataloging-in-Publication Data
Lubet, Steven.
  Fugitive justice : runaways, rescuers, and slavery on trial / Steven Lubet.
      p. cm.
  Includes bibliographical references and index.
  ISBN 978-0-674-04704-4 (alk. paper)
  1. Trials (Treason)—United States.   2. United States. Fugitive slave law (1850).   3. Fugitive
slaves—Legal status, laws, etc.—United States.   4. Slavery—Law and legislation—United
States.   5. Antislavery movements—United States.   6. Loring, Edward G. (Edward Greely),
1802–1890. I. Title.
  KF221.P6L83 2010
  342.7308'7—dc22

                                                                                    2010012950

To Sarah Nomi

CONTENTS

FUGITIVE JUSTICE

INTRODUCTION

From the days of John Marshall to the outcome of *Bush v. Gore,* American political and social institutions have been deeply influenced by judicial decisions. Some landmark decisions of the U.S. Supreme Court have become so influential and famous (or infamous) that they can be recalled by the name of a single party: *Marbury, Dred Scott, Lochner, Korematsu, Brown, Miranda, Roe.* Most cases, of course, no matter how momentous, never reach the rarified precincts of the Supreme Court. Rather, they begin and end in the far more chaotic and uncertain environment of a trial courtroom, where a judge, a jury, and the public first encounter the facts of the case.

By their nature, trials are almost always far less significant than Supreme Court decisions, seldom affecting anyone other than the parties themselves. Even the numerous so-called trials of the century—from the Lindbergh kidnapping to the prosecution of O. J. Simpson—usually became notorious only because of the celebrities involved and the near-prurient subject matter.

Only a relative handful of trials have had a broader impact on American politics and culture—perhaps the Scottsboro case, the Scopes Monkey Trial, the Chicago Seven, and the first Rodney King case. One might add the treason trial of Aaron Burr and the impeachment of Andrew Johnson, but the list is quite limited. Law and history are made by the Supreme Court, and in that context even a major trial is at most a preliminary event, and usually only a dramatic sideshow.

The decade before the Civil War, however, saw a series of tumultuous trials that contributed greatly to the growing discord between the free and slave states. In each of these cases, a fugitive slave escaped to the North, only to be tracked down by southern slave hunters. Under the Fugitive Slave Act of 1850, it was supposed to be a very simple matter for a slave catcher to obtain an "order of removal," authorizing the return of a runaway, but abolitionists and their allies often intervened. The resulting trials—some of "rescuers" and some of the slaves themselves—helped to build the antislavery movement in the

1

North, but they also outraged public opinion in the South, where they were seen as the product of a conspiracy against the "property rights" of slave owners. Thus, the reluctance of Northerners to comply with the Fugitive Slave Act was frequently cited as a grievance justifying secession.

The fugitive slave trials are inherently fascinating, built as they were around the vivid narratives of daring fugitives, devoted rescuers, and despicable slave catchers. They are historically significant for other reasons as well. First, they underscore the important role that slaves themselves played in exacerbating the tensions that led to the Civil War. Every Fugitive Slave Act case was generated by a slave who decided to take control of his or her own destiny, undertaking enormous risks for the sake of freedom. Of course, the runaways had no intention of appearing in court—they were hoping to avoid detection and to live in obscurity—but the simple act of absconding had the potential to lead to a trial, and the trials in turn created highly visible political platforms for antislavery agitators. Individual African-Americans played little part in antebellum congressional debates over the extenstion of slavery, or even on the battlefields of "Bleeding Kansas," but they were prime movers (if not vocal participants) in the fugitive slave trials that intensified the irrepressible conflict between North and South.

The fugitive slave trials also help us understand the way that law—as reflected in the tactics of practicing lawyers—can be influenced by public opinion. In the earliest trials, defense lawyers were reticent to challenge the legitimacy of the Fugitive Slave Act, which had been part of the grand Compromise of 1850. Supporters of the Act, including local prosecutors in most northern cities, argued adamantly, and not unconvincingly, that the rendition of fugitives was essential to the preservation of the Union. In that environment, even abolitionist lawyers understood that a frontal attack would be unavailing—both in the courtroom and in the court of public opinion—and they therefore tended to confine their defenses to less provocative factual claims. As the decade progressed, however, antislavery sentiment became much stronger in the North—prompted by such outrages as the Kansas-Nebraska Act and the *Dred Scott* decision—and lawyers' advocacy followed suit. By 1859, some lawyers were openly calling for judges and juries to embrace civil disobedience in the name of "higher law," which only stirred up more secessionism in the South.

Finally, the fugitive slave trials provide us with uncomfortable but meaningful insights into the nature of slavery itself. In form and structure, the trials were quite similar to modern cases. Apart from some differences in the rules of evidence, a contemporary reader might very easily imagine a comparable trial—over, say, stock fraud or homicide—occurring today. But while the components of the fugitive cases are all recognizable—opening statements, direct and cross-examinations, final arguments, jury instructions—much of the testimony is jarring. We read the words of slave catchers casually describing their jobs, detailing how they hunted their quarry, and explaining why the condemnation of a human being to slavery should be treated no more seriously than recovering a stray horse or cow. We see rulings in which a man's skin color—was he black or copper colored?—is a sufficient description to determine his fate. And in every case, we hear slavery described as a benevolent institution to which simpleminded fugitives would gladly return, if only the meddlesome abolitionists would stop interfering. Such words were not spoken on some benighted cotton plantation, nor in a secession-seeking southern legislature, but rather in northern courtrooms presided over by federal judges. With all apparent sincerity, those judges—including some who professed personal opposition to slavery—calmly considered whether human beings should be treated as property. We are thus both shocked and edified by the juxtaposition of familiar-seeming judicial proceedings with such grotesque abuses of human dignity. How could something so evil be treated so routinely by such otherwise fair-minded men? The answer tells us much about how deeply the institution of slavery had penetrated American government even in the free states.

This book tells the stories of three of the most important fugitive slave trials of the 1850s, which together illustrate the tremendous courage of the fugitives, the dedication of their rescuers and lawyers, and, alas, the inability of American legal and political institutions to come to grips with slavery short of civil war.

Abraham Lincoln was elected president of the United States on November 6, 1860, without receiving a single electoral vote in the South. By the following day, the nation was in turmoil, as bitter crowds throughout the slaveholding states held angry demonstrations against the president-elect's antislavery policies. Nowhere was the reaction more fierce than in South Carolina, where a huge throng cheered as an effigy of Lincoln was mounted on a scaffold and burned. Southern leaders had been threatening disunion for decades, but Lincoln's election turned rhetoric into a looming political reality.

Within a few weeks the South Carolina legislature called for a state convention to consider seceding from the Union. Meeting in Charleston on December 20, the convention unanimously passed a resolution dissolving "the union between the State of South Carolina and other States united with her under the compact entitled 'The Constitution of the United States of America.'" The Ordinance of Secession—a single paragraph of only 158 words—was signed in an elaborate ceremony before thousands of spectators, attended by marching bands and fireworks displays. Four days later, again acting unanimously, the convention approved the *Declaration of the Immediate Causes Which Induce and Justify the Secession of South Carolina from the Federal Union.*

That document recited a list of grievances and "encroachments" that would today be immediately recognized by even the most casual student of American history. The northern states had "denounced as sinful the institution of slavery" and allowed the establishment of abolitionist societies "whose avowed object is to disturb the peace" and to deprive Southerners of their property. And most recently, all of the northern states had

> united in the election of a man to the high office of President of the United States, whose opinions and purposes are hostile to slavery. He is to be entrusted with the administration of the common Government, because he has declared that that "Government cannot endure permanently half slave, half free," and that the public mind must rest in the belief that slavery is in the course of ultimate extinction.

But of all South Carolina's enumerated reasons for secession, the first listed, and the one elaborated at greatest length, was the refusal of the northern states to enforce the Fugitive Slave Act of 1850. Compared to Lincoln's determination to place slavery on the path to "ultimate extinction," it would seem to most modern readers that noncompliance with the Fugitive Slave Act should have been at worst a minor irritant, rather than the leading cause of secession. Repeal of the law had been proposed in Republican circles as a possible campaign issue, but the idea was rejected as too inflammatory, and it was not even mentioned in the party's 1860 platform. And in any event, the number of slaves who escaped to the North may have been as few as a thousand each year out of an enslaved population of about four million—with the great majority of the successful runaways coming from the border states of Maryland, Virginia, Kentucky, and Missouri. Only a relative handful of slaves ever could have gotten from South Carolina to the free states.[1]

Nonetheless, the South Carolina Declaration of Immediate Causes complained bitterly about northern perfidy in applying the Fugitive Slave Act. It was asserted that "fourteen of the States have deliberately refused, for years past, to fulfill their constitutional obligations" to "deliver up" fugitives upon the claims of their owners, and that "increasing hostility on the part of the non-slaveholding States to the institution of slavery, has led to a disregard of their obligations" under the federal fugitive statute. Thus, it was claimed, "the constituted compact has been deliberately broken and disregarded by the non-slaveholding States, and the consequence follows that South Carolina is released from her obligation."

The reality, however, was rather different. Judges in the free states had been, in the main, very careful to fulfill their responsibilities under the Fugitive Slave Act. Despite several highly publicized rescues, and a few court decisions in favor of fugitives and rescuers, the overwhelming majority of cases under the Act resulted in returning the fugitive to bondage. Of 191 known proceedings between 1850 and 1861, only 34 slaveholders' claims were denied. The other 157 men and women were remanded to slavery, usually with the cooperation of local officials, and in 68 cases with the assistance of federal authorities.[2] It is true that most northern states had enacted "personal liberty laws" to protect free blacks from legalized kidnapping, but jurisdictional disputes were almost always resolved in favor of the federal system, thus denying state courts any power to intervene.

Why, then, was the South Carolina secession convention so exercised over the problem of fugitive slaves? Indeed, why had the demand for the return of runaways generated so much friction on both sides of the Mason-Dixon Line, becoming a frequent cause célèbre in the North and a constant cri de coeur in the South?

———————

Most fugitive renditions proceeded efficiently and peacefully. In a small but significant number of cases, however, Southerners met with furious resistance when they attempted to reclaim "property" in a northern state. These cases became the subject of sharply politicized courtroom confrontations that pitted slavery opponents against slave owners and, to a greater or lesser extent, local authorities against the federal government.

Enforcing the Fugitive Slave Act of 1850 had become a point of honor for the South and the source of deep resentment for many in the North. Resistance to the Act took place both in the streets and in the courtrooms. Angry crowds, often led by free blacks, overwhelmed slave catchers and spirited their quarry to freedom. Lawyers, in turn, defended the rescuers or, when rescues failed, attempted legal maneuvers to defeat "removal" of the captured fugitives.

The dominant actors in the legal proceedings were, of course, lawyers and judges. Outside the courtrooms, political leaders on both sides of the slavery issue rallied their supporters and inveighed against their opponents, endeavoring to exploit the cases to their best advantage. Often the fugitives themselves may have seemed to fade into the background, treated as symbols in a far larger struggle. But in fact, the fugitives were central to the legal and political issues in ways that were not fully appreciated at the time. Escaping from slavery was always an act of individual courage and defiance, but the Fugitive Slave Act turned it into a political event as well.

Every time slave hunters apprehended a fugitive in a northern state, they became part of a small invasion, temporarily imposing slavery on otherwise free soil. Some runaways—including Frederick Douglass, Lewis Hayden, and Jermain Loguen—went on to become leaders of the abolitionist movement. But in one of history's great unintended consequences, the Fugitive Slave Act potentially empowered every absconding slave to provoke a minor confrontation between North and South. These tensions could only intensify as long as slaves continued to flee bondage and masters continued to demand their return.

To Southerners, anything less than the immediate rendition of fugitives amounted to a betrayal of the Compromise of 1850, which had been intended to provide a final resolution of the slavery question that threatened to destroy the Union. Under its terms, California was admitted to the Union as a free state, the slave trade was abolished in the District of Columbia, the New Mexico Territory was organized without any reference to slavery (neither allowing nor forbidding it), and a new, stronger fugitive slave law was enacted. For many southern leaders, the Fugitive Slave Act had been the most significant feature of the package, because it signified northern acceptance of slavery as a legitimate national institution. Resistance to the Act was therefore seen not merely as insulting and dishonorable, but also as a repudiation of the Union-saving compact and the Constitution itself.

Many Northerners, however, despised the Act for precisely the same reason. It represented the ultimate intrusion of slavery onto free soil, requiring not only that they tolerate the peculiar institution in the South, but also that they actively assist in arresting and detaining runaways. Under the Act, the free states could not be wholly free, because slave hunters had federal authorization to range at will among them. Slavery, therefore, ceased to be an abstraction—limited to the benighted southern states and some of the remote territories—but instead became an acute local concern from Massachusetts to Wisconsin. Within weeks of the Act's passage, committees were established in many northern cities with the avowed purpose of preventing the new law from taking effect and promising "bold action as well as fiery words."[3] There were celebrated rescues in Boston and Syracuse, where angry crowds, often led by free blacks, overwhelmed slave catchers and spirited their desperate quarry to freedom.

Cases inevitably came to court, almost always with prominent lawyers on both sides. From the beginning, prosecutors (and private lawyers for the slave owners) viewed the cases as intensely political, recognizing that resistance to the Fugitive Slave Act represented a challenge to the authority of the national government and therefore, as they explained it, to the viability of the Constitution itself. In many cases, local prosecutors received instructions directly from cabinet officers, and even from the president. Their legal arguments never failed to invoke the alleged "disloyalty" of rescuers and the dire consequences to the Union should the prosecutions fail.

Defense lawyers, in contrast, were compelled to walk a finer line, concerned at least as much for the fate of their individual clients as for the political ramifications of the case. As opposed as they might have been to slavery, defense counsel had to take account of the existing law, which had been specifically framed to protect slavery and to benefit slave owners. Purely as a tactical matter, a frontal assault on slavery could have led to disaster for a defendant, as federal judges showed little indulgence for fugitives and even less for resisters and rescuers. It is therefore unsurprising that the defense lawyers in the earliest trials tended to focus on technicalities, while downplaying the political significance of the cases and sometimes even disclaiming opposition to the fugitive law.

As the decade progressed, however, the issues became ever more sharply drawn. Developments such as the Kansas-Nebraska Act (repudiating the Missouri Compromise and expanding slavery into new territories) and the *Dred Scott* decision (observing that a black man had no rights that a white man was bound to respect), made northern opposition increasingly militant. Abolitionists such as William Lloyd Garrison had long condemned the Constitution, given its implicit recognition of slavery, as a "covenant with death" and an "agreement with Hell." More moderate slavery opponents, such as New York Senator William Seward, cautioned that there was a "higher law" than the Constitution.

Eventually the claims of the "higher law" found their way into courtrooms, as lawyers reflected the anger that was building in the North. It was an evolutionary process, however, with the tactics of defense counsel becoming more radical over the course of a decade. As we will see in the following chapters, the stories of three dramatic trials—in 1851, 1854, and 1859—convey the increasing militancy of antislavery lawyers and the eventual transformation of higher law from an abstract inspiration to an unapologetic legal defense.

In 1851 a white Pennsylvania miller named Castner Hanway faced treason charges based upon his alleged participation in the so-called Christiana slave riot, in which a Maryland slave owner had been killed while attempting to recapture several fugitives. In fact, Hanway's involvement had been peripheral. The actual rioters—or resistance fighters, as they should more accurately be called—had all been black, led by an escaped slave named William Parker. But Parker had fled to Canada, and Hanway provided an accessible target for a federal prosecutor determined to obtain at least one conviction for the outrage. Hanway was represented by a formidable group of attorneys, including Congressman Thaddeus Stevens, who was one of the most prominent antislavery lawyers in the United States. Stevens and his colleagues, however, were careful to keep the notion of abolitionism as far from the courtroom as possible. They accepted the legitimacy of the Fugitive Slave Act, and even the civic duty to apprehend runaways, while defending their client strictly on the basis of the facts. They conceded that resistance to the Fugitive Slave Act was unjustifiable, while arguing somewhat implausibly that Hanway had been only a bystander. The famously eloquent Stevens even chose to forgo addressing the jury, fearing that his well-known abolitionism would raise the specter of higher law.

By the spring of 1854, some lawyers had become far less willing to accept the legitimacy of the Fugitive Slave Act. In late May, the passage of the Kansas-Nebraska Act extended slavery into territories where it had previously been prohibited, thus undermining the basis of the Compromise of 1850 and calling into question the political premise of the Fugitive Slave Act itself. Outraged reactions to the Kansas-Nebraska Act were especially intense in Boston when, at the height of the political controversy, Anthony Burns was arrested as a fugitive slave. The city's abolitionist leaders rushed to Burns's defense, holding mass meetings and mounting an abortive rescue attempt in which a jail guard was killed. On the legal front, Burns was defended by Richard Henry Dana and Charles Ellis, both leading members of the antislavery bar. In a lengthy trial before a fugitive slave commissioner, Ellis and Dana argued that the enormity of sending a man into slavery obligated the court to "multiply" the ordinary burden of proof and thereby, in essence, to sidestep the harsh requirements of the Fugitive Slave Act. Although they were not quite ready to appeal openly to the higher law, Dana and Ellis clearly built their case around moral claims, asserting that "fundamental considerations of freedom and justice" required the court to stretch and reinterpret, or even to nullify, the statute in favor of freedom and against slavery. That was as close as any lawyers yet had come to asking for legalized resistance from the bench.

No attorney ever resorted to Garrisonian rhetoric in court—denouncing the Fugitive Slave Act as a statute from hell—but some came as close as nineteenth-century decorum would allow. In late 1858 a fugitive named John Price was captured by Kentucky slave hunters in the abolitionist stronghold of Oberlin, Ohio, and taken to the nearby town of Wellington. Students and faculty from Oberlin College learned of the arrest and hurried to Wellington, where they forcibly rescued the prisoner. Price was soon taken safely to Canada, but thirty-seven Oberlin rescuers were indicted for violations of the Fugitive Slave Act. The first two defendants—Simeon Bushnell, a white bookseller, and Charles Langston, a free black man who worked as a schoolteacher and journalist—were brought to trial in Cleveland the following spring. By this time, there had been killings in Kansas and the U.S. Supreme Court had issued its infamous *Dred Scott* decision, holding that a black man could not be a citizen of the United States. The "Slave Power" seemed in many ways ascendant, but that only heightened the militancy of the rescuers and their counsel. Defense attorney Albert Riddle drew gasps in the courtroom when he declared himself "a votary of the higher law," calling flatly for the court and jury simply to disobey the Fugitive Slave Act in order to free his clients. Even more stunning, defendant Charles Langston told the court that he repudiated the Fugitive Slave Act and would not hesitate to violate it in the name of higher law. That was perhaps the first time an African-American had claimed the right to civil disobedience as a legal defense.

Only a handful of fugitive arrests led to extended trials, and even fewer resulted in decisions in favor of runaway slaves or their supporters. But those celebrated cases, and the emergence of increasingly provocative justifications for resistance, infuriated the South Carolinians into accusing the northern states of violating their constitutional obligations to "deliver up" fugitives. As historian William Freehling explained, "Myth may convey a more significant reality than [the actual] count. Newspapers publicized the few Yankee defiances of the law. The many undramatic compliances went unnoticed."[4] Nonetheless, the secessionists had at least one thing right. The origin of the struggle— and the reason for its disproportionate impact on national politics—could be found in the Constitution itself.

∽ 1 ∾

SLAVERY AND THE CONSTITUTION

Many issues divided the delegates to the Constitutional Convention who met in Philadelphia during the summer of 1787. Although there was a general recognition that the Articles of Confederation suffered "important defects . . . of a nature so serious as to . . . render the situation of the United States delicate and critical,"[1] it was far from clear how a better, stronger central government could be structured.

Slowly and methodically, the framers debated their way through complex problems of politics and political economy, but the vexing issue of slavery often cast a disquieting shadow over their work. As James Madison presciently noted, "The states were divided in different interests not by their difference of size, but by other circumstances; the most material of which resulted partly from climate but principally from the effects of their having or not having slaves."[2] In fact, nearly all of the states had at least some slaves in 1787. Only Massachusetts had eliminated slavery, while Pennsylvania, Rhode Island, and Connecticut were in the process of gradual emancipation. In all, about 40,000 slaves lived in the northern states, only a minority of whom could expect to see freedom in their lifetimes. Still, there could have been no doubt that the future of American slavery was in the southern states, where more than 650,000 slaves accounted for 40 percent of the total population, and where emancipation was not even on the horizon.[3] As Madison observed, "It was pretty well understood that the institution of slavery & its consequences formed the line of discrimination" between North and South.[4]

The perpetuation of slavery had been the great moral failing of the American Revolution of 1776—a movement that was based on the self-evident truth that "all men are created equal," although its foremost leaders, such as George Washington and Thomas Jefferson, themselves owned hundreds of slaves. It is not that they failed to recognize the stark hypocrisy of proclaiming inalienable human rights while simultaneously buying and selling human flesh. "Virtually all the most prominent founders recognized that slavery was an embarrassing contradiction that violated all the principles the American Revolution claimed to stand for."[5]

Rather, they were unwilling to forgo the benefits of the system that provided the underpinning for so much of their prosperity. When the signers of the Declaration of Independence pledged "our lives, our fortunes, and our sacred honor," it should not have escaped notice that a good deal of their collective fortune was in the form of human beings. And when Samuel Johnson scornfully asked, "How is it that we hear the loudest yelps for liberty among the drivers of negroes?" the founders had no ready answer.[6]

Some of the founders, to be sure, believed in eventual emancipation. John Adams was firmly opposed to slavery (as was his wife, Abigail, who wrote that "it always appeared a most iniquitous scheme to me to fight ourselves for what we are daily robbing and plundering from those who have as good a right to freedom as we have").[7] Benjamin Franklin, John Jay, and Alexander Hamilton all served as officers of antislavery organizations. Washington—whose will manumitted many slaves at his death, although he freed none in his lifetime—once said, "There is not a man living who wishes more sincerely than I do to see a plan adopted for the abolition [of slavery]."[8] But for every delegate in Philadelphia who actually opposed slavery, or who at least hoped for its eventual demise, there were many others who staunchly defended the institution on moral, economic, and practical grounds. South Carolina's Charles Cotesworth Pinckney explained bluntly that "Georgia and South Carolina can not do without slaves. . . . The more slaves," Pinckney continued, "the more produce to the carrying trade [and] the more revenue for the common treasury." Connecticut's Oliver Ellsworth, later chief justice of the Supreme Court, was more than willing to go along with the slave trade for the sake of his state's lucrative commerce in slave-produced goods. In opposition to any "intermeddling," he argued that "the morality or wisdom of slavery are considerations belonging to the States themselves."[9]

When it came to realpolitik, alas, virtually none of the framers proved willing to take a resolute stand against slavery, and for good—in the sense of pragmatic, if not admirable—reasons. "With the exception of real estate, slaves were the most valuable form of privately held property in the United States at the end of the revolution."[10] It is therefore hardly surprising that no one was ultimately inclined to jeopardize the "species of property" that accounted for nearly 60 percent of the entire wealth of the southern states.[11] Thus, when delegates to the Constitutional Convention arrived in Philadelphia, it was obvious that any revision of the Articles of Confederation would have to recognize and accommodate the institution of slavery as a condition of forming a "more perfect" union. "No delegate came to Philadelphia intending to grapple with the social and moral issues of slavery."[12] Slavery was so much a part of American life and culture, however, that they could not avoid wrestling with its sordid details.

The most contentious issue, with seemingly the most at stake, was apportionment of the House of Representatives. Would the size of each state's delegation to Congress be determined by its total population, by some measure of property, or by its number of free inhabitants? Political power hung in the balance, with the slave-heavy southern states insistent on counting their entire populations and delegates from northern states proposing alternate methods based either on the free population (excluding slaves) or on property valuation (including the value of slaves along with houses and livestock).

The showdown came at the end of a four-day debate that covered questions of taxation as well as representation. Southern delegates made it clear that some representation of slaves would be essential to their agreement. North Carolina's William Davie objected loudly to any attempt "to deprive the Southern States of any share of Representation for their blacks."[13] Pennsylvania's Gouverneur Morris countered with perhaps the sharpest antislavery speech of the entire convention, asserting that he "never would concur" in a plan that rewarded slavery:

> It was a nefarious institution. It was the curse of heaven on the States where it prevailed. . . . Upon what principle is it that the slaves shall be computed in the representation? Are they men? Then make them Citizens and let them vote. Are they property? Why then is no other property included?[14]

Morris's moral reasoning was powerful, but his argument ran aground on the hard rock of political reality. The southern states were not going to budge, thus making representation of slaves a prerequisite to establishing the Union. Northerners, including the antislavery delegates among them, valued "harmony at the convention"[15] more highly than they cared about the rights or condition of southern slaves. Even New York's Rufus King, who delivered one of the convention's few speeches flatly condemning slavery, was in the end "ready to yield something in the proportion of representatives for the security of the Southern states."[16]

Thus, when a compromise solution was first broached, it was tellingly introduced by James Wilson of Pennsylvania, a well-known critic of slavery, and seconded by Charles Cotesworth Pinckney of South Carolina, who boldly defended slavery as morally superior to free labor. The Wilson-Pinckney proposal was eventually embodied in the three-fifths provision, which provided in its final form that representation would be apportioned among the states "according to their respective Numbers, which shall be determined by adding to the whole Number of free Persons . . . three fifths of all other Persons." Although delicately phrased to avoid the word "slavery," which many framers found too distasteful to include in the Constitution, "euphemisms and indirection could never disguise its accommodation of slavery as a fundamental element in the structure of American politics and law."[17]

Along with that achievement, which ensured their political dominance in the House of Representatives, the slave-state delegates pressed their advantage in other areas as well. As approved at the convention and subsequently ratified by the states, the Constitution ultimately included numerous provisions that protected slaveholding, either directly or indirectly. At the time, the slaveholders no doubt believed they had accomplished a great victory, guaranteeing the future of slavery in the new United States. Charles Pinckney later reassured his fellow South Carolinians that "we have a security that the general government can never emancipate them. . . . We have obtained a right to recover our slaves in whatever part of America they may take refuge, which is a right we had not before. In short, considering all circumstances, we have made the best terms for the security of this species of property it was in our power to make."[18]

In fact, the southern delegates had gone too far. The newly won "right to recover slaves," which Pinckney extolled as a constitutional virtue, would eventually turn slavery into an irresolvable political problem that pitted state against state.

For the most part, the Constitutional Convention dealt with slavery through a process of compromise. The three-fifths provision was an obvious case of splitting the difference between counting slaves fully or not at all, and the same ratio was applied to the levy of direct taxes. Congress was prohibited from interfering with the importation of slaves, but only until 1808. The southern delegates clearly got the best of these bargains but they were nonetheless the products of give-and-take negotiation. Once those matters were settled, however, a final slavery-favoring provision was added almost without debate. Although seemingly uncontroversial at the time, it would later have almost unimaginable consequences.

Pierce Butler and Charles Pinckney, both of South Carolina, jointly introduced a motion "to require fugitive slaves and servants to be delivered up like criminals." Two Northerners—James Wilson of Pennsylvania and Roger Sherman of Connecticut—briefly objected, although not out of any concern for the protection of free blacks or escaped slaves. Wilson worried that the provision would obligate each state to track down fugitives "at the public expense," with Sherman adding that he "saw no more propriety in the public seizing and surrendering a slave or servant, than a horse."[19] Butler quickly agreed to revise his proposal, substituting the following language:

> If any person bound to service or labor in any of the [United] States shall escape into another State, he or she shall not be discharged from such service or labor, in consequence of any regulation subsisting in the State to which they escape, but shall be delivered up to the person justly claiming their service or labor.

This provision was unanimously adopted by the convention "without any serious debate or discussion," and without recorded dissent.[20] It was later slightly refined following the report by the Committee of Detail, with the final version reading:

> No Person held to Service or Labour in one State, under the Laws thereof, escaping into another, shall, in Consequence of any Law or Regulation therein, be discharged from such Service or Labour, But shall be delivered up on Claim of the Party to whom such Service or Labour may be due.

Historians have questioned the northern delegates' immediate acquiescence to the Fugitive Slave Clause, with Paul Finkelman suggesting that they either "did not understand the importance of the issue or were too tired to fight it."[21] It is equally interesting to consider why the southern delegates believed that the provision was so necessary in the first place.

The Articles of Confederation did not have a fugitive slave clause (although there was a provision for the extradition of criminals), but its absence does not appear to have occasioned any great dissatisfaction or controversy. There were hardly any cases during the Confederation years in which state officials declined to cooperate, much less interfered, with slave hunters in search of runaways. According to historian Don Fehrenbacher, the flight of slaves across state lines was "far from being a significant problem in 1787," no doubt because only Massachusetts had abolished slavery at the time (Vermont had abolished slavery in 1777 but would not become a state until 1791). Pennsylvania's 1780 gradual emancipation act would not take full effect for decades, and in any event it included the stipulation that "the right of an out-of-state owner to recover a fugitive remained unimpaired."[22] While it is true that by 1787 the northern states were clearly headed toward emancipation, there was no great reason to think that northern leaders seriously intended to challenge slavery in the South. Indeed, their conduct at the Constitutional Convention had demonstrated just the opposite. Not a single delegate had questioned the sovereign power of the southern states to maintain black people in perpetual bondage.

And yet the southern delegates remained deeply apprehensive about the "security" of their human property, missing no opportunity to build structural protection into the new Constitution. Several factors may explain their concern.

First, there remained an irreconcilable inconsistency between the ideals of the revolution and the practice of slavery. Even in the South, slavery's grip had loosened slightly in the years since 1776. Every state except Georgia and the Carolinas had prohibited slave importation, and a 1782 Virginia statute had liberalized, and therefore somewhat encouraged, manumission. In 1784 the Confederation Congress almost passed a bill, introduced by Thomas Jefferson, that would have prohibited slavery in the territories (it failed by a single vote). Perhaps these marginal gestures toward freedom caused sufficient alarm in South Carolina to suggest the need for additional protection in the form of the Fugitive Slave Clause.

Other fears would have been more concrete, as Southerners surely recalled that the British army had abetted thousands of absconding slaves during the American Revolution. In late 1775, Lord Dunmore, the last British colonial governor of Virginia, "unequivocally promised outright liberty to all slaves escaping from rebel plantations" who reached British lines and served in some capacity with the army. That promise was later sanctioned by the royal government, reiterated by leading British generals, and eventually expanded to include women and children. During the following six years, between 80,000 and 100,000 slaves fled southern plantations to seek emancipation by the British army.[23]

Not all of the runaways were successful—many were recaptured by their masters; others were betrayed by the British and returned to slavery—but Lord Dunmore's promise clearly had a powerful effect on slaves and slaveowners alike. Many of the leading founders had been among the masters who lost their human property to the British army. As they contemplated the new Constitution in 1787, they would have been acutely aware that slaves could gain freedom, at least theoretically, by fleeing from one jurisdiction to another.

Most of all, the framers were mindful of the 1772 British decision in *Somerset v. Stewart*, in which Lord Mansfield, chief justice of the King's Bench, had granted freedom to James Somerset, a runaway Virginia slave. Somerset had been taken to England by his owner, Charles Stewart, in 1769. He managed to escape at one point, but he was recaptured and placed on a slave ship headed for Jamaica. Fortunately, Somerset had become known to leaders of the British antislavery movement, including Granville Sharp, who filed a petition for a writ of habeas corpus on his behalf. There was no doubt that Somerset was a slave under the law of Virginia, but there was no comparable statute authorizing slavery in England itself. The high court therefore had to determine which law would govern Somerset's status, Virginia's (where he had been born enslaved) or England's (where the court encountered him). Lord Mansfield's famous judgment left no room for doubt:

> The state of slavery is of such a nature that it is incapable of being introduced on any reasons, moral or political, but only [on the basis of] positive law. . . . It's so odious, that nothing can be suffered to support it but positive law. . . . Therefore the black must be discharged.[24]

According to Lord Mansfield's construction of the common law, a slave's servile status did not travel with him from place to place. In the absence of a specific statute ("positive law") to the contrary, he became a free man once he set foot upon free soil.

The *Somerset* decision was limited to England; it had no immediate legal effect in the colonies, and almost none when the Constitution was drafted in the newly independent United States. As noted, all of the states in 1787 (except Massachusetts) had some positive law allowing slavery, so there was scant likelihood that an American court would render its own version of Lord Mansfield's ruling anytime soon. If anything, the northern states had shown themselves sympathetic to the recovery of fugitive slaves. Of the states that were at all proximate to the slaveholding south, Pennsylvania had a statute that specifically provided for the return of runaways, while New York and New Jersey, with more than 30,000 slaves between them, could hardly be considered free soil. In 1788, the New York legislature would enact a comprehensive slave code, "systematizing and strengthening the regulations underlying the system of chattel bondage."[25]

Nonetheless, the *Somerset* precedent was frightening to southern slaveholders. It had been widely published in America, and often over-interpreted as having completely abolished slavery under British law. News of the ruling had spread by word of mouth among slaves, which of course was troubling to their masters.[26]

Thus, southern slaveholders were responding to a real, if then remote, risk when they added the Fugitive Slave Clause to Article IV. In an abundance of caution of historic proportions, they took steps to ensure that the northern states could never adapt the *Somerset* ruling such that any fugitive "black must be discharged." James Madison himself recognized as much during the subsequent ratification debate in Virginia, when he explained that the provision was "expressly inserted, to enable owners of slaves to reclaim them." This, Madison reassured his fellow slave owners, "is a better security than any that now exists."[27]

As legal scholar Akhil Amar explains, Article IV was fashioned to contravene the "background choice-of-law rules and general principles of comity."[28] Without the provisions of the Fugitive Slave Clause to the contrary, an escapee could hypothetically be "discharged from . . . service or labor" upon reaching a jurisdiction where the local law was simply silent (or nonexistent) on the subject of slavery. While that may not have been a pressing issue regarding the northern states—nearly all of which recognized slavery in their own positive law—the national territories were a somewhat different matter.

British common law continued in force following American independence. Therefore, in the absence of legislation specifically authorizing slavery in the territories, the *Somerset* rule might well have been applied by default.

The Confederation Congress—meeting in New York even as the Constitutional Convention made plans in Philadelphia to replace it—recognized precisely that problem when it enacted the Northwest Ordinance to govern the territories north of the Ohio River recently ceded to the national government. Motivated largely, it seems, by the desire to support land speculation and encourage settlement, the Congress provided that "there shall be neither slavery nor involuntary servitude" in the Northwest Territories.[29] Then, to negate any possible *Somerset* effect, the Ordinance continued,

> That any person escaping into the same [territories], from whom labour or service is lawfully claimed in any one of the original states, such fugitive may be lawfully reclaimed, and conveyed to the person claiming his or her labour or service as aforesaid.

The Northwest Ordinance was enacted on July 13, 1787, only two months before the Constitutional Convention adopted the final version of the Fugitive Slave Clause. The Ordinance was obviously a model for the constitutional provision, but there were two significant differences. First, the Ordinance referred to slaves as persons "from whom labour or service is lawfully claimed," while the Constitution substituted the term "held to Service or Labour in one State, under the Laws thereof." Thus, the Constitution implied that the ultimate legality of a fugitive's slave status was not to be questioned or litigated in the asylum state, but rather would be determined exclusively under the laws of the state from which the person escaped. In addition, the Constitution called for fugitives to be actively "delivered up" like criminals, rather than merely allowing them to be "lawfully reclaimed" as provided by the Northwest Ordinance.

As they did throughout the convention, the slaveholders believed they had left nothing to chance, but in fact they had placed far more at risk than they realized at the time.

When the Constitution was adopted, America's slaves were among the most powerless people on earth. They were regarded merely as property and used, as Elbridge Gerry put it during the apportionment debate, just "as horses and cattle."[30] In modern terms it might be said that slaves were completely denied agency—they were unable to control their own lives or maintain their own families, let alone participate in political events.

No one in 1787 would have suggested that the Constitution had actually (albeit quite unintentionally) empowered the boldest of the slaves, but that in fact is what happened. The Fugitive Slave Clause transformed the recapture of runaways from an essentially private problem into an issue of government responsibility. After the Constitution was ratified, masters could demand of right that their slaves be "delivered up" by local authorities anywhere in the country, thus making state governments (and later the federal government) crucial players in the business of slave hunting. In other words, the Fugitive Slave Clause "made interstate rendition of slaves part of the national purpose and did so in the language of legal command."[31]

Under the Fugitive Slave Clause, it was inevitable that slave catching would become the frequent subject of interstate disputes, and therefore a political issue. And thus, the runaways themselves became de facto political actors, able to throw the machinery of government into motion, and often into confusion, simply by crossing the boundary between one jurisdiction and another. Running away, which had previously been only an act of individual defiance, became under the Fugitive Slave Clause an act of public significance and the cause of constant and increasing tension between states. The fugitives' motives, of course, remained personal.[32] They ran away to seek freedom, to evade punishment, to search for separated relatives. But the possible consequences of an escape had changed dramatically under the Constitution, inexorably setting state against state, and not merely slave against master.

The first state-versus-state confrontation came almost immediately. In 1788, a black man named John Davis was seized by three slave catchers and dragged from freedom in Pennsylvania into slavery in Virginia. Davis's legal status was complicated. He claimed to have been freed by operation of Pennsylvania's 1780 Emancipation Act, but his erstwhile owner maintained that Davis was still a slave (under a loophole in the law) and "rented" him to a man in Virginia. Davis succeeded in making his way back to Pennsylvania, only to be apprehended by three slave catchers and returned south. All further efforts to free Davis failed, but Pennsylvania had recently enacted a law against enslaving (or re-enslaving) a free person, and a court subsequently indicted the slave hunters for kidnapping. Pennsylvania Governor Thomas Mifflin attempted to extradite the slave catchers, sending a copy of the indictment to Virginia's Governor Beverley Randolph and invoking "the provisions contained in the second section of the fourth article of the constitution of the United States."[33]

Randolph declined to comply with the request. Following the advice of his attorney general, he asserted that the kidnapping of a free person constituted only "a trespass . . . as between the parties" under Virginia law. Randolph, in other words, was attempting to dispose of the case as a purely local matter, treating wrongful enslavement as nothing more serious than a minor "breach of the Peace."[34] Under Article IV, however, it was impossible to cabin the dispute, which ripened into a national controversy.

Unwilling to accept Virginia's local characterization of the crime, Governor Mifflin complained to President Washington, requesting the "interposition of the Federal Legislature." After some equivocation, Washington forwarded Mifflin's petition to Congress, where the issue was considered at length by both houses. Congress eventually produced a bill, although it did not exactly respond to Governor Mifflin's request. Rather than address the problem of kidnapping, Congress instead enacted what became known as the Fugitive Slave Act of 1793. Passed in the Senate without recorded opposition, and in the House by an overwhelming margin of 48–7, the law provided:

> That when a person held to labor in any of the United States . . . shall escape into any other part of the said States or Territory, the person to whom such labor or service may be due . . . is hereby empowered to seize or arrest such fugitive from labor, and to take him or her before any Judge . . . of the United States . . . or before any magistrate of a county, city, or town corporate, wherein such seizure or arrest shall be made, and upon proof to the satisfaction of such Judge or magistrate . . . it shall be the duty of such Judge or magistrate to give a certificate thereof to such claimant . . . which shall be sufficient warrant for removing the said fugitive from labor to the State or Territory from which he or she fled.[35]

Another section of the Act made it an offense to obstruct or hinder the claimant of a slave, or to rescue, harbor, or conceal a fugitive, providing for a

$500 fine as well as damages to the claimant. It is ironic, to say the least, that Pennsylvania's attempt to deter kidnapping resulted in the first federal statute for the specific benefit of slave catchers, no doubt "enhancing opportunities for kidnapping" in the process.[36]

John Davis died in bondage. Governor Mifflin was willing to expend considerable energy attempting to vindicate Pennsylvania's laws, but he did not prove quite so interested in obtaining one slave's freedom. Nonetheless, Davis had a resounding impact on American history. The repercussions of his effort to flee slavery reached the U.S. Congress, setting forces in motion that would generate irresolvable antagonism between the states and regions, thereby hastening the day of emancipation. To paraphrase Thomas Jefferson's mordant remark, Congress had taken a wolf by the ears and could neither hold him nor safely let him go.

❧ 2 ❧

THE MISSOURI EQUILIBRIUM

James Madison proved tragically prescient. The institution of slavery had indeed formed a "line of discrimination" between the northern and southern states. By 1804, all of the original northern states had either abolished slavery or had enacted gradual emancipation statutes, and slavery would be prohibited in the new states created from the Northwest Territories. In the meantime, slavery flourished in the southern states and spread, with the blessing of Congress, to the new territories south of the Ohio River. The total number of southern slaves grew from about 650,000 in 1790 to nearly 900,000 in 1800. In 1820 there were approximately 1.5 million slaves in the South, and their number would continue to increase, reaching 3.2 million in 1850 and 4 million in 1860.[1]

By the early nineteenth century it was already obvious that the United States was becoming a "house divided" into two different economic systems—with slavery in the South and free labor in the North. The initial challenge was to ensure that the nation's political balance could be maintained as, more or less, half slave and half free, reflecting what legal scholar Mark Graber has called the bisectional power-sharing arrangement.[2] For a while, that balance could be achieved through the alternating admission of new states: free Vermont (1791) and slaveholding Kentucky (1792); slaveholding Tennessee (1796) and free Ohio (1803). The Louisiana Purchase of 1803, however, added an immense new territory to the country, where slavery had long been legal under both the French and Spanish, and with vast reaches attractive to slave-based agriculture. At the same time, the nation's population began shifting northwestward into free territory, a trend that would later accelerate and undermine the slave states' domination of the House of Representatives (which had once seemingly been ensured by the three-fifths provision of the Constitution).

The creation of new states from the Louisiana Territory eventually provoked the Missouri crisis of 1819–1820, which constituted "the first major sectional controversy over the expansion of slavery."[3] At issue was the admission to the Union of Missouri as a slave state, which would have tipped the congressional balance decidedly in favor of slavery—Louisiana had been admitted in 1812, Mississippi in 1817, and Alabama would be admitted in late 1819—while also setting a precedent for even more slave states to follow. Eventually a compromise was reached, in which Missouri was admitted as a slave state, Maine was admitted as a free state, and, crucially, slavery was prohibited in the remainder of the former Louisiana Territory north of the 36° 30' parallel. This new geographic "line of discrimination" appeared to settle the political question of slavery, at least for the time being, but the operation of the fugitive slave laws meant that the problem could not be ignored. No matter where politicians drew lines—whether it was along the Ohio River or at Missouri's border—slaves continued to seek freedom on the other side. Slave hunters were equally undeterred by state lines, and they did not only seize fugitives. There were numerous "free blacks who were kidnapped, carried to a slave market, and auctioned off to the highest bidder."[4]

Although the free state governments were generally willing to go along with the rendition of actual fugitives, they were unwilling simply to accept the abduction of free blacks. As early as 1808, New York had passed "An Act to Prevent the Kidnapping of Free People of Color." Similar statutes were enacted in other states, generally requiring some form of hearing before a captive could be taken back to slavery, and providing criminal penalties for wrongful enslavement. In 1826, the Pennsylvania legislature passed a strengthened antikidnapping statute, motivated by a series of incidents involving alleged runaways from Maryland. The new law sought to eliminate the private "recaption" of slaves by requiring slave hunters to bring their prisoners for adjudication before state magistrates. This provision (and others like it) had the effect, if not the purpose, of making it considerably more difficult, or even legally risky, for masters to reclaim their slaves. The ensuing disputes would cause significant antagonism across the Mason-Dixon Line, with one case eventually resulting in the crucial U.S. Supreme Court decision *Prigg v. Pennsylvania*.

To be sure, most northern courts in this period were receptive to slave owners' claims. In 1823 the Massachusetts Supreme Judicial Court upheld the constitutionality of the Fugitive Slave Act of 1793, and other courts held likewise in Indiana, Pennsylvania, and New York.[5] Even judges uncomfortable with slavery were constrained by a constitutional duty to respect the Fugitive Slave Clause. Pennsylvania Chief Justice William Tilghman thus cautioned his colleagues that "whatever may be our private opinions on the subject of slavery, it is well known that our southern brethren would not have consented to become parties to a Constitution . . . unless their property in slaves had been secured."[6] But no matter how accommodating the courts were in the end, southern leaders were deeply offended by the very existence of free-state statutes and the occasional requirement of extended judicial proceedings. Southern anger would only increase in the 1830s, with the development of a well-organized abolitionist movement.

The origin of militant abolitionism is often dated to 1831, with the first publication of William Lloyd Garrison's *The Liberator*. Garrisonian abolitionism differed from earlier antislavery movements by demanding an immediate and complete end to slavery, even in the southern states, and by eschewing both gradualism and the "colonization" of freed blacks to Africa. Garrison recognized the proslavery nature of the Constitution, which he denounced as "a covenant with death and an agreement with Hell." His newspaper called for *northern* secession, arguing that an independent North would be released from the fugitive slave laws and could therefore offer freedom to escapees from the South. Whether in or out of the Union, however, Garrison and his followers "stressed the dichotomy between natural and positive law."[7] To the leaders of the new movement it was self-evident that man-made laws such as the Fugitive Slave Act or, indeed, the Constitution, were entitled to no deference when they conflicted with the "higher law" of natural human rights.

That same decade saw the development of an ideological antislavery bar—a cadre of lawyers who were determined to press the courts on behalf of freedom. Lawyers, of course, could hardly renounce the Constitution in favor of higher law, even if they were inclined to, and remain effective. Rather, they attempted to use every conceivable legal and tactical means to thwart slave owners, or at least to delay the return of escapees. Although not all of the noted antislavery lawyers were radicals—Richard Henry Dana, for example, was a Free-Soiler but not an abolitionist—many would go on to political leadership in the antislavery movement. Salmon Chase, Thaddeus Stevens, Charles Sumner, and William Seward would all serve in Congress and would all become leaders of the Republican Party. In the 1830s, however, their electoral victories were still far in the future, and courtroom victories would be hard to come by as well.

In 1837, Salmon Chase first came to national attention when he undertook the representation of a young runaway slave named Matilda, who had been seized by slave catchers in Cincinnati. Matilda was the natural daughter of her master, Larkin Lawrence of Missouri; she could pass for white and had been raised and educated in his household. Accompanying her father on a trip to Ohio, she had begged him for a certificate of freedom. When Lawrence refused to free his own child, she ran away and sought refuge in the home of James Birney, a well-known abolitionist lawyer. After working for some time as Birney's housekeeper, Matilda was tracked down by slave hunters in her father's employ, who had obtained an arrest warrant from an Ohio magistrate pursuant to the federal fugitive slave law.

Fearing that he might be prosecuted for harboring a fugitive, Birney retained Chase to represent Matilda in a proceeding before Judge David Este. Chase was in a difficult position, and not only because Judge Este had allowed him just one day to prepare his case. Matilda was admittedly a slave, and she had been seized by lawful process. Chase believed that Matilda was surely entitled to freedom as a matter of higher law, but he still had to frame his case in terms that a court could accept. Chase therefore began his argument by conceding that only positive law could govern the case, but he quickly added that "there is such a thing as natural rights, derived not from any constitution or civil code, but from the constitution of higher nature and the code of heaven." Although higher law could not in itself govern the case, Chase argued that the court was bound to construe the statute and Constitution in the way most consistent with respect for natural rights. Matilda could not be considered a fugitive, he continued, because she had been brought voluntarily into Ohio. Thus, the Fugitive Slave Act could not be applied, and the warrant for her arrest was invalid. Chase raised additional points along the same line—Matilda was entitled to a jury trial; the state court lacked jurisdiction to enforce a federal statute—arguing that the court was obliged to harmonize natural and positive law.[8] But to no avail. Judge Este took only a few minutes to issue a certificate of removal, remanding Matilda to her master.

Just as we can only marvel at Matilda's courage—she ran away from her master and family, leaving a relatively comfortable life in bondage solely because she wanted to be free—we can only imagine her despair when the court ruled against her. There is no record that she was ever returned to Lawrence's Missouri household, and Chase's biographer speculates that she was instead sold in a slave market. Like so many before her, Matilda simply disappeared into slavery. But she did leave an enduring legacy.

Chase's argument in Matilda's case was printed and distributed nation-wide, marking the beginning of his career as the "Attorney General for Run-away Negroes."[9] His approach to the law—attempting to embed recognition of natural rights into the construction of the Constitution—would be repeated and refined over the years, by himself and others, but the courts by and large continued to hold that positive law favored slavery. Even in the occasional victories for antislavery lawyers—such as the famous U.S. Supreme Court decision in the *Amistad* case—the courts made a point of noting that slavery was cognizable under both American law and the law of nations.

The interplay of higher law and positive law may have been a conundrum for lawyers and the courts, but it posed no such problem for antislavery activists who saw their crusade in religious terms. For them there was no doubt that natural law superseded any statutory or constitutional obligation, and that laws establishing or facilitating slavery, however enacted, were morally invalid. As early as the 1820s, Quakers in southeastern Pennsylvania sheltered significant numbers of runaway slaves from neighboring Maryland, in a precursor of the movement that later came to be known as the Underground Railroad.[10] Similar efforts took place throughout the northern border states, most notably Pennsylvania and Ohio, but also in Indiana and Illinois.

In late May 1842 nine slaves escaped from the northern Kentucky farm of Wharton Jones. Making their way across the Ohio River, they were met on the other side by John Van Zandt, a devout Methodist and committed abolitionist. Van Zandt secreted the fugitives in his wagon and headed north, only to be intercepted by suspicious slave hunters. The slave catchers restrained Van Zandt's team and, following a brief struggle, managed to open the wagon and discover the blacks. "Have you a load of runaways?" came the obvious question. "They are, by nature, as free as you or I," said Van Zandt.[11] Asked whether he knew he was carrying slaves, Van Zandt defiantly replied, "They ought to be free."

The slave catchers were unimpressed by Van Zandt's invocation of higher law. They seized seven of the nine fugitives (two succeeded in breaking free), whom they returned to their owner in exchange for a $600 reward. The owner, in turn, filed suit against Van Zandt under the Fugitive Slave Act of 1793, claiming a total of $1,700 in damages. Facing a ruinous judgment, Van Zandt retained Salmon Chase as his defense counsel.

The case came for trial before two judges, Humphrey Howe Leavitt of the U.S. District Court and U.S. Supreme Court Justice John McLean (sitting as a circuit judge, as did all Supreme Court justices until 1869). McLean was a friend of Chase's and was well-known for his religious opposition to slavery. He had dissented earlier that year in *Prigg v. Pennsylvania,* when the Supreme Court invalidated state antikidnapping laws. (In 1856 he would place second to John Fremont in the contest for the Republican presidential nomination.) Thus, despite the evidence against him, Van Zandt seemed to have at least some chance at acquittal. As legal scholar Robert Cover put it, "Chase was not simply a lawyer trying to win a case, but a friend trying to win a convert."[12]

Chase began his argument by claiming that Van Zandt had been unaware he was ferrying escaped slaves and thus had not "harbored" them within the meaning of the Fugitive Slave Act. There was some slight support for that position, as the slave hunters had no warrants and had not shown Van Zandt any documentation. Still, the weight of the evidence showed that Van Zandt had known exactly what he was doing. Not only had he tried to flee with his passengers, but he also had made several incriminating statements in front of witnesses, at one point declaring that "it was a Christian act to take slaves and set them at liberty." Chase must have known that he was raising a spurious, if not flatly false, defense, but that gave him little pause. Then as now, it was the job of a defense lawyer to raise every favorable inference from the facts, and Chase was able to make his argument strictly on the basis of gaps in the prosecution testimony. Moreover, he likely believed that the higher law granted him license to embellish or mislead for the sake of freedom. As we will see, other antislavery lawyers in later years would be at least equally imaginative in their presentation of facts, perhaps even to the extent of producing perjured testimony.

As he had in Matilda's trial, Chase attempted to use natural law as a means to narrow the reach of a punitive statute. He claimed that the fugitive slave laws should be applied only to escapees from the original thirteen states (and thus not Kentucky), and he argued that the Fugitive Slave Clause of the Constitution had not given Congress the power to enact penalties against rescuers. He relied on Lord Mansfield's *Somerset* opinion, and on a similar judgment entered by the Massachusetts Supreme Judicial Court in *Commonwealth v. Aves* in 1836, without acknowledging that the Constitution itself made those rulings inapplicable in the case of fugitives.

Justice McLean was sympathetic only to some of Chase's arguments. In his charge to the jury, he agreed that "every person in Ohio, or any other free state, without regard to color, is presumed to be free," explaining that "no presumption, therefore, arises, from the color of these fugitives, alone, that the defendant had notice that they were slaves."

More significantly, however, McLean continued, "If, at the time the defendant was connected with the Negroes, he had a full knowledge of the fact, however acquired, that they were slaves and fugitives from labor, it is enough to charge him with notice" and thus to convict him of violating the law.

And when it came to the higher law, McLean had no patience at all. He cautioned the jury to apply only the law as written:

> In the course of this discussion, much has been said of the laws of nature, of conscience, and the rights of conscience. This monitor, under great excitement, may mislead, and always does mislead, when it urges any one to violate the law.
>
> I have read to you the Constitution and the act of congress. They form the only guides in the administration of justice in this case.

The jury convicted Van Zandt and fined him $1,500. Following the verdict, McLean was even more severe in rebuking Chase's trial tactics. "We are not here to deal with abstractions," he reprimanded his friend. "We cannot theorize upon the principles of our government, or of slavery. The law is our only guide. If convictions . . . of what is right or wrong, are to be substituted as a rule of action in disregard of the law, we shall soon be without law and without protection." Undeterred, Chase prepared to take the case to the Supreme Court, where it would be decided several years later.

Prior to 1842 the disquieting conflict between free states and slave catchers had reached a rough, if not always satisfactory, equilibrium. Most runaways were rather quickly recaptured, usually without resort to courts or legal formalities, not unlike the slaves in John Van Zandt's wagon who found themselves back in Kentucky within a matter of days. At the same time, many northern states attempted to impede the rush to bondage by enacting personal liberty laws—not out of great concern for runaways, but rather to protect free blacks—that required some measure of legal process as a condition of lawful removal. Neither side was particularly happy with the situation: most slaveholders viewed the state laws as gratuitous harassment; many Northerners were concerned that far too many abductions were still taking place. Nonetheless, as Matilda's trial had shown, it was possible for a state court to provide a fair hearing and make a reasoned decision regarding the status of an alleged slave. At the very least, the various participants—claimants, lawyers, and judges—all knew their respective places in the system.

That relatively tolerable status quo was permanently disrupted by the U.S. Supreme Court decision in *Prigg v. Pennsylvania*. In 1832 a slave named Margaret had moved from Maryland to Pennsylvania to live with her husband, a free black man named Jerry Morgan. The Morgans resided together undisturbed for five years with the tacit consent of Margaret's owner, John Ashmore. The couple had several children, at least one of whom had been born in Pennsylvania and was therefore free under Pennsylvania law. Then Ashmore died and his estate passed to his widow. Slaves across the South had good reason to fear the death of their masters, realizing that the settlement of an estate could very well involve the division or distribution of every "species of property," or its sale to cover debts, and hence the separation of families. That appears to be what happened to the Morgans, as Mrs. Ashmore retained an attorney to recover her inherited slave. The lawyer, Edward Prigg, obtained a warrant for the seizure of Margaret and her children, and then executed it by dragging them out of bed in the middle of the night. "The mother, father and children [were] put into an open wagon in a cold sleety rain, with scarcely their ordinary clothes on" and taken before a Pennsylvania magistrate. The state judge, however, refused Prigg's request for a certificate of removal because the lawyer had not complied with the strict requirements of the Pennsylvania personal liberty law.[13]

Rather than appeal the ruling, Prigg simply forced Margaret and her children into a waiting carriage and hustled them across the border into Maryland, where "by the morning light they were sold to a negro trader and in a calaboose ready for shipment to the South."[14] In a near repetition of the painful story of John Davis, Margaret Morgan and her children were irrevocably condemned to slavery, while the free-state authorities proceeded to bring criminal charges against their kidnapper. Prigg was extradited from Maryland and convicted by a jury of violating Pennsylvania's 1826 antikidnapping statute. By agreement between the two states, the conviction was appealed directly to the U.S. Supreme Court. Thus, *Prigg v. Pennsylvania* "might with more accuracy have been titled 'Maryland versus Pennsylvania,' or even 'Slave States versus Free States.'"[15]

The Supreme Court's primary opinion was written by Justice Joseph Story, who just the previous year had ordered the release of the rebellious slaves who had seized the Spanish schooner *La Amistad*. The precocious son of a prominent Massachusetts family, and the author of the three-volume *Commentaries on the Constitution of the United States*, Story was known for his opposition to slavery, but also for his insistent respect for positive law.[16] Although his *Prigg* opinion gave a slight nod toward natural rights, citing the *Somerset* case for the proposition that slavery was a "mere municipal [local] regulation," unrecognized by international law, Story quickly noted that slavery occupied a favored place in the U.S. Constitution:

> Historically, it is well known, that the object of this [fugitive slave] clause was to secure to the citizens of the slave-holding states the complete right and title of ownership in their slaves, as property, in every state in the Union into which they might escape from the state where they were held in servitude. The full recognition of this right and title . . . was so vital to the preservation of their domestic interests and institutions, that it cannot be doubted, that it constituted a fundamental article, without the adoption of which the Union could not have been formed.

Moreover, Story held, the Fugitive Slave Clause was self-executing, entirely independent of any legislation, thus securing to every slaveholder the "positive, unqualified right" to recapture his slaves anywhere in the Union, without restraint or regulation by any state law. Therefore, "any state law or state regulation, which interrupts, limits, delays or postpones the right of the owner to the immediate possession of the slave, and the immediate command of his service and labor" would necessarily violate the owner's constitutional right of self-help recapture. Consequently, the Pennsylvania personal liberty law was unconstitutional because it interfered with the owner's right to immediate possession of her slave.

Finally, Story held that the power to legislate for the recovery of fugitives belonged exclusively to Congress and could not be concurrently exercised by the states. While the states could exercise their "police powers" to arrest or detain runaways, just as they could detain "idlers, vagabonds and paupers," they could "never be permitted to interfere with, or to obstruct, the just rights of the owner to reclaim his slave."[17]

The implications of Story's opinion were startling. Slave catchers were suddenly vested with extraterritorial rights, essentially allowing them to impose southern laws on northern states, by compelling the "free states to accept the slave-state principle that a Negro or mulatto was a slave unless he could prove otherwise." Indeed, under the rule of federal exclusivity, it did not even appear that a northern state could provide a forum in which an alleged slave could prove his own freedom: "One-half of the nation must sacrifice its presumption of freedom to the other half's presumption of slavery."[18]

Story and most of his colleagues quite evidently hoped that national uniformity would resolve the sectional tensions created by fugitive slave captures. "The agitations on this subject," he opined for the Court, "which have had a tendency to interrupt the harmony between [the states], may subside, and the conflict of opinion be put at rest." Not for the last time, however, the Supreme Court seriously misjudged the likely impact of its ruling. In fact, the *Prigg* decision would ultimately do more to exacerbate tensions than to put them at peace.

Under the theory of federal exclusivity, Story's opinion had strongly suggested that free states' governments could choose to abstain completely from the recovery of runaway slaves.[19] Thus, many states were prompted to enact new versions of their personal liberty laws, prohibiting the involvement of their courts and sheriffs, or the use of their jails, for the rendition of fugitives. The resulting statutes only increased the widespread southern belief that Northerners would never voluntarily assist in the return of runaways. John C. Calhoun denounced the personal liberty laws as "one of the most fatal blows ever received by the South and the Union." At the same time, even non-abolitionists in the North bridled at the wholesale eradication of their own "states' rights" and the intrusive nationalization of "the brutal relations between slave and slave holder."[20]

The trouble became apparent later that year, with the apprehension in Boston of a slave named George Latimer. Acting without a warrant or other legal process (as was his "positive, unqualified right" under the *Prigg* decision), Latimer's alleged owner, James Gray of Virginia, had him seized and taken to the city jail. Gray then requested an order of removal from Justice Story, who was coincidentally sitting as the federal circuit judge in Boston (where he also taught at Harvard Law School). Story obligingly ordered the detention of Latimer, in order to allow Gray additional time to produce sufficient evidence of ownership.

Attorney Samuel Sewall volunteered his services on behalf of Latimer and applied to Lemuel Shaw, chief justice of the Massachusetts Supreme Judicial Court, for a writ of habeas corpus. The habeas petition argued that Latimer was entitled to a jury trial under Massachusetts's 1837 personal liberty law. That claim was not ill-founded. Latimer had been arrested without process or even written documentation of his alleged status as a slave and, although he was a federal prisoner pursuant to Story's order, he was being held in a Massachusetts jail. At the time, the law was not clear whether a state court could order the release of a federal prisoner. Given that Shaw was as close to a confirmed opponent of slavery "as existed on the bench," there was good reason to think that he might grant the writ.[21]

Shaw, however, badly disappointed Boston's abolitionists by denying the writ to free Latimer. As reported in *The Liberator,* he ruled that "an appeal to natural rights and to the paramount law of liberty was not pertinent." Rather, the case was only "to be decided by the Constitution . . . and by the Law of Congress," which were to be strictly "obeyed, however disagreeable to our natural sympathies or views of duty."[22]

To William Lloyd Garrison, Shaw's contra-conscience fidelity to the law only proved that the Constitution was indeed a proslavery compact that merited no respect. Conceding that judges could not intentionally violate the law, Garrison nonetheless castigated Shaw's decision:

> For rather than to have been made an instrument in sending Latimer back to prison and ultimately to slavery . . . he had it in his power, and as an honest and humane man was duty bound, to resign his office and to bear his testimony against all such legal diabolism. . . . Villainy is still villainy though it be pronounced equity in the statute book.[23]

Garrison argued that no judge should willingly cooperate with slavery, even though Latimer's counsel had not made such a claim, and indeed could not have, in the habeas corpus proceeding. Shaw's resignation would not have freed Latimer, who would nonetheless have remained subject to Story's original order. In fact, even Story's resignation (impossible to imagine as that was, post-*Prigg*) would still have left Latimer in the custody of Gray's agents.

Fortunately for Latimer, the affair had generated so much outrage that the Boston jailer was pressured into releasing the slave to his master's custody, even without the issuance of a writ. That placed Gray in a parlous position, as he no longer had any effective means of holding his captive. When a committee of prominent Bostonians offered to buy Latimer's freedom, Gray jumped at the chance "to cut his losses." But that was only one case. The complicity of the judiciary, along with the gutting of the 1837 personal liberty law, made it obvious that a more forceful and enduring measure was needed if future recaptures were to be prevented in Boston.[24]

The solution was the Latimer law, enacted in 1843 by the Massachusetts legislature following the submission, by Charles Francis Adams, of a petition bearing the signatures of more than 65,000 citizens. The new law prohibited all state officials from participating in the detention of fugitive slaves, and forbade the use of state facilities for their confinement. Vermont and Ohio passed similar laws the same year, followed by Connecticut in 1844, Pennsylvania in 1847, and Rhode Island in 1848. Indirectly triggered by Margaret Morgan and George Latimer, new personal liberty laws were eventually adopted in nearly every northern state.[25] At a time when there were few federal judges and marshals, and virtually no federal jails, the denial of state facilities was potentially a major impediment to the arrest, detention, and eventual return of fugitives. Typical of the outraged reaction in the South, a Virginia legislative assembly would later characterize these statutes as "disgusting and revolting exhibition[s] of faithless and unconstitutional legislation."[26]

When the appeal in *Jones v. Van Zandt* reached the Supreme Court in 1847, nearly five years after the trial, Salmon Chase was joined as counsel by William Seward, the former governor of New York. It was one of the most exceptional legal teams in history. Seward would later be elected to the U.S. Senate, and then would serve as Lincoln's secretary of state. Chase would likewise serve Ohio as both governor and U.S. senator, later becoming Lincoln's secretary of the treasury, and finally chief justice of the U.S. Supreme Court. In 1847, however, they were just two lawyers in private practice, facing an uphill battle before an unsympathetic Court. (The case was submitted entirely on the basis of written briefs; Chief Justice Roger Taney refused to set the matter for oral argument, notwithstanding the intercession of Chase's friend Justice McLean.)[27]

Chase's main brief began by describing Van Zandt as a "rather hapless geriatric drawn into a situation for which he could not be held accountable." According to Chase, the defendant—"an old man, of limited education and slender means"—had merely "found in the road a company of Negroes" to whom he had innocently provided a wagon ride. Conceding that the blacks had apparently escaped from slavery, Chase argued that Van Zandt "had nothing to do with their escape" and "had no notice whatever . . . that the Negroes had been held to service or labor in Kentucky." Chase's description of his client was at best highly implausible, given Van Zandt's known involvement in the abolitionist movement, not to mention that he had taken on his passengers at three o'clock in the morning—an appropriate hour to hide fugitives, but an extremely unlikely time to pick up random hitchhikers. As before, Chase was quite willing to stretch the facts in furtherance of natural law, even as he insisted that the Court limit the reach of a federal statute.

"No court is bound to enforce unjust law; but on the contrary every court is bound, by prior and superior obligations, to abstain from enforcing such law," Chase expounded to the justices, noting that "multitudes, in all parts of the country, regard the act of the defendant . . . not merely as no crime, but as an act of humanity and mercy."[28] In language that other lawyers would adapt in later cases, Chase argued that "no legislature can make right wrong; or wrong right. No Legislature can make men things; or things men."[29]

Moving as it was, Chase's argument never had a chance. In an opinion written by Justice Levi Woodbury of New Hampshire, the Supreme Court ruled unanimously against Van Zandt, upholding the constitutionality of the Fugitive Slave Act of 1793, while dismissing out of hand any appeal to either morality or higher law:

> It may be expected by the defendant that some notice should be taken of the argument, urging on us a disregard of the constitution and the act of Congress in respect to this subject, on account of the supposed inexpediency and invalidity of all laws recognizing slavery or any right of property in man. But that is a political question, settled by each State for itself; and the federal power over it is limited

and regulated by the people of the States in the constitution itself, as one of its sacred compromises.

Whatever may be the theoretical opinions of any as to the expediency of some of those compromises, or of the right of property in persons which they recognize, this court has no alternative, while they exist, but to stand by the constitution and laws with fidelity to their duties and their oaths.[30]

At that point, it must surely have seemed that the courtroom struggle against slavery had reached a dead end. The Supreme Court had declared itself firmly on the slaveholders' side, by (1) authorizing the broadest possible right of self-help recapture; (2) denying the free states any power to demand minimal due process in their own courts; and (3) refusing to indulge even the slightest flexibility in interpreting the "sacred" constitutional stature of fugitive slave rendition.

Although Latimer-type laws may have created a standoff in some locales, the fact is that many northern communities were tolerant of southern slavery (and often hostile to blacks, whether runaway or free). Moreover, every community was under intense political and economic pressure to cooperate with slave hunters, if only for the sake of profitable commercial relations with the South. By the late 1840s, therefore, the landscape had definitely become less hospitable for fugitives, as well as for their rescuers and defenders.

In 1850, however, things got much worse. Prompted by strident southern demands, Congress passed a new Fugitive Slave Act that represented the ultimate intrusion of slavery into the North, thus setting the stage for a renewed and intensified series of confrontations in the streets and in the courts.

⚭ 3 ⚭

THE COMPROMISE OF 1850

In late December 1845, President James Polk signed a joint resolution of Congress admitting the Republic of Texas to the Union as a slave state. The annexation was sharply protested by the government of Mexico. It was also unpopular among many Americans, especially Northerners who objected to the admission of another slave state and feared the likelihood of a war with Mexico.

The war came soon enough, beginning in the spring of 1846. Political leaders, from the young Abraham Lincoln to the elderly John Quincy Adams, condemned the war as an unprincipled land grab for the purpose of expanding slavery. It was opposition to the Mexican War that led Henry David Thoreau to resist paying his taxes—famously spending a night in jail—and to write the historic essay later published under the title "On the Duty of Civil Disobedience."

Initial wariness about the war, however, was quickly eclipsed by the overwhelming success of the military campaigns. General Winfield Scott captured Mexico City in 1847, while other American forces were also successful in California and in what was then northern Mexico. In the ensuing Treaty of Guadalupe Hidalgo, Mexico was forced to cede nearly half its territory to the United States—an area now comprising California, Nevada, and Utah, parts of Wyoming, Arizona, New Mexico, and Colorado, as well as a disputed portion of Texas—in exchange for the payment of $15 million and the assumption of an additional $3 million in debt.

Polk had added more territory to the United States than any other president in history. But he also upset the balance created a generation earlier by the Missouri Compromise, once again raising the question of slavery in the federal territories. Fearing both the spread of slavery and the attendant divisiveness of the issue, Ralph Waldo Emerson accurately predicted that "Mexico will poison us."[1]

Even before the treaty, a certain northern congressman had attempted to ensure that new slave states—beyond Texas—would not be created from

Mexican lands. In August 1846, at the very beginning of the war, a first-term Pennsylvania congressman named David Wilmot offered an amendment to a funding bill, providing that "as an express and fundamental condition to the acquisition of any territory from the Republic of Mexico . . . neither slavery nor involuntary servitude shall ever exist in any part of said territory." The Wilmot Proviso, as it came to be known, passed the House of Representatives, where Northerners held a majority, but it failed in the Senate—a pattern that would be repeated many times over the following years.

The persistent reintroduction of the Wilmot Proviso became a flashpoint in national politics, as both North and South jockeyed for control of the Mexican Cession. Unlike the Louisiana Purchase, where slavery had been well established long before the American acquisition, the Mexican Cession was free territory, Mexico having abolished slavery in 1829. To Northerners, then, the Wilmot Proviso was merely an attempt to protect the status quo by preventing the spread of slavery into new regions. To Southerners, however, the proviso seemed to raise a question of survival. The growing population in the North had created a significant majority in the House of Representatives, and the admission of additional free states threatened to weaken or overcome southern dominance in the Senate.

By the 1840s, no ambivalence remained in the South about the morality of slavery. Once considered perhaps a necessary evil, the peculiar institution had come to be regarded as morally beneficial not only to the master, but also to the slave (who was said to receive the blessings of Christian civilization along with lifetime economic security). Senator Robert M. T. Hunter of Virginia proclaimed that "there is not a respectable system of civilization known to history whose foundations were not laid in the institution of domestic slavery." John C. Calhoun declared slavery "a positive good . . . the most safe and stable basis for free institutions in the world."[2]

The blessings of civilization—including forced labor, family separation, constant beatings, and rape—were understandably less obvious to the slaves themselves, who continued to run away and sometimes to rebel. Convinced that abolitionist agitators were responsible for the slaves' discontent, southern legislatures adopted a series of measures intended to limit the baleful lure of freedom. Every slave state made it a felony to incite or even indirectly encourage discontent or servile insurrection. With the complicity of the federal postal service, it became illegal to distribute abolitionist literature through the mail. "On numerous occasions local postmasters, public officials, or mobs seized and destroyed antislavery publications."[3]

In those instances when slave rescues were actually attempted, southern justice came down hard on the offenders. In 1844 Jonathan Walker was caught attempting to help seven slaves escape from Florida on his fishing boat. After two months shackled to the wall of a prison cell, Walker was brought to trial in Pensacola. "The charges against him included every crime of which a slave owner dreamed an abolitionist ought to be accused,"[4] and the court disallowed his defense that it was no crime to assist men escaping slavery. Walker was quickly convicted and sentenced to pay a huge fine and, savagely, to have the palm of his hand branded with the letters *SS,* for "slave stealer." The sentence was executed by a federal marshal.

Walker became a hero in the North. To slaveholders, however, he was the symbol of "a vast and powerful . . . conspiracy to undermine the institutions of the South." A report by the Florida legislative council condemned the abolitionists' "vicious fanaticism clothed in the garb of religion" and declared that "negro-stealing" should no longer be regarded as "a mere larceny, but a species of treason against the state" punishable by death.[5]

From the southern perspective, slavery was a besieged institution, and the South was therefore a region under siege. Attempted escapes or rescues such as Walker's—or that of Daniel Drayton and Edward Sayres, who were captured in 1848 attempting to smuggle seventy-eight slaves out of Washington, D.C., by boat—were viewed as the leading edge of an abolitionist assault. The near-paranoid reactions were in fact wildly out of proportion to any actual threat to the viability of slavery. There was no looming abolitionist invasion in the 1840s—nor would there ever be one, until John Brown's pyrrhic expedition in 1859.

The Wilmot Proviso, however, was another matter. The prohibition of slavery in the Mexican Cession, and the consequent admission of additional free states, was a real threat to southern political dominance, and by extension to the long-term perpetuation of slavery itself. Lincoln would later recognize as much, when he said that banning slavery from the territories would put it on the path to "ultimate extinction." In 1847 Calhoun was no less certain when he warned that the proviso would lead to "political revolution, anarchy, civil war, and widespread disaster."

Driven by "the region's anti-Proviso frenzy," the southern congressional leadership followed a two-track strategy. The first was to argue that the Constitution itself protected the right to hold property in slaves and that Congress therefore lacked the power to prohibit slavery in any U.S. territory. In other words, slavery followed the flag. And in the event that slavery was not acknowledged as a national institution, then perhaps the integrity of the nation itself was at peril, as the "more militant southerners [discussed] the possibility of disunion quite freely."[6]

By 1849 "nearly every northern legislature had passed resolutions endorsing the principle of the Wilmot Proviso," while Southerners responded with plans for a "southern convention" in Nashville where the agenda would include "the alternative of dissolving the partnership." There could no longer be any doubt that "the sectional quarrel over slavery [had] reached the level of a national crisis," and it was a secession crisis at that.[7]

On January 29, 1850, Henry Clay introduced eight resolutions on the floor of the Senate, intended to quell the controversy and save the Union. Among other measures, Clay called for the admission of California as a free state, counterbalanced by the organization of the New Mexico and Utah territories "without any restriction or condition on the subject of slavery"; for the abolition of the public slave trade in the District of Columbia, but without limiting slavery itself; and finally for the enactment of a stronger fugitive slave law. Although negotiation of the eventual Compromise of 1850 took much of the following year, its prospects were greatly enhanced in early March when Daniel Webster took the floor to speak in favor of Clay's proposals.

Previously known as an opponent of slavery, Webster created a commotion at the very opening of his Seventh of March Address: "I wish to speak today, not as a Massachusetts man, nor as a northern man, but as an American. I speak today for the preservation of the Union. Hear me for my cause." The "preservation of the Union," as everyone well understood, meant an accommodation with slavery. Webster announced that he would not join other Northerners who wanted to to prohibit slavery in New Mexico and he denounced "the Wilmot" as a "taunt or indignity" toward the South.

When it came to the recapture of fugitive slaves, Webster went even further. The complaints of the South, he said, had a "just foundation," in that there has been found at the North, among individuals and among legislators, a disinclination to perform fully their constitutional duties in regard to the return of persons bound to service who have escaped into the free States. In that respect, the South, in my judgment, is right, and the North is wrong.

Northern political leaders and legislatures, he said, had indeed engaged "excuses, evasions [and] escapes" to avoid fulfilling their lawful obligations to deliver up fugitives. Webster therefore called upon "all sober-minded men at the North . . . who are not carried away by some fanatical idea or some false impression" to join him in supporting the proposed fugitive slave law "with all its provisions, to the fullest extent." This, he advised, was "a question of morals and a question of conscience," unequivocally concluding that "the South has been injured in this respect, and has a right to complain; and the North has been too careless of what I think the Constitution . . . enjoins upon her as a duty."[8]

Not everyone was willing to go along, especially Webster's fellow northern Whigs, many of whom were infuriated "that he could charge the North with wronging the South over the elimination of a moral evil."[9] William Seward— who had represented John Van Zandt three years earlier before the U.S. Supreme Court—had recently been elected to the Senate from New York. In his first major floor speech, on March 11, 1850, he accepted Webster's challenge and rejected the very idea of a compromise on "the questions which have arisen out of slavery."

I am opposed to any such compromise in any way, and in all the forms in which it has been proposed. They involve the surrender of the exercise of judgment and conscience.

Seward rejected completely the proposed Fugitive Slave Act. There could be "no guaranty for the return of fugitive slaves," he said, "because you cannot roll back the tide of social progress."

Most famously, Seward added that "there is a higher law than the Constitution." He did not mean to declare that the Constitution could be flouted in the name of conscience, even for the protection of fugitives, but rather that it had to be interpreted in keeping with "the common heritage of mankind, bestowed upon them by the Creator of the universe."[10] Nonetheless, the juxtaposition of Seward's statement with Webster's position—respect for the higher law versus enforcement of slaveholders' constitutional rights—became the framework for much of the public, political, and courtroom debate over the following decade.

The Compromise of 1850 took an extended and tortuous route through Congress, following the death of President Zachary Taylor (who did not support it) and the inauguration of Millard Fillmore (who did), the appointment of Daniel Webster as secretary of state, the semiretirement of Henry Clay, and the subsequent assumption of leadership by Senator Stephen Douglas of Illinois. In the end, the ultimate compromise more or less adhered to Clay's original outline, with an enhanced fugitive slave law as its most prominent provision.

Initially proposed by Senator James Mason of Virginia, the new fugitive slave bill (technically an amendment to the Act of 1793) was designed to respond to the Supreme Court ruling in *Prigg v. Pennsylvania* by completely federalizing the apprehension of runaways while denying states any power to interfere. Even though a majority of northern congressmen and senators opposed the new law, it managed to pass both houses when President Fillmore persuaded a sufficient number of Northerners to abstain on the final vote.

The central feature of the bill was the authorization of U.S. court commissioners to preside over all aspects of fugitive slave proceedings. Commissioners were low-level quasi-judicial officers appointed by circuit judges, but not subject to confirmation by the Senate, whose authority was otherwise quite limited. The Fugitive Slave Act increased the number of commissioners and allowed them to exercise "concurrent jurisdiction" with federal judges, and to issue warrants, appoint deputies, hold hearings, and issue "certificates of removal" for the return of fugitives to their asserted masters.

Virtually every aspect of the Fugitive Slave Act was tilted against the alleged runaway, who was denied the right to a jury trial, to appeal, or to seek relief from another court. The law specifically provided that "in no trial or hearing under this act shall the testimony of such alleged fugitive be admitted into evidence."[11] The latter provision was not quite as draconian as it now must seem. In 1850 plaintiffs and defendants in lawsuits, including criminal defendants, were not permitted to testify on their own behalf in any state or federal court, pursuant to the so-called interested-party rule. Strictly speaking, then, the no-testimony provision of the Fugitive Slave Act merely put an alleged slave (the subject of the proceeding, but not a formal party) on the same footing as the alleged master (the plaintiff or claimant), neither being allowed to testify. But of course their true positions were far from equivalent. The claimants had resources to call upon other witnesses—agents, employees, neighbors—to testify to the identity and servile status of a prisoner, while the fugitives almost invariably had only themselves.

Other features of the Act were also calculated to make rendition as simple as possible. A claimant had the right simply to seize an alleged fugitive, or alternatively to obtain a warrant, and assistance if necessary, from a commissioner. When it came to proof of status, the certification of a southern court, issued ex parte to a slaveholder, was to be taken by the commissioner as "full and conclusive evidence of the fact of escape." The only issue left open was identity—whether the captured prisoner was in fact the person sought—but even that was subject to summary determination by the commissioner, who was authorized to rely on "a general description of the person so escaping, with such convenient certainty as may be." No appeals were allowed from a commissioner's ruling, nor was the writ of habeas corpus available. As one last, and gratuitous, thumb on the scale, a commissioner was to be paid $10 for granting a certificate of removal, but only $5 for ruling in favor of an alleged slave.

Supporters of the Act defended its obvious one-sidedness by asserting that fugitive rendition was only a preliminary proceeding and that an alleged slave could obtain a full trial upon return to his or her purported master.[12] The disparity in payment to the commissioner was justified on the ground that additional paperwork was necessary to grant a certificate of removal. Those arguments were rationalizations at best, and makeweights at worst. The promise of a postrendition trial, for example, was illusory, given that the captured fugitive could not testify and other slaves and free blacks were prohibited in every southern state from appearing even as supporting witnesses.[13] In truth, it was evident from the start that the entire purpose of the Act was to make it nearly impossible for judicial process to delay the restoration of slaves to claimants. Virginia Senator James Mason, one of the principal sponsors of the bill, all but conceded as much when he asserted that no person or court should have "a right to interpose between the claimant and the fugitive, or to inquire whether the slave be his, or whether he is a slave at all, far less to molest or hinder him in the capture."[14]

For all of its blatant unfairness, the Act might have been considered tolerable in the North—at least among non-abolitionists—if it had been directed only at blacks. Additional aspects of the law, however, were demeaning to state governments and burdensome to white citizens.

The statute made it a crime, subject to fine and six months' imprisonment, to obstruct or hinder the seizure of a fugitive—even when a claimant was acting without a warrant—as well as to aid, abet, assist, rescue, harbor, or conceal a fugitive. "Molestation" by legal process—meaning the use of free-state courts to protect fugitives—was prohibited. More offensive still, federal marshals or other "suitable persons" appointed by commissioners were given the power to "call to their aid the bystanders, or *posse comitatus,* of the proper county" and command them to assist "in the prompt and efficient execution of this law." Citizens who refused to be pressed into slave catching risked being charged with "indirectly" assisting an escape, in which case they could be held liable for the value of the lost slave.

Leaving no insulting stone unturned, the Act also imposed penalties on any conscience-stricken federal marshals who hesitated to participate in the capture of slaves or who otherwise failed to "use all proper means diligently to execute" the law. It even imposed liability on marshals for the escape of a fugitive, "whether with or without the assent of such marshal." On the other hand, if a slave owner feared that a fugitive would be rescued, he was entitled to demand that the marshal, with as many deputies as necessary, "remove [the fugitive] to the State whence he fled, and there to deliver him to the said claimant."

It would be difficult to imagine a more intrusive law, or one more calculated to provoke resistance in the North. Not only did the law belittle the role of state courts while mocking the very idea of due process in its own rigged tribunals, but it also put the federal government itself in the business of manhunting, while requiring "every free-born American to become a man-hunter on occasion." The Fugitive Slave Act of 1850 had no redeeming qualities, even for the Southerners who demanded its passage as the price of maintaining the Union. The law has been called "futile," "gratuitously obnoxious," and "a firebrand vastly more inflammatory than the Wilmot Proviso." Its "unrelieved abrasiveness" turned it into "the most divisive legacy" of the entire decade.[15]

Surely the southern sponsors of the bill must have had at least some apprehension that it might backfire. In fact, northern senators had offered several amendments to make the bill more palatable, providing for jury trials, access to habeas corpus, and the elimination of conscripted posses. (Even President Fillmore had momentary qualms about the bill's abridgement of habeas corpus, until he was reassured by a written opinion from Attorney General John J. Crittenden.)

It should have been obvious that northern communities would far more faithfully comply with a "just and reasonable" law than with an "arbitrary, oppressive" one, and yet the Southerners persisted. Senator Mason, the bill's sponsor, ridiculed the idea that Northerners would ever willingly assist in the recapture of runaways. In the absence of the statute's most coercive measures, he said, "You may as well go down into the sea, and recover from his native element a fish which has escaped you."[16] Maybe so, but at least some Northerners might have been attuned to the unintended irony in Mason's metaphor. Whatever similar challenges faced both anglers and slave catchers, it was obvious that fish had no natural rights in any part of the country. And in any event, most fishermen would have been just as eager to catch a freeborn fish as one that had escaped.

But who worries about irony when regional honor is at stake? Not Virginia's Mason, when explaining the need for his harsh bill: "Although the loss of property is felt," he said, "the loss of honor is felt still more." For the South, the Fugitive Slave Act was far more important symbolically than practically, signaling as it did an important victory over the forces of free soil and abolition. If nothing else, the law promised to make Northerners, no matter how reluctant, complicit in the preservation of slavery, inherently conceding, therefore, the legitimacy of slavery as a national institution. Of course, that in turn would depend on enforcement. "The continued existence of the United States as one nation," according to one southern newspaper, "depends upon the full and faithful execution of the Fugitive Slave Bill."[17]

The Fugitive Slave Act, by its very terms, contemplated that Northerners would have to be dragooned into fulfilling their duties as slave catchers. Otherwise, there would have been no need for such intimidating provisions. Resistance to the law was no doubt anticipated, although the vehemence of the confrontations—ignited by the volatile admixture of desperate fugitives, self-righteous slave owners, and ardent abolitionists—sent recurrent shock waves across the national body politic.

There have been various attempts by historians to describe the typical fugitive slave, but records are by their nature incomplete and no strong consensus has emerged. Were the runaways mostly young, single men who were able to travel unencumbered? Were they families, or husbands and wives, frantically trying to avoid the degradation of forced separation? Did they tend to be hired slaves who worked as store clerks or as skilled laborers, and thus had access to a broader community? Or were they field hands, reacting to cruelty and abuse? In fact, fugitive slaves came in every description. Some ran away on impulse, while others made elaborately plotted attempts in groups of two, three, nine, or more. Some acted entirely on their own, while others were led to freedom by "conductors" such as Harriet Tubman. Of course, most fugitives in the North fled from border states, where they had only to cross a river—or in the case of Maryland's boundary with Pennsylvania, simply walk across an imaginary line—to reach free territory. Some, however, made it from Georgia or South Carolina all the way to Boston or New York.

Whatever the precise demographics, the fugitives all "acted on an intention to transform their position from property to persons."[18] That presented an intolerable contradiction for southern slavocrats who were eager to present slavery as a benevolent institution. Of course, there was nothing benign about slavery. Its entire structure depended on the implicit brutality of each master's "uncontrolled authority over the body" of the slave, although that cruel reality was usually denied or obscured as much as possible in polite company.[19] To maintain the masters' genteel worldview, every runaway therefore had to be portrayed as an aberration—either foolishly errant or, worse, lured from home by unscrupulous abolitionists or, worst of all, dangerously unstable and rebellious. Frederick Douglass, perhaps the most famous fugitive in American history, epitomized slaveholders' most grave fears—militant and charismatic, he dared anyone to try to recapture him[20]—but every successful runaway, no matter how anonymous, was in some way a silent rebuke of the southern way of life.[21]

To explain the fugitive phenomenon, Dr. Samuel Cartwright of New Orleans developed the theory of drapetomania, a supposed mental illness that was said to cause slaves to run away. Derived from the Greek words for runaway slave and crazy (literally, "mad slave disease"), drapetomania was said to be curable, at least in the first instance, with the provision of adequate food and shelter. Repeated occurrences, however, had to be treated with vigorous whippings until the subjects fell "into that submissive state which it was intended for them to occupy in all aftertime." Dysaesthesia, a similar "disease" that was said to cause overwhelming sloth, was likewise curable, according to Dr. Cartwright, by administering sufficient beatings to stir the blacks' "molasses-like" blood.[22]

In a culture where repeated whippings could be seriously recommended as medicinal, it was only a small step to believe that recapture was merely an exercise of responsible paternalism or even kindness. In that light, there could be no valid reason for Northerners' squeamishness, much less their obstinacy, at returning runaways.

But if the dominant myth—childish slaves and benevolent masters—had ever been credible in the North, it was demolished by the life stories of the real fugitives who increasingly came to public attention following enactment of the Fugitive Slave Act. For many Northerners, it had been possible to look away from the fugitive problem in the years before 1850. Recapture then had been the work of private slave hunters, whose efforts were at least blunted by state statutes such as the Latimer law. Although a majority of Northerners may have come to consider slavery distasteful, only a minority of abolitionists and activists attempted to protest, much less intervene, when fugitives were seized.

After 1850, however, the federal government took over the active management of that disagreeable enterprise—empowering the slave catchers, putting the federal courts at their service, and potentially commanding all good citizens "to aid and assist in the prompt and efficient execution of this law." At that point, it became far harder to remain uninvolved. There was nothing hypothetical or remote about the emotional impact of the Fugitive Slave Act. It brought home the plight of hundreds of flesh-and-blood people who had risked their lives to reach New York, Philadelphia, Boston, and many smaller towns and hamlets, and who now might be tracked down by slave catchers.

That lesson became clear in the autumn of 1850 when slave hunters sought to arrest George and Ellen Craft, only weeks after the passage of the Act. Two years earlier, the Crafts had made a daring escape from slavery in Georgia, traveling by steamer and train from Macon through Baltimore and Philadelphia, and finally to Boston. The fair-skinned Ellen had disguised herself as an invalid young white man, headed north to seek medical attention. She kept her right arm in a sling so that she would not have to write, and bandaged her face to muffle her voice. William played the part of her "servant," accompanying his "master," who was too ill to travel alone.[23]

In Boston, the Crafts obtained the assistance of Rev. Theodore Parker, who was well known for his ministry to escaped slaves, and Lewis Hayden, a merchant and the acknowledged leader of the city's black abolitionists. Under Parker and Hayden's guidance, the Crafts attempted to take up normal lives in Boston, he as a cabinetmaker and she as a seamstress. Seemingly safe in their new home, the Crafts also became frequent lecturers on the antislavery circuit, achieving considerable prominence with the tale of their dramatic flight through the South.

The publicity surrounding the Crafts attracted the attention of their owner, Robert Collins, although Massachusetts's Latimer law made it impractical for him to attempt to reclaim his property. The enactment of the Fugitive Slave Act, however, changed the balance of power. Almost as soon as President Fillmore signed the bill, Collins dispatched two agents, named Hughes and Knight, to Boston with orders to seize the Crafts. The slave hunters initially had some difficulty obtaining a warrant; the fugitive law was new and controversial, and a number of federal judges were reluctant to be the first to authorize its use. Hughes and Knight eventually persuaded a court to issue the necessary papers, but their repeated efforts and inquiries had by then alerted the abolitionist Vigilance Committee, which swung into action to protect the fugitives. The Crafts were separately sheltered by the abolitionist community—William lived with Hayden, whose house was strongly barricaded and well stocked with guns and ammunition; Ellen was hidden more quietly by Parker—while crowds of abolitionists denounced and threatened the slave catchers. Members of the Vigilance Committee put up handbills warning of the "man-stealers," who were taunted on the streets and at one point briefly arrested for conspiracy to commit kidnapping.

Hughes and Knight at first met the resistance with bravado, vowing to capture the Crafts "if [we] have to stay here to all eternity."[24] The Fillmore administration encouraged the slave catchers to remain in the hunt, but eventually the harassment, including multiple arrests and physical threats, became too much for them and they left empty-handed.

In this early instance, the higher law had prevailed in the streets of Boston. The abolitionist community had not been willing to acquiesce to the Fugitive Slave Act and, in fact, had been energized by the challenge. "We must trample this law under our feet," Wendell Phillips had declared, and his cohorts proceeded to do just that by sending Hughes and Knight packing, warrants and all. Appalled by the failure of federal power, President Fillmore offered assistance to the Crafts' owner if he were willing to try again. While Parker, Hayden, and Phillips were no doubt primed for another showdown, the Crafts themselves prudently concluded that their situation had become too parlous. Rather than risk capture, they fled to England, where they continued to write and speak in opposition to slavery.

Contrary to the hopes of Henry Clay and Daniel Webster, the Fugitive Slave Act had become a major source of intersectional conflict, and matters would only get worse as the federal government was drawn ever more deeply into its enforcement on behalf of the South. Far from putting the question of national slavery to rest, the Act had actually transferred the controversy from remote, and barely settled, territories to the population centers of the East, potentially entangling the federal government in every escape, warrant, seizure, rescue, and trial until the advent of the Civil War.

To risk mixing a metaphor, the key to the Compromise of 1850 had in fact become its Achilles' heel. Although politicians in the North and South had reached a cautious agreement, they had overlooked or underestimated the importance of a third force—black Americans—who were never part of the deal and who could not be bound, or even influenced, by its terms. With the increasing support of abolitionist allies, they would continue to upset the balance, undermine the compromise, break the armistice, and shatter the truce.

∞ 4 ∞

BUT WE HAVE NO COUNTRY

President Millard Fillmore signed the enhanced Fugitive Slave Act on September 18, 1850, creating a near panic in African-American communities throughout the North. From large eastern cities to small communities in the western states, black families suddenly faced the very real prospect of capture and enslavement. The Latimer-type laws had previously offered at least some protection to northern blacks, but that had been ripped away by the federalization of slave catching and the command that "all good citizens" assist in the "prompt execution" of the law. Free blacks could hope to fare only slightly better than escapees, because the new law provided them scant opportunity to prove their freeborn or manumitted status. The certification of a southern court was to be taken as conclusive proof of slavery, supported only by a general description of the person sought, while the alleged fugitive was not allowed even to speak on his or her own behalf. With no right to appeal or to petition a real court, black people, no matter how lawfully free, could easily find themselves on the block at a slave market within days of capture.

Barely a week after the passage of the new statute, northern blacks learned just how callously the law would be applied. On September 26 a young porter named James Hamlet was arrested in New York City and taken before fugitive slave commissioner John Gardiner. Hamlet protested that he was legally a free man, by virtue of his birth to a free woman, but Commissioner Gardiner would not allow him to testify in his own defense. Instead, the commissioner accepted the hearsay testimony of the alleged owner's agents and ordered Hamlet into slavery. Hamlet's friends and supporters were later able to purchase his freedom for $900, but that provided little comfort to others who might become trapped by the Fugitive Slave Act. It was a rare black person who could raise such an enormous ransom, and Hamlet's release would prove to be an exception indeed. By the end of 1850, there would be nineteen successful proceedings under the fugitive law, with only two dismissals.[1]

The Fugitive Slave Act left runaways with only a few options. They could flee to Canada, disrupting their lives and dividing their families, but at least finding freedom under the protection of the British Crown. Many did just that. The *Pennsylvania Freeman* reported that 40 percent of Boston's black residents left for Canada in the first day after the law was enacted. That number may well have been exaggerated, but there is no doubt that numerous black communities suddenly began to shrink. Church congregations became smaller across New England, New York, and Pennsylvania, and the leading hotels in Pittsburgh announced that they were without servants because so many blacks had left for Canada.[2]

For those without the funds or contacts to reach Canada (or England, as in the case of William and Ellen Craft), a common alternative was to remain as inconspicuous as possible in their northern homes, while relying on popular sentiment for protection. Rev. Theodore Parker, whose Boston congregation included hundreds of fugitives, urged the "fugitive and colored inhabitants of Boston and the neighborhood to remain with us, for we have not the smallest fears that any one of them will be taken and carried off to bondage." An article in *The Liberator* argued that "more can be accomplished by the all-controlling power of *public sentiment* than by guns, bowie knives, or pistols."[3] That was easier advice to give than to follow, and many African-Americans were understandably skeptical about the effectiveness, if not the virtue, of nonresistance.

The third alternative was to organize active resistance among the fugitives themselves. Rev. Jermain Loguen, a fugitive from Kentucky who had established a ministry in Syracuse, told his followers that they must crush the law or be crushed by it. "I will not live a slave, and if force is employed to reenslave me, I will make preparations to meet the crisis as becomes a man." William Powell, of the Manhattan Anti-Slavery Society, argued that the law "must be resisted and disobeyed at all hazards and by all means, non-violent and violent." A meeting of blacks—both free and fugitive—at New York's Zion Chapel resolved to "arm themselves with the surest and most deadly weapons; to resist unto death." A member of Boston's League of Freedom was yet more specific, simply advising "every fugitive to arm himself with a revolver." Vigilance committees were organized in virtually every city and town with a significant black population, many after hearing Frederick Douglass's call to "resist the execution of the Fugitive Slave Law, even to the taking of a life."[4]

The most stunning instance of black resistance to the Fugitive Slave Act took place in Christiana, Pennsylvania, on September 11, 1851, when a party of slave catchers was routed as they attempted to capture four runaways. In the course of "Freedom's Battle," as Douglass later called it, one Maryland slave owner was killed and three of his relatives were gravely wounded, while the federal marshal who led the raid was sent running for his life. The Fillmore administration responded furiously by issuing forty-one indictments—against thirty-six black men and five whites—for the capital crime of treason against the United States. Never before (or since) in the history of the United States had so many people faced the death penalty for participation in a single event. The case was heard in Philadelphia's Independence Hall, the same building where the Fugitive Slave Clause had been affixed to the Constitution sixty-four years earlier.[5]

In the end, however, only one person was actually brought to trial for the Christiana Riot (as it came to be known), a white miller named Castner Hanway who had been present, but unarmed, at the scene of the killing. Hanway was alleged to be part of a dangerous conspiracy—fanatical abolitionists who adhered to the "monstrous doctrine" of higher law and who used "colored people [as] instruments of war" against the government.[6] To the defense, however, Hanway was the innocent target of a political vendetta intended to intimidate the abolitionist movement and its sympathizers. Hanway's life depended on the jury's decision. Was he the wicked instigator of a murderous insurrection, or a hapless bystander victimized by a show trial? Whichever view prevailed in court, there was no doubt at the time that Hanway's prosecution was a test case for the vigorous enforcement of the Fugitive Slave Act.

—•—

In the autumn of 1851, Frederick Douglass was surely the most notorious escaped slave in the United States. William Parker—a much more obscure fugitive, then living near Christiana, Pennsylvania—was in many ways more dangerous.

After several failed attempts to escape from slavery in Maryland, Douglass had finally succeeded in 1838, using false papers to make his way first to Philadelphia and then onward to New Bedford, Massachusetts. In 1841 Douglass attended an antislavery meeting in Nantucket, where he met William Lloyd Garrison. With Garrison's encouragement, Douglass soon became a frequent lecturer at antislavery meetings across the United States. He joined the staff of The Liberator in Boston and in 1845 published his first autobiography, which helped establish him as the nineteenth century's "foremost black agitator, intellectual, political leader, orator, and reformer." Initially committed to the Garrisonian philosophy of nonresistance and nonviolence, Douglass began to break with Garrison over both personal and tactical issues in the late 1840s. With the passage of the Fugitive Slave Act, Douglass abandoned his earlier pacifism in favor of forcible resistance to the law, asserting that he "who would be free must himself strike the first blow" even if that led to blood in the streets. The "law of God," declared Douglass, "required the death of the kidnappers."[7]

If Frederick Douglass was the leading theorist of black resistance, William Parker was certainly one of his most indomitable adherents. About four years younger than Douglass, Parker too was born in Maryland, where the two men met briefly while both were still slaves. Like Douglass, Parker had endured a fairly humane form of slavery, working for relatively "good" masters on a series of plantations. Also like that of Douglass, the moderate nature of Parker's bondage only encouraged his desire for freedom. As Douglass wrote, "Whenever my condition was improved, instead of its increasing my contentment, it only increased my desire to be free, and set me to thinking of plans to gain my freedom."[8]

In 1839 Parker and his brother ran away from their owner, traveling by foot to southeastern Pennsylvania and ultimately settling near the village of Christiana. Unlike Douglass, Parker did not make his way farther into the abolitionist stronghold of New England, but rather stayed, as did many fugitives, within a day's journey of southern slavery.

Boston may have been the command center for American abolitionism, but southern Pennsylvania was definitely the front line in a series of running battles between fugitives and slave catchers. For decades slaves had been escaping from Maryland into Pennsylvania, where they attempted to hide themselves among the fairly substantial free black population. As Parker explained in his 1865 memoir, most slaves were unaccustomed to traveling and therefore thought that a few hours' walk was a long journey. As a result, fugitives tended to cluster near the border, in part because they did not understand how close they remained to their former owners. The slave hunters, on the other hand, knew full well that it would be easiest to capture the fugitives who remained closest to "home." Nor were they always very particular to distinguish between fugitive slaves and the many free blacks who lived in the area. A healthy black adult could fetch a good price in Maryland, and it was a fairly simple matter to transport an unlucky captive the relatively few miles necessary to reach a slave market.

Parker and his brother encountered one such gang of slave catchers on their very first night in Pennsylvania, but they were not easy prey. "See here," said one of the slave hunters, "you are the fellows that this advertisement calls for. . . . I have taken back many a runaway, and I can take you." The white man reached into his pocket, as if to draw a pistol, when Parker struck him a heavy blow on the arm with his walking stick. The slave catcher "fell as if it was broken [and then] he turned and ran."[9] That was the beginning of Parker's career as a guerrilla fighter and defender of fugitives, which in its own way was every bit as remarkable as Douglass's career as a writer and lecturer.

Some years after he arrived in Pennsylvania, Parker had "the great privilege of seeing that true friend of the slave, William Lloyd Garrison, who came into the neighborhood accompanied by Frederick Douglass." It was a transformative experience for Parker, who was surprised to hear another former slave's "free-spoken and manly language against slavery" and impressed by how much it embodied his own "crude ideas of freedom." Parker came away from the lecture vowing that "I would assist in liberating everyone within my reach at the risk of my life, and that I would devise some plan for their entire liberation." The result of Parker's resolution was the establishment of a mutual protection organization, composed of runaways and free blacks who were determined to use as much force as necessary to repel slaveholders and kidnappers.

Over the following years, Parker's organization fought numerous skirmishes with slave catchers, including an incident at a place called Gap Hill, where Parker and his band overtook a gang of slave hunters who were dragging a young girl back to Maryland. After freeing the frightened girl, Parker and his men beat the slave catchers so badly that two of them later died. The girl had denied being a runaway, but was she telling the truth? It is entirely possible that the slave catchers had never inquired and did not really care. It is certain, however, that her status made absolutely no difference to Parker, who treated every slave catcher, lawfully empowered or otherwise, like a kidnapper. He and his group confronted slave hunters on the roads, at jails, and once even in the midst of a trial. Whether the capture of a black person was "clothed with legal authority or not, I did not care," he explained, "as I never had faith in nor respect for the fugitive slave law."[10]

Parker developed a reputation as a fearless defender of fugitives who was willing to back up his principles with violence. His small home—a two-story stone farmhouse that he rented from a Quaker, Levi Pownell—became a meeting place for runaways, who would come to Parker for protection when it was rumored that slave hunters were on the prowl in Lancaster County. Thus, when four young men escaped from the plantation of Edward Gorsuch in nearby Baltimore County, Maryland, it was only a matter of time before several of them found their way to Parker's house, where they had good reason to believe they would be safe from recapture.

Gorsuch, however, proved to be more resourceful and more daring than most slave owners. With the assistance of informants and federal authorities, he managed to track his slaves all the way to Parker's front step. The ensuing armed confrontation between Parker's resistance fighters and Gorsuch's posse might well be called the first pitched battle of the Civil War.

———

On November 6, 1849, four slaves—Nelson Ford, Noah Buley, and George and Joshua Hammond—escaped from Gorsuch's plantation under cover of darkness. The young men had been for some time stealing grain from their master, and they may have run away out of fear of punishment when they realized that their pilfering had been discovered. Or perhaps their thefts had been part of a longer-standing plan to finance an escape—they sold the grain, through an intermediary, to a local miller—although that seems less probable. Gorsuch was another "good" master who, in fact, had promised freedom to his slaves when they reached the age of twenty-six. The youngest of the runaways was already nineteen and the oldest was about twenty-two, so it seems unlikely that all four would have jeopardized their certain freedom—which lay only a few years off—unless they had some compelling reason to flee.[11]

It was not unusual for slaves to slip away from their owners when they feared trouble. In the great majority of cases, absent slaves would only hide in the nearby woods or in the slave quarters of another local plantation, until they were finally spotted or returned home voluntarily. Gorsuch may have expected his absent slaves to follow the same pattern, but he soon came to believe that they had fled to Pennsylvania. By the end of November he had sent his son Dickinson to Harrisburg, hoping to enlist state officials in the search for his missing men. Under the *Prigg* decision, however, the Pennsylvania authorities were under no obligation to provide any assistance, and Dickinson came home disappointed. Gorsuch made a similar attempt in early 1850, but again the Pennsylvania government declined to help him.[12]

In the fall of 1850, the Fugitive Slave Act made it possible for slave owners to bypass local authorities in their search for missing property. Under the new law, Gorsuch could apprehend his own slaves, if only he could discover their whereabouts. Less than a year later, in late August 1851, Gorsuch received the information he had been waiting for, in the form of a handwritten letter from an informant named William Padgett. According to Padgett, Gorsuch's slaves could be found living in Lancaster County, within two miles of each other. He advised Gorsuch to travel immediately by way of Philadelphia, where he could assemble a "force of the right kind" with the assistance of a deputy U.S. marshal. Padgett promised to meet Gorsuch in a tavern "at the gap" where he optimistically predicted they could perfect a plan to "divide and take them [all] within half an hour."[13]

Padgett had well chosen the meeting location. The "Gap" was a region near the Maryland border where slave hunters were known to gather, and the area had become the home of the Gap Gang, "a loosely organized band of working-class whites who terrorized the black community of Lancaster County."[14] Padgett, himself a member of the Gap Gang, evidently made a living by spying on suspected runaways and then reporting them to their alleged masters. He may have later acted as a guide for Gorsuch, but he otherwise left to others the dirty work of actually restraining suspected fugitives.

Upon receiving Padgett's letter, Gorsuch quickly assembled a slave-hunting party of friends and relatives, including his son Dickinson, his elderly cousin Joshua Gorsuch, his nephew Dr. Thomas Pearce, and two neighbors, Nathan Nelson and Nicholas Hutchings. After making sure that his posse was well armed, Gorsuch set off alone for Philadelphia, with plans to meet up with the others near the Gap.

On September 9 Gorsuch arrived in Philadelphia, where he found the federal authorities much more accommodating than the Pennsylvania officials had ever been. He easily obtained four fugitive slave warrants from Commissioner Edward Ingraham, who was known for his cavalier approach to proof in fugitive cases. The previous December Ingraham had relied on a second-hand identification to issue a certificate of removal against a black man named Adam Gibson, despite substantial testimony that he had been born free.

Gibson was duly chained and shipped to Maryland, where his purported owner recognized that a mistake had been made. Luckily the slave owner was an honest man, who released Gibson and returned him to freedom.[15] Ingraham was not known to have apologized for the error.

Gorsuch also secured the assistance of federal Deputy Marshal Henry Kline. Thus armed with federal warrants, and backed up by federal firepower, Gorsuch was ready to meet the rest of his posse in the Gap. To avoid arousing suspicion, Kline and Gorsuch agreed to travel separately by rail to the town of Penningtonville, where they would rendezvous with the rest of their crew. Gorsuch made the trip without incident, but Kline ran into difficulty almost immediately.

Because he was well-known as "a professional kidnapper of the basest stamp," Kline was often closely watched by a "Special Secret Committee" of black abolitionists in Philadelphia.[16] Once he was seen huddling with Gorsuch, it was not hard for the committee to figure out that Kline had a new assignment. Samuel Williams, a committee member and the owner of the Bolivar Tavern in Philadelphia, was assigned to carry a warning to the fugitives in Lancaster County.

As it happened, Kline and Williams arrived almost simultaneously at a tavern in Penningtonville, a few hours after midnight on September 10. Realizing that he had been followed, Kline attempted to throw Williams offtrack by announcing that he was on the trail of horse thieves. Williams was hardly fooled. Hoping that he might be able to abort the deputy's entire manhunt, he told Kline that "your horse thieves were here and gone. You might as well go home."[17] Kline did not get the message. He was either too confident or too dense (or perhaps too greedy; he was being paid for his work) to realize that his mission had been compromised before it could get under way.

In any event, Kline continued on to the Gap Tavern to meet his confederates, while Williams proceeded to Christiana, where he began to raise the alarm. Word of the slave hunters "spread through the vicinity like a fire in the prairies,"[18] reaching Parker's house by that afternoon.

Parker lived with his wife, Eliza, and their two children, as well as Hannah and Alexander Pinckney, Eliza's sister and brother-in-law. Three other men were also at Parker's on the night of September 10: two of Gorsuch's slaves, who had changed their names to Samuel Thompson and Joshua Kite, and Abraham Johnson, who was also a fugitive from Maryland. Anticipating an attack, the seven adults sat up late into the night wondering when it might come. Parker attempted to reassure his friends and family that they needn't worry, but he sent his children, and those of the Pinckneys, to their grandmother's house for safety.

News of the slave catchers was not limited to Christiana's black community. Sarah Pownell, Parker's neighbor and landlady, also heard the reports, and she hurried over to warn him. Pownell knew Parker's reputation as a fighter but, as a Quaker, felt compelled to urge him to flee to Canada rather than take arms. As Douglass later reported,

> He replied that if the laws protected colored men as they did white men, he too would be non-resistant and not fight, but would appeal to the laws. "But," he said, "the laws for personal protection are not made for us, and we are not bound to obey them. If a fight occurs, I want the whites to keep away. They have a country and may obey the laws. But we have no country."[19]

"But we have no country." The caustic observation was Parker's, but the expression may well have been Douglass's, as it captured in a few words much of his philosophy about the relationship between African-Americans and the slavery-dominated government. Slaves were under no obligation to obey the laws that had robbed them of their own liberty, Douglass believed, because "the morality of *free* society can have no application to *slave* society." Thus, it was no crime at all for a slave to kill in defense of his freedom.[20] Douglass also recognized that the rejection of ordinary morality would be difficult for his white supporters to accept or adopt, even those who recognized that the higher law superseded the Constitution. Perhaps that is why he made a point of noting Parker's admonition that his white friends stay away from the impending fight. Invocations of morality would only get in the way on the battlefield.

A different problem would arise whenever the struggle shifted from the battlefield to the courtroom, where virtually all of the lawyers were white and trials were held under the government's laws. Could any conception of the higher law excuse tactics such as suppressing evidence or using perjured testimony? Runaway slaves were surely entitled to lie without hesitation when escaping—as had the Crafts, as had Parker, and as had Douglass himself in his use of false papers—but could the same justification be invoked by their white rescuers or their lawyers? That question would be presented—sometimes implicitly, sometimes as an accusation from the prosecution—in all of the trials held under the Fugitive Slave Act. Douglass, and no doubt Parker, would have laughed at the idea that a slave owed any duty of truthfulness to a white judge. As we will see, however, the answer was more complicated for even the most ardent of the antislavery lawyers.

Parker and his friends were hardly concerned about moral philosophy on the night of September 10, as they steeled themselves for the next morning. For them, freedom fighting was a matter of survival, not a subject for debate. Parker had fearlessly confronted slave hunters across Lancaster County, and he was not about to quail before them in his own home.

Marshal Kline, meanwhile, was still trying to collect his troops. The stratagem of traveling separately turned out to be a fiasco, failing to provide anonymity and making it difficult for the group to assemble at their destination. It took the full day of September 10 for the entire party—Kline, Gorsuch, and the other Marylanders—to finally reconnect at the Gap Tavern. After obtaining the service of a local guide, the slave hunters were finally able to coordinate an approach to Parker's in the early morning of September 11. By that time they may have been among the few people in the Christiana area who did not realize that an armed confrontation was about to take place.

The posse of seven left the Gap Tavern an hour or so after midnight. Their guide led them overland for seven or eight miles until they reached Parker's house just before sunrise. As the guide departed—if it was indeed Padgett the informer, he obviously wanted no part of the trouble to come—a young black man stepped out of the house, alerted by the trampling in the surrounding field. It took him only an instant to realize what was happening. "O William! Kidnappers! Kidnappers!" he shouted as he raced back indoors.[21]

Parker and the others were still in their sleeping quarters on the second floor of the stone building, where they had also stockpiled firearms and other weapons. Kline and Gorsuch barged through the open front door but paused at the foot of the narrow staircase. Gorsuch, believing that he had recognized one of his slaves, began to head up the stairs but Kline temporarily restrained him. "I am the deputy Marshal," shouted Kline, perhaps expecting a quick surrender.

By that time Parker had come to the landing. Looming over the slave catchers below, he warned them to go away or risk the consequences. "I told him to take another step, and I would break his neck," Parker later recounted. Surprised by the black man's defiance, Kline repeated that he was a U.S. marshal, to which Parker replied that he "did not care for him nor the United States." Kline may not yet have realized the gravity of his situation, as he attempted to match Parker's bravado. "I have heard many a negro talk as big as you," he called up the stairs. "And I have taken him; and I'll take you." "You have not taken me yet," said Parker calmly.[22]

Gorsuch insisted that Kline proceed up the stairs but the marshal thought better of it. Instead, he read out the warrants for the four fugitives and repeated his call for surrender. "You see, we are commanded to take you, dead or alive; so you may as well give up at once." There was no response, other than the sound of guns being loaded. "Go up, Mr. Kline," prompted Gorsuch, but the marshal would not make a decisive move. Gorsuch grew impatient and began to lead the charge himself, only to turn back when a hail of sharp objects—first a five-pronged fish gig, then an ax—came flying at him down the stairway.[23]

Gorsuch and Kline retreated but continued their dire warnings to the fugitives. Then Eliza Parker took matters into her own hands. She went to an attic window and blew several loud blasts on a horn as a signal for friends and supporters to come to their aid. The slave-hunting party responded with gunfire, but Eliza knelt below the window ledge and, behind the safety of the stone walls, continued to sound her alarm.

There was a momentary standoff, as each side attempted to trick the other into giving up. Parker came to the second-story window and shouted to the slave owner, "Am I your man?" "No," answered Gorsuch. He then called his brother-in-law Alexander Pinckney forward. "Is that your man?" "No," again said the slave owner. Abraham Johnson was called next, "but again Gorsuch said he was not his man." At that point Parker was running out of decoys. "The only plan left was to call both Pinckney and Johnson again; for had I called the others, he would have recognized them, for they were his slaves."

Kline did not fall for Parker's ruse, but countered it with one of his own. He hastily scribbled a note and handed it to one of his men. "Take it," he said loudly enough to be heard inside the house, "and bring a hundred men from Lancaster." The siege had taken its toll on Alexander and Hannah Pinckney, who suggested to Parker that they might well have to give up in the face of superior firepower. Parker later claimed that he had not been intimidated, but he did briefly negotiate with the posse, asking for and receiving fifteen minutes to consider whether to surrender.[24]

Before the allotted time could expire, however, reinforcements began to arrive—but not for the slave hunters. In response to Eliza Parker's trumpet call, the members of Parker's self-defense organization came running across the nearby fields. Kline and other witnesses would later testify that as many as 150 blacks came to Parker's rescue, although likely there were no more than forty or fifty. Whatever their number, "almost all were armed, some with pistols, shot guns, or hunting rifles; others carried corn cutters, scythes, or other farm tools that would serve nicely as swords in hand-to-hand combat."[25]

The posse now found itself on the defensive, exposed and surrounded by hostile blacks while their quarry remained secure in Parker's stone house. Frustrated and growing frightened, Kline thought he saw a way out of the dilemma. In addition to the dozens of blacks, several white men had also come to the scene, and the marshal turned to them for assistance. Kline was badly mistaken in thinking that the white men were potential allies. In fact, they were sympathetic to the fugitives, although they had not been summoned by Eliza's horn.

Earlier in the morning, a black man named Isaiah Clarkson had observed the confrontation at Parker's house and set off to get help. His first stop was a store owned by a Quaker named Elijah Lewis. Clarkson told Lewis that kidnappers were attacking Parker's house and asked the shopkeeper to spread the word in order "to see that justice was done." Lewis started toward Parker's, but first he went to Castner Hanway's mill, where he found the miller eating breakfast. "Parker's house was surrounded by kidnappers," he told Hanway, who pushed aside his meal and grabbed his hat. Hanway was feeling poorly that morning, so he saddled his horse rather than accompany Lewis on foot. Lewis had at least one more stop to make—at the home of a black farmer named Jacob Woods—so Hanway was apparently the first local white man to arrive at Parker's that morning. To Hanway's eventual misfortune, he was definitely the first one Kline noticed.

As the miller rode up on his sorrel horse, Kline approached him to enlist his assistance in arresting the runaways. Invoking the authority of the Fugitive Slave Act, Kline showed Hanway his warrants and demanded his help.

Hanway declined, and so did Elijah Lewis, who joined the two men midway in their conversation. Kline and other posse members would later elaborate on this encounter, testifying that Hanway had angrily rejected the marshal's plea for help and had encouraged the deadly violence that followed. The testimony may have been embellished but there is no doubt that both Hanway and Lewis rebuffed Kline's lawful command that they "aid and assist in the prompt and efficient execution of this law." Nor is there any doubt that the discussion was heated, as both men admonished Kline that "the colored people had a right to defend themselves," with Lewis adding that the posse had better "clear out, otherwise there would be blood spilt."[26]

While Kline and the two white men were arguing, Gorsuch remained at his post on Parker's front step, oblivious to the mounting danger all around him. Dozens of armed black men kept arriving, and they became increasingly aggressive and hostile—a development that several witnesses would blame on incitement from Hanway—such that the prospect of a successful arrest, or even a safe retreat, was growing dimmer by the moment. Kline apparently saw the situation far more clearly than the intransigent slave owner, and he called for Gorsuch to withdraw. "Your property is secured to you, provided this man is worth it," he assured Gorsuch, explaining that Hanway's refusal to help had made the miller liable for the slaves' value under the terms of the Fugitive Slave Act. The agitated Gorsuch was not persuaded. "I will have my property, or die in the attempt," he exclaimed.[27]

At that moment, one of Gorsuch's slaves defiantly emerged from the house. "Old man, you had better go home to Maryland," he said. "No," retorted Gorsuch, "you had better give up and come home with me." That would never happen. The runaway slave clubbed his master with a pistol, beating him to the ground. As Gorsuch attempted to draw his own gun, the slave fired one shot and then another, again knocking the old man off his feet. Gorsuch gamely struggled to rise, but then the nearby crowd of black men surged toward him. Shouting loudly, they struck Gorsuch with clubs and corn-cutters until he was senseless. Finally, according to Parker, "the women put an end to him."[28] Southern newspapers would later report that Gorsuch's body had been mutilated, but there was no such evidence in the subsequent coroner's report or inquest.

Gun in hand, young Dickinson Gorsuch attempted to come to the aid of his beleaguered father, only to be met by two blasts from Alexander Pinckney's shotgun. With blood gushing from his mouth, Dickinson staggered about one hundred yards and fell unconscious at the base of an old oak tree. Remarkably, Dickinson survived the shooting, although he had been hit by eighty scattershot in his arms, thigh, and chest. Most of the pellets were later removed by surgeons, although some remained in his body for the rest of his life. When he was prepared for burial in 1882, his torso was still "pitted like a sponge" with the marks of the resistance at Christiana.[29]

Badly outnumbered and outgunned, the remaining members of Kline's posse turned and ran, but they did not all escape injury. Nathan Nelson and Nicholas Hutchings got away unharmed, but Dr. Pearce was hit four or five times by shotgun balls and bullets, and Joshua Gorsuch was beaten severely about the head by everyone "that could get a lick at me."[30] Deputy Kline also ran for cover. He would later testify that he had attempted to hold the ground until some time after Edward Gorsuch was killed, but most other witnesses said that he fled much sooner, refusing to stand by Gorsuch and leaving him to his fate.

Lewis and Hanway had warned that blood would be spilled, but they had no interest in staying around to assess the accuracy of their prediction. Both men headed for safety as soon as the firing began, Lewis on foot across a field and Hanway on horseback down a long lane that led away from the Parker house. At one point Thomas Pearce and Joshua Gorsuch caught up with Hanway in the lane. For a while, both men were able to use Hanway's horse as a partial shield—Pearce would later admit that the maneuver probably saved his life—but the miller eventually galloped ahead of them. Pearce ducked off the road and managed to hide in a field, but Joshua Gorsuch was overtaken and beaten again.

In time, the fury of the riot subsided, which is probably the only reason that Joshua Gorsuch and Thomas Pearce survived. Parker wrote that his men kept firing until their guns "got bent and out of order," but it is also probable that they simply became weary of killing and concerned about arranging their escape. With one slave owner dead and another who appeared to be mortally wounded, there was not much time before the law would descend on Christiana, making it unsafe for even the most steadfast fugitive to remain.[31]

Realizing that they were in great danger, the Parker and Pinckney families abandoned their home within hours of the riot. By nightfall William Parker and Alexander Pinckney were already on their way to Canada. Their escape was surprisingly easy, given the notoriety of the crime. Within two days they were in Rochester, New York, at the home of Frederick Douglass, who received them warmly and introduced them to other members of the abolitionist community.

Douglass interviewed Parker at some length, later reporting the story under the title "Freedom's Battle." Not a trace of his earlier commitment to nonviolence remained in Douglass's account. "The only way to make the Fugitive Slave Law a dead letter," he wrote, "is to make a half a dozen or more dead kidnappers."[32] Parker and Pinckney were heroes to Douglass—they had "already tasted blood"—but it was not safe for them to stay long in his house. "They were not only fugitives from slavery but charged with murder, and officers were in pursuit of them," he recalled. "The hours they spent at my house were therefore hours of anxiety." Douglass hurriedly made preparations for his guests to travel across Lake Ontario to Toronto. When Douglass personally escorted them to the boat he had arranged, Parker handed him, as a "memento of the battle for Liberty," a pistol that he had taken from the dying Edward Gorsuch.[33]

Eliza Parker and Hannah Pinckney had initially stayed behind with their children, but they too, after some harrowing times, reached Canada, where they were reunited with their husbands. The other central figures in the resistance also managed to escape—none of the Gorsuch slaves was ever captured, nor was anyone ever specifically identified and charged with shooting Edward Gorsuch or wounding the others—but that did not prevent the authorities from engaging in a massive roundup.

News of the so-called Christiana Riot had spread quickly, first in Lancaster County and then across the nation. A local posse was assembled by the end of the day, soon supplemented by "gangs of armed ruffians" from Maryland, to hunt down the perpetrators and suspected perpetrators. By the following morning, "a strong force" of about forty-five U.S. Marines had arrived, as well as a contingent of Philadelphia police, both of which joined the numerous county constables and deputy sheriffs who were already in action. The following search paid little heed to such niceties as constitutional rights or actual evidence of guilt. The result was a "reign of terror" in which blacks were arrested indiscriminately and virtually "hunted like partridges."[34]

From the beginning, there was an argument between state and federal law enforcement authorities. The U.S. Attorney and the federal marshal believed that they should have been in charge of the manhunt, while the local district attorney claimed that the crimes fell under Pennsylvania's jurisdiction. The controversy was temporarily "adjusted by an agreement that each party should make its own arrests," but it would resurface as soon as formal court proceedings were initiated, with Maryland also joining the quarrel.[35] Once again the actions of escaped slaves had triggered a dispute among states and the federal government—exactly the sort of conflict that the Compromise of 1850 was intended to prevent.

∽ 5 ∾

A TRAITOROUS COMBINATION

L egal proceedings in the Christiana case began almost immediately, but their course was at first confused and uneven. There were competing state and federal preliminary hearings, and the ultimate nature of the charges— would it be a Pennsylvania murder case or a federal treason prosecution?— remained in some doubt for several weeks.

Within a day of the riot, U.S. Deputy Marshal Henry Kline met with state prosecutors from Lancaster County and swore out murder warrants for five white men and more than a dozen blacks. Without waiting to be arrested, Hanway and Lewis promptly turned themselves in at Zercher's Hotel in Christiana, which had been set up as a temporary courthouse. Unfortunately, Kline was present at the time, and he took the opportunity to assault the two defendants. "You white-livered scoundrels," he shouted. "When I plead for my life like a dog and begged you not to let the blacks fire upon us, you turned round and told them to do so." That was the first intimation that Lewis and Hanway would be charged with directly inciting Gorsuch's murder, and it was delivered with such force that Alderman J. Franklin Reigart, who was to preside over a preliminary hearing, felt compelled to defend the prisoners. He took Kline by the shoulder and ordered him to "say nothing to produce a disturbance."[1] The marshal, however, continued to confront the defendants and later tussled with a guard who attempted to intervene. In the end, Kline was ejected from the room.

Federal Commissioner Edward Ingraham arrived the following day and began taking testimony as well. Kline testified at the hearing, as did a young black man named George Washington Harvey Scott. Kline identified a number of men as present at the riot, and provided a relatively equivocal account of Hanway's involvement. He did not repeat the previous day's accusation that Hanway had called upon the blacks to fire at the slave catchers, but instead said only that Hanway had declared that the "negroes had a right to defend themselves." As to Kline's demand for assistance under the Fugitive Slave Act,

66

Hanway had replied that "he did not care for any act of Congress, or anything else."

Scott's testimony was less oblique, at least with regard to the offense of murder. He testified that he had gone to the scene at the urging of two colored men, John Morgan and Henry Simms, whom he later saw killing Gorsuch— Simms by shooting and Morgan by striking him with a corn cutter. He also identified Hanway as present and attempted to implicate him as a conspirator by testifying that the mob had gathered "to resist all slaveholders." At the close of the day, Scott was "committed as a witness," meaning that he would be held in custody to secure his presence at trial, even though he had not been charged with an offense.[2]

The defendants, too, were held in prison as the case continued to take shape. Ingraham heard additional testimony for several days until September 16, when all proceedings were suspended. The ostensible reason was that Kline, a key witness no matter how the cases were brought, was unavailable, but in fact the hiatus was necessary to give the federal government an opportunity "to prepare and coordinate treason charges against the prisoners."[3]

It had not been immediately obvious that the Christiana riot would lead to a federal prosecution. The most serious crime had been the killing of Edward Gorsuch, and murder fell exclusively under Pennsylvania's jurisdiction. Violating the Fugitive Slave Act was a federal offense, but it carried a maximum penalty of only six months imprisonment and a $1,000 fine. That was hardly likely to satisfy an outraged southern public, which demanded blood for blood. Under federal law, however, the only available capital offense was treason—a charge particularly difficult to prove under the requirements of the Constitution.

On September 16 Maryland Governor Louis Lowe wrote a letter to President Fillmore demanding federal action. Receiving no immediate reply, Lowe published an open letter to the president urging that the Christiana rioters be prosecuted for treason. Lowe's demand for federal involvement was motivated at least in part by his mistrust of Pennsylvania Governor William Johnston, who had opposed the Compromise of 1850 and the Fugitive Slave Act. Compounding matters, Johnston had been inexplicably sluggish in responding to the riot. He made no public statement for three days, and then he seemed to minimize the entire affair. It took Johnston nearly a week to issue a statement of regret and offer a $1,000 reward for the apprehension of the murderers, but by that time "the political damage was done." Johnston had marked himself as reluctant to enforce the Fugitive Slave Act and "soft" on blacks and abolitionists.[4]

It is likely, however, that Maryland's Lowe would have called for federal intervention even if Pennsylvania's Johnston had been a proslavery zealot. Enforcement of the Fugitive Slave Act was a fundamental aspect of the Compromise of 1850, and federal inaction would be seen as a signal that the Union-saving concordat had failed. Could the federal government be relied upon to protect the rights—and indeed the lives—of southern slaveholders who had in good faith complied with every element of the law? If not, the Fugitive Slave Act was little more than an empty promise.

Lowe was not a secessionist, but he well understood the potential consequences of a federal default in the Christiana matter. "I do not know of a single incident that has occurred since the passage of the Compromise measures," he said, "which tends more to weaken the bonds of Union." Calling upon President Fillmore to impose the "most prompt, thorough, and severe retribution upon the murderous treason," Lowe cautioned that the citizens of Maryland "would not remain one day" in the Union if it turned out that the federal government was "inadequate" to the task of ensuring the safe recapture of fugitive slaves.[5]

The Fillmore administration did not need much convincing. Having shepherded the compromise through Congress only a year earlier, the president understood that a show of strength would be necessary to demonstrate that the Fugitive Slave Act could not be violated with impunity. Although the Act had in fact been implemented rather effectively during the previous year, several high-profile "rescues," most notably in Boston, had created the impression that it might become unenforceable, thus adding to the pressure to take the strongest possible steps against anyone connected to the Christiana outrage.

The political case for a treason prosecution relied on a simple syllogism. Enforcement of the Fugitive Slave Act was essential to the unity of the nation. Opposition to the statute therefore threatened the integrity of the Union. Consequently, organized resistance to the Fugitive Slave Act was treasonous. Numerous political leaders had presented versions of that argument on both sides of the Mason-Dixon Line, but none more vigorously than Secretary of State Daniel Webster. In a series of speeches delivered in May 1851, Webster argued repeatedly that slave rescues and other resistance to the Act amounted to treason and that encouraging resistance, even in the name of conscience or higher law, was criminal as well. He castigated abolitionism as a "whirlwind of fanaticism," and he denounced abolitionists as traitors to the Constitution. Physical resistance to the Fugitive Slave Act was "treason, and nothing else," as was even vocal opposition:

> But they meet and pass resolutions; they resolve that the law is op-pressive, unjust, and should not be executed at any rate, or under any circumstances. . . . These proceedings, I say it upon my profes-sional reputation, are distinctly treasonable. Resolutions passed in Ohio, certain resolutions in New York, and in the conventions held in Boston, are distinctly treasonable.[6]

Legally, however, there was more to treason than contempt for the Con-stitution or disobedience to the law. Treason is the only crime specifically defined in the Constitution and it is strictly limited to "levying war" against the United States or adhering to its enemies. Even the most violent resistance to the Fugitive Slave Act could not be characterized as adhering to the na-tion's enemies, but the concept of "levying war" had been given a broad scope in the early nineteenth century. According to the leading antebellum treatise on American criminal law, it was treasonous for any "body of men" to forcibly "resist or oppose the execution of any statute of the United States."[7] In other words, simply violating a statute in any one instance was an ordinary crime, but attempting to nullify the law—by rendering it ineffective in all cases—amounted to levying war. As Webster explained it,

> If men get together, and combine together, and resolve that they will oppose a law of the Government, not in any one case, but in all cases . . . and carry that purpose into effect . . . either by force of arms or force of numbers, that, sir, is treason. . . . When this pur-pose is proclaimed, and it is proclaimed that it will be carried out in all cases, and is carried into effect, by force of arms or num-bers . . . that constitutes a case of levying war against the Union.[8]

Nonetheless, a treason prosecution was not a step to be taken lightly. Ear-lier that year Webster had balked at bringing treason charges following the rescue of a slave named Shadrach Minkins from a Boston courthouse. Despite the rescuers' "flagitious offense," Webster had directed that they be charged only with violating the Fugitive Slave Act, a decision that he later attributed solely to the administration's lenient forbearance.[9] The Christiana case was more serious—no one had been killed in the Minkins rescue—and besides, the prosecutions in Boston obviously had not deterred resistance in Pennsylvania. In many ways, therefore, the Christiana case presented Webster with just the opportunity he wanted.

As early as September 16, John W. Ashmead, the U.S. Attorney for Eastern Pennsylvania, had been requested by his superiors "to ascertain whether the facts would make out the crime of treason."[10] Shortly afterward Ashmead met with President Fillmore and his cabinet—including Webster and Attorney General John Crittenden—and received instructions to seek treason indictments.[11] Many decades later Ashmead's son would claim that the treason case had been forced upon his father, but at the time of the prosecution there was no evident dissent on the government side. All of the prosecutors—and all of the political figures behind them—seemed unanimous and enthusiastic about the scope of the case. The Fillmore administration's credibility depended on bringing a federal indictment, rather than deferring to Pennsylvania, and treason was the only offense available that carried a penalty adequate to the crime of murder.

When the preliminary hearing resumed in Lancaster on September 23, there was little reason to doubt that the defendants would be charged with treason against the United States. The prosecutors recalled Kline to the stand so that the marshal could expand on his earlier story by providing additional details essential to the treason charge. This time Kline was far more specific about Hanway's role in encouraging the violence:

> Hanway walked his horse up to where the crowd of negroes were, and he spoke something low to them, and they gave one shout—he walked his horse about twenty or thirty yards and looked towards them, and they fired up where Mr. Gorsuch was . . . it was at Mr. Gorsuch and his son—by that came another party and they fired.[12]

Kline's intention was to tie Hanway more closely to the shootings by accusing him of conspiring with "twenty or thirty blacks" immediately before the gunfire began. This characterization would be elaborated in the following trial, until it was made to seem that Hanway had actually given a signal to commence firing. Kline also added the names of several black men whom he claimed had been at the scene with weapons, although he did not explain how he was able to identify them. Perhaps to fill this obvious gap, George Washington Harvey Scott was recalled to confirm the participation of the men named by Kline.

Dr. Thomas Pearce, the nephew of Edward Gorsuch and a member of the slave-hunting party, was also called to support Kline's testimony by directly implicating Hanway in the violence. According to Pearce, the fighters in William Parker's house had been on the verge of surrendering until they saw Hanway ride up on his sorrel horse. At the moment of the white man's arrival, however, the blacks began to cheer and shout, renewing the resistance that led directly to Gorsuch's death.[13] Pearce's account supported the prosecution claim that white abolitionists were the true leaders of the black rebellion and thus collaborators in a traitorous conspiracy.

Several other important witnesses were heard for the first time at this hearing, providing evidence—essential to a treason charge—that the resistance had been planned in advance. A white man named Henry Young testified to a conversation between two black men and Dr. Augustus Cain that occurred on the evening before the riot. The black men—Josephus Washington and John Clark—had informed Dr. Cain that "kidnappers and the Marshal were coming up, and they must be prepared to meet the Marshal, and also notify the [fugitives]."[14] Washington and Clark were then "committed as witnesses," both black men having apparently agreed to testify for the prosecution, just as Scott had been earlier.

The defendants were represented by formidable counsel at the reconvened preliminary hearing in Lancaster. Thaddeus Stevens, U.S. congressman and fiery abolitionist, led the defense team in presenting a surprisingly extensive case. As would be expected, Stevens vigorously cross-examined Kline and the other prosecution witnesses, but he also presented a series of witnesses of his own, which was an unusual maneuver for the defense at a preliminary hearing.

Stevens's approach to Kline was scornful, challenging the marshal's claim that he had joined the battle and had witnessed Gorsuch's death. Hadn't he run when the shooting started? Stevens asked. "When I saw the negroes pointing their guns at me I got over the fence into the cornfield," Kline was forced to admit.[15] Stevens also pressed him on his impressive ability to identify so many black men by name, none of whom he had ever known before.

Kline's imprecision made Scott's testimony even more important regarding identification of the black defendants, many of whom had been arrested at random and had been linked to the riot only by the black informant. Stevens called alibi witnesses for several of the black defendants, including Henry Simms and John Morgan, whom Scott had identified as Gorsuch's killers. Most surprisingly, Stevens also called four witnesses who swore that Scott could not possibly have been at Parker's house when the riot occurred at dawn on September 11. Scott lived with a blacksmith named John Carr, who was also his employer. Carr and three members of his family testified that Scott had been securely "buttoned" into his room on the night of September 10, and that he was still there the next day at breakfast time when Carr undid the lock. Scott had worked with Carr throughout that morning, they claimed, making it impossible for him to have traveled the six miles to and from the Parker house.

Stevens took a chance by revealing so much of his case at a preliminary hearing. Other lawyers might have held back their witnesses for trial, rather than give the prosecutors a preview of the defense strategy and an opportunity to adapt their own case in advance. Stevens pressed forward, however, because he sensed an opportunity to cripple the government's case right at the outset. With all of his clients detained in Philadelphia's Moyamensing Prison, which was notorious for its austere and unsanitary conditions, Stevens gambled that his frontal assault might be able to get some of the charges dismissed before trial.

And there were surely political considerations as well. The public outrage following Gorsuch's murder had hardly begun to fade by the time of the hearing. Much of the immediate anger was directed at Castner Hanway and Elijah Lewis—there had even been talk of lynching the presumed abolitionist leaders of the riot—but Lancaster County's black population also continued to suffer considerable insecurity. One local newspaper inveighed against "the white and black murderers," while another pointedly blamed the white prisoners for having "urged the blacks to this horrid measure."[16] By exposing the weaknesses in the government's case, Stevens probably hoped to create a shift in public opinion, blunting some of the hostility that had been indiscriminately directed against both his movement and his clients.

Stevens argued that the evidence against the defendants was far from adequate and that it rested almost entirely on the shaky credibility of Kline and Scott, both of whom had been contradicted by other witnesses. The crimes alleged against Hanway and Lewis were "a bold perfidy of the creature Kline," who had "perjured himself in the course of the investigation in more than a dozen instances." And Scott had committed even more "wicked perjury" by falsely claiming that he had been at the scene. Upon showing these facts, Stevens said, "Nothing [was] left to implicate any of the accused but the undoubted perjury of Kline and Scott. The proof of the absence of the other prisoners [was] equally conclusive."[17]

Most notable were the arguments that Stevens did not raise. Militant abolitionist as he was, there was not a trace of militancy in the presentation of his case. He allowed from the start that "a great crime—the crime of murder—had been committed in this county," making no attempt to argue that the killing of Gorsuch had been in any way justified. And he did not stop there, but rather added that "a citizen from Maryland had been murdered by his own slaves, in the unlawful attempt to secure their freedom."[18]

Thus, Stevens appeared to accept not only the constitutionality of the Fugitive Slave Act, but also the legitimacy of slavery itself, conceding as he did that it was unlawful for slaves to seek freedom. By declining to attack, or even question, the institution of slavery, Stevens put himself at odds with other leading abolitionists, most of whom agreed with Frederick Douglass that the Christiana resistance had been not only justified but also heroic. Ohio Congressman Joshua Giddings, for example, openly rejoiced that the fugitives had "stood up manfully in defense of their God-given rights and shot down the miscreants, who had come with the desperate purpose of taking them again to the land of slavery." But even though Stevens was himself deeply opposed to slavery, the lawyer determined that his clients would only be hurt if he invoked the higher law on their behalf. Despite his "unchangeable hostility to slavery in every form in every place," all of the defendants would be far better off, Stevens reckoned, if he defended them strictly on the facts of the case.[19]

Stevens's tactic was sound, but it did not work at the preliminary hearing stage. While the court did dismiss charges against a few of the prisoners, nearly all of them were remanded to a grand jury to face the charge of treason.

The grand jury convened in Philadelphia on September 27, 1851, with Federal District Court Judge John Kane presiding. A former district attorney and attorney general of Pennsylvania, Kane was a firm supporter of the Fugitive Slave Act. Just a year earlier he had warned a grand jury that the country had been "convulsed in its length and breadth" by "fanatics of civil discord" who "inveighed against obedience to [the fugitive] statute, obstructing officers of the law, and deeds of violent resistance against them." Kane's well-known views "did not afford a very encouraging outlook for those who were about to be tried before him," and the judge proceeded to remove any question about his sympathies when he delivered his instructions to the Christiana grand jury.[20]

After first informing the jurors of the alleged facts, Judge Kane broadly defined the crime of treason, explaining that it included "any combination forcibly to prevent or oppose the execution or enforcement of a provision of the Constitution or of a public Statute, if accompanied or followed by an act of forcible opposition." Moreover, he continued, it was "not necessary to prove that the individual accused was a direct, personal actor in the violence," but only that he was present "counselling [sic] or countenancing it."

Kane's charge was aimed nearly as much at the abolitionist movement as it was at any of the individual defendants. "For some months past," he pointed out, it was alleged that "gatherings of people . . . have been held from time to time in the vicinity of the place of the recent outbreak, at which exhortations were made and pledges interchanged to hold the law for the recovery of fugitive slaves as of no validity, and to defy its execution." According to Kane, proof of conspiracy could be found "in the declared purposes of the individual party before the actual outbreak," and it could even be derived from the "proceedings of meetings" he either had taken part in or had somehow made effective. That was an expansive interpretation of the criminal law, but one of the defense lawyers would later agree that "if the circumstances mentioned had taken place, the Judge was correct in saying the highest crime known to the laws of the United States had been committed at Christiana."[21]

The court concluded with a rebuke to abolitionists everywhere, threatening that they could be held accountable for preaching allegiance to higher law. In words that might just as easily have been written by Daniel Webster, Kane warned:

> If it has been thought safe to counsel and instigate others to acts of forcible oppugnation to the provisions of a statute,—to inflame the

minds of the ignorant by appeals to passion, and denunciations of the law as oppressive, unjust, revolting to the conscience, and not binding on the actions of men,—to represent the Constitution of the land as a compact of iniquity, which it were meritorious to violate or subvert,—the mistake has been a grievous one.

He then instructed the grand jurors to indict any men "who, under whatever mask of conscience or of peace, have labored to incite others to treasonous violence."[22]

It did not take long for the jurors to reach the expected decision. On October 6 the grand jury began issuing "true bills," ultimately indicting five white men and thirty-six blacks (nine of whom, including William Parker and the Gorsuch slaves, had never been arrested and were to be tried in absentia) for the crime of treason.

The five-count indictment accused the defendants of forming a "traitorous combination to oppose, resist, and prevent the execution" of the Fugitive Slave Act "by means of force and intimidation." In the florid and repetitive legalese of the nineteenth century, it alleged that "upwards of one hundred persons had assembled with guns, swords, and other warlike weapons" with the intent to "levy war" against the United States. The defendants were charged with assaulting Henry Kline, a federal marshal, and with preventing him from executing lawful warrants against men "who had been legally charged . . . as being persons held to service or labor in the State of Maryland, and owing such service or labor to a certain Edward Gorsuch." While only some of the defendants did "liberate and take out of [Kline's] custody . . . persons held to service or labor," the indictment charged that all participated in a conspiracy that "maliciously and traitorously did meet, conspire, consult, and agree among themselves, further to oppose, resist and prevent, by means of force and intimidation, the execution of the said laws."

Perhaps most ominously, the indictment concluded that defendants and unknown others had "prepared, composed, published, and dispersed divers books [*sic*], pamphlets, letters, declarations, resolutions, addresses, papers and writings [containing] incitement, encouragement, and exhortations, to move, induce, and persuade" fugitives to resist the law. That language was broad enough to cover almost anyone who had ever attended an abolitionist meeting or who had spoken out against the Fugitive Slave Act.

Stevens's approach had been to depoliticize the case, treating the riot as he would any other homicide. The only question, he had argued at the preliminary hearing, was "who are the guilty parties?"[23] As the indictment showed, however, the prosecutors viewed the case far differently. To them, the political implications of the riot far outweighed any questions of individual responsibility. Their goal was not really to identify Gorsuch's killers—his death was not even mentioned in the indictment—but rather to demonstrate the perils of opposing the arrest of fugitive slaves, in either word or deed. Thus, the sweeping allegations in the indictment were framed to cover not only the resistance fighters and their active supporters, but also many vocal critics of the Fugitive Slave Act. A successful prosecution therefore threatened to criminalize—as treason, no less—the publication of books, pamphlets, resolutions, and writings that encouraged slaves to escape or exhorted fugitives to resist recapture.

Plea bargaining was unknown in 1851, so every treason case was an all-or-nothing proposition leading either to an acquittal or the death penalty. Because the Christiana prosecution was "politically motivated, however, it was not absolutely necessary for the government to win." Simply securing the indictments and pursuing the case was enough to establish Fillmore's settled determination to enforce the law, with the added benefit of intimidating the more militant elements in the abolitionist movement. Both Webster and Crittenden counseled the president "that even if a conviction were not obtained, the effect of the trial would be salutary in checking Northern opposition to the enforcement of the Fugitive Slave Act." That was more than wishful thinking. While devotion to the higher law had inspired many abolitionists to shelter runaways or to openly violate the fugitive law, it would be a far more daunting matter to face a possible death penalty. U.S. Attorney John Ashmead made precisely that point in his correspondence with Fillmore, inviting the president to "look to the overt act alleged" in comparison to the abolitionist "pamphlets and resolutions" that had been circulated in opposition to the fugitive law. "If you will examine the last overt act in the Indictment, that which respects speeches and pamphlets," he wrote to his superiors, "you will perceive it may alarm some of the persons who are travelling through the country preaching treason."[24]

Although the treason charges were extreme, they were not unsustainable. Several earlier courts had convicted defendants of levying war against the

United States based solely on their forcible resistance to a particular statute. The prominent legal scholar Francis Wharton—at the time the nation's leading authority on criminal law—had advised Ashmead that those precedents could be applied to the Christiana case, which clearly placed the actual participants in the riot (even the passive ones, such as Hanway and Lewis) in considerable jeopardy.[25] There were no similar treason precedents for merely encouraging violations of the law through writing or speaking, but never before had a slave owner been killed while attempting to execute a federal warrant. Moreover, there had indeed been numerous public calls to nullify the new Fugitive Slave Act through forcible resistance, which virtually dared the government to respond with its heaviest legal artillery. If ever a court was going to accept an expansive theory of treason culpability, the Christiana riot would likely provide the case.

There were two groups of defendants in the Christiana case. In theory, most of the black defendants could be directly tied to the violence by eyewitness testimony (although in fact, many had been arrested without cause and had no connection to the riot), while the white defendants could only be accused of encouraging or inciting the resistance. For both groups, the government could obtain treason convictions only by proving that the defendants had intended to prevent all enforcement of the Fugitive Slave Act, as opposed to simply rescuing several slaves from slave catchers. And for the white defendants there was an additional challenge—establishing a link between antislavery advocacy and the violence that followed—that could be met only through exceptional prosecution lawyering in every phase of the process, from investigation through trial.

The breadth of the treason indictment presented the prosecutors with a series of difficult problems, although they certainly had sufficient manpower to address them. There were seven lawyers on the government side. U.S. Attorney John Ashmead was assisted by his cousin George Ashmead, as well as R. M. Lee, the Philadelphia city recorder, and James Ludlow, a Philadelphia attorney. In addition, the State of Maryland engaged three attorneys to participate in the trial: State Attorney General Robert Brent, Pennsylvania Senator James Cooper, and Baltimore District Attorney Z. Collins Lee.

With all of that talent available, it should have been possible for the prosecution to divide the work at hand and apportion tasks to present the strongest possible unified case. As it turned out, however, the prosecution team was riven by dissent and professional jealousies that made cooperation difficult if not impossible. The result was a deeply flawed case, characterized by a series of miscues and blunders that Thaddeus Stevens and his colleagues were ready and eager to exploit.

———

John Ashmead, the U.S. attorney for the Eastern District of Pennsylvania, was a seasoned prosecutor who was proud of his work. As one of the chief federal law enforcement officers in the area, he had wasted little time responding to the Christiana Riot. Arriving at the scene the following Saturday, Ashmead directed a company of U.S. Marines and federal marshal's police, who promptly began rounding up suspects. Ashmead's warrantless investigation may have lacked prudence and accuracy, but that was more than counterbalanced by its arbitrary aggression and sweeping extent. The federal forces "went from house to house," making some good-faith arrests but also seizing "by wholesale, men who afterwards were found to have been miles from the scene of action."[26]

Given his official position and evident zeal, Ashmead had every reason to expect that he would lead the prosecution of the Christiana rioters, and at first it did seem that he would be strongly supported by his superiors in Washington, D.C. He was authorized to hire additional counsel and to incur "extraordinary expenses" for the "management of these important cases."[27] Soon, however, Ashmead's control over the case began to unravel.

Maryland's Governor Lowe had not been content merely to prod the federal government into seeking a treason indictment. He also wanted to play a part in directing the prosecution, both to ensure that "full justice" was provided to the Gorsuch family and to "vindicate the insulted dignity" of his state. Having dispatched his own attorney general, Robert Brent, to observe the preliminary hearings, Lowe later decided that Maryland would also have to be represented at the trial. In addition to Brent, the governor retained Pennsylvania Senator James Cooper for that purpose, reasoning that "policy as well as propriety" dictated engaging at least one Pennsylvania lawyer.[28]

At Lowe's urging, Brent wrote to U.S. Attorney Ashmead, offering to join the prosecution team. Ashmead, however, had mixed feelings about the offer. He had already recruited several local attorneys to assist him but his request to hire even more lawyers had been turned down by Washington, leaving him at least slightly understaffed. Brent's offer, therefore, might have been welcomed, if it had not seemed somewhat high-handed—intimating, as it did, that oversight from Brent and Cooper was necessary to ensure that the federal government would take every necessary step to punish the rioters.

Ashmead responded "defensively, and a bit officiously," accepting Brent's offer of assistance, but only if it was "distinctly understood" that the Maryland lawyer would take a secondary position at counsel table. Ashmead would be the lead attorney and, most important, would present the final argument to the jury. Such restrictive terms were apparently offensive to Brent, who replied that he "could not possibly accept preliminary conditions on his participation." Ashmead did not back down, however, preferring to remain short-handed rather than cede significant responsibility to an interloper.[29]

From there, the contretemps only got worse. Brent appealed to his patron, Governor Lowe, who forwarded the complaint directly to the president. Fillmore and Webster were in no mood to "create a national incident of the very kind they were trying to prevent by prosecuting the Christiana prisoners" in the first place.[30] In short order, Webster sent a rebuke to Ashmead, instructing him to accept both Maryland representatives onto the prosecution team, and ordering him to relinquish the final argument in favor of Brent.

Ashmead had no choice but to swallow his pride. Compelled to retract his earlier position, he wrote conciliatory letters to Brent and Lowe accepting their proposed arrangement. The sniping continued, however, eventually finding its way into the press, to the embarrassment of Ashmead and (one suspects) to the secret delight of Brent. Only on the very eve of trial did Brent and Ashmead finally reconcile their differences. As Brent later reported, the "difficulty" regarding his appearance as counsel was "satisfactorily adjusted" at a meeting with Ashmead in Philadelphia only two days before the beginning of jury selection. Ashmead "tendered to me the position of leading counsel in these trials, which I promptly declined. . . . It was then agreed that the Hon. James Cooper, of Pennsylvania . . . should occupy the position of leading counsel, which he did with fidelity and signal ability."[31]

Senator Cooper was indeed a fine lawyer, and Brent would later prove himself to be both an excellent cross-examiner and an outstanding tactician. In fact, Brent's keen understanding of the complex relationship between allegation and proof would prove far better than Ashmead's at several crucial points in the prosecution case. As it was, however, the resolution between Ashmead and Brent came far too late for the prosecution to settle upon a unified theory, much less to select an effective leading counsel. The squabbling among lawyers and politicians had consumed crucial weeks that should have been devoted to concerted investigation and preparation. Brent himself later conceded that "the unfortunate preliminary difficulty" had hampered "the development of the evidence, by preventing that early interchange of views and information, which was necessary to a thorough preparation of these important cases." That was an understatement. A member of the defense team later put it more bluntly, observing that the late addition of Brent and Cooper resulted not only in wasted time but also in "a misapprehension of both the law and the facts of the case."[32] The lack of coordination among counsel, as well as their continuing jealousies and disagreements, would severely damage the prosecution case from beginning to end.

One of the most important prosecution decisions was made well before Brent and Cooper arrived in Philadelphia. It appears that Ashmead himself had decided to hold a series of individual trials rather than join all (or even several) of the defendants in a single case. As Ashmead explained it,

> [A] jury would be terrified at the idea of returning a verdict of guilty which would involve so great a sacrifice of human life and also because the evidence would be uncertain and indistinct as to some, and in this way might so involve the whole transaction in doubt as to lead to the acquittal of all. Separate indictments would enable us to select the strongest cases for trial first.

There were logical reasons as well to try the cases in succession, as that would simplify the proof in each case, while potentially giving the prosecutors multiple "bites at the apple." On the other hand, this strategy definitely depended on starting with the strongest cases, as the first trial would necessarily be a test case, "determining the character of the following prosecutions."[33]

It is not known precisely how Ashmead chose which defendant to try first. About a week before the trials were to begin—and several days before his "satisfactory adjustment" with the Maryland attorney general—Ashmead "announced that Castner Hanway would be tried on the following Monday" and that John Jackson, one of the black defendants, "would be tried immediately after Hanway."[34]

Given Fillmore and Webster's fixation on the antislavery movement, it was not surprising that Ashmead chose to begin with a white defendant. As part of the Great Compromise, the Fugitive Slave Act was, above all else, a compact among white men—an agreement that the *white* men of the North would assist in recapturing the slaves who belonged to the *white* men of the South. Although it was "certainly the objective of the black resisters" to render the fugitive law void and inoperative, it was white defiance (or complicity) that truly endangered the entire structure of the agreement. Blacks, after all, could be expected to run away, and sometimes even fight when cornered. Especially in the South, however, it was thought that the encouragement of white sympathizers had turned the slaves' troublesome tendency into a national crisis. Thus, "the prosecution needed to convict white men to avenge Edward Gorsuch's death in the eyes of Southerners."[35]

There was also a considerable amount of racism underlying the assumption that the black resistance movement must have depended on white leaders. Hence the charge that Hanway had used "colored people as instruments of war" against the government. And hence the allegation that "declarations, resolutions, addresses, papers and writings" had induced the fugitives to resist the law—as though slaves were not inclined to fight for their freedom without instructions from white men in Boston or Philadelphia. Perhaps, too, the prosecutors were wary of staking the validity of their case on a treason charge against any of the black prisoners, even if one could be shown to have fired the fatal shot. There was something paradoxical, almost illogical, about charging black men as traitors. Six years later, in the Dred Scott case, the U.S. Supreme Court would rule that blacks could not be citizens. But even in 1851, the most adamant slaveholder would have had to agree with Frederick Douglass that the government could not actually demand loyalty from fugitives who had been disenfranchised and enslaved.[36] The alternative would have been to concede that blacks could choose either to extend or withhold allegiance. The prosecutors may have recognized, as Douglass observed, the implicit acknowledgment that "the treason arraignment . . . admits our manhood."[37] That was ultimately an admission of political agency, contrary to both the myths and needs of a slaveholding republic, and it could not easily be presented in court.

Even so, it is unclear why Ashmead singled out Hanway as the lead defendant, rather than any of the other white prisoners, several of whom might have been more seriously implicated than the unarmed miller. Joseph Townsend, for example, "had lent his loaded gun to a black man" for use against the "kidnappers" at Parker's house.[38] Elijah Lewis and Joseph Scarlett both helped spread the alarm, and both actively recruited others to rush to the scene—a level of involvement that supported the government's conspiracy theory far more than did Hanway's almost coincidental presence following his interrupted breakfast. Scarlett and Lewis were also both Quakers—as Hanway was not—which further tied them to Lancaster County's antislavery movement.

Then again, it was Hanway who had the most extended interchange with Kline, and who had most rudely brushed off the marshal's request for assistance, refusing to provide his name and asserting that he "did not care for any act of Congress." On the day after the riot, Kline had also confronted Hanway at Zercher's Hotel in Christiana, where Hanway had remained maddeningly silent when the deputy marshal accused him of telling the blacks to begin shooting. Perhaps it was nothing more than Hanway's misfortune that Kline— the prosecution's indispensable star witness—was able to identify him best and had the most to say about him.

Whether by happenstance or plan, Castner Hanway found himself first in the dock when the Federal Circuit Court convened on Monday, November 24, 1851. After the clerk of the court read the indictment, Hanway was asked for his plea:

"Not guilty."

"How will you be tried?" asked the clerk.

"By God and my Country."

∽ 6 ∾

PROSECUTION AT INDEPENDENCE HALL

T he term "trial of the century" had not yet been coined in 1851, but it might very well have been applied to the Christiana prosecution. The gravity of the charge alone was sufficient to attract the attention of the entire country. Not since 1799 had an American been convicted of treason, and there had never before been a case in which more than thirty defendants faced capital punishment. Add to that the drama of a slave owner killed by black fugitives, the open hostility between citizens of Maryland and Pennsylvania, and the Fillmore administration's claim that the future of the Union was suspended in the balance, and it was no wonder that the courtroom was completely packed with both spectators and reporters while many more stood outside in the hall, in the lobby, and on the street.

The jurisdiction of U.S. courts was limited in the 1850s, consisting largely of patent and admiralty cases, and a narrow category of federal crimes. Thus the federal courtroom, located on the second story of Independence Hall, was not designed for huge crowds, although the two presiding judges—John Kane of the District Court and Robert C. Grier, a Supreme Court justice riding circuit—had done their best to accommodate the great number of spectators. Extra benches were placed on both sides of the courtroom, and gaslights had been installed so that the court could hold evening sessions. Ventilators "of the most appropriate pattern" were mounted on the ceiling to bring fresh air into the stuffy room. "Nothing was wanting but space to promote the ease and comfort of those who were to figure in the solemn investigation about to take place."[1]

On the opening day of trial, many of the available seats were taken by the eighty-one prospective jurors who had been assembled by federal Marshal Anthony Roberts. The composition of the jury caused the trial's first controversy. Roberts was a political ally of Thaddeus Stevens's, and the prosecutors suspected that he had loaded the panel with men who were "unfavorable to a conviction." In addition, U.S. Attorney John Ashmead had learned that the defense lawyers had conducted an investigation of the potential jurors—his superiors had denied him funds for the same purpose—which only heightened the fear that the prosecutors were facing a stacked deck. In fact, Stevens was not entirely happy with the panel—there were too few jurors from Lancaster County and too many in total, thus making it more difficult for the defense to make the best strategic use of its limited number of peremptory challenges.

The prosecution and defense lawyers jockeyed for advantage when court convened, neither side wanting to take responsibility for delaying the trial, and each hoping to bait the other into moving to disqualify the jury panel. When Stevens cautiously sought to have the court summon more jurors from Lancaster County (who presumably would have been sympathetic to their neighbor Castner Hanway), Ashmead saw an opening and seized the opportunity. "I wish to say that if they desire to quash the array, we will cordially agree to it."[2] Stevens, however, recognized the ploy and quickly countered it:,

> If the prosecution will add to that agreement that the prisoner
> shall be admitted to bail to appear at the next session of the Court,
> and that . . . the trial shall be ordered in the County of Lancaster,
> it is our desire; otherwise not.

Justice Grier was not amused by the lawyers' maneuvers. "We have a great deal of business before us," he snapped. "Let us not take up the time in useless discussion." Thus, the first exchange of the trial ended in an apparent draw, with the jury panel remaining as Roberts had gathered it. More significant than that particular outcome, however, was Justice Grier's display of impatience. He had taken a no-nonsense attitude toward the work before him, and as the trial progressed he would prove quite unwilling to indulge anything other than the most straightforward approach to the facts and the law.

Whatever their misgivings about the jury array, the prosecutors had every reason to believe that the two judges would be favorably disposed toward their case. Judge Kane's charge to the grand jury had been a virtual roadmap to the prosecution's theory, right down to his thinly veiled warning to abolitionist agitators. Justice Grier, too, was known as a firm supporter of the Fugitive Slave Act, having once vowed to enforce it "as the Lord liveth and as my soul liveth . . . till the last hour it remains on the books."[3] A lifelong Democrat and staunch Unionist, Grier well understood the high stakes involved in the Christiana trial, and he rejected any implication that the treason charge had been brought in bad faith. At one point early in the trial, he complained about northern editorialists who had "taken upon themselves to settle the whole law with regard to these proceedings, that this transaction is not treason," and later he disparaged Boston newspapers—"from what is called the Athens of America"—for their sympathy toward the defense, "thinking, perhaps, that we have not the same degree of illumination here as they have there."

Although he was no friend of either fugitives or abolitionists, Grier was a strict student of the law. The son and grandson of Presbyterian ministers, he had received a classical education and had served as an instructor at Dickinson College before he turned to law practice. Perhaps because of his religious and academic background, there was a certain rigidity about Grier, especially when it came to matters of procedure. He insisted on a tightly run courtroom in which the lawyers were prompt and precise, and he was willing to take extreme steps to enforce his sense of protocol and efficiency.

There was also a matter of timing. As a member of the Supreme Court, Grier was required to ride circuit for part of each year, presiding with local district judges over certain serious felonies. Grier's principal responsibility, however, was to the Supreme Court itself, which was scheduled to meet in mid-December. He was anxious to return to Washington and he could not have been pleased at the prospect of hearing numerous individual trials, each covering much of the same ground as the others. Although he perfunctorily assured the lawyers that he was not inclined to "hurry or drive either party," he made it clear that he wanted to dispose of at least Hanway's trial within two weeks.

Stevens recognized Grier's concern and assured the court that the case could be finished quickly. "I hope it will not take that time to get through with one case—in our country, we hang a man in three days, and I hope [the prosecutors] will not take so long a time." Maryland Attorney General Robert Brent, however, seemed to miss the point. "This is a civilized country," he retorted, refusing to commit himself to a speedy time frame. That was the beginning of a pattern in which Stevens and company would successfully play to the court, while the disorganized prosecutors appeared to bicker and stall.

The five defense attorneys were well situated to take advantage of Justice Grier's proclivities. Not only were they among the very best lawyers practicing in Philadelphia, but they were also unified in their approach to the trial. Unlike the prosecutors—who were variously answerable to Daniel Webster, Governor Louis Lowe, and the Gorsuch family—the defense lawyers advocated only for Hanway, strenuously avoiding any suggestion that they were beholden to a larger cause. Also in contrast to the prosecutors—whom their superiors had committed to a complicated theory of treason-by-encouragement—the defense counsel were able to simplify the case, reducing it to the single question of Hanway's own actions during the riot.

We do not know whether the defense lawyers ever disagreed among themselves, because they quite obviously put aside both their egos and their personal beliefs to present a united front. As the most prominent among them, Stevens was entitled to be designated "chief counsel," but he declined the position in order to distance Hanway from any presumed connection to abolitionism. Instead the leading role was officially taken by John M. Read, a prominent Philadelphia attorney and a "respectable Democrat," who would later serve as chief justice of the Pennsylvania Supreme Court.[4] The other defense attorneys included Joseph Lewis and Theodore Cuyler, both leaders of the Pennsylvania bar and neither of whom identified with radical causes, and W. Arthur Jackson, a talented young lawyer who acted as junior counsel.

The defense team enjoyed a clear organizational advantage as the trial began, which also put them in a position to adapt their tactics to accommodate the court. The prosecutors, however, continued to claim the political high ground, positioning themselves as the defenders of law and order, as well as national cohesion. Those grand themes would be hard for the court and jury to ignore. The shocking murder of Edward Gorsuch continued to reverberate in Pennsylvania and Maryland, and eyewitness testimony about the bloody circumstances of his death was sure to create sympathy for the prosecution's case and pressure for Hanway's conviction.

The national mood had, if anything, become even more tense in the months since the riot, as opponents of the Fugitive Slave Act continued to clash with federal authorities. One of the most dramatic confrontations—which came to be known as the Jerry Rescue—took place in Syracuse that autumn, just as the Christiana grand jury was completing its work. A fugitive slave named William McHenry but known to everyone as "Jerry" had been working for some years as a cooper in Syracuse, one of the most pro-abolitionist cities in the country. Jerry may have hoped that he was fairly safe among his antislavery neighbors, especially in early October 1851, when the abolitionist Liberty Party convened its national meeting at Syracuse's Congregational church. Jerry would have felt considerably less secure, however, if he had been aware of Daniel Webster's very specific threat to enforce the fugitive slave law in Syracuse "in the midst of the next Anti-Slavery Convention, if the occasion shall arise."[5]

Unfortunately, Jerry's Missouri owner had somehow discovered his whereabouts and sent an agent named James Lear to recapture him. Arriving in Syracuse in late September, Lear obtained a warrant from U.S. Commissioner Joseph Sabine. On October 1, accompanied by a posse of deputy marshals, Lear located Jerry at his place of work and, after a brief struggle, managed to subdue and shackle him. The slave hunters dragged Jerry into Commissioner Sabine's office, where they expected to quickly obtain a certificate of removal.

In the meantime, news of Jerry's arrest had reached the Liberty Party convention. Someone shouted out that a slave had been arrested, and the assembled delegates, both black and white, rushed into the street. Led by Rev. Jermain Loguen and Gerrit Smith (one of the most notable abolitionists in the country), the crowd soon reached Sabine's second-story office, where the commissioner was attempting to hold a hearing. That proved impossible, however, as the packed room became so noisy and chaotic that testimony could not be heard. In frustration, Sabine adjourned the proceeding, but he did not clear the room or take other steps to secure the prisoner.

Recognizing his opportunity, Jerry made a sudden dash for freedom, pushing aside Lear and racing for the exit. The abolitionist crowd cleared the way for him, while doing their best to prevent the officers from giving chase. Though still manacled, Jerry made it into the street, half running and half stumbling toward the Erie Canal. Just as he reached a bridge across the canal, the fugitive was intercepted by several local constables, who knocked him to the ground and beat him into submission. They threw their prisoner into a waiting cart and took him to the local police station under heavy guard.

But that was not the end of it. Even while Jerry was being dragged back into custody, a group of several dozen abolitionists—again including Loguen and Smith, and joined by Rev. Samuel May—were meeting to consider their next move. Some of the white abolitionists counseled restraint, suggesting that they wait for the commissioner's ruling before taking any action. But Rev. Loguen—himself a fugitive from Kentucky—was adamant that there had to be a second rescue. "If white men won't fight," he told the group, "let fugitives and black men smite down marshals and commissioners—anybody who holds Jerry—and rescue him or perish."[6] After that there was no dissent, and a plan was soon developed. Rev. May was dispatched to the jail, ostensibly to counsel the despondent prisoner, but in fact to alert him that a renewed rescue was in the works.

Later that evening Jerry was brought from his cell into an adjacent courtroom, where Commissioner Sabine again attempted to convene a hearing. A crowd of thousands had gathered outside the building, chanting, "Let him go! Let him go!" At a prearranged signal, a band of perhaps fifty men, both black and white, charged the courtroom, smashing the doors and windows and "sweeping the vastly outnumbered constables in a stumbling tangle before them." As the officers scattered, the rescuers found Jerry in the back of the room and carried him out of the police station and into the street. From there he was taken into hiding and, after several weeks underground, smuggled into Canada.[7]

The abolitionists were triumphant, and they were not shy about proclaiming their victory over the Fillmore administration. Within twenty-four hours of the rescue, the Liberty Party convention had adopted a provocative resolution, introduced by Gerrit Smith. The resolution praised the "recent resistance to kidnappers in Pennsylvania," while noting that "if any class of criminals deserve to be struck down in instant death it is kidnappers." As to the Jerry rescue itself, the resolution taunted Daniel Webster for the government's failure to "replunge a poor brother in the horrors and hell of slavery":

> *Resolved,* That we rejoice that the City of Syracuse—the anti-slavery city of Syracuse—the city of anti-slavery conventions, our beloved and glorious city of Syracuse—still remains undisgraced by the fulfillment of the satanic prediction of the satanic Daniel Webster.[8]

The government responded by indicting twenty-six men—fourteen white and twelve black—for their participation in the Jerry rescue. The charges were severe—including interference with a federal marshal and assault with intent to kill—but they did not include treason. It is not known why Fillmore and Webster responded less harshly in Syracuse than they did in Christiana. The Christiana riot had been much more violent, but violence was not the sole determinant of treason. The Jerry rescue had been much more clearly the work of organized abolitionists—indeed, it had been all but an official project of the Liberty Party—which should have made it far easier to prove that there had been a "traitorous combination to oppose, resist, and prevent the execution" of the Fugitive Slave Act. It would not have been hard for prosecutors to identify speeches and statements in which Loguen, May, Smith, and others had promised to make the fugitive act unenforceable, thus supplying a key element of the government's treason theory.

We can imagine various reasons for the two cases to be treated differently. Perhaps Fillmore and his cabinet advisers realized that treason was a hard charge to prove, and they did not want to undertake two difficult trials simultaneously. Perhaps they reasoned that the chances of a test-case conviction were better in Philadelphia than in Syracuse. There was, after all, considerable hostility toward the many runaway slaves in southeastern Pennsylvania, while Syracuse was the heartland of abolitionism. Or perhaps the dramatis personae made the difference. Governor Lowe and the Gorsuch family had pressed hard for treason indictments in Pennsylvania, but there were no aggrieved relatives or important political figures to exert comparable pressure in Syracuse. Jerry's owner, in distant Missouri, evidently lacked influence or connections in Washington. Moreover, Gerrit Smith was one of the wealthiest men in the United States, so charging him with treason would have been a steep uphill battle at a time when the government's resources were already stretched thin.

If anything could be certain, it would be that Webster must have taken the Jerry rescue as a personal affront. His public boast—"Depend upon it, the law will be executed . . . in Syracuse"—had been thrown rudely back in his face, as he was mocked and vilified by the very abolitionists he had sworn to suppress. That may have made the Christiana case even more important, both for Webster and the administration that he served. A successful treason prosecution, no matter where it was achieved, would at least dampen the spirits of the exultant abolitionists. Castner Hanway was the easiest target at hand, as the prosecutors attempted to make him an unwilling proxy for everything they despised and feared about abolitionism.

It took two full days to select twelve jurors from among the eighty-one citizens who responded to the summons from Marshal Roberts. Many of them seemed anxious to be released from service, some pleading business necessity and more claiming ill health. Justice Grier was skeptical of the numerous requests, refusing to excuse a bank president who stated that the company could not function without him. "Could not the cashier attend to the business of the bank, in the absence of the president?" he asked. Several jurors claimed to be deaf, one of whom added that he labored "under a very severe cold in the head, and it affects my hearing," gratuitously continuing that "I should be unwilling to sit upon a case of so great importance, unless I could hear all the evidence presented." That was almost too much for Grier. "Your disease has become epidemic to-day," the justice growled in reply. In the end, however, the court was indulgent, excusing the cold-afflicted juror and eighteen others for various reasons, ranging from rheumatic gout to vertigo.

Once the excuses were resolved, the first potential juror was called by the clerk. Solomon Newman, of Pike County, answered to his name. "Juror look upon the prisoner," said the clerk. "Prisoner look upon the juror. What say you, challenged or not challenged?"

Hanway conferred briefly with Stevens, who then immediately accepted the juror. "Not challenged," he said. The speed of the response—without a single question asked by counsel—came as a jolt to the prosecutors, confirming their suspicions that the defense already had investigated the jurors' backgrounds and associations. Believing themselves at an extreme disadvantage, the prosecutors therefore proposed that the court ask each juror six questions, designed to reveal their sympathies and beliefs. The first question was whether the juror had "any conscientious scruple, upon the subject of capital punishment that would prevent him from rendering a verdict of treason." The next four asked whether the juror had any prior knowledge, opinion, or bias about the facts of the case or "the guilt or innocence of the accused." The sixth question asked whether the juror had an opinion concerning the constitutionality of the Fugitive Slave Act and whether he could "convict a person indicted under it."

Read responded for the defense, feigning surprise. "We have never seen these questions, nor heard them till this moment," he complained. Notwithstanding that protestation, Read was immediately able to launch into an extended discussion of the proposed questions, complete with case citations relevant to each one. Quite obviously well prepared for the argument, Read allowed that the first five questions were acceptable, though redundant. He saved his fire for the last one, to which he strenuously objected: "We are not here to dispute the constitutionality of that law—and we do not intend to argue it."

The unconstitutionality of the Fugitive Slave Act could have provided a complete defense to the treason charge—it would have been no crime to prevent the enforcement of an invalid law—and yet Hanway's counsel specifically disclaimed the issue. The decision was, in part, pragmatic. With a defense based entirely upon Hanway's noninvolvement in the riot, there was simply no need to take on the burden of challenging the Fugitive Slave Act. And there was a tactical side as well. The jury panel selected by Marshal Roberts very likely included opponents of the Fugitive Slave Act who would have been strongly inclined to vote for acquittal whatever the facts of the case. The proposed question about constitutionality could serve only to expose any antislavery jurors, thereby allowing the prosecutors to remove them from the panel. The defense thus objected to any question that could "bind the conscience" of the jurymen.

The prosecutors needed a jury that respected or, better yet, revered the sanctity of the law, and they were wary of what we might now call sleepers or moles. "It is essential to the rights of the United States," argued James Ludlow, "that every juror who goes into that box should believe the law to be constitutional, and if the question is not put, any juror may take his seat and be guilty of the same traitorous intention in heart as is charged in the overt act upon the prisoners."

Explaining only that "as far as possible every juror ... shall be entirely without bias of any sort whatever," the court ruled in favor of the prosecution and agreed to make all six inquiries of each juror, including a slightly modified version of the question about the constitutionality of the Fugitive Slave Act.

As the voir dire proceeded, it became increasingly apparent that the defense lawyers had considerable information about the jury panel. A number of jurors were accepted without questions, forcing the prosecution to have at least twenty men "set aside" for further interrogation, as procedures then allowed. Other jurors were peremptorily challenged by the defense, again without significant inquiry. When John Miller was called, for example, Theodore Cuyler asked him only whether he had "formed or expressed" an opinion concerning the issues in the case. Miller answered that he had not, but Cuyler nonetheless had him struck from the jury.

Even more intriguing was the dismissal of Erskine Hazard, who declined to be sworn when called by the clerk. "Are you conscientiously scrupulous about taking an oath?" asked Justice Grier. "I am," answered Hazard, who was then allowed to affirm. This time Read handled the questions for the defense, asking only whether Hazard had formed an opinion "as to the guilt or innocence of the accused." "I am not aware that I have," came the answer. Although Hazard was presumably a Quaker or Mennonite and therefore likely to oppose the fugitive law, Read challenged him on behalf of the prisoner. Judge Kane could not understand why the defense would strike such a seemingly favorable juror. "Peremptorily?" he asked in disbelief. "We challenge peremptorily," replied Read. He must have had his reasons, but he kept them to himself and his colleagues.

If the defense had the upper hand when it came to questioning the jurors, the prosecution had an advantage when arguing to the court. Grier repeatedly ruled for the prosecution on challenges "for cause," refusing to remove jurors who seemed biased against Hanway. One juror admitted having previously expressed an opinion about the case, saying "if it is not treason, I do not see how treason against the United States can be levied." Another had "formed an opinion upon the outrage against the laws in the Christiana affair." Still another had "expressed an unfavorable opinion towards the course" of the defendants. Justice Grier, however, ruled that all three men were qualified to sit in judgment of Hanway, requiring the defense to expend their limited peremptory challenges to remove them from the jury. In contrast, the court sustained a prosecution challenge for cause to a juror who had "formed an opinion that the act does not constitute treason," but who stated that he would change that opinion "if directed by the court."

The court's favoritism during jury selection was palpable, but that may not have mattered in the end. By law, the defense team had sufficient peremptory challenges to strike every juror to whom they objected and, in fact, they concluded the selection with ten such challenges still in reserve. For whatever reason—thorough investigation, Marshal Roberts's collusion, or pure luck—Hanway had some cause for optimism when he faced the jury box.

The trial began in earnest on Friday, November 28, 1851, following a one-day recess for Thanksgiving. Although John Ashmead had ceded the role of leading counsel to Senator James Cooper, the U.S. attorney was still officially in charge of the case. It was Ashmead's prerogative, therefore, to give the government's opening statement, which he presented in painstaking detail. As the architect of the indictment, Ashmead was greatly invested in establishing the precise elements of treason and was loathe to skip over even the smallest point. He therefore addressed the jury by reading aloud from his prepared text, which included the entire indictment, several statutory and constitutional provisions, and extended references to legal precedents dating back more than fifty years. Cooper, for one, was unimpressed by Ashmead's prose reading, observing that "none but extempore addresses are ever effective when addressed to courts and juries."[9]

As wooden as he might have been in style, Ashmead did set out the legal and factual bases for the prosecution case. Hanway, he claimed, had "wickedly devised" and participated in a "concerted and combined resistance, by force, of a statute of the United States" with the "declared intent . . . to render its provisions void, and to make the act altogether inoperative." Summarizing Henry Kline's earlier accusations, Ashmead described what he called the "pre-concerted action" of the blacks at William Parker's house: resisting the marshal's party, blowing a horn to summon assistance, and ultimately firing the shots that killed Edward Gorsuch and wounded his relatives. Hanway had arrived on the scene in response to the bugle call, prompting the blacks to give "a shout of satisfaction; when before that they had appeared discouraged." After informing Marshal Kline that "he did not care for [the Fugitive Slave Act] or any other act—that the negroes had rights and could defend themselves," the defendant "rode up to them and said something in a low tone of voice. He moved his horse out of the way of the guns; the negroes shouted, and immediately fired from every direction."

There was not much more to be said about Hanway's involvement, so Ashmead spent the greater part of his speech establishing his political objectives. Open resistance to the law might be justifiable under a monarchy or tyranny, he explained, but "no such excuse . . . exists with us; for our institutions are based upon the inherent right of the people to change and modify their form of government." Hoping to deflate any sympathy for Hanway's defiance of the unpopular fugitive law, Ashmead continued, "If obnoxious acts of Congress are passed they can be changed or repealed."

But the Fugitive Slave Act was not just any law. Without the Fugitive Slave Clause, Ashmead argued, "the Constitution of the United States never could have been adopted," and therefore the "solemn obligations of the Constitution [require the] surrender of the absconding slave to his rightful claimant" even if that is sometimes "unpalatable." The conviction of Hanway was therefore necessary not only to punish him for shedding "the blood of an unoffending American citizen [who was] acting under the sanction of the laws of the Union" but also to ensure that the law could be enforced in the future. Should Hanway be acquitted, "then a dark and heavy cloud will have passed over the sunlight of the American Union."

Arthur Jackson, the youngest member of the defense team, would later criticize Ashmead's opening statement for "the common error" of promising more than he could prove,[10] but in fact the opening statement was more remarkable for what it left out. Apart from reading the indictment, Ashmead referred to no evidence of the abolitionist meetings, pamphlets, declarations, and writings that were said to have induced the fugitives to commit their crimes. Nor did he mention the previous testimony of Harvey Scott, who had identified so many of the participants in the riot, or that of Josephus Washington and John Clark, who had provided a link between Philadelphia's black "Special Secret Committee" and white Lancaster County abolitionists. Before any testimony was taken, it already seemed as though the prosecution's case had been significantly curtailed. Judging from Ashmead's opening statement, almost everything would depend on Henry Kline.

———————

Deputy U.S. Marshal Henry Kline was called as the prosecution's first substantive witness. Under direct examination by George Ashmead, the chief prosecutor's cousin and assistant, Kline testified to his receipt of the warrants for the four fugitives and his arrangement with the Gorsuch posse. He described his encounter with Samuel Williams—the black man who had tailed him from Philadelphia and who had spread the alarm in the Christiana area—and his eventual rendezvous with Gorsuch at the Gap Tavern.

The examination then moved to the events at Parker's house, including the initial confrontation on the stairway when Parker threw a fish gig at Gorsuch. After regrouping his forces, Kline read out the warrants and demanded that Parker surrender. Kline said "I then called one of [my] men . . . and told him to go to the sheriff and fetch over a hundred men. I thought that would intimidate [the blacks]. They began to get scared then and asked me to give them time to consider." Before Kline's ruse could take full effect, however, Hanway arrived, and things took a sharp turn for the worse.

Kline, who was not otherwise known for good manners, testified that he politely approached Hanway—"Good morning, sir"—and asked his name and whether he lived in the neighborhood. "He allowed it was none of my business." Maintaining formality, Kline then read Hanway the warrants, "not only once, but twice," and told him that "I was a Deputy Marshal, and came to arrest two fugitives." Hanway, however, threateningly "allowed that the colored people had a right to defend themselves," as there were "some fifteen or twenty standing there . . . with their guns loaded." According to Kline, the armed black men had arrived just after Hanway, and they had come from the same direction.

By that time Elijah Lewis had also arrived, joining the conversation between Kline and Hanway. "Mr. Lewis replied in the same way" to Kline's request for help. "He said the colored people had a right to defend themselves, and I had better clear out, or otherwise there would be blood spilt." Kline informed the two white men of their obligations under the Fugitive Slave Act, but Hanway "said he did not care for any act of Congress or any other law."

As more and more armed black men arrived, Kline grew fearful that the situation was getting out of control. Believing that Hanway and Lewis were in charge of the mob, he began to beg. "I then told them that if they would not let these colored people fire on us, I would withdraw my men." Hanway's response, however, was just the opposite of Kline's request:

> Mr. Hanway walked his horse over to the negroes, some fifteen or twenty, and he sat on his horse and kind of stooped over and said something to them in a low voice, what that was I don't know, but he rode his horse some twenty or thirty yards. [The blacks] made one shout and one of them . . . hallooed out that "he was only a deputy"—up the lane they went and fired.

Kline also testified about his confrontation with Hanway on the day after the riot, when Hanway turned himself in at Zercher's Hotel. Realizing that the episode reflected badly upon him—he had been ejected from the makeshift courtroom for threatening the prisoner—Kline's revised version of the incident was decidedly low key. "I told him [Hanway] you are one of the men and he would not deny it." Kline claimed that he could not recall the rest of the conversation "because somebody bothered me."

Hanway's seeming failure to deny his participation in the riot—a purported admission-by-silence in the face of Kline's accusation—might have been one of the highlights of the direct examination, but it was muffled by Kline's self-serving reluctance to describe the circumstances in detail. That was far from the least of Kline's shortcomings as a witness.

Earlier in the examination, Kline had been asked to describe the weapons in the hands of the black mob. "They were armed with guns, scythes, and clubs," he answered. Then he further volunteered, "I saw Harvey Scott there, he had no arms." The reference to Scott probably caused teeth to clench at the prosecution table. John Ashmead had deliberately omitted Scott from his opening statement, no doubt because the informant's credibility had already been severely damaged at the preliminary hearing. It was nearly impossible that Scott had actually been at Parker's on the day of the riot, but now Kline had sworn to his presence. That remark could open up the marshal to a devastating line of cross-examination, which the prosecutors had surely hoped to avoid by simply excluding any mention of Scott from the Hanway trial.

What had caused such a stunning blunder? Had the Ashmead cousins failed to share their plan for the trial? Had the preparation of Kline's testimony been adversely affected by the squabbling among counsel? Or had the headstrong deputy marshal spontaneously decided to embellish his testimony, without regard to the prosecutors' instructions? In any event, the damage was done. Contrary to John Ashmead's best-laid plans, Scott's credibility—and therefore Kline's—would become a major issue in the case.

Although John Read was nominally lead counsel for Hanway, it was clear to everyone that Thaddeus Stevens was the chief strategist for the defense. Thus, it came as no surprise when Stevens rose to cross-examine Kline. As everyone fully expected, the cross-examination was stingingly acerbic from the outset.

Stevens began by pointing out a series of inconsistencies between Kline's trial testimony and his testimony at the two preliminary hearings. Although none of the individual discrepancies could be considered momentous standing alone—they dealt mostly with Kline's precise position and line of sight at various times during the riot—Stevens fired so many questions, with so much scorn and speed, that the witness soon became flustered. At one point Ashmead objected that Kline had not been allowed to complete his answers.

Justice Grier admonished Stevens to "let the witness speak for himself," but the pace of the cross-examination continued unabated.

Then Stevens turned to the heart of the cross-examination, Kline's claim that Scott had been present at Parker's:

> **Stevens:** When you were examined at Lancaster you stated, you had seen George Washington Harvey Scott there, did you?
> **Kline:** Yes, sir.
> **Stevens:** And you saw him on the ground?
> **Kline:** Yes, sir.
> **Stevens:** What time did you see him on the ground?
> **Kline:** I saw him there with the first party [of blacks].
> **Stevens:** Did you see him there after Hanway came?
> **Kline:** I saw him after Hanway came, because no one came after Hanway.
> **Stevens:** Might you not be mistaken about its being Harvey Scott?
> **Kline:** No, sir. I took a good look at him. He seemed scarish and back'd off a little before the second firing.

With that, Stevens had irrevocably committed Kline to the story that Scott was present during the riot. That was potentially a crippling blow to the prosecution, because four trustworthy witnesses were available to swear that Scott had been working at John Carr's blacksmith shop that entire morning. Even if Scott never testified at the trial, Kline's own credibility had been severely damaged, as he had now sworn repeatedly to an impossible set of events. If Kline had lied about Scott, or even if he had merely been mistaken, the balance of his testimony was also open to serious doubt.

Stevens next demanded that Kline provide the names of other blacks he claimed to have seen at Parker's. Kline answered at first that he knew them "only by sight," realizing that it would obviously stretch the truth to claim that he could identify men he had never seen before. But Stevens had the transcript of the Lancaster preliminary hearing, where Kline had indeed identified several black men by name. "Have you seen all those in jail?" asked Stevens. "I think I have," answered Kline, once again providing an opening for the defense. It had become obvious, at least to the lawyers, that Kline's identifications were based on arrest records, rather than on any actual observations at Parker's. So his identification of Scott was clearly bogus, and his

identification of the other black men had now been made highly questionable as well.

Stevens had not yet finished making his point. "The course of our defense,"
he told Judges Kane and Grier, "requires that these prisoners should be brought
into Court, that the witness should see them." That was necessary, he explained
to the court, because

> Mr. Kline has heretofore identified most of these men. I want to
> prove what he says is false, and thereby to show that he don't know
> who are and who are not prisoners.

Ashmead argued that Kline's ability to identify other prisoners was "col-
lateral" to the prosecution of Hanway, but Stevens had a ready reply: "If there
is war made, we must see the soldiers." Grier was persuaded, and ordered that
the black prisoners be produced in court the following day.

Stevens hoped to demonstrate that Kline had been duplicitous, or at least
wildly misguided, in his testimony about the events at Parker's. Although it
was not possible to deny Hanway's presence at the resistance, the black defendants had been rounded up so indiscriminately that many of them had iron-
clad alibis for the morning of September 11, 1851. It would therefore be nearly
impossible for Kline to accurately match the prisoners' faces to names, and
extremely likely that he would identify several men who were indisputably
miles from the scene. Not only would Kline's anticipated misidentifications
damage the Hanway prosecution, but they could also cripple the cases against
many of the black men whose trials were yet to come.

With so much at stake, the defense team was not about to take chances with
Kline's recognition skills. Some of the black defendants had in fact participated
in the resistance and, though they could not be hidden, they could be camou-
flaged. When court opened on Saturday morning, November 29, twenty-four
black men sat on the north side of the courtroom, all dressed identically in new
clothing, and each wearing a red, white, and blue scarf. They were all freshly
shaven, which was clearly an attempt to thwart Kline's earlier description of one
of the rioters with "military whiskers."

The appearance of the black men outraged Brent, who fumed that "these
negroes were . . . sitting in a row, supported on each side by white females,
who, to the disgust of all respectable citizens, gave them open sympathy and
countenance."[11] Brent was exaggerating, if not imagining, the extent of the pris-

oners' female escort. While it is true that a great number of women attended the trial, filling more than half of the spectators' section on some days, there is no other source for his agitated claim that two white women sat with each defendant in the courtroom. Defense lawyer Arthur Jackson appropriately ridiculed Brent's comments as "bullying and bravado."[12]

Fevered southern stereotypes aside, Brent was certain that the defense ploy "was manifestly done with the privity, sufferance and consent of the officers having charge of the prisoners." He was suspicious with good cause. Shortly before the beginning of the trial, two of the prosecution's key witnesses—Josephus Washington and John Clark, who had been held in custody to ensure their appearance at trial—had "escaped" from the Moyamensing Prison, where the guards had been under the supervision of Marshal Roberts. The disappearance of Washington and Clark, which appeared to have been accomplished "without breaking a lock," was a severe setback for the prosecution.[13] The volatile Brent had many reasons to be furious at Roberts and his subordinates, who seemed to be openly and perhaps even illegally assisting the defense case, but he had previously managed to hold his tongue. Perhaps he had been restrained by the more sedate Ashmead and Cooper or perhaps he was simply waiting for the right opportunity.

Fortunately for the prosecution, Justice Grier had reconsidered the usefulness of bringing the prisoners into court. Stevens explained that he intended to cross-examine Kline about the identities "of those he spoke of as being present" and then to "contradict him by proving that they were not present," but the court ruled that the proposed evidence was inadmissible. There was only one relevant exception. "It may be possible," Grier said,

> that a man may mention matters in the examination-in-chief, and you may bring it out more broadly in cross-examination, and you could bring other witnesses to show that he falsified.

That was clearly a reference to Kline's testimony about Scott, and the defense would later take full advantage of the court's invitation to produce evidence of Kline's perjury. For the time being, however, the prisoner parade had failed, and Stevens regretfully requested that the black defendants be taken out of the courtroom.

The prosecution next called the five surviving members of the Gorsuch party. The direct examinations were all conducted by George Ashmead, although he was frequently interrupted when Brent and Cooper chimed in with additional questions. The two lawyers for Maryland either mistrusted their colleague's thoroughness or were determined to play a larger role in the trial than they had thus far been allotted by the Ashmead cousins.

Dr. Thomas Pearce, Joshua Gorsuch, Dickinson Gorsuch, Nicholas Hutchings, and Nathan Nelson each testified at some length about the events at Parker's and the killing of Edward Gorsuch. Their accounts of the incident were generally consistent, including the assembly of the posse, the first encounter with Parker, the blowing of the horn, and the arrival of the numerous armed blacks. Each witness also told the story of his own escape, with Pearce and Joshua Gorsuch describing Hanway's refusal to help them. Joshua and Dickinson Gorsuch both testified that they recognized several of the Gorsuch family slaves, thus proving the applicability of Kline's warrants and establishing an essential element of the indictment. Most moving by far was Dickinson Gorsuch's testimony about his father's death and his own near-fatal wound.

Each of the five witnesses also testified to Hanway's apparent responsibility for the riot. Pearce claimed that before "Hanway rode up to the [area], the negroes seemed to give up, but on seeing him they raised a yell and became fully confirmed, in my opinion, to repel to the very last." He also heard Hanway angrily warn Kline, "You had better go home, you need not come here to make arrests, for you cannot do it," while also saying "something about blood." According to Joshua Gorsuch, the people in Parker's house had been on the verge of surrender, but "after the man on horseback came up, they appeared to be inspired. . . . They appeared to rally." Dickinson Gorsuch testified to Hanway's arrival: "Before this the negroes seemed as if they would have given up . . . now they seemed to be determined." In Hutchings's version, the blacks had "appeared to be rather intimidated" by the posse, but at Hanway's arrival "they appeared to be in great spirits—all of them hallooing and shouting and singing." Nelson told essentially the same story, that the "negroes seemed to rejoice" at the sight of Hanway, as "they made a jumping and a great noise."

The essential implication, crucial to the prosecution case, was that Hanway had been the leader, or at least an instigator, of the resistance. The similarity of the five witnesses' testimony might therefore be attributable to coordination among them, although they might also have been simply describing the same incident. It seems highly improbable, however, that all five men, positioned at different locations and under extreme stress, would have independently observed and remembered the same precise sequence of events: dejection among the blacks at Parker's, followed by Hanway's arrival some distance from the house, followed immediately by signs of renewed determination among the resisters. Distracted, as they must have been, by sporadic gunfire from the Parker house and an army of hostile blacks flowing in from every direction, wasn't it likely that at least one of the slave hunters would have failed to notice the exact moment of Hanway's arrival? The great probability, therefore, is that the five witnesses had been prompted by the prosecutors, who were anxious to make sure that they all supported and agreed about Hanway's involvement in the "traitorous combination."

For tactical reasons, the defense attorneys had decided that they would not cross-examine Joshua or Dickinson Gorsuch, as that would later allow them to profess sympathy for the bereaved Gorsuch family. That courtesy, however, apparently did not extend to Pearce, whom Stevens vigorously cross-examined even though he was Edward Gorsuch's nephew. Stevens's first objective was to establish that Pearce had not heard any shooting in the "long lane" leading from the Parker house, where Kline had confronted Hanway. That was extremely important because the absence of gunshots in Hanway's vicinity would tend to undermine the theory that he had inspired the blacks to begin firing. Pearce resisted the implication, but Stevens was persistent:

> **Stevens:** From the time you looked for the Marshal until you retreated did you see any body firing in the long lane?
> **Pearce:** I heard no firing in the long lane. My attention was not directed to the long lane.
> **Stevens:** Did you hear any firing in the long lane?
> **Pearce:** My attention was not directed there and of course I did not hear.
> **Stevens:** I did not ask where your attention was directed, I asked if you heard any in the long lane.
> **Pearce:** I stated I did not.

Using the same dogged technique, Stevens also compelled Pearce to admit having once declared that Hanway had saved his life during the escape, by placing his horse between Pearce and the pursuing rioters. Pearce also reluctantly conceded "that the whole difficulty or at least the fatal part of it arose from the imprudent conduct of [his] uncle."

Attorney General Brent conducted the redirect examination of Pearce, marking his first significant contribution to the trial. He had gotten only three questions out of his mouth when Stevens objected to his "insinuations with a witness." That sparked a testy exchange between the two attorneys, in what had until then been a mostly courteous proceeding. Brent retorted that there had been no insinuation and that Stevens's remark was "unwarrantable." The defense and prosecution continued to spar over whether Brent's questions, any insinuations aside, were beyond the scope of the cross-examination and thus impermissible on redirect. Justice Grier finally ruled in favor of the prosecution, noting that "where a party may have overlooked a point, he then may have leave to ask it again." That was a temporary victory for Brent, but it might have come at great cost. The prosecutors would later become perilously lax about the formal order of their proof, perhaps relying to their detriment on Grier's initial permissiveness.

The final two witnesses of the trial's first week were Miller Knott and his adolescent son John. Both had seen the shooting of Edward and Dickinson Gorsuch, but neither contributed anything damaging to Hanway. Once again the direct examinations were conducted by George Ashmead, and once again Brent insisted on pursuing redirect examinations—in both cases at greater length than the original directs—although he did not succeed in implicating the defendant. The redirect examination of young John Knott droned on so long that defense counsel finally objected that it was simply repeating material that should have been covered during direct examination.

Brent's reply was more revealing than he intended. "I can only say in regard to these facts that I was not aware what the witnesses could prove" when they first testified. "We determined on consultation to re-examine both of these witnesses." In other words, the prosecution was so ill-prepared and uncoordinated that they had not conferred about the witnesses' testimony before putting them on the stand. Even worse, it appeared that Brent had access to information relevant to the testimony but had not shared it with George Ashmead (or had not trusted him to present it). Justice Grier remained indulgent, although only to a point. He allowed Brent to continue the redirect examination of John Knott for a while, before finally cutting him off: "It is no use examining him as to what he was examined on before."

⸺◆⸺

Monday morning, December 1, brought a new set of prosecution witnesses and a new line of attack. J. Franklin Reigart, who had presided over one of the preliminary hearings, testified to the heated confrontation that occurred when Hanway and Elijah Lewis turned themselves in at Zercher's Hotel. He recounted Kline's angry accusation: "When I plead for my life like a dog and begged you not to let the blacks fire upon us, you turned round and told them to do so." Although Elijah Lewis immediately denied the charge, "Mr. Hanway said nothing, he didn't deny it." Constable William Proudfoot then testified to the same exchange, reporting both Kline's words and Hanway's guilty silence. The cross-examinations could not challenge the accuracy of Reigart's and Proudfoot's testimony, so instead they emphasized Kline's offensive belligerence—Reigart recounted how he had to take Kline by the shoulder to prevent a disturbance—in contrast to Hanway's relative composure.

At that point the trial finally turned to evidence of "preconcert and combination." Charles Smith was called to testify about the warning that had been spread in Christiana just before the riot. He had encountered Samuel Williams just before daylight, and the black agent of the Philadelphia Vigilance Committee told him that slave hunters were at work in the area. Hoping to alert the runaways "that their masters were after them," Williams had left a note in Christiana, and he implored Smith to help spread the word.

The defense objected bitterly to Smith's testimony. It might have constituted proof of someone's preconcert, but there had been no mention of Hanway and the testimony was therefore irrelevant. "What is wanting here is the connecting link," argued defense counsel, because there was no evidence of any communication between Williams or Smith and Hanway. U.S. Attorney John Ashmead was ready to defend his theory of the case, arguing that Williams's warning had been the starting point of the ultimate offense:

> This is the beginning of the transaction and was the first information which led to the assembling of the band of armed negroes and the other parties at Parker's house. . . . And after the information was taken by this man, [Hanway] was seen there, acting in concert

with them, encouraging them, and he is responsible for all that happened from the beginning.

Grier ruled in favor of the prosecution. Because Hanway "was at least present at an outrage in which a hundred men were concerned," Grier reasoned, "the acts of all the parties concerned in it became evidence against him to show the nature of the offense. Otherwise it would be impossible to make out treason or conspiracy."

Seizing that opening, the prosecution next called Dr. Augustus Cain, who was a "well-known abolitionist and active underground railroad agent."[14] Appearing involuntarily under subpoena, Cain was far from a cooperative witness. Testimony had to be dragged out of him, bit by bit. Under questioning by George Ashmead, Cain allowed that he had spoken to Josephus Washington and John Clark—the two government informants who had absconded from prison, perhaps with Marshal Roberts's connivance—on the day before the riot. He also admitted that they had given him a paper—presumably from Samuel Williams—with the names of three runaways who needed to be warned. At that point Brent jumped in, interrupting Ashmead's orderly examination to ask when Cain had first heard "of the murder of Edward Gorsuch." "Not of the murder, I didn't hear," answered Cain, "but I heard that the kidnappers had been at Parker's."

Grier was not pleased by the witness's characterization: "I suppose in the language of that region, any master seeking to recover his slave, is called a kidnapper. I want to know what the witness means by it." Cain, however, would not give ground, even to the court. "I gave the words as they were told to me by a colored man," he snapped, "that there were kidnappers at Parker's."

Grier did not pursue the point, but Brent was not about to miss an opportunity to sully the witness. After you learned of Gorsuch's death in the riot, he asked, "Were you at any time . . . called upon to dress any wounds of any colored persons?" Cain answered that he had treated two black men for gunshot wounds but had not asked them how they had come to be injured. "Did you give any information to have these men arrested?" asked Brent. Cain admitted that he had not.

If not technically guilty as an after-the-fact collaborator, Cain had definitely been exposed as a fugitive sympathizer and perhaps worse. Brent hoped that Cain might even provide the key to the case, by linking abolitionist agitation to the planning of the Christiana resistance. Cain, however, saw where the examination was headed and did his best to derail it:

> **Brent:** Have you any knowledge of meetings having been held in that neighborhood in regard to fugitive slaves?
>
> **Cain:** No, sir.
>
> **Brent:** Had you knowledge of any meeting in which that was considered, though called for other purpose?
>
> **Cain:** I think it is likely I had.
>
> **Brent:** When was it and where?
>
> **Cain:** It was at Westchester, at the Horticultural Hall.
>
> **Brent:** Were there speeches made at that meeting against [the fugitive slave] law?
>
> **Cain:** There were speeches disapproving of the law, I believe.
>
> **Brent:** Did you see the resolutions published in the papers afterwards?
>
> **Cain:** I didn't.
>
> **Brent:** Do you know whether Hanway was present?
>
> **Cain:** I don't—I don't recollect seeing him at it.

George Ashmead suddenly seemed to realize that Brent was making a potentially decisive point that he apparently had not previously discussed with his cocounsel. Ashmead immediately interposed a series of his own questions, returning Brent's earlier interjections:

> **Ashmead:** Was it a society that met?
>
> **Cain:** I believe it was.
>
> **Ashmead:** What society was it?
>
> **Cain:** I understood it [to] be the Anti-Slavery Society. . . . It was the annual convention.
>
> **Ashmead:** In what paper in Westchester are the resolutions of that society generally published?
>
> **Cain:** I don't know if any resolutions were adopted at that meeting.
>
> **Ashmead:** Do you know in what papers in Westchester the resolutions of that society are generally published?

Cain: I am not aware of there having published any of the proceedings in any paper in Westchester.

Not to be outdone, Brent reasserted his control of the examination:

Brent: How many attended in that convention from Sadsbury [Christiana] Township?

Cain: I can't tell. . . . I don't recollect. . . . I was there as a spectator; I didn't receive any invitation to go.[15]

That was as much as the prosecution was able to establish (or intimate). Cain had evidently known something in advance about plans to thwart the slave catchers, and afterward he had been trusted enough to secretly treat the black men wounded in the riot. He was also tied closely to the abolitionist movement in the Christiana area, and the manner of his responses hinted—if only by his hesitation—that he knew more than he was willing to tell about Hanway's possible associations as well. Still, there had been many problems in Cain's direct testimony; the combative witness had refused to supply details or name names. The defense wisely chose not to cross-examine him, lest they open areas of inquiry that could be exploited on redirect examination.

The prosecution's conspiracy theory rested on a series of implied links, leading from the Anti-Slavery Society to Samuel Williams to Josephus Washington and John Clark to Augustus Cain to Castner Hanway. But thus far the story was full of holes. Some of the gaps could conceivably be filled by inferences—just as Justice Grier had ruled that Hanway's mere presence at the riot could be used to tie him "to the acts of all the parties concerned"—but a jury was likely to want hard proof somewhere along the line. Perhaps Washington and Clark might have supplied the necessary connection—there is no telling who else they warned or recruited to the resistance, in addition to Dr. Cain—but they had mysteriously fled government custody and were not available to testify.

There were other cooperating witnesses, however, including two black men who testified that they had been alerted to the "kidnappers" at Parker's house. John Roberts had been roused on the morning of the resistance by Joseph Scarlett, a Quaker who was also among the indicted white men. Under instructions from Scarlett, Roberts had first attempted to round up other "colored people," and he then headed to Parker's himself, carrying a loaded gun that had been given to him by a man named Jacob Townsend. Roberts was obviously under considerable pressure to testify favorably for the prosecution, having admitted to being armed at the scene of the killing. By the time he took the stand, Roberts had spent seventy-two days in custody at the Moyamensing Prison, where he had shared quarters with Washington and Clark, and he testified that the two missing witnesses had escaped but did not "break any locks or any thing of that kind."

Jacob Wood had been recruited in a similar fashion. He testified that he had been at work digging potatoes on the morning of the riot when Elijah Lewis "came along and informed me that . . . it was no time to take up potatoes, when Mr. Parker's house was all surrounded by kidnappers." With that, George Ashmead announced, "We close the testimony . . . in this case, on the part of the United States."

Senator Cooper, putative lead counsel for the prosecution, allowed that he was relatively satisfied with his and his colleagues' work. "I think we have established the material overt act, by *more* than two witnesses," he wrote to Governor Lowe. "It is to be feared however, that the character of the principal witness, Kline, will be successfully assailed by the prisoner, and especially inasmuch as there are some discrepancies between him and our other witnesses and some contradictions of his former statements made at various times."[16]

Cooper had more reason to worry than he confided to Governor Lowe. Although the prosecution had indeed produced adequate evidence of a material overt act, Hanway's personal culpability was supported only by the tenuous inference that every person present at the resistance was accountable for the acts of the rioters. The government had also presented significant evidence of preconcert. There had clearly been a general plan in the area to resist slave hunters in which it appeared that Joseph Scarlett, Elijah Lewis, and others had gone from house to house gathering men to join the crowd at Parker's. But Hanway had been loosely tied, if at all, to that effort. Most glaringly, there had been no solid proof of Hanway's intention, in a case where intent was the most important element of the crime. To gain a treason conviction, the prosecutors had to prove that Hanway intended to render the fugitive law a nullity, not merely that he had provoked resistance to the recapture of certain slaves.

Thus, the prosecution case was uncomfortably dependent on the credibility of Marshal Kline, the witness who most directly implicated Hanway in the resistance. It was Kline who had Hanway whispering to a gang of armed blacks immediately before they began firing in the long lane, and it was Kline who had generated Hanway's alleged admission-by-silence at Zercher's Hotel. Kline was also the only witness to Hanway's arrogant assertion that "he did not care for any act of Congress," including the Fugitive Slave Act—an avowal that was more incriminating at the time than it may appear today. In the nineteenth century, the term "care for" was not synonymous with "appreciate." Instead, it was often used in the sense of "heed," in which case Hanway's statement could have been interpreted to mean that he would not recognize or obey the law, with the following implication that he intended to interfere with its general enforcement.[17] Such a supposition might have been reinforced by the introduction of the promised abolitionist books, pamphlets, resolutions, and writings—or, better yet, some evidence of Hanway's own attachment to abolitionism—but no such evidence had been offered during the prosecution's case-in-chief.

Despite Cooper's cautious optimism, defense counsel Arthur Jackson's evaluation was closer to the mark. It came "to the surprise of every one," he observed, when "the case of the United States was announced to be concluded" with so many of the prosecution's promises unfulfilled.[18]

∽ 7 ∽

SIR–DID YOU HEAR IT?

Theodore Cuyler opened the case for the defense, and he wasted no time getting directly to the point. He assailed the "total inadequacy" of the prosecution case and he expressed "painful surprise, that a charge so grave has been founded upon evidence so weak." Yes, there had been a terrible murder at Christiana, but Hanway had taken no part in it. Far from a traitorous conspirator, the defendant was "as free of participation in this offence as you who sit in the jury-box; or his honor, upon the bench." Hanway had gone to William Parker's only to determine whether unlawful kidnappers were at work, as had often been the case over the years in the region. Once he saw that Henry Kline had legitimate authority, Hanway retired from the scene "before any firing."[1]

If the case had taken on political significance, explained Cuyler, it was only because the State of Maryland, as personified by Attorney General Robert Brent, "distrusts the justice of Pennsylvania." That was most unfair to Hanway, amounting almost to a thirst "for the blood of this man" who "is not here through his counsel to defend those sad deeds which disgraced the sweet and peaceful valley near Christiana." Indeed, the defense explicitly accepted the constitutional obligation to return fugitive slaves when sought by proper means.

The treason charge itself was absurd, argued Cuyler, as was the prosecution claim that the fate of the Union might somehow turn on the outcome of the case:

> Sir—Did you hear it? That three harmless, non-resisting Quakers, and eight-and-thirty wretched, miserable, penniless negroes, armed with corn-cutters, clubs, and few muskets, and headed by a miller, in a felt hat, without a coat, without arms, and mounted on a sorrel nag, levied war against the United States. Blessed be God that our Union has survived the shock.

One leg of the defense strategy was to show the frequency of illegal kidnapping in the vicinity of Christiana, thus providing a context for Castner Hanway's and Elijah Lewis's rush to Parker's house. To that end, Thaddeus Stevens called Thomas Pennington as his first witness and asked him to testify "to the kidnapping and carrying away of coloured persons in the neighborhood of the Gap within the past year."

U.S. Attorney John Ashmead immediately objected. Illegal kidnappings had nothing to do with the case, he argued, because Kline and Edward Gorsuch had been acting under lawful process. "There is no crime in the world that could not be justified in some way . . . by showing that somebody had done a wrong anterior to it."

Stevens countered that the proposed evidence was material to Hanway's defense "to show what might have brought him there." The Gap Gang, he said,

> had not only upon one, but on two or three occasions, in the dead of night, invaded the houses of the neighbors, of white people, where black men lived, and black people, and by force and violence and great injury and malice, without authority from any person on earth, seized and transported these men away.

Grier looked to the prosecutors for a cogent response, but instead Ashmead and James Cooper openly quibbled with each other over whether the date of the alleged kidnappings was relevant. They should have been more attentive to the court.

Their objection would be valid, Justice Grier told them, if "you had indicted this man simply for resisting an officer of government; but when you have accused him of treason, it is a position founded upon some previous conspiracy or agreement." Hanway, therefore, should be allowed to show that he had come to Parker's "merely upon the spur of the moment [rather than] in open war." The prosecution had been given "the widest scope to prove either by proclamation or meeting, or a mere publication that it was a levying of war," and it was only fair that the defendant be allowed the same latitude. The prosecutors could only grimace as Grier continued to rule against them. While the Fugitive Slave Act had been "unjustly treated with odium," he said, it was not necessarily proven that Hanway and Lewis had known from the first alarm that "masters were there with proper process to arrest a runaway." Thus, it was permissible for the defendant to "show that kidnappers had been about, and there was a degree of insecurity among the free negroes who resided in that neighborhood."

Stevens took full advantage of the court's ruling, producing four witnesses to a brutal abduction. Pennington testified to the kidnapping from his home of a black man named John Williams, who was seized at gunpoint by six or seven members of the Gap Gang. Williams struggled for his freedom, but he was beaten bloody and dragged to a waiting carriage. On cross-examination, Cooper attempted to show that Williams had been a runaway who presumably had been lawfully captured, but Pennington would not agree with either proposition. Pennington's son and daughter-in-law were later called to back him up, but their direct testimony added few details and they were barely cross-examined.

The next defense witness was Henry Rhay, who testified to the same encounter. This time Brent conducted the cross-examination, and his approach may well have come as a surprise to his prosecution colleagues. "Do you know of any meetings, large or small," he asked, "in that neighborhood, on the subject of the Fugitive Slave Law?" This was an obvious attempt to remedy the earlier deficiencies in the prosecution case, especially in light of Justice Grier's recent comment about the need for evidence of a "proclamation or meeting, or a mere publication" to support the theory of treasonous intent.

Stevens, of course, objected that Brent had gone well beyond the scope of the direct examination. Justice Grier agreed. "It is irregular to cross-examine a witness, except on the subject matter of his examination-in-chief. If you want the witness, you should produce him yourself."

"We will reserve it," said Brent, attempting to salvage something from the situation. But that only made things worse. "You have already made your case upon which the United States must stand or fall," admonished Grier. "You have a right to cross-examine, to show how far the defendant's witnesses have told the truth . . . but not to start new subjects with the cross-examination."

That may have been the moment when the prosecutors fully realized how badly their case had faltered, in part because each lawyer seemed to be acting independently of the others. Not only had they constantly interrupted one another, but Ashmead and Cooper could not even agree on so simple a matter as the relevance of evidence. And Brent, it appeared, had his own ideas—perhaps his own information—about how to prove the existence of an abolitionist conspiracy.

———————

It was only the first day of the defense case, and the prosecution was already reeling. It appears that the prosecutors retreated to confer among themselves, because John Ashmead was not in the courtroom when Elijah Lewis was called as the next witness. That may have been a defensive maneuver on Ashmead's part. Lewis was going to create more trouble for the prosecution, and this time the problem would be attributable solely to the U.S. attorney himself.

As soon as Lewis took the stand, Justice Grier asked whether the court should delay the proceeding until Ashmead's return. Speaking cryptically, Brent explained "it was understood that Mr. Ashmead would offer an objection to this testimony," but then he proceeded to present the argument himself. Lewis was disqualified, said Brent, because he had been indicted as part of a "joint offense." The rules of evidence in 1851 did not permit a criminal defendant to testify in his own behalf, and Brent insisted that the "interested party" rule applied equally to codefendants, even if they were not then being tried. Justice Grier was not persuaded. "Having indicted the prisoners severally," he told the prosecution, "you cannot deprive one of them of the testimony of his fellow" by holding separate trials.

Ashmead's decision to proceed with separate trials had backfired badly. Without Lewis, there would have been no eyewitness for the defense. Hanway was barred from testifying, and the only other witnesses to the relevant exchange had been Kline and the surviving members of the Gorsuch party. But now, following Grier's ruling, the defense would be able to provide its own firsthand account of Hanway's reaction to the riot. Whether he was angry or embarrassed by the turn of events, Ashmead did not return to court until Elijah Lewis was off the stand.

Under questioning by Stevens, Lewis explained that he had first been approached by Isaiah Clarkson at about sunrise, as he was first opening his shop. Clarkson was spreading the alarm that Parker's house "was surrounded by kidnappers" and he insisted that Lewis join him "to see that justice was done." Lewis readily agreed, but Hanway's involvement seemed almost like an afterthought: "Having to pass Castner Hanway's house, I called upon him and requested him to accompany me." Hanway was not feeling well that morning, so he saddled his horse for the one-mile ride to Parker's, while Lewis continued on foot.

By the time Lewis arrived at Parker's, Hanway was already conferring with Kline. At Lewis's request, Kline produced his warrants, and then asked the two local men to assist in arresting the fugitives. Lewis and Hanway replied that they "would have nothing to do with it." By then there were "several negroes" nearby who "had guns and threatened to shoot." Hanway shouted, "'Don't shoot! don't shoot! for God's sake, don't shoot!' and advised Kline that it would be dangerous to attempt making arrests, and that they had better leave." As more armed blacks arrived, all three white men retreated; Kline ran into a nearby copse before the fatal shooting began.

Stevens concluded the examination with a masterful series of pointed questions that summarized the entire defense case:

> **Stevens:** Did [Hanway] ride across to the other side of the lane where the negroes were, to speak to them?
> **Lewis:** He did not.
> **Stevens:** Did he, or did he not say that he cared nothing about the Act of Congress or any other law?
> **Lewis:** He did not, that I heard him.
> **Stevens:** Did you say that?
> **Lewis:** I did not.
> **Stevens:** When the firing commenced, Kline was in the woods?
> **Lewis:** He was.

Lewis was triple-teamed on cross-examination, with Cooper, George Ashmead, and Brent each taking a turn. Cooper began by questioning whether Lewis (and therefore Kline) had departed before the shooting began. "Why did you leave?" he asked. "Our object being accomplished—to ascertain that there was authority there, we had no further business," Lewis replied. "Why didn't you go back at the time and assist?" challenged Cooper, hoping to embarrass the witness or at least make him seem callous and untrustworthy. "It is a hard question to answer," stammered Lewis, whose only explanation was that "I felt repugnant to going there."

George Ashmead took over at that point, with a set of questions intended to implicate the black prisoners. Had Lewis seen Harvey Scott at the scene?

John Morgan? Henry Simmons? Lewis answered no to all three. Well, then, asked Ashmead, "who were the colored persons that you saw there, whom you knew?" Lewis named William Howard and James Dorsey, who were not among the indictees. He also named Ezekiel Thompson, who had been charged, but added that "he had nothing in his hands that I saw."

Brent followed up with a relentless cross-examination that turned out to be one of the best in the entire trial. He began with Isaiah Clarkson's request to Lewis:

> **Brent:** He wished you to see justice done?
> **Lewis:** He called upon me to go and see justice done.
> **Brent:** Had you promised him or anyone before that, you would see justice done?
> **Lewis:** I had not, that I know of.
> **Brent:** Why did he call on you?
> **Lewis:** I don't know.
> **Brent:** Had he particular reasons for calling on you to see justice done?
> **Lewis:** None that I know of.
> **Brent:** You hadn't promised it before?
> **Lewis:** No.

Brent had successfully insinuated that Lewis (and perhaps also Hanway) had been part of a preexisting network of resisters. He then moved on to address Lewis's disrespect for the law, pointing out that the witness had seen Kline's four warrants:

> **Brent:** Did you tell the negroes that there was authority?
> **Lewis:** I did not speak to them.
> **Brent:** Why didn't you give them that information which you had obtained from the papers? You went there to see justice done?
> **Lewis:** I went there to see if they had authority.
> **Brent:** You were invited to see justice done. I want to know why you did not inform these men you saw there about to proceed to violence, that there was authority?

Lewis: I don't know that I can give any reason; I felt myself in danger and wished to get away.

Had Lewis really been in danger? Or had he been more a partisan of the resistance than he let on? Brent had one more point to make along that line:

Brent: Did you sell any powder or shot the day before?
Lewis: I have no recollection of selling any.
Brent: Have you sold to colored persons?
Lewis: I sell to all who ask me.
Brent: Then you have sold to colored persons?
Lewis: Yes, to colored, and to white, too.

The cross-examinations had done some damage to Lewis, but on balance his testimony was still extremely helpful to the defense. Contrary to the prosecution theory, Lewis had provided a plausible alternate account of Hanway's actions at Parker's and, even more important, an innocent explanation of Hanway's motive for being there in the first place.

Nine defense witnesses testified to minor contradictions in the prior statements of prosecution witnesses. Four of them had heard Kline admit that he fled before the shooting began, while blaming the debacle on Gorsuch's refusal to join him in retreat. Four others heard Dr. Pearce brand Kline a coward for abandoning his posse. The voluble Pearce had apparently spoken frequently about his experience at Parker's, because three of the witnesses also heard him concede that Hanway had saved his life. Only one of the witnesses had actually been present during the resistance. Isaac Rogers had seen Hanway fleeing along with Dr. Pearce and Dickinson Gorsuch, and he testified that Hanway had shouted, "Don't shoot!" to the pursuing colored men. Once again, Brent demonstrated his astute understanding of the case, pointing out on cross-examination that it "would have endangered Hanway" if the black men had fired while he and Pearce were both running away down the same lane.

If that barrage had not been enough, the defense followed with twenty-nine witnesses, many of them leading figures in Philadelphia's legal and political communities, who testified to Henry Kline's poor reputation for truth and veracity. Their testimony varied in minor detail, but they declared unanimously that Kline was an undependable character who could not be trusted under oath. The prosecutors could do little more than sit and watch as their key witness was persistently vilified, although they did make sure he was present in the courtroom for all of the character testimony—no doubt in the vain hope that the defense witnesses might be more restrained if they had to face Kline in person.

Interspersed among the general character witnesses, the defense also called members of the Carr family to testify that Harvey Scott could not have been present during the resistance at Parker's. The prosecution objected on the ground that they had never called Scott as a witness in the Hanway trial itself, but Stevens pointed out that Kline had mentioned Scott's presence during direct examination. Carr's testimony, therefore, would show that Kline's testimony was "utterly and totally false." Cooper replied halfheartedly that the prosecution had not asked any "questions to ascertain whether Harvey Scott was there; the witness volunteered to state it," but he must have known that he was fighting a losing cause. Grier ruled the testimony admissible and the defense proceeded to devastating effect.

John Carr testified that Scott had been "buttoned" into his second-story room on the night of September 10, and released only at sunup the following day. Scott then worked in Carr's blacksmith shop the entire morning of September 11, and therefore could not possibly have made a secret six-mile round trip to Parker's. Carr's testimony was corroborated by his son-in-law and one of his customers, both of whom saw Scott in the blacksmith shop during the hour of the riot. On cross-examination, Cooper was reduced to asking whether "a man of ordinary size" could have climbed out of the window at Carr's. That was unlikely, said the witness, but even so it would not explain Scott's presence the entire morning in the smithy.

In what may have been his only misstep in the entire trial, Stevens called Enoch Harlan as a character witness for the defendant. Harlan, a Quaker who had known Hanway for twenty-eight years, described him as "a peaceful, good, loyal, and orderly citizen."

That was one adjective too many, as Ashmead eagerly jumped on the description of Hanway as "loyal." How could Hanway be loyal, Ashmead asked, when he had refused to assist Kline in the execution of the fugitive slave law? "What I mean by loyal," replied Harlan, "would be a man that would not resist the laws of his country." That was not enough for Ashmead. Wouldn't a loyal citizen have to "perform any duty and any obligation that the law of the land lays upon him?" That put the witness in a bind, but he answered candidly:

> I would say there were some duties which the laws of our country might impose upon me which I could not conscientiously perform; which if not performing them I am not loyal, [then] I am not a loyal citizen.

The implication hung over the courtroom. Hanway had admittedly refused to fulfill his legal obligations under the fugitive act, and now a defense witness conceded that might have been "disloyal." While there was a constitutional difference between disloyalty and treason, it was a fine distinction that might easily elude a jury. Stevens therefore hastened to repair the damage by pointing out that Harlan was a Quaker, whose religion prevented him from bearing arms or fighting the enemies of the country. "Does Mr. Hanway belong to your sect?" Stevens asked. "He is not a member of either branch of the Society of Friends that I know of," replied Harlan.

Defense counsel would close their case with twelve more character witnesses, who variously vouched for Hanway's quiet, orderly, well-disposed, innocent, good-hearted, unblemished, and remarkably peaceable nature, but they would not again make the mistake of raising the "loyalty" issue. On Thursday, December 4, the defense rested.

<hr />

George Ashmead was assigned the task of outlining the prosecution's rebuttal case to the jury, and he began with a straightforward refutation of the defense case. He defended Deputy Kline from the multi-witness character assault, explaining that "it is impossible for a police officer to have continued for several years in his office without raising round him, in all probability, a host of enemies." More surprisingly, he committed the prosecution to "produce Harvey Scott himself before you [to] corroborate the statement of Kline." Ashmead also denied the claim that illegal kidnappers had previously enjoyed a free hand in Christiana, promising to prove that the man allegedly seized by the Gap Gang had in fact been a fugitive slave taken by a lawful warrant. But even if it had been a kidnapping, said Ashmead, it was only a single incident—far from the epidemic of abductions Theodore Cuyler had described in the opening statement for the defense. "Do you believe," asked Ashmead, "if the learned counsel for the defence had had it in their power to prove another case even of alleged kidnapping, that they would not have done it?"

Ashmead's statement at last showed a sign of coordination among the prosecuting attorneys. Pursuing the themes of Brent's cross-examinations, Ashmead promised to show that in the Christiana region, "meetings have been held, speeches have been made, and resolutions adopted . . . to sustain that higher law, which . . . overrides the laws and the Constitution." Indeed, it would be proven that "organized bands of negroes [had] paraded the streets of Lancaster, on the hunt for slave hunters, and showing the determination that if they caught them, they would kill them." The latter claim was more or less true, as we know from William Parker's memoir, and Ashmead was on relatively solid ground when he argued that there had been "a general, long-continued determination, acted upon by signals, to prevent the execution of the laws." It was still necessary to tie Hanway to the conspiracy, but the prosecutors had another problem. They had not produced any such evidence during their case-in-chief, and it also seemed beyond the strict scope of rebuttal.

Ashmead attempted to remedy the procedural difficulty by claiming that "the matter [had] been opened to us on the part of the defence." But that was wishful thinking. Rather than claim a right to produce new evidence, the prosecution's best hope lay in appealing for the court's indulgence. It would not have been the first time that judges had allowed an extra degree of latitude to disorganized prosecutors. For the time being, however, Grier was noncommittal. He responded to a defense objection only by cautioning the prosecutors against describing evidence that "would not be received as testimony."

With that warning in mind, the prosecution began the rebuttal case by calling an exhausting array of character witnesses for Marshal Kline, including six police officers, a deputy district attorney, numerous lawyers, four innkeepers, two aldermen, a doctor, and a tax collector. After sixty-eight witnesses had assured the jury of Kline's veracity (as opposed to the defense's mere twenty-nine detractors), Justice Grier observed that "two to one is as good as three, or four, or five to one," and he complained that "there is no use of multiplying them." Somewhat reluctantly—apparently because he had still more Kline supporters waiting in the wings—Ashmead agreed to go on to more substantive matters.

A crucial showdown began when George Ashmead called William Noble as the first of several proposed witnesses who would prove that the Christiana area had been "patrolled by armed bodies of negroes" who were part of "a regular organization for the purpose of resisting, upon every and all occasions, the execution of the laws of the United States." The defense objected to improper rebuttal but the prosecutors argued there were extenuating circumstances. Ashmead assured the court that "the very existence of all the witnesses whom we intended to offer upon this point were not known, to any of the counsel on the part of the United States, until after the defence had opened the testimony on their part." Brent made the same point, although he put it more obliquely. "I was not conscious that this testimony was in the power of the United States, when the evidence on the part of the prosecution closed."

Ashmead and Brent were protecting themselves from charges of ineptitude, and neither was very credible. How could the prosecution have been unaware of murderous bands of negroes and their white supporters, especially after having spent weeks on a county-wide roundup of every suspicious black man in sight? And having alleged the existence of a "traitorous combination," how could the prosecutors now claim to have been totally unaware of the witnesses necessary to establish the conspiracy? The gist of their excuse was to blame each other for the woeful gap in their case, both men disclaiming the knowledge that each one should have had. There was sufficient blame to go around. The Ashmead cousins had prepared inadequately, before and after the indictment. Brent, as indicated by the propositions in his cross-examinations and his subsequent correspondence with Governor Lowe, had prior knowledge of the allegedly treasonous meetings and organizations, but he did not share that information with his cocounsel.

In any case, the defense lawyers were having none of it. "This is perhaps the most extraordinary offer I ever heard in rebutting testimony," sputtered John M. Read. The prosecutors had "deliberately withheld" an essential part of their case "for the express purpose of bringing it as evidence in rebuttal. . . . I say that this is unprecedented. This is unprecedented." Read might endlessly have reiterated his indignation, but it was not necessary.

"Every thing tending to show there was an intention to make public resistance to a particular law, was entirely a matter of evidence in chief," ruled Justice Grier, "and should have been given as such." The testimony now proposed by the prosecution was "not at all rebutting," and was therefore inadmissible.

"By omitting evidence of preconcert," the prosecutors had "fail[ed] in their original case" and could not be permitted to make up the ground in rebuttal.

That ruling was a severe blow to the prosecution. Without any leeway to offer new evidence on rebuttal, there was no chance of tying Hanway to any prearranged resistance. Therefore, the only hope of conviction now rested even more fully on Kline's shaky assertion that Hanway had whispered to the rioters and encouraged them to shoot, thereby joining, even if spontaneously, an armed conspiracy in progress. But Kline's account had been badly undercut by the Carrs' testimony regarding the whereabouts of Harvey Scott. Thus, the prosecutors had little choice but to call Scott himself to the stand, in a last-ditch attempt to bolster the credibility of their own star witness.

George Ashmead conducted Scott's direct examination, hoping to prove that Carr and the other defense witnesses had been incorrect. "Were you at the battle?" asked Ashmead.

"I gave my evidence that I was there once," said Scott equivocally. "I was frightened at the time," he continued, "and I said I was there, but I was not."

Ashmead could not believe his ears. "Were you there?" he demanded.

"I was proved to be there, but I was not there," the witness replied.

Ashmead pressed on, repeating himself as though in shock. "On the morning of the 11th of September, last?"

"No, sir—Kline swore I was there . . . and they took me to Christiana, and I was frightened, and I didn't know what to say, and I said what they told me."

For a moment there was silence in the courtroom, but then everyone realized what had just happened. The most important witness in the prosecution's rebuttal case had just recanted, and the spectators erupted into laughter and applause. Far from reinforcing Kline's testimony, Ashmead's direct examination had placed his own credibility on the line. "I had a conversation with this witness three or four days ago," he frantically explained to the court, "and he said he was there."

"Yes," noted Grier sardonically, but "others have had a conversation later than you."

Still, George Ashmead could not accept the reversal. "Have you had conversation with any one, since you conversed with me?" he asked the witness.

"No, sir," said Scott.

That was quite enough for U.S. Attorney John Ashmead. Smarting from the laughter of Hanway's friends and supporters, he reminded the court that Scott had testified under oath at the preliminary hearing and had "detailed all the transactions that had occurred" at Parker's. In light of the witness's altered testimony, the prosecutor had no choice but "to ask that he may be now committed to [stand] trial for perjury."

The defense attorneys objected. Scott was "a poor negro with a weak mind," said Read, "who was entrapped into saying what was untrue." Having seen Scott's demeanor, Grier apparently concurred. "Poor devil, it is not worth while for the United States to do it," he told the prosecutors as he adjourned court for the day. "Let him go, and if you owe him anything, pay him, that he may not be tempted to steal."

But that was not yet the end of the Scott affair. Mortified by the unanticipated turn of events, the prosecutors attempted to blame the defense team or its allies for tampering with their witness. Brent was certain that Scott had been "influenced by bribes or some other corrupt consideration," but George Ashmead was somewhat more circumspect, arguing for the admission of Scott's testimony from the preliminary hearing.[2] The prior testimony was more reliable, claimed Ashmead, because "yesterday in the Marshal's office he was conversed with, by several negroes" who presumably convinced him to change his story. "We think that we have a right to show these things . . . in justification for having offered him as a witness."

Cooper put it more colorfully. "I think it perfectly competent to show that the enemy have ploughed with our heifer," he said, accusing Marshal Anthony Roberts of foul play. Although the black defendants had been treated well by the prison authorities—provided with ample food, new clothing, and even barbering—Cooper claimed that Scott had been kept "ragged, dirty, and filthy," thus making him susceptible to abolitionist enticements.

Stevens took umbrage at the accusation of witness tampering. "Our people had (and could have) no intercourse with him," he huffed. And besides, "It is not proved that we have spoken to him." The latter was a rather weak denial, but it was adequate under the circumstances. Grier had little patience for even more testimony concerning Kline's credibility and he was anxious to close the case. The prosecutors were compelled to withdraw their proffer and, after reestablishing a few technical points, they rested on rebuttal.

Jury argument was a fine art in the nineteenth century—usually lasting hours; frequently extending for days—and the lawyers in the Hanway case were understandably eager to display their oratorical skills in front of a national audience. They agreed among themselves that three attorneys would argue for each side, perhaps because no one was willing to forgo his potential star turn. Grier was far from enthusiastic about such a protracted round of oratory, but he agreed to accommodate counsel and let the arguments begin.

J. R. Ludlow presented the opening speech for the prosecution, beginning with a summary of the evidence pointing to Hanway's guilt. "An infuriated, lawless, determined band of negroes [had] assembled together," he said, "for the express purpose of rescuing slaves [and] defying authority." Hanway had been their acknowledged leader, visibly raising the spirits of the mob just as they were about to surrender. After announcing that "he did not care for that [fugitive] law or any other Act of Congress," he huddled with the armed resisters. Then,

> He whispers to them those important words which shall never be known, but the effect of which was a bloody onslaught upon every white man upon the ground, except the prisoner and his friend Lewis.

Ludlow then turned from facts to politics. Men such as Hanway, he said, "have not the fear of the Constitution." Their resistance to the law "would bring upon this country of ours, civil war, disunion, and all that is horrible." And though he had been the "general" of the negroes at Parker's, Hanway himself was a small player in a larger conspiracy. "He was but acting upon principles which had been dictated to him by men in high authority," by whom "the compromises of the constitution are proclaimed to be odious."

If Hanway's conspiracy threatened the foundation of the Republic, there was little doubt that it would also stoop so low as to tamper with a witness such as Harvey Scott. While Ludlow would *never* suggest that his "learned friends upon the other side [had] bribed him," he flatly charged that there were "others in the Court house who would have done it." How else to explain the difficulties that beset the prosecution? Scott recanted, and "two of our witnesses . . . escaped from the jail." That could only have been the work of the "bigots, fanatics, and demagogues [who] have endeavored to stimulate the populace to illegal and monstrous acts."

Ludlow's political attack on abolitionism was restrained compared to the following assault from Brent. There was no principle more crucial to the Constitution, he said, than the commitment "that the master should have his fugitive slave surrendered to him upon claim being made." And yet, there were those who proclaimed "in this very courtroom" that the "higher law" absolved them of any obligation under the Constitution of the United States. It was a "monstrous doctrine" that led to "the conniving, inciting, aiding, and abetting" resistance to the law, and which threatened to "snap and rend asunder, one by one, the cords which bind [the Union] together."

Brent's animus was not reserved for Castner Hanway. He also assailed Enoch Harlan, "one of the witnesses here . . . who said he was loyal but who reserved to himself the right, when summoned . . . of not assisting though he saw an officer of the United States threatened and menaced with death." Perhaps because he was a stranger to Pennsylvania, the Maryland attorney general did not seem to recognize the significance of nonviolence in Harlan's Quaker faith. But there were at least four Quakers or other pietists on the jury—those who had affirmed rather than sworn when seated—and they surely would have been offended by Brent's implicit denigration of their religion.

Brent may have been tone-deaf to local conditions, or he may no longer have cared. By that point in the case he believed that the trial had turned into a "broad farce," writing to Governor Lowe that the entire environment was "tainted and rotten." Still, he expressed hope that a "calm, collected, but severe speech" might yet save the day, which makes it all the more baffling that such an otherwise capable lawyer would risk insulting a third of the jurors.

Only after several hours of argument did Brent finally begin to address the question of Hanway's actual guilt or innocence. Brent was a talented attorney and he marshaled the evidence nimbly and adroitly once he turned to the facts of the case. Regarding Kline's questionable credibility, for example, he pointed out that the deputy had never testified to the words of Hanway's whispered conversation that seemed to have triggered the shooting. That was the stamp of truth, Brent explained, because "it would have been just as easy for him to have sworn that he heard Hanway order the blacks to fire." But rather than embellish, Kline had "contented himself with facts" and he should therefore be believed. Ultimately, however, Brent's argument was as much about honor as it was about treason. The State of Maryland had been "insulted and traduced," he complained at the close of his speech, and subjected to "low, false, groveling and contemptible imputations." Respect for Maryland and its institutions required a conviction, he argued. And should the jury decide otherwise, he concluded portentously, "I have discharged my duty and the people of Maryland will act for themselves."

Joseph Lewis presented the first argument for the defense, beginning on the morning of December 6, 1851. His much anticipated presentation drew perhaps the largest crowd of the entire trial, including the famous abolitionist Lucretia Mott. But if Mott expected counsel to deliver a stirring condemnation of slavery, she was quickly disappointed.

Lewis began by informing the jury that Castner Hanway did not belong to "any sect or any class which have set themselves in opposition" to the Fugitive Slave Act. Hanway was "altogether unconnected with those to whom are attributed these unpatriotic sentiments." He accepted the constitutionality of the fugitive law, and even the legitimacy of slavery itself: "What the laws of the southern states have made property, is property here by the constitution, and may be reclaimed." Indeed, "If the issue were on the Fugitive Slave Law, and the question here was, whether Mr. Hanway disapproved of it; he could not be convicted even of that offense," because he had never stated "any opinion either one way or the other on that subject."

As to the resistance, Lewis ignored Hanway's admirable assertion that the "colored people had a right to defend themselves." Instead, counsel insisted that "no man regrets the lamentable events of that day more than Castner Hanway," emphasizing that "we are here neither to justify, excuse, or palliate it." To show his client's compassion for the "unfortunate man, who lost his life in that bloody affray," Lewis reminded the jury that defense counsel had refrained from cross-examining members of the Gorsuch family.

The closest Joseph Lewis came to denouncing slavery was his expression of disdain for "man and woman hunting," which he found "revolting to the sensibilities of Pennsylvanians." But when it came to explaining Hanway's and Elijah Lewis's refusal to assist Kline, Joseph Lewis's explanation was based not on sympathy for runaways, but on fear:

> Had one or two white men of the neighborhood ventured to interfere between those Southern gentlemen and the negroes, they would have incurred the peculiar resentment of the negroes, and would have been the first to be sacrificed.

Hanway's innocence, said counsel, was obvious and beyond question. The entire prosecution was based on Kline's trumped-up testimony, which had been contrived in an effort to conceal the deputy's own blundering. But even then, Joseph Lewis faulted only the execution of the slave hunting mission, not its objective. Kline was a reckless fool, but "Marshal Roberts might and would have apprehended all the fugitives named in Kline's warrants without a single revolver."

Though Joseph Lewis was soft on the question of slave catching and aloof from the abolitionist movement, he was not wholly without emotion. He showed absolute fury at the suggestion that "Harvey Scott has been seduced to perjure himself, by person or persons connected with this defence." He accused the prosecutors of engaging in "a slander villainous and atrocious to the last degree."

John Read also presented a lengthy closing argument for the defense. He agreed that Hanway was "bound by the Constitution and by the laws of the land," and he informed the jury that "we have told the Court in advance that we never intended to dispute the constitutionality of this [fugitive slave] law." Read pronounced himself—and by extension, his client—ready "at this moment at all times" to render any necessary assistance to "our Southern brethren" in enforcing the law. On the other hand, said Read, Pennsylvanians also had a duty to protect free blacks from kidnapping and would not "permit any Southern master to come into Pennsylvania . . . and contrary to the express provisions of the Fugitive Slave Law, to carry [an alleged runaway] into slavery."

Of course, not even Brent and Ashmead were plainly in favor of seizing blacks in violation of the Fugitive Slave Act. And the evidence had been indisputable that Gorsuch and Kline had complied scrupulously with the law, having secured proper warrants and having displayed and read them out loud at every opportunity. Unfortunately, only the first few pages of Read's lengthy speech were included in the printed record of Hanway's trial, so we do not know how he intended to show the relevance of illegal kidnapping to Hanway's defense. According to the court reporter's notes, Read's lost address "was marked throughout by eloquence and profound learning, being a thorough and complete dissertation on the law of Treason."

Even if the assembled audience was surprised by Lewis's and Read's relatively anodyne arguments, they still had every reason to expect fireworks when Thaddeus Stevens rose to speak. One of the most prominent abolitionists in the United States, he was also a famed orator. If anyone was likely to deliver a singing jeremiad on the evils of slavery, it was surely Congressman Stevens. But once again, the crowd was disappointed. Stevens simply announced that he "declined speaking in the cause" and yielded the floor for the prosecution's third and final argument. Stevens was acutely aware of his reputation as an extremist and no doubt wanted to avoid making "his well-known abolitionism part of Hanway's defense."[3] Indeed, Stevens's abstention was a powerful statement to the jury. He had already participated fully in the trial, cross-examining nearly all of the prosecution witnesses and often sparring sharply with Brent and the other prosecutors. There was no question that the "woolly-headed Whig" was Hanway's main counsel, so the jurors were unlikely to suddenly disassociate Stevens from the defense merely because he declined to deliver a closing argument. Rather, Stevens's deference would have been taken as a declaration that abolitionism was irrelevant to the case. The expected tirade against slavery was not going to be delivered, thus signaling Stevens's endorsement of the apolitical positions Lewis and Read had already taken. Silence, as it turned out, was the most eloquent statement Stevens could make.

Senator Cooper, however, saw things far differently. As the final lawyer to address the jury, he wanted to leave no doubt about the political nature of the case. "Since the foundation of the government there has not been submitted to a jury for its decision a question of greater importance . . . to the peace, harmony and welfare of the Union," he began. "There must be no refusal, no holding back, no hesitancy to comply with the obligations which the constitution imposes."

Cooper sketched out the case against Hanway, emphasizing the evidence of conspiracy.

> His arrival is greeted by huzzas, shouting and the clashing of the weapons of the negroes, who preceded him to the scene of action. Why is this? Why these manifestations of joy at his approach, if it were accidental?

There could be only one answer, Cooper maintained: "Because all had been arranged beforehand." Then he returned with a vengeance to the prosecution's main theme. It was every citizen's obligation to obey the Fugitive Slave Act, and treasonous to resist. "He whose conscience . . . forbid[s] him to support and maintain it in its fullest integrity, may relieve himself from the duties of citizenship by divesting himself of its rights."

After eighteen days of testimony and argument, it was finally time to commit the case to the jury. Unlike today's practice, in which jury instructions are generally limited to neutral statements of law, antebellum judges enjoyed great latitude in their jury charges. It was expected that the judge would comment at length on the nature of the crime, the quality and sufficiency of the proof, the credibility of the witnesses, and the significance of the verdict. Thus, it was well understood that Justice Grier's jury charge could make all the difference in the case. Although the prosecution theory was problematic and the evidence less than overwhelming, a conviction was still possible if Justice Grier defined treason broadly enough or if he instructed the jury to infer Hanway's responsibility for the acts of the rioters.

When at last Grier spoke, it seemed as though he had taken the prosecutors' side. Making no effort to conceal his anger, he condemned the fact that:

> A citizen of a neighboring State, while in the exercise of his undoubted rights, guaranteed to him the Constitution and laws of the United States, has been foully murdered by an armed mob of negroes.

Grier was convinced that the responsibility for the murder rested upon white instigators who, "if they did not directly . . . participate in the outrage, looked carelessly and coldly on." He inveighed against the "male and female vagrant lecturers" and the "infuriated fanatics and unprincipled demagogues" who had openly counseled "a bloody resistance to the laws of the land." The more Grier fulminated, the more it sounded as though he accepted the prosecution's abolitionist conspiracy theory:

> The guilt of this foul murder rests not alone on the deluded individuals who were its immediate perpetrators, but the blood taints with even deeper dye the skirts of those who promulgated doctrines subversive of all morality and all government.

He was referring, of course, to the adherents of the higher law who had organized opposition to the Fugitive Slave Act. If Hanway had participated in the agitation against the law—if he had "attended any of these conventions got up to fulminate curses against the Constitution . . . and to exhort to a seditious and bloody resistance"—then he was guilty. But there was no such evidence, observed Grier, noting with approval that "the learned counsel for the prisoner" had "not made . . . objection to this law which had been so clamorously urged by many presses and agitators."

Incensed as he was at the abolitionist movement, Grier was ultimately too much of a judge to allow Hanway to hang without direct evidence of his culpability. "There was no proof of any previous connection of the prisoner with the [rioters] before the time the offense was committed," and none that he had "counseled, advised or exhorted the negroes to come together with arms." That conclusion alone would have been sufficient to acquit Hanway, but Grier went even further, rejecting the prosecutors' expansive view of the crime of treason.

"A number of fugitive slaves may infest a neighborhood," he said, and along with white supporters they may "resist with force of arms, their master or the public officer, who may come to arrest them." If so, they would all then be guilty of felonies. But they would not be traitors, he explained, because "their insurrection is for a private object, and connected with no public purpose." Such was also the case at Christiana. Heinous as it was, the resistance did not rise "to the dignity of treason or a levying of war. Not because the numbers or force was insufficient [but] for want of any proof of previous conspiracy to make a *general and public resistance to any law* of the United States." There was just too little evidence that the rioters, much less Castner Hanway, "had any other intention than to protect one another from what they termed kidnappers." That was bad enough, according to Grier, but he could not bring himself to call it treason.

The jury retired to deliberate, though their conclusion was all but foregone. Grier told the jurors that he would remain in court only "for a short time, for the purpose of receiving their verdict," and they did not defy him. After only fifteen minutes, the jury returned with a verdict of not guilty, to the tremendous relief of Hanway and his friends.

Grier had attempted to soften the blow to the prosecutors by commending their "zeal and ability." He singled out Brent for praise and pronounced the government "perfectly justified" in having brought the treason charge in the first place. That did little to alleviate their total defeat. Brent complained bitterly to Governor Lowe about nearly every aspect of the trial: the court had erroneously disallowed crucial evidence, misconstrued the law of treason, indulged the defense lawyers, and all but encouraged "black regiments with white allies, in their work of murdering Southern masters."[4]

Not only was Hanway acquitted under the treason indictment, but the charges against all of the other defendants—both state and federal—were soon dropped as well. The Christiana defense team had won a remarkable courtroom victory. Facing an openly hostile court, Stevens and company had devised a strategy that could appeal to Justice Grier's and Judge Kane's strict constructionism while neutralizing the judges' blatant antagonism toward abolitionism. In contrast to the prosecution approach, which invoked and exploited the nation's impending sectional crisis, defense counsel sought to depoliticize the case by explicitly repudiating any link between the defendant and the antislavery movement.

Hanway's acquittal was cheered in abolitionist quarters as a defeat to the slave power and a rebuke to the administration of Fillmore and Webster. Speaking at a post-trial victory rally, Ohio Congressman Joshua Giddings "made no secret of his approval of the conduct of the blacks in fighting for their freedom, and said that if he were a slave, he would take his liberty if he had to walk over the dead bodies of slaveholders all the way from the borders of Kentucky to the Canada line." One of Giddings's constituents, a then-obscure free black schoolteacher named Charles Langston, sent a similar message of support, praising the actions of the "Christiana patriots [as] worthy the imitation of every colored man in the country, whether bond or free, when his liberty is assailed." Seven years later, Langston would become famous for his role in the Oberlin fugitive slave rescue. Other abolitionists, however, were somewhat more restrained. Lucretia Mott, speaking from the same platform as Giddings, dissented from his apparent approval of violence, but otherwise applauded the "vindication of the rights of the slave."[5]

To Maryland's Governor Lowe and other Southerners, the response to the verdict was part of an "incalculable calamity." Gorsuch's blood had flowed on American soil, Lowe reported to his state legislature, and yet "venal politicians are found, in the open day, to glory in the human sacrifice."[6] Among those incensed at the acquittal was a young John Wilkes Booth, who attended a Maryland boarding school with a son and a nephew of the murdered Edward Gorsuch.[7]

It is ironic that Hanway's exoneration was alternately celebrated and excoriated as a victory for violent resistance to the Fugitive Slave Act, given that his counsel had done all they could to deny the existence of any such connection. At one point, in fact, defense attorney Theodore Cuyler had interrupted Attorney General Brent's final argument—in a rather unusual breach of nineteenth-century decorum—to insist urgently that Hanway's defense "has not been conducted on the principle that the fugitive slave law is not binding upon us all." No contemporary observer commented publicly on the incongruity, although we can imagine what William Parker and Frederick Douglass might have thought silently to themselves. White lawyers had saved a white man's life, but only by disclaiming any support for black people's right of self-defense. To Douglass and Parker, "Self-defense was the backbone of the concept of redemptive violence because blacks could not depend on the system to protect them." Thus, Douglass had sarcastically derided the very notion that Gorsuch had been a "*law abiding* citizen" engaged in a "patriotic expedition," and he certainly would have scorned defense counsel's expression of sympathy for the slave master and respect for the fugitive law. Far from condemning "the lamentable events" at Christiana, as attorney Lewis put it on Hanway's behalf, Douglass applauded the "heroic defenders of the just rights of man against manstealers."[8]

Where one man stands on principle, others are concerned only with tactics. Hanway's attorneys were necessarily pragmatists, interested more in results than in moral or ideological consistency. Their overriding objective was to win the case, to the exclusion of almost every other consideration. Indeed, they were quite evidently ready and willing to take advantage of impropriety at the Moyamensing Prison. Even if the lawyers played no direct role in the chicanery, it seems certain that someone connected to the defense released Josephus Washington and John Clark—thus depriving the prosecution of crucial testimony—just as someone connected to the defense no doubt surreptitiously persuaded Harvey Scott to abruptly change his story. Perhaps the defense lawyers were shocked—*shocked!*—to learn about the back-channel communications with a prosecution witness. From the available record, however, it appears that they knew in advance of Scott's conversion and rather disingenuously sandbagged the opposition, exploiting an opportunity to make the prosecutors look foolish and unprepared.

It was not unusual for abolitionist attorneys—motivated by the higher law and fighting for the cause of human freedom—to push the boundaries of professional conduct. Salmon Chase had raised a patently spurious defense in the

Van Zandt case and, as we will see, other antislavery lawyers would later employ subterfuges that flirted with outright perjury. In that light, it seems almost trivial that Hanway's counsel would feign allegiance to the Fugitive Slave Act, which in fact they strenuously opposed. After all, their efforts resulted in a tremendous success for Hanway and the other defendants, both black and white, leading Maryland's Governor Lowe to predict with complete accuracy that "no resistance to the fugitive slave act, henceforth, can be brought within the law of treason."[9]

If there was a drawback to the defense approach, it was only that it provided little or no guidance for the lawyers who followed. The Christiana defense could not be emulated, because few future defendants would be able to make such a powerful claim of prosecution overreaching. The government would never again bring a treason case to trial for resistance to the Fugitive Slave Act, confining itself to more modest prosecutions for lesser offenses. Those cases would call for significantly different defense tactics. Claims of innocence would be much less availing, and that very circumstance would create far greater latitude for invoking higher law in the courtroom.

⌇ 8 ⌇

ATHENS OF AMERICA

I n the course of the Hanway trial, Justice Robert Grier had barely troubled
to conceal his dislike for the abolitionist movement in general and for the
city of Boston in particular. He derided the intellectuals of the "Athens of
America" for their arrogance, and he scoffed at the "ecclesiastical assemblies
in the north" that had passed resolutions condemning the Fugitive Slave Act
as unconstitutional. Although he did not identify the specific assemblies he
had in mind, there is no doubt that they included many Congregational, Unitarian, and other churches in Massachusetts (and elsewhere in New England)
that were well-known for their antislavery activism.

Grier was far from alone in his disdain. In a nation torn along sectional
lines over the slavery issue, Boston had indeed attained a well-deserved reputation as the center of abolitionist and free soil agitation. Other regions—
including upstate New York and northern Ohio—also included important
abolitionist strongholds, but no other place had achieved such a critical mass
of antislavery sentiment, especially among the intellectual classes. Boston's
many clergy, professionals, and literary figures were notably vocal, and frequently rather haughty, in their condemnation of slavery. Although the city's
bankers, manufacturers, and laborers were generally quite sympathetic to the
South, dependent as they were on commerce in cotton and other commodi-
ties, the city as a whole was probably more unfriendly to slavery than any
other comparable locale in the United States. It was extremely meaningful,
therefore, that Daniel Webster began his "Seventh of March" address, in which
he announced his support for the Fugitive Slave Act, by declaring that he
spoke "not as a Massachusetts man." The recapture of runaway slaves had
long been anathema in Boston and it was fairly well understood, until Webster's historic defection in 1850, that a true "Massachusetts man" wanted as
little as possible to do with the rendition of fugitive slaves.

The Massachusetts Constitution of 1780 included a Declaration of Rights,
providing that "all men are born free and equal, and have certain natural,

essential, and unalienable rights." Shortly afterward, the Supreme Judicial Court held that the Declaration of Rights meant that "slavery is . . . as effectively abolished . . . by the granting of rights and privileges wholly incompatible and repugnant to its existence."[1] In the 1836 case of *Commonwealth v. Aves,* Chief Justice Lemuel Shaw elaborated on the meaning of natural rights, holding that "slavery cannot exist" in Massachusetts, and consequently that "an owner of a slave in another State where slavery is warranted by law, voluntarily bringing such slave into this State, has no authority to detain him against his will, or to carry him out of the State against his consent, for the purpose of being held in slavery."[2] In other words, slaves became free upon entering Massachusetts. This American application of the *Somerset* decision went well beyond the law in other northern states, where slave owners were allowed the right of "transit," meaning that they could bring their slaves along during temporary or even extended visits.

Runaways were not covered by the *Aves* case, which applied only to slaves whose masters voluntarily brought them into Massachusetts. In 1837, however, Massachusetts enacted a personal liberty law that guaranteed every alleged fugitive the right to trial by jury (with the implicit recognition that local juries would be reluctant to rule in favor of southern slave owners). When that protection proved inadequate in the 1842 *Latimer* case, the Massachusetts legislature responded by passing a new personal liberty statute (often called the Latimer law) that prohibited state officials from assisting in the arrest of alleged fugitives and that barred the use of state facilities for their detention, thus making it nearly impossible for a slave catcher to succeed. It was precisely that sort of passive resistance that Daniel Webster had in mind when he complained of the northern states' "disinclination to perform fully their constitutional duties in regard to the return of persons bound to service." The federal Fugitive Slave Act was designed to circumvent Latimer-type laws by creating a purely federal forum for slave catchers and by dragooning state officials into the rendition process.

Nowhere did the new law generate more protests than in Boston, where numerous speakers harshly condemned the Fugitive Slave Act virtually from the moment it was signed by President Fillmore. In September 1850 a meeting of Boston's black leadership formed the League of Freedom, resolving to "manfully assert their independence" and declaring that "they who would be free, themselves must strike the first blow." At a conference of the Massachusetts

Free Soil Party in October 1850, Charles Sumner—later to become a U.S. senator and a near-martyr to the abolitionist movement—proclaimed that Boston's populace, "like the flaming sword of the cherubim at the gates of Paradise . . . shall prevent any Slave Hunter from ever setting foot in the Commonwealth." That same month, thousands of black and white Bostonians gathered at Faneuil Hall and resolved to "trample this law under foot." The meeting called for the establishment of a "Committee of Vigilance and Safety" for the protection "by all just means [of] fugitives and colored inhabitants of Boston."[3]

As we have already seen, Boston's first great challenge came in October 1850 when a Georgia slave owner sent his agents to arrest William and Ellen Craft. The Crafts' daring escape had made them celebrities on the antislavery lecture circuit, and therefore prime targets for a test of the fugitive law's effectiveness. The slave hunters—Willis Hughes and John Knight—had hoped to avoid public attention while they attempted to apprehend the Crafts. Their Boston attorney, an established practitioner named Col. Seth Thomas, made repeated attempts to obtain the necessary warrants in chambers, but he was turned away by several federal judges who were skittish about applying the brand-new law. Fugitive Slave Commissioner George Ticknor Curtis was finally persuaded to issue the required papers, but he insisted that Hughes and Knight request the writs in open court, for fear of creating the appearance that he had given a secret hearing to southern kidnappers. Curtis had no intention of facilitating the concealment of fugitives—he was a protégé of Webster's and would later be his executor and biographer—but his decision to hold a public hearing alerted the Crafts and made an unobtrusive arrest impossible.

Word quickly spread that Georgia slave hunters were abroad in Boston, turning Hughes and Knight into marked men. Once their mission was exposed, the two Georgians were relentlessly hounded wherever they went. They were besieged in their hotel, accosted on the streets, and subjected to daily arrests on trivial and trumped-up charges including smoking in the streets, slander, swearing and cursing, carrying concealed weapons, reckless driving, and failure to pay bridge tolls.[4] Many of the complaints against Hughes and Knight were devised by lawyers associated with the Vigilance Committee, and whose sense of professionalism obviously did not prevent them from utilizing spurious means to accomplish a worthy end.

Bogus arrests were small beer compared to the other measures undertaken by members of the Vigilance Committee. For example, Lewis Hayden's home, where William Craft had taken refuge, was conspicuously booby-trapped with barrels of gunpowder, making it clear that it could be deadly for anyone to attempt to execute a fugitive warrant. With merchants threatening mayhem and clergymen promising mutually assured destruction—all in the name of the higher law—the least a lawyer could do was to draft frivolous writs or swear out unsupportable warrants.

Hughes and Knight were never physically attacked, but they were subjected to threats of violence whenever they ventured onto the street. Finally a delegation of the Vigilance Committee arranged a private meeting with the slave hunters, at which Rev. Theodore Parker delivered a blunt ultimatum. The two men "were not safe in Boston another night." Shaken by such an overt threat from a man of the cloth, Hughes and Knight realized that they had no choice but to abandon their quarry. The two men soon left town, rationalizing that even "if we had succeeded in arresting the negroes, that they would have been rescued by the citizens."[5]

But even as members of Boston's Vigilance Committee were congratulating themselves on protecting the Crafts, federal officials were preparing to ensure that the Fugitive Slave Act could indeed be implemented in Boston. Webster himself had traveled to Boston in the hope that he could "put this business of the attempt to arrest the Crafts into a better shape," but he arrived too late—Hughes and Knight had already been chased out of the city, and the Crafts were on their way to safety in England. Nonetheless, the secretary of state would continue, as long as he remained in office, to "intrude[] his presence to guarantee enforcement of the law in Massachusetts." President Fillmore was of the same mind, vowing that if necessary, military detachments would be used in the future "for the purpose of overcoming such forcible combinations against the law." Fillmore would soon have an opportunity to make good on his commitment, although it is unlikely that he anticipated just how much force would be necessary to remove a slave from Boston.[6]

Aside from the Craft debacle, the Fillmore administration's initial enforcement of the fugitive law was rather effective. By early 1851 at least one hundred fugitives had been returned to the South, almost always without incident.

Most of the runaways were apprehended in the northern border states—Pennsylvania, Ohio, Illinois—but some were also taken in Michigan and New York. Slave rendition had been so successful through the end of 1850 that Fillmore was able to report to Congress that the Fugitive Slave Act "was in its character final and irrevocable" and that "the great majority of our fellow citizens . . . in the main approve, and are prepared, in all respects, to sustain" enforcement of the law.[7]

But not everywhere. The Act had yet to be enforced in Boston, where abolitionists boasted that they had already "whipped Webster, and turned Massachusetts right side up." With a black population upward of 2,000, including many runaways, Boston would have attracted a certain number of slave hunters under any circumstances, but the city's reputation for resistance turned it into a three-way proving ground. Unionists were determined to show that the Fugitive Slave Act could reach even the most recalcitrant corner of New England. Southern extremists, on the other hand, hoped that repeated failures in Boston would demonstrate the uselessness of the Compromise of 1850 and thus reinvigorate the secessionist movement. Finally, abolitionists and Free-Soilers regarded Boston as the strongest and most important bastion in the struggle against the slave power. In the words of Charles Francis Adams, "It remained to be seen whether the solemn act of Congress or the resolve of the political gathering was law in the State."[8]

Some fugitives became willing players in the tripartite drama. The intrepid William and Ellen Craft, for example, were energetic antislavery lecturers and publicists well before their encounter with slave catchers. After Hughes and Knight had their nefarious warrants in hand, William Craft rejected a plan to have supporters buy his and Ellen's freedom. Even if his freedom "could be bought for two cents," Craft said, he "would not consent to compromise the matter in such a way."[9] Instead he made a point of continuing to work at his carpentry shop, in a well-armed and remarkably composed show of faith that Boston's abolitionists would be able to protect him.

Only a few fugitives were as politically active as the Crafts. But thanks to the dynamics surrounding the Fugitive Slave Act, every runaway was in fact a potential political actor—even those who would far rather have chosen a life of peaceful anonymity. One such person was a slave named Shadrach Minkins.

Shadrach Minkins was born a slave in Norfolk, Virginia, sometime around 1820, the property of a tavern owner named Thomas Glenn. Following Glenn's death, Minkins was sold in fairly quick succession to several new masters, until he was eventually acquired by John DeBree in November 1849. Whatever were the conditions for slaves in DeBree's household, Minkins did not stay there very long. By early May 1850 he had escaped, making his way by sea to Boston, either as a stowaway or with the assistance of an accommodating ship's captain or crewman.

In Boston Minkins found work as a waiter at the Cornhill Coffee House, where he no doubt would have been content to remain, earning a modest but adequate living and fitting himself quietly into the city's black community. Minkins had been in Boston for only a few months when the Fugitive Slave Act was signed into law, causing him to panic along with every other escaped slave in the North. He briefly left the city, but for reasons of his own he soon returned to Boston. Perhaps he lacked the wherewithal or support system necessary for flight to Canada, or perhaps he felt reassured by the pronouncements of the Vigilance Committee. In any case, he kept his job serving lavish meals to Boston's bankers and businessmen.

Unfortunately, DeBree had learned of Minkins's whereabouts, and he made plans to reclaim his property under the new law. DeBree's first step was a visit to the Norfolk courtroom of Judge Richard Baker, where he obtained legal certification that Minkins owed him "service or labor" and had escaped into another state. DeBree then executed a power of attorney authorizing John Caphart, a well-known and particularly effective slave catcher, to take all steps necessary for Minkins's "apprehension, prosecution, transportation, and restoration to the present claimant."[10] Finally, DeBree arranged for Caphart to travel to Boston, where he hoped to avoid the notoriety that had thwarted Hughes and Knight in their similar pursuit of William and Ellen Craft.

Caphart arrived in Boston on Wednesday, February 12, 1851, and at first it seemed that everything would go smoothly. Embarrassed by the Craft incident, federal officials were eager to provide him with as much assistance as needed. This time Commissioner George Ticknor Curtis showed no reticence about issuing a warrant, having learned the perils of proceeding in open court. Curtis met privately with Caphart on Friday evening, signing the necessary warrant and turning it over to Deputy Marshal Patrick Riley for execution.

The next morning, Saturday, February 15, Riley and his men quietly staked out the Cornhill Coffee House, hoping to catch Minkins unawares. Caphart wisely stayed away from the scene of the arrest, realizing that the presence of a known slave hunter might alert the Vigilance Committee. When Minkins briefly stepped out of the dining room and into a hallway, he was seized by two deputies, each of whom "took the negro by an arm, and walked him out of the back passage way."[11]

For the first time, a black man had been arrested in Boston under the Fugitive Slave Act, and no one in the abolitionist community had any idea that it had happened. Minkins himself made no resistance as he was hustled through the streets and into the courthouse. Still in his apron, he was taken to the third-story federal courtroom, where the doors were barred and placed under guard. So far everything had gone well for the slave catchers, but the situation could not remain calm for long. Boston's Court Square was a busy place on Saturday mornings, and word quickly spread that federal marshals had been seen escorting a black prisoner into the building. In less than an hour, a predominantly black crowd had surrounded the building and pushed its way into the courtroom.

Alerted to the grave situation, lawyers for the Vigilance Committee quickly gathered to plan a response. The leaders of this ad hoc legal team were Ellis Gray Loring and Samuel Sewall, both lions of the Massachusetts bar. Loring belonged to an influential Boston family and was a founder of the New England Anti-Slavery Society. Sewall came from an even more impressive background. He was a descendant of a much earlier Samuel Sewall who had served as chief justice of Massachusetts and who, in 1700, published one of the first antislavery pamphlets in colonial America. (The first Samuel Sewall had also been one of the judges at the Salem witch trials; he later distinguished himself by openly apologizing for his role and calling for a day of public fasting and repentance.) The meeting was also attended by Robert Morris, Loring's protégé and only the second black man to be admitted to the bar in the United States,[12] and Richard Henry Dana, another well-known antislavery lawyer who would come to play a leading role in Boston's most important fugitive cases.

While Morris and Dana commenced work on a petition to the Massachusetts Supreme Judicial Court, Loring and Sewall hurried to the courtroom, hoping to be able to prevent, or at least delay, any further action on the fugitive warrant. They were surprised to find Commissioner Curtis already on the bench. As a part-time commissioner, Curtis did not keep regular hours at the courthouse. There was no particular reason for him to be there on a Saturday morning other than by arrangement with Caphart's attorney, Seth Thomas, who had learned all about the drawbacks of procrastination when he represented the slave hunters in the Craft case.

Loring and Sewall asked Commissioner Curtis for a postponement to allow them to meet with Minkins and prepare a defense. Thomas naturally objected. His papers were all in good order, he argued, and the Virginia court's certification was "conclusive" under the Fugitive Slave Act on every issue that might otherwise be contested. The only question before Curtis was the identity of the prisoner, and that could be established with only a few minutes of testimony.

Curtis was inclined to grant Thomas's request for a summary ruling, as the statute seemed to require. The commissioner was, after all, a devoted friend of Daniel Webster's and a strong supporter of the Fugitive Slave Act. Along with his older brother, Benjamin R. Curtis, who would later be appointed to the U.S. Supreme Court, he had sponsored a reception for Webster shortly after the "Seventh of March" address. The two Curtis brothers had also been among the main organizers of a pro-Compromise meeting at Faneuil Hall in November 1850. Speaking at the rally, the elder Curtis declared that "Massachusetts has nothing to do" with the rights of fugitive slaves. "They have no right to be *here*," he told the cheering crowd. "*This* is not the soil on which to vindicate [their rights]. This is *our* soil, sacred to *our* peace, on which we intend to perform *our* promises."[13] The younger Curtis held the same commitment to perform the promises of the Fugitive Slave Act.

On the other hand, there was no precedent for holding such a truncated hearing in Massachusetts, and much sentiment against it. It was likely that public opinion would only be inflamed if a black man was returned to the South without any chance to present a defense, especially with such patrician lawyers as Loring and Sewall making the request. It must have appeared to Curtis that a short delay could do no harm, so the commissioner agreed to postpone the hearing until the following Tuesday morning. Caphart was not able to take immediate custody of Minkins, who was therefore detained in the courtroom under the rather tenuous control of Deputy Riley.

Following the adjournment, Curtis ordered the courtroom cleared of spectators, many of whom, however, remained milling about angrily in the outside hallway. He allowed several defense lawyers—including Robert Morris, who by then had joined the other attorneys in court—to stay in the locked room to confer with the prisoner. That small group was joined by Elizur Wright, an antislavery newspaper editor, and Rev. Leonard Grimes, one of the most important African-American clergymen in Boston. Deputy Marshal Riley continued to stand guard with a small contingent of about fifteen men, but the much larger city constable's office declined to provide assistance, in keeping with the Latimer law of 1843.[14] The lack of a backup force was not Riley's only problem. He was responsible for maintaining custody of Minkins for the next two nights, but he had nowhere to keep him. Massachusetts law prohibited the use of state facilities and there was no federal jail in Boston. For the time being, it appeared that Minkins could be held securely in the courtroom, but it was obvious that the situation could not last for long.

Riley's dilemma was resolved much sooner than he anticipated. As editor Wright was leaving the courtroom, a group of about twenty black men began to shove their way through the open door. Riley and his officers attempted to repel the crowd, but they were soon overwhelmed. Within moments, several of the rescuers had grabbed Minkins and carried him out of the courtroom, down the stairs, and into the street. Watching from his office across Court Square, Richard Henry Dana observed "two huge negroes bearing the prisoner between them with his clothes half torn off." As the crowd cheered Minkins's freedom, the two "powerful fellows hurried him through the square" in the direction of the Charles River.[15]

As the rescuers rumbled through the streets "like a black squall," as Dana put it, Lewis Hayden and Robert Morris realized that the federal marshals would soon be in pursuit. Taking control of the volatile situation, the two black leaders worked their way to the head of the disorganized crowd and managed to guide Minkins to a safe house, where he remained hidden while plans were made for his removal from the city. Over the next few days, Minkins was taken by wagon to Cambridge and then to Concord, and finally to Canada. Minkins ultimately settled in Montreal, where he operated a series of restaurants, one of which he named Uncle Tom's Cabin.

Abolitionist Boston was jubilant at what came to be called the "Shadrach Rescue." William Lloyd Garrison's *Liberator* boasted that Minkins had been freed in "proud defiance to President Fillmore and all his Cabinet" and that the rescuers, just like the patriots of the American Revolution, had acted "in obedience to the higher law of their generation." Elizur Wright's *Boston Com-*

monwealth trumpeted the news under a bold print headline—KIDNAPPERS DISAPPOINTED—and explained below that Minkins had been freed "by a writ of Deliverance issued under the Higher Law."[16]

The reaction was just as intense on the other side, not least because the rescue had been the work of African-Americans. News of the rescue spread through the South "like a spark over a powder magazine." In Washington, an aged Henry Clay called for an investigation of the incident, demanding to know whether "a government of white men was to be yielded to a government by blacks." Fillmore and Webster responded with a joint proclamation calling upon "all military and civil authorities in Boston to prevent further rebellious acts and to assist in recapturing the fugitive," and promising that prosecutions would be "commenced against all persons who have made themselves aides or abettors in this flagitious offense." Embarrassed by the charge that the city had provided lax security for the federal courtroom, and recognizing the potential for damage to the city's commercial interests, Boston's mayor and common council penned their own resolution, "heartily approving" of the presidential proclamation and promising "to carry out its recommendations."[17]

Within days of the rescue, ten men—three whites and seven blacks—were arrested, most notably including the white journalist Elizur Wright, and black leaders Lewis Hayden and Robert Morris. Although some consideration had been given to a treason prosecution, the defendants were charged only with assisting Minkins's escape. Almost at the outset, three of the cases were dismissed for lack of evidence, leaving seven men to face trial. The three most important defendants—Wright, Hayden, and Morris—were all represented by Richard Henry Dana, who was then only thirty-six years old.

Hayden's trial came first, before Judge Peleg Sprague of the U.S. District Court. Sprague was an experienced judge, generally regarded as "equitable & firm," but he was also strongly inclined to favor the prosecution in cases where "his party & political friends are at stake."[18] Numerous witnesses named Hayden as a leader in the rescue. One witness testified that Hayden had carried Minkins down the courthouse steps, while others placed him at various locations along the escape route. According to Thomas Garrety, an Irish cab driver, Hayden had at one point stopped and cautioned the crowd to disperse so the authorities would not easily be able to follow them.

In response, the defense produced a series of alibi witnesses who testified that Hayden had been elsewhere than the rescue scene, either at his home eating dinner or working in his clothing shop. That testimony was surely inaccurate, and more likely false. How could Lewis Hayden—the militant leader of Boston's black community; the man who had threatened explosive mayhem rather than allow the capture of William Craft—possibly have gone home for dinner rather than remain at the Minkins hearing, if only to protest?

Historian Gary Collison allows that the alibi witnesses may have been confused as to the actual times when they saw Hayden, but he also suggests more realistically that "it was perfectly possible that they were lying."[19] Dana, of course, had been in the courtroom with Hayden, and he had then watched the rescue from his law office window. If he did not know the precise details of his client's involvement in the incident, he must certainly have realized that the defense witnesses were stretching the truth—if not forsaking it entirely—by placing Hayden so far from the scene of the crime. But whether it was justifiable or not, the defense tactic worked. The jury was unable to reach a unanimous verdict, causing Judge Sprague to release the defendant. "I cannot detain you further upon the facts," he said.

The next defendant to face trial was Robert Morris, who was perhaps the most important black professional in all of Boston. Morris was born free in Salem, Massachusetts, in 1823, his father having been emancipated when the Commonwealth abolished slavery in 1780. As a teenager, Morris came to the attention of prominent attorney Ellis Gray Loring, who hired the young man as a "copier" in his law firm. Morris performed his office duties so carefully that soon he was promoted to clerk, and he was eventually encouraged to read for the bar. In 1847 Morris was admitted to the Suffolk County bar, becoming one of the first black lawyers in the United States. In his first trial, he represented a black plaintiff seeking to recover unpaid wages from a white man. Although opposing counsel treated him with scorn and outright hostility, Morris persuaded the jury to enter judgment for his client. The many black spectators in the courtroom were thrilled by the unprecedented victory. Morris himself remarked that "it made me feel like a giant. . . . My heart pounded up, and my people in the courtroom acted as if they would shout for joy."[20]

Morris went on to develop a thriving practice, primarily representing the city's free blacks and immigrant Irish laborers. In 1850 he joined Charles Sumner as counsel for the plaintiff in a lawsuit that challenged racial segregation in Boston's school system. Although the suit was not successful—Chief Justice Lemuel Shaw ruled that separate but equal facilities were sufficient to satisfy the state constitution—it helped establish Morris as an unquestioned leader in both the state bar and the black community. In the ensuing years, he discreetly provided counsel to the city's "black underground."[21]

Even more so than the trial of Lewis Hayden, the prosecution of Robert Morris constituted an enormous threat to Boston's black citizens. A conviction would probably result in disbarment, depriving the community of one of its most important voices and its sole representative in the judicial system.

Unfortunately, the evidence against Morris was powerful and the court was decidedly unfriendly. District Judge Sprague, who had presided alone over the Hayden case, was joined on the bench by Benjamin R. Curtis, who had recently been named to the U.S. Supreme Court and was therefore sitting as circuit judge in Boston. In a comparable situation today, judicial ethics would prevent a judge from participating in a case that had so badly embarrassed his own brother. But no such rule existed in 1851, leaving Justice Benjamin Curtis free to rule in a matter involving an escape from Commissioner George Curtis's courtroom. Even without the family connection, Benjamin Curtis's own background bode ill for the defendant. Curtis had begun his legal career as counsel for the thwarted slave owner in the landmark *Aves* case and he was a staunch political ally of Daniel Webster, who had spoken forcefully in favor of prosecuting Minkins's rescuers. Curtis had also been involved in the attempted arrests of the Crafts in 1850, providing the federal marshal with a legal opinion supporting the constitutionality of the Fugitive Slave Act. If ever a court was going to be unreceptive to claims based on the immorality of slavery—or the unconstitutionality of the Fugitive Slave Act—it was the one Dana faced on behalf of Robert Morris. To gain an acquittal, therefore, defense counsel would have to appeal to something other than the judges' consciences.

At the outset of the proceeding, Dana raised a series of technical objections—the indictment was invalid; a juror had been wrongly dismissed; the case had been improperly delayed—all of which were rejected by the court for reasons that Dana considered "small & second rate."[22] That cleared the way for the prosecution to present a parade of witnesses to establish Morris's guilt. First to testify was John DeBree himself, who traveled all the way from Norfolk to vindicate his rights as a slave owner. "Shadrach was [my] slave," DeBree told the jury. He had "purchased him in November, 1849," the court record showed, "and he remained in the service of the witness until May, 1850, when he left secretly, and without his consent."[23]

DeBree was followed to the stand by John Caphart, the slave hunter whose efforts had been frustrated by Minkins's rescue. Caphart was not demure about his occupation. "I am often employed by private persons to pursue fugitive slaves," he said, and "I never refuse a good job of that kind." Caphart continued that he had known Minkins in Norfolk for sixteen years, and knew both of his parents to be slaves. Moreover, Caphart had once actually seen Minkins "sold by the sheriff at a public venue, at the door of the court-house."[24]

Defense counsel objected that the evidence was insufficient to prove that Minkins was actually a slave. Because Minkins had been described by both DeBree and Caphart as a mulatto, that meant his ancestry was at least partially white and the presumption of slavery "did not obtain in reference to persons who had some white blood." Because slavery followed the maternal line, Dana argued, it was necessary for the prosecution to establish that Shadrach was descended from a black woman who had been held in slavery prior to 1795, as required under Virginia law. Once again the court rejected Dana's argument. It was inconceivable, Curtis ruled, that the prosecution should have to "trace a pedigree for upwards of sixty years." Rather, it was sufficient "for the master to testify that the person mentioned in the indictment was his slave." "By the common law," Curtis concluded, "possession is evidence of property," with no exceptions for human beings.[25]

With that troublesome detail resolved, the prosecution was able to move on to the facts of the case. Numerous witnesses testified to Morris's involvement in the rescue, placing him at various locations on the escape route. One witness testified that Morris had encouraged the crowd to storm the courtroom. A deputy marshal said that Morris had been whispering to Minkins only moments before the rescue, to which the prisoner replied loudly, "If I die I die like a man." Other witnesses had seen Morris and Minkins together several blocks from Court Square, with the lawyer apparently leading the fugitive by the arm.[26]

Once again, the defense produced a sequence of alibi witnesses. Some of them had seen Morris at the courthouse but said that he had not participated in the rescue. Somewhat inconsistently, others placed him at a good distance from the events by the time the rescue took place.[27] The first set of witnesses probably testified honestly, at least to the extent that they had not happened to see Morris actively involved in freeing Minkins. The second group, as in Hayden's trial, might well have been lying. Morris had unquestionably been in or near the courtroom when the crowd first surged through the door, and it is almost unimaginable that he would have gone elsewhere during the ten or so minutes of the actual rescue.

At the close of the evidence, the defense attempted to argue that the jury should refrain from enforcing the Fugitive Slave Act "if any of them conscientiously believed [it] to be unconstitutional." Justice Curtis, however, jumped in at midsentence. Quite aware of the jurors' "proclivities to acquit," Curtis wanted to afford them as little discretion as possible. Instructing counsel "that he could not be permitted to argue this proposition to the jury," Curtis announced that it was the prerogative of the court alone "to decide every question of law which arises in a criminal trial," and the constitutionality of the Fugitive Slave Act was therefore no concern of the jury's.[28]

Notwithstanding the limitations placed on the defense argument—not to mention the sketchy nature of Morris's alibi—the jury returned a finding of not guilty. The verdict was a tremendous victory for the antislavery bar in Massachusetts. Robert Morris was exonerated, and thus free to continue both his activism and his law practice. At the same time, Richard Henry Dana was catapulted into the very front rank of the profession, having secured acquittals in two high-profile, hotly contested cases (he would later perform the same service for Elizur Wright, whose trial was delayed until 1852).

It is impossible to say whether Dana knowingly made use of perjured testimony in the Hayden and Morris trials. Some of the defense testimony was extremely dubious, as should have been apparent at the time, but that does not mean that Dana was complicit in obtaining it. It is at least plausible that the witnesses simply presented themselves to defense counsel (or that they were recruited by members of the Vigilance Committee), and Dana then considered it his duty to place them on the stand.

In public Dana often expressed his fidelity to the positive law. In one of the Shadrach Rescue cases, for example, he conceded the legitimacy of the Fugitive Slave Act (though arguing, of course, that the defendant was factually innocent of any violation):

This law was constitutionally passed. . . . It is the law until repealed or judicially abrogated.

The higher law had its place—in the pews; perhaps in the streets—but it definitely had no overt role in the courtroom:

We talk about a higher law on the subject of resistance to the law. And there is a higher law. But what is it? It is a right our fathers took to themselves, as an ultimate remedy for unsupportable evils. It means war and bloodshed. It is a case altogether out of the law.[29]

In private Dana's view of the law was more complex. Immediately following the Shadrach Rescue, he wrote in his personal journal that "it would be the duty of a citizen not to resist [the Fugitive Slave Law] by force, unless he was prepared for revolution and civil war." He went on to add, however, that "we rejoice in the escape of a victim of an unjust law, as we would in the escape of an ill-treated captive deer or bird."[30] Thus, Dana apparently did not find it contradictory to respect the law himself, while cheering as others violated it. That outlook might indeed have allowed him to make use of seemingly untruthful witnesses to avoid injustice, so long as they had been procured by others who had acted without his encouragement or approval. Perhaps he even considered that the equivalent of a "writ of Deliverance issued under the Higher law."

By any measure, the Shadrach Rescue trials turned out to be among the "greatest defeat[s] suffered by the national government in the enforcement of the Fugitive Slave Law." Not one of the ten defendants was ever convicted, notwithstanding Webster's behind-the-scenes maneuvering. According to the Massachusetts district attorney, Webster had controlled the cases from the beginning, deciding whom to prosecute and virtually taking the "cases into his own hands." "It is of great importance to convict" at least some of the rescuers, Webster wrote to President Fillmore, to establish the effectiveness of the Fugitive Slave Act and maintain the Compromise of 1850.[31]

It was widely understood that the Fillmore administration was determined to see another fugitive captured and then returned to the South. As Charles Francis Adams observed, there was a "general impression abroad that an attempt at seizure would be made. . . . The law was to be vindicated; a fugitive was to be taken back to slavery from Massachusetts soil."[32]

—————

Webster and Fillmore were not the only Northerners determined to see the Fugitive Slave Act executed in New England. Boston's civic and mercantile life had long been dominated by a group of "Cotton Whigs" whose fortunes— both politically and literally—were closely tied to southern commodity producers. As individuals, the "State Street brokers and Milk Street jobbers" may have found slavery somewhat disagreeable, but as a class they were far more distressed by anything that threatened the security of their mortgages on slave property, or that might otherwise disrupt their lucrative relationship with southern planters. The cotton spinners of the North had deep financial ties to the cotton producers of the South—Charles Sumner called it an alliance between "the lords of the loom and the lords of the lash"—that they were unwilling to jeopardize for the sake of a few runaway slaves.[33]

Following the Minkins rescue, many mainstream political and business leaders considered it more than "a matter of pride . . . that a fugitive should be seized in Boston and taken back to slavery."[34] They considered it a virtual necessity. For better or worse, they did not have long to wait for an opportunity. On Thursday, April 3, 1851, less than two months after Minkins's escape, a young black man named Thomas Sims was seized as the property of James Potter, a rice planter and slave owner from Chatham County, Georgia.

In his slave life, Sims had been hired out as a bricklayer in the port of Savannah, which gave him access to the city's docks. In late February 1851 he had managed to stow away on a Boston-bound merchant brig, the *M. & J. C. Gilmor*, where he somehow remained hidden in the forecastle for two weeks until the ship entered Boston Harbor. Only as the *Gilmor* finally approached port was Sims discovered by one of the sailors, who angrily brought him before the captain. Sims was locked in a cabin overnight as the ship waited to make land. Incredibly, Sims somehow pried off the cabin door lock and, stealing a dinghy, rowed himself to shore while the brig's crew slept.

Sims was not able to enjoy freedom very long. Lonely and destitute, he attempted to contact his wife and children in Georgia, but the message was intercepted by James Potter. Within days Potter appeared before a Georgia court, where he obtained a declaration that Sims was a person "bound to service or labor" who had escaped from his lawful master. Having secured the necessary papers, Potter hired an agent named John Bacon, who arrived in Boston on April 3. Not surprisingly, Bacon immediately sought out Seth Thomas—who had represented the slave owners in both the Craft and Minkins cases—to act as his attorney.

The abolitionist press had vilified Colonel Thomas as "the legal pimp of the slave catchers,"[35] but that was a matter of perspective. Southerners such as John Bacon thought Thomas was just the man they needed—a talented and experienced advocate, well able to counsel them through the toils of the Massachusetts judicial system. Although Minkins and the Crafts had escaped rendition, it had not been through any flaw in their owners' legal representation. Once again Thomas proved his worth. On the very day Bacon arrived in Boston, Thomas brought his client before the cooperative Commissioner George Ticknor Curtis, who obligingly issued an arrest warrant.

Federal Marshal Charles Devens was out of town at the time, so the warrant was turned over for execution to a deputy, Asa Butman, who recruited several members of the city police to assist him (in apparent violation of the Latimer law). At about nine o'clock that night, the posse located Sims on a dark street and seized him from two sides. But Sims did not give up easily. Freeing himself momentarily from the officers' grip, he drew a knife and stabbed Butman in the leg, seriously wounding the deputy. By sheer force of numbers, however, the other policemen were eventually able to subdue him, and they dragged their captive to a waiting carriage. The resourceful Sims made one last effort, shouting to passersby, "I'm in the hands of kidnappers."[36]

Sims's cry was enough to alert members of the Vigilance Committee that yet another fugitive had been taken into custody. Theodore Parker, Elizur Wright, and Samuel Sewall rushed to the courthouse, where they encountered Deputy Marshal Patrick Riley. "Is the prisoner to be examined to-night? Tell me at your peril," demanded Sewall, who then, "in his earnestness, laid his hand on Mr. Riley."[37] The deputy responded by placing Sewall under arrest, although the lawyer was released after only a few hours in the nearby watch house.

While Sewall and Riley were arguing, Sims had been taken into a jury room adjoining the same federal courtroom from which Minkins had escaped. This time the jailers were taking no chances. In addition to establishing a round-the-clock guard, extreme measures were taken to secure the entire building to prevent another "black squall" from getting anywhere near the prisoner. By morning, a heavy iron chain had been placed around the entire courthouse, and additional ropes and chains cordoned off all the approaching walkways. A city police force of more than sixty men was deployed to guard the building's entrances, reinforced by numerous special police and a regiment of militia.

The intimidating barricade was the work of City Marshal Francis Tukey, but attorney Seth Thomas should probably receive some credit as well. The warrant for Sims had been issued in secret the previous evening, at a hearing attended only by Thomas, Commissioner Curtis, and Bacon the slave hunter. One of those three men must have then contacted Tukey and his superiors overnight, persuading them to sidestep the Latimer law by providing extraordinary security at the courthouse. Among the three, Thomas was surely the most likely candidate. Bacon was a stranger in Boston with no direct access to city officials, and Curtis was a judge who valued at least the appearance of neutrality. Although there is no documentary evidence of Thomas's involvement in facilitating the blockade, it is certainly reasonable to conclude that the slave owners' advocate of choice—or "pimp"—would have readily provided that particular service.

However it had been arranged, the barricade served its purpose. Individuals were allowed to cross the police line only with authorization from Marshal Tukey, and then they were compelled to bend over to pass underneath the chain. Even Chief Justice Lemuel Shaw was required to "bow down under these chains" to attend to the business of his court. Writing in his journal, Henry Wadsworth Longfellow bemoaned Shaw's humiliating deference to the slave power. "This is the last point of degradation. Alas for the people who cannot feel an insult."[38]

On the morning of Friday, April 4, 1851, Commissioner Curtis convened a hearing under the Fugitive Slave Act. Seth Thomas was present and eager to proceed on James Potter's claim. Despite the indignity of Marshal Tukey's gantlet, two attorneys from the Vigilance Committee appeared on behalf of Sims—Charles G. Loring and Robert Rantoul, the latter a sitting U.S. congressman. Sims himself was surrounded by nine armed men—two on each side, and five more in the row behind him. Only the prisoner's lawyers were allowed near him, and they could approach him only from the front.

Thomas presented five witnesses. Two Georgians identified Sims as a slave from Savannah, testifying that they knew him "perfectly well as the property of James Potter." The captain and two crewmen from the *Gilmor* provided the circumstances of Sims's arrival in Boston Harbor, including his near admission that he was "not exactly a slave." Thomas also produced a certified record from a Savannah court, attesting that Sims "had escaped from the state of Georgia, while owing service or labor to James Potter, the claimant."[39]

Loring and Rantoul had no witnesses to present. Sims himself was prohibited from testifying, and there was no one else in Boston who might creditably controvert Potter's claim. They did, however, attempt to circumvent the strictures of the Fugitive Slave Act by offering an affidavit from Sims in which he swore he had been emancipated. Claiming that his real name was Joseph Santiana, Sims averred that his "free papers were left by him, many years ago, with Morris Porter of Savannah," and that he did not know and had never "heard of such a person as James Potter."[40] It was extremely unlikely, to say the least, that a free man would stow away aboard a ship while leaving his crucial documents behind, but in any event Curtis found the affidavit inadmissible, ruling that it was the equivalent of testimony and therefore barred by the Fugitive Slave Act. With nothing further to be offered by the defense, Curtis scheduled the case for argument the following Monday.

With little reason to expect a favorable decision from Curtis, members of the Vigilance Committee concentrated on other ways to free Sims. The more militant members, led by Rev. Thomas Wentworth Higginson, explored various rescue plans, including "all sorts of fantastic and desperate projects." At one point Higginson proposed obstructing the proceeding by stealing the Georgia court record, "which lay invitingly . . . among lawyers papers on the table," but attorney Ellis Gray Loring squelched the idea.[41] For Higginson and other radical abolitionists, the higher law was all of a piece, justifying virtually any deed or ploy that could liberate a slave. Lawyers necessarily saw things differently. Higher law might have an occasional role in the courtroom, but it also had its limits. Presenting questionable evidence or an improbable affidavit could be rationalized as zealous advocacy, but outright theft of documents was out of the question.

Samuel Sewall and Richard Henry Dana had meanwhile prepared a habeas corpus petition to the Massachusetts Supreme Judicial Court, asserting the unconstitutionality of the Fugitive Slave Act. Chief Justice Lemuel Shaw had rudely brushed off Dana when the attorney tried a similar maneuver on Shadrach Minkins's behalf, and the aging jurist was barely more receptive this time around. At first Shaw refused to consider the matter at all, but he was eventually persuaded—perhaps because the case was to be argued by the estimable Richard Rantoul—to set the petition for argument before the full court.[42]

On Monday morning, April 7, Rantoul urged the Supreme Judicial Court to declare the Fugitive Slave Act unconstitutional on two grounds. First, asserted Rantoul, the law impermissibly conferred judicial power on mere commissioners who lacked the authority to render final judgments under Article III of the Constitution. Moreover, he continued, the entire statute was invalid because Congress had "no power . . . to legislate at all on the subject of fugitive slaves," as that power had been reserved to the states under Article IV.[43] Rantoul's argument was highly technical. Much of it turned on the precise definition of the word "case," and whether a commissioner's finding was legally conclusive that a prisoner was "held" to service.

The justices probably had their minds all but made up before the hearing began. They did not bother to request a response from federal Marshal Charles Devens, who legally held Sims in custody pursuant to Curtis's warrant, or from Seth Thomas, who represented the real party in interest. Instead they issued a unanimous ruling—written by Chief Justice Shaw—a scant two hours after the conclusion of oral argument. Shaw left no doubt where he stood on the Fugitive Slave Act, finding it fully constitutional in every regard. A determination under the Act was primarily administrative rather than judicial, he said, and therefore the summary proceedings could be conducted by a commissioner rather than a judge. As for the other issues raised by Rantoul—the question of congressional power; the absence of trial by jury—those had been resolved by the U.S. Supreme Court in *Prigg v. Pennsylvania* when Justice Story upheld the Fugitive Slave Act of 1793. "The law of 1850 stands," he said, "precisely on the same ground with that of 1793, and the same grounds of argument which tend to show the unconstitutionality of the one, apply with equal force to the other; and the same answer must be made to them."[44]

Shaw's ruling was roundly condemned in abolitionist quarters. "What a moment was lost," lamented Ralph Waldo Emerson, "when Judge Shaw declined to affirm the unconstitutionality of the Fugitive Slave Law." Theodore Parker took only slight solace in the public spectacle of "old stiff-necked Lemuel visibly going under the chains" to enter his own courthouse. Richard Henry Dana, however, placed at least some of the blame on Rantoul's advocacy. It had been "a very striking and forcible argument," he wrote, "considered as a speech to the people, or as a piece of abstract reasoning, but not one calculated to meet the difficulties in the minds of the court."[45]

Dana evidently believed he could have done better, but it is not obvious that any argument would have persuaded Shaw to rule in Sims's favor. Rantoul's "abstract reasoning" had been based firmly on constitutional principles of the sort that high court judges usually considered. A more emotional appeal, based on the immorality of slavery or the demands of natural law, almost certainly would have failed even more resoundingly. Shaw was willing to concede that slavery was "abhorrent to the dictates of humanity and plainest principles of justice and natural right," but he was nonetheless committed to enforcement of the positive law. Each state had the right and power, Shaw believed, "to judge for itself, and to allow or prohibit slavery by its own laws." It was the duty of the free states, therefore, to respect the institution of slavery where it existed, even if that meant enforcing all of "the rights flowing from it." Thus, the rendition of fugitive slaves was "essentially necessary to the peace, happiness and highest prosperity of all the states."[46] Richard Henry Dana had a gift for jury persuasion, as was obvious in his effective representation of Robert Morris and Lewis Hayden, but it is hard to see how any lawyer could have overcome Lemuel Shaw's commitment to the Fugitive Slave Act.

Rantoul had little time to ponder Shaw's opinion (or to worry about Dana's critique of his performance). He was due back in Curtis's courtroom that same afternoon for the final argument in Sims's rendition hearing. Rantoul's argument before Curtis was a prolonged elaboration of the morning's presentation; he spoke for six hours, until the close of the day's session. His construction of the Constitution was so intricate, however, that at one point the commissioner asked him to "remind me of the bearing of the argument."[47]

The following morning, Charles G. Loring continued the argument on Sims's behalf. He began with an apology for his lack of time to prepare, but that did not prevent him from speaking for more than four hours. He astutely disclaimed any connection to the protesters in the street, or to the Shadrach Minkins rescuers, realizing that he could succeed only by disentangling the case from its political context. Thus, Loring strenuously avoided making any broad moral claims, while likewise urging Curtis to ignore the potential "political effect" of the case and to concentrate instead on "first principles of civil liberty and personal security under the laws and Constitution."[48] By that time, however, the Shaw opinion had already been issued, placing Loring in a tricky position. The Massachusetts Supreme Court had just unanimously rejected the very points he was attempting to make. The best he could do was to criticize the Supreme Court for an "unavoidably hasty" decision, "without much if any deliberation, and without full discussion." He added somewhat condescendingly that he had not participated in the Supreme Court hearing, suggesting that the habeas corpus petition had been a poor idea in the first place.

Seth Thomas responded briefly on behalf of the slave owner. The question, he remarked sarcastically, was not merely whether Potter was entitled to the services he claimed, "but whether there was any Constitution in the United States." All of the defense arguments were simply "obstacles in the way of this law," given that the actual evidence was overwhelming. Thus, the commissioner was obligated to "secure to the claimant the peaceable exercise of a right guaranteed" by the Constitution itself.[49]

Unlike Justice Shaw, Commissioner Curtis was not prepared to issue an immediate opinion. Following the arguments of counsel, he simply recessed court on Tuesday afternoon. Over the next few days, while the case before Curtis was in limbo, the lawyers attached to the Vigilance Committee pursued all manner of additional writs, warrants, and legal ploys, none of which succeeded. Radical abolitionists, such as Thomas Wentworth Higginson, had never placed much faith in the judicial process, and they grew increasingly frustrated as the lawyers' work brought no results. "Absolutely nothing could be accomplished in the court-room," Higginson believed, and he continued to press his closest colleagues to show some "fighting quality" by planning a rescue.[50]

Eventually a handful of conspirators agreed upon an imaginative scheme to rescue Sims from the upper-story courtroom where he was held and which, as Higginson observed, "had no gratings at the windows." Under the plan as conceived, Sims was to jump from the window at a "specified hour" in the evening, only to land safely on a stack of mattresses that the plotters would pile below at that exact moment. Rev. Leonard Grimes had permission to visit and console Sims, so the black clergyman used that opportunity to convey the escape plan. Sims readily agreed, and the arrangements were quickly made. The mattresses were assembled at a lawyer's office across the street from the courthouse and a fast carriage was engaged to hurry Sims to safety. At the last minute, however, the defenestration was thwarted, as workmen arrived to install bars across the window. "Whether we had been betrayed, or whether it was simply a bit of extraordinary precaution, we never knew," wrote Higginson.[51]

For two days, while the Vigilance Committee members pursued their various futile petitions and plots, Commissioner Curtis was busy preparing his judgment in the Sims case. He delivered it on Friday morning, April 11. As expected, Curtis ruled in favor of Potter's claim, systematically rejecting every argument raised on Sims's behalf. Much of Curtis's reasoning followed precedent, but some of it was clearly improvised. For example, Curtis announced that he would not accept the $10 statutory fee for granting the claimant a certificate of removal, as though that remedied the inequity of the Fugitive Slave Act itself, which would have allowed him only $5 had he ruled in Sims's favor.

At times, Curtis's opinion seemed almost intentionally obtuse. To uphold his authority to hear the case as a quasi-judicial officer, he insisted that his order was not a final adjudication of Sims's slave status. Rather, it was only a preliminary finding that would do nothing more than return Sims to Georgia, where he would then have "the means of testing his alleged owner's right to hold him." Conceding that Sims might face "difficulties or improbabilities" once he was returned to Georgia, Curtis was satisfied that the government of the United States was justified in trusting each slave state to provide "a full and final trial" to returned fugitives.[52] Horace Mann, then serving in the House of Representatives, ridiculed Curtis's faith in southern justice: "He might as well doom a man to be hurled from the Tarpeian rock and say that the act is not final because he only commits the victim to the laws of gravitation, as he has committed Sims to the laws of Georgia."[53]

Lest he appear completely heartless, Curtis expressed his belief—based on the testimony of one of Potter's agents—that Sims's mother had begged "for God's sake to bring him back again," even if he was in a free state. Reuniting the slave family, explained Curtis, "certainly disarms this case of any unpleasant features."[54] Thomas Sims could be forgiven if he did not quite see it that way. Once the gist of Curtis's ruling became clear, he began to scream in protest. "I will not go back to Slavery," he cried. "Give me a knife," he implored his counsel, "and when the Commissioner declares me a slave I will stab myself in the heart, and die before his eyes! I will not be a slave."[55] The knife was withheld, reported Theodore Parker, as Sims's attorneys reluctantly took leave of their client in the courtroom.

It was thought that Sims's "removal" would take place the following day, so only a handful of abolitionists kept watch on the courthouse Friday night. The authorities, however, were determined to take no chances with another rescue attempt, or even a public disturbance. Several hours after midnight, about one hundred city police officers began to gather at the courthouse, and soon they were joined by an additional two hundred armed volunteers and members of the city watch. Their plan was to sneak Sims to the harbor under cover of darkness, where they would then place him aboard the brig *Acorn*. "It was not the bravest way to uphold the Constitution, but it was the safest."[56]

At about four o'clock in the morning, the column began its march, with the shackled Sims securely in the middle of three hundred men carrying swords and pistols. Perhaps a score of abolitionists had been alerted to Sims's removal, and they dogged the parade with shouts and jeers. The troop proceeded smartly to Long Wharf, where the prisoner was delivered to the waiting ship. By the following week, the *Acorn* had arrived in Savannah, where Sims was given thirty-nine lashes in the public square.

Boston had at last returned a fugitive slave to the South. The Cotton Whig establishment rejoiced, and James Potter, once again in possession of his slave, published a notice in the Boston newspapers thanking the city's commercial leaders, who had been "conspicuous in their efforts to serve us."[57] Although the process had cost about $20,000, Webster was well satisfied with the outcome. He reported to Fillmore that the "abolitionists & free soilers . . . are insane, but it is an angry & vindictive insanity" that had been effectively overcome. The president responded effusively: "I congratulate you and the country upon the triumph of law in Boston. She has done nobly. She has wiped out the stain of the former rescue."[58]

In the midst of the Sims case, when the abolitionists first realized the great degree of force that was arrayed against them, Wendell Phillips remarked that "one thing is certain; courts obliged to sit guarded by bayonets will not sit long in Massachusetts. The Commissioner who grants certificates shielded by armed men, will not have many certificates to grant."[59] Three years later he would be proven right, in ways he could not have predicted at the time.

∽ 9 ∾

KIDNAPPING AGAIN!

The first fifteen months following the enactment of the Fugitive Slave Act saw a series of high-profile cases, including the escape of the Crafts, the rescue of Shadrach Minkins, the rendition of Thomas Sims, the Jerry rescue, and the Christiana resistance. In fact, roughly one-quarter of all known fugitive slave cases occurred during that period, and 1851 was the single most active year for fugitive renditions during the entire decade before the Civil War. In 1852 the number of recaptured slaves fell by two-thirds, and the number of proceedings before federal commissioners plummeted by more than 80 percent.[1] As would be expected, the furor over the fugitive law also subsided, "perhaps because the legions of law and order finally prevailed [or perhaps because] nearly all of the eligible fugitives had decamped to Canada."[2] In any event, the next few years provided Unionists with some reason for optimism. The Compromise of 1850—including the Fugitive Slave Act—actually seemed to be working.

In 1854, however, sectional tensions reemerged with the eruption of the Kansas-Nebraska controversy. Initially, the "Nebraska question," as it was often called, had very little to do with slavery and everything to do with the construction of a transcontinental railroad. Beginning in 1852 Illinois Senator Stephen A. Douglas had championed the development of a central route for the proposed railroad, which would encourage economic growth in Illinois and, not coincidentally, enhance the value of his own real estate holdings. The key to Douglas's plan lay in organizing the vast Nebraska territory that lay directly west of Missouri.

Douglas's efforts were blocked by southern senators, who naturally favored a southern route. In addition, Missouri Senator David Atchison also opposed organizing the Nebraska territory, all of which was situated north of the 36°30" parallel and was therefore barred to slavery under the terms of the 1820 Missouri Compromise. Even though a central railroad would greatly benefit his own state, Atchison could not tolerate seeing Missouri "surrounded by free territory," with

the free states of Iowa and Illinois to the north and east and a free-soil Nebraska to the west. It was preferable, in his view, to leave Nebraska unorganized
rather than create an opening for the "emissaries of abolitionists"[3]

The impasse between Douglas and Atchison, and their respective allies,
continued for several years, but they finally agreed upon a resolution in January 1854. Douglas introduced a bill organizing the area into two territories—
Kansas and Nebraska—and providing that "all questions pertaining to slavery in the Territories . . . are to be left to the people residing therein through
their appropriate representatives."[4] The bill included a provision specifically
repealing the Missouri Compromise of 1820, and therefore immediately opening both new territories to slavery. (It was understood at the time that Nebraska's climate would preclude a slave-based economic system but that slave
owners from Missouri would find a congenial environment in Kansas.)

Douglas expected his bill to "raise a hell of a storm," and so it did. Abolitionists, Free-Soilers, and many other Northerners were aghast at the idea
of opening previously free lands to the introduction of slavery. A group of
"Independent Democrats"—including Salmon Chase, Charles Sumner, and
Gerrit Smith—denounced Douglas's bill "as a gross violation of a sacred
pledge, as a criminal betrayal of precious rights, as part and parcel of an atrocious plot" to turn the new territory into a "dreary region of despotism, in-
habited by masters and slaves." At that point, the bill "ceased to be primarily a
railroad question and became primarily a slavery question."[5]

Nonetheless, the Kansas-Nebraska Act passed the House on May 23 and
the Senate on May 26. It was signed into law by President Franklin Pierce on
May 30, 1854. To many in the North, the bill represented not only a repeal of
the Missouri Compromise, but also a repudiation of the Compromise of 1850.
If Southerners were no longer willing to respect the 36°30" line of demarca-
tion, it was argued, why should Northerners adhere to the Fugitive Slave Act?

The Kansas-Nebraska Act caused particular outrage in Boston. Richard
Henry Dana, for example, believed that the bill threatened to turn the United
States into "a slave-holding and slavery propagating" republic. Its passage, he
declared, put "compromises at an end," making it "time to take up the gaunt-
let [in a] war against the extension of slavery into new territory." Even erstwhile Cotton Whigs retracted their support for the Compromise of 1850, with
wealthy merchants such as Amos Lawrence warning that "the Fugitive Slave
law could no longer be enforced" in Massachusetts.[6]

Almost as if on cue, another resourceful fugitive reached Boston. The arrest of Anthony Burns—only one day after the House of Representatives passed the Kansas-Nebraska Act—and his subsequent trial underscored the symbolic connection between slavery in the federal territories and the capture of runaways in the northern states. In both circumstances, the southern slave power seemed to be relentlessly extending its reach onto free soil, thus rewarding compromise with aggression.

———

Anthony Burns was born in the early 1830s in the village of Stafford, Virginia, as the property of John Suttle and his wife.[7] The Suttles both died when Burns was a child, and he was inherited along with a dozen other slaves by Charles Francis Suttle, who owned a store in nearby Falmouth. Charles Suttle was a prominent citizen, having served as county sheriff and a colonel in the state militia, but he could not profitably employ the many slaves devised by his parents' estate. Consequently, he hired out his slaves to others, while of course keeping their wages for himself. Anthony Burns began his life as a hired slave at the tender age of seven or eight, working first as a babysitter on a local plantation, and later as an errand-runner for three elderly women. Somewhere along the way he had an opportunity to observe white children at their studies, and through the kindness of a teacher he obtained a primer and learned to read and write.

As he grew older, Burns was hired out for more strenuous work, including two years with a friend of Suttle's named William Brent. In 1849 Burns was working at a steam-powered sawmill where his right hand was badly mangled in an accident. The injury left Burns with a disfigured arm—almost an inch of bone protruded through the skin at his wrist—that was later used to identify him in court. Following his recovery, Burns was once more placed under the supervision of William Brent. In a complex arrangement, Burns was first "leased" to a Richmond pharmacist named Millspaugh for $125 per year, but then allowed to find his own work as a day laborer. In return, Burns agreed to pay back the $125 out of his daily wages, with the understanding that he could keep the balance. This sort of bargaining was technically illegal under Virginia law, but it was not unusual among urban slaves.

Burns found regular work on Richmond's wharves, loading and unloading cargo. Over the course of a year, he was able to amass a small sum of money and, more important, he made the acquaintance of sailors from northern ports. One sympathetic sailor from Boston became his confidant and helped him plan an escape. On a cold morning in early February 1854, Burns slipped away from his slave quarters and, with the assistance of the unnamed sailor, stowed away on a Boston-bound ship. Burns spent three weeks in the ship's hold, living on bread and water supplied by his friend, until he finally arrived in Boston sometime toward the end of the month.

In Boston Burns was able to find temporary work as a cook, but he was fired after a week because he "was unable to make his bread rise."[8] Finding himself unemployed and out of funds, Burns took to the streets in search of work. To his good fortune, he soon encountered a black man named William Jones, who proved more than willing to aid a stranger in distress. Jones took Burns into his home and over the next few days helped him make the rounds of potential employers. Together they approached several shopkeepers, but no work was available. Finally, on March 3, Jones secured work washing windows at the Mattapan Works in South Boston, and he agreed to pay Burns 8 cents per window as his assistant. The two men worked on the windows for nearly a week, after which they found some odd jobs at City Hall. Although they had a slight dispute over the amount of Burns's payment for the Mattapan job, they appear to have parted friends sometime around the middle of the month.

At some point afterward Burns obtained work as a helper in the Brattle Street clothing store of Coffin Pitts, a deacon of the black Twelfth Baptist Church who was known as "a respectable colored trader." Fatefully, however, Burns attempted to contact his brother, who was a slave in Richmond. Burns somehow managed to have a letter posted from Canada, thinking that would conceal his whereabouts, but he carelessly mentioned that he was living in Boston, trusting his brother to keep his secret. Burns must not have realized that southern postmasters never delivered mail directly to slaves, but rather to their masters. Thus, the letter was forwarded to Suttle, who was then living in Alexandria. Alerted to Burns's location, Suttle made plans to retrieve his missing property.

Suttle's first step was to appear before the Alexandria County Circuit Court, on May 16, 1854, where he "proved to the satisfaction" of the presiding judge that "Anthony Burns was held to service and labor by him" in Virginia and that "the said Anthony has escaped from the State." The transcript of the court proceeding also included a description of Burns, as required by the

Fugitive Slave Act, calling him "a man of dark complexion, about six feet high, with a scar on one of his cheeks, and also a scar on the back of his right hand, and about twenty-three or four years of age."[9]

Armed with the necessary documents, Suttle then recruited William Brent—Burns's nominal overseer, and an essential witness—and headed to Massachusetts. By Wednesday, May 24, the two Virginians had arrived in Boston, where of course they obtained the counsel of Col. Seth Thomas. In short order, Thomas arranged for Suttle to appear before Fugitive Slave Commissioner Edward Greely Loring—George Ticknor Curtis being for some reason unavailable—who promptly issued a warrant for Burns's arrest. Loring's warrant, directed to U.S. Marshal Watson Freeman, recited the allegations of Suttle's ownership and noted that Burns had escaped on March 24, 1854. That seemingly unimportant detail, which was not included in the Virginia court record, would become extremely significant in the trial that followed.

The warrant was entrusted to Deputy Marshal Asa Butman for execution, the same man who had arrested Thomas Sims in 1851. Sims had fiercely resisted arrest and the deputy was anxious to avoid another violent struggle. He and his henchmen therefore devised a plan to trick Burns into surrendering peacefully. The posse staked out Coffin Pitts's clothing store until they saw Burns depart at closing time. They followed Burns down a dark street and then called on him to stop. The startled Burns froze in his tracks, fearful that he was being "beset by a street brawler." He was therefore rather reassured when he heard Butman inform him that he was being arrested for the robbery of a jewelry store. "Conscious of [his] innocence, and feeling assured that he could easily clear himself of the charge," Burns willingly submitted to the arrest, expecting that the misunderstanding could be quickly resolved with a simple explanation. Instead, however, he was immediately seized by a half-dozen ruffians who picked him up "as they would a dead person" and rushed him off to the courthouse.[10] Still believing that he was being erroneously charged with robbery, Burns made no outcry or attempt to escape.

Butman and company were greeted at the courthouse by federal Marshal Watson Freeman, "who stood with a drawn sword" on the front steps. Taking command of the situation, Freeman directed Burns and his captors to the federal jury room, on the third floor of the building. Once he was securely behind locked doors, Burns was finally informed that he had been arrested as a fugitive and not as a thief.

Burns realized just how desperate his situation had become when Charles Suttle and William Brent entered the room. Suttle was well prepared to confront his slave, having been advised by Seth Thomas to obtain admissions that could be useful in court. "Why did you run away from me?" the Virginian demanded.

As he had no doubt learned during his life as a slave, Burns tried to divert his master's anger. "I fell asleep on the vessel where I worked," he said, "and before I woke up, she set sail and carried me off." Burns evidently hoped that he could minimize his punishment by pretending that he had not intentionally run away, but Suttle was having none of it.

"Haven't I always treated you well, Tony?" the slave owner continued. "Haven't I always given you money when you needed?" Burns tried to avoid the questions, but he finally replied, "You have always given me twelve and a half cents once a year."[11] The answer, whether contrite or sarcastic, did not matter at all to Suttle. He was simply prompting Burns to acknowledge, in front of witnesses, that he was a slave. With that object accomplished, Suttle and Brent informed Marshal Freeman that he had captured the right man. Then they retired for the night, leaving Anthony Burns in the callous care of Asa Butman (who did not bother to provide either a bed or food for his prisoner).

Early on the morning of Thursday, May 25, Burns was manacled and escorted into the nearby federal courtroom, still under heavy guard. News of his capture had not yet reached the general public, so the courtroom was nearly empty. Suttle and Brent were there along with their attorneys, Seth Thomas and a young lawyer named Edward Griffen Parker, who, unlike Thomas, was not known as a proslavery man. Commissioner Edward Loring would soon take the bench, and at first it appeared that Burns's rendition hearing would be conducted entirely in secret.

Before the formal proceeding could begin, however, Rev. Leonard Grimes and Richard Henry Dana separately entered the room. Each man had heard rumors that another fugitive slave had been captured, and hastened to the courthouse to investigate. Grimes arrived first, and the prominent clergyman was allowed to confer briefly with Burns. Dana arrived shortly afterward. Scanning the courtroom, he saw Burns sitting "in the usual place for prisoners, guarded by a large corps of officers." Dana was appalled by Burns's condition—

manacled, exhausted, terrified—and observed that he was "completely cowed & dispirited."[12] Dana also immediately noticed Burns's unmistakable physical injuries, which would later play an important role in the trial of the case, describing "a large scar on his cheek [which] looks like a brand, a broken hand, from [which] a large piece of bone projects, and another scar on his other hand."[13]

Making his way through the ring of guards and deputies, Dana went over to Burns and offered to represent him. Burns, however, was unresponsive. With Suttle and Brent sitting only yards away, he was fearful that any effort at defense would only make his eventual punishment more severe. "It will be of no use," he finally said. "They have got me." Dana attempted to press the issue, explaining that "there might be some flaw in the papers, or some mistake [and] that he might get off," but Burns knew his own mind. "They will swear to me & get me back; and if they do, I shall fare worse if I resist." Without Burns's authorization, Dana reluctantly concluded that he had no choice but to allow the hearing to proceed. And in any event, he understood Burns's cruel predicament. "Any delay & expense he cause his master would be visited upon him when he got back," Dana wrote in his journal. Therefore, "his best policy was to conciliate his master as best he could."[14]

Commissioner Loring called court to order at about 9:00 a.m., inviting Suttle's lawyers to present their case. Parker, the junior counsel, began by offering the relevant documents. He first read the complaint and the warrant. Then he introduced the official record of the Alexandria County Court, which established that Anthony Burns was the property of Charles Suttle and that "the said Anthony [had] escaped" from Virginia. Under the Fugitive Slave Act, all that remained was to prove that the prisoner was indeed the same person who was named in the warrant. For that purpose, Parker and Thomas called William Brent to the stand. (Suttle himself was barred from testifying under the "interested party rule," which had made it necessary for Brent to accompany him to Boston.)

Dana watched helplessly as Brent began to testify. "I know Anthony Burns," he said, and "now see him at the bar in front; he is the man referred to in the record which has been read; he is owned by Mr. Suttle as a slave."

By that time the news of the hearing had spread around Court Square and numerous spectators had taken seats in the courtroom. Among them were the Vigilance Committee lawyers Charles Ellis and Robert Morris, as well as

Rev. Theodore Parker and the noted abolitionist Wendell Phillips. Ellis begged Dana to intervene in the proceeding, but Dana replied that his hands were tied because he had not been retained.

Theodore Parker, however, was not bound by Dana's lawyerly professionalism. Approaching Burns on his own, Parker explained that he had been appointed "minister at large" to Boston's fugitive slaves, and in that capacity he urged Burns to accept representation. Burns was still unconvinced. "If I must go back," he told Parker, "I want to go back as easy as I can."

"But surely, it can do you no harm to make a defence," pressed Parker.

"Well," said Burns, relenting under pressure from the persistent white man, "you may do as you have a mind to about it."[15]

Taking Burns's equivocal response as assent, Parker implored Dana to mount a defense. Dana continued to hesitate, however, until he heard Brent's testimony take an ominous turn.

"I knew that [Burns] was missing from Richmond on or about the 24th day of March," the witness said, adding that "last night I heard Anthony converse with his master."[16]

That was more than Dana could tolerate. The Fugitive Slave Act specifically excluded the testimony of the subject slave, yet here was the claimant's counsel blithely introducing Burns's own words as evidence against him. With no one else able to object to the damaging testimony, Dana took it upon himself to approach the bench. "May it please your Honor," he said,

> I rise to address the court as amicus curiae, for I cannot say that I am regularly of counsel for the person at the bar. . . . I am satisfied that he is not in a condition to determine whether he will have counsel or not . . . or whether he will defend or not.
>
> I submit to your Honor's judgment that time should be allowed to the prisoner to recover himself from the stupefaction of his sudden arrest . . . and have opportunity to consult with friends and members of the bar, and determine what course he will pursue.

Suttle's attorneys were irate at the interruption. Dana had no standing in the court, and the prisoner himself had shown no interest in either representation or postponement. Any adjournment would come at considerable additional cost and inconvenience to Suttle and Brent, argued Edward Parker, while the "only object of delay, is to try to induce [Burns] to resist the just claim which he is now ready to acknowledge."[17]

Dana retorted that "counsel for the prosecution misapprehends my statement." It was too soon to tell whether the prisoner wanted to raise a defense, because "he was not in a fit state to decide for himself what he will do." Even if there was some reason to think that Burns wanted to "plead guilty to the claim, the court ought not to receive the plea under such circumstances." Although he maintained that he was acting only as amicus and not as counsel, Dana had skillfully started to frame the case in Burns's favor. The proceeding before Loring was only an action for the recovery of property, yet Dana characterized the case in the language of criminal law, referring to "counsel for the prosecution" and the possibility of a "guilty" plea. Those were not casual references, but rather the subtle prelude to his later argument that Suttle's case would have to be proven beyond a reasonable doubt.

Just as he had intended, Dana's request for a continuance placed the court in a difficult spot. In addition to his part-time position as a U.S. commissioner, Loring was also judge of the Suffolk County Probate Court and a faculty member at the Harvard Law School, making him one of the most highly visible members of Boston's legal community. There had not been a fugitive case in Boston since 1851, and much had happened since then, so Loring knew his decisions would be closely watched on all sides. As a Cotton Whig, his natural inclination was simply to enforce the Fugitive Slave Act, which had been found constitutional by both the Massachusetts Supreme Court and Commissioner George Ticknor Curtis (who was Loring's relative by marriage). And even though Daniel Webster had died in 1852 (and the Whigs had fallen out of power nationally, with the election of Democrat Franklin Pierce that same year), there was still much support for the Fugitive Slave Act among Boston's ruling classes. On the other hand, the Kansas-Nebraska Act had shaken the foundations of the Compromise of 1850, leading many responsible leaders to question the viability of the Fugitive Slave Act. Although the claimant was probably entitled to an immediate hearing under a strict reading of the law, it was also undeniable that the trembling Burns was in no condition to make a decision involving "freedom or slavery for life."

Recognizing that Loring would be torn between the demands of justice and the requirements of the positive law, Dana adroitly appealed to the commissioner's conscience (and his vanity). "Even without a suggestion from an amicus curiae," he said, Loring surely would not "weigh liberty against convenience and freedom against pecuniary expense." "I am confident," Dana continued, that "your Honor will not decide so momentous an issue against a man without counsel."[18]

Loring was not willing to adjourn the case solely on the basis of Dana's request, as that would have appeared too dismissive of Suttle's legitimate claim to a speedy resolution. Instead the judge called Burns up to the bench and told him "that he had a right to a defence and could have counsel, if he desired it." Burns, however, was "distracted and uncertain." He had already declined counsel twice, attempting to comply with his master's demand that he return willingly to slavery. But now the white judge seemed to demand something else of him. With Suttle and Brent glowering from across the courtroom, and Loring watching expectantly from the bench, the bewildered Burns "looked around the courtroom timidly, and made no reply" to the question.

Once again Loring asked whether Burns would like "time to think about this. Do you wish to go away and meet me here to-morrow or next day, and tell me what you will do?" This time Burns mumbled something inaudible. After an awkward silence, Loring interpreted Burns's hesitant words as acquiescence. "I understand you to say you would," prompted the court.

Burns turned his eyes from Loring to Suttle, and then back to the bench. He finally answered softly. "I would," said Burns, in his only recorded words for the duration of the proceeding.[19]

"Then you shall have it," announced the court. Loring continued the hearing for two days, until the following Saturday, as he was scheduled to lecture Friday at Harvard.

Suttle and his attorneys were troubled by the court's ruling, but Marshal Watson Freeman was visibly distressed. He had hoped that the case would be resolved that morning and that Suttle and his slave would depart for Virginia before mass protests could be mounted. Now, however, he was faced with the task of guarding Burns for at least two additional nights, again with no federal jail at his disposal. Freeman rushed to the bench, pleading quietly with Judge Loring to change his decision.

"No, Sir, he must have the time necessary," said Loring.

Freeman tried again, whispering urgently to the judge.

This time Loring replied severely. "I can't help that, Sir, he shall have the proper time."[20]

With that, court adjourned. Anthony Burns was saved from a precipitous return to slavery, but only at the cost of further angering his master. Meanwhile, attorney Richard Henry Dana and Commissioner Edward Loring were able to congratulate themselves on having ensured at least procedural fairness in the execution of the fugitive law. Dana thought that Loring's conduct had been "considerate and humane," observing that a judge "could not act better in his office than [had] Judge Loring."[21]

It is true that the forms of law had been followed, and even expanded upon. The Fugitive Slave Act did not contemplate allowing counsel to runaways, who were afforded no more protection under the statute than any other piece of property. Thus, Loring's statement that Burns had "a right to a defence" was in part exaggeration, in part self-indulgence, and in part deference to Dana's request. Absent the intervention of amicus curiae—not to mention the presence in court of Leonard Grimes, Theodore Parker, Charles Ellis, Robert Morris, and other notables—it is highly unlikely that Loring would have been so concerned about affording Burns any sort of delay.

But even as they were ostensibly protecting the prisoner's rights, Dana and Loring were treating Burns almost as a bystander at his own rendition. In the same vein, Theodore Parker had naively assured Burns that "it can do you no harm to make a defence," without appreciating that the prisoner might know better. More than anyone else in the courtroom—save Suttle and Brent, and perhaps Seth Thomas—Burns understood that difficulty for the master inevitably resulted in punishment for the slave. Dana was hopeful that there might be "some flaw in the papers," but Burns had no reason to trust any lawyer's judgment, or even his good intentions, much less expect freedom from the court.

Dana was not quite ready to begin working for Burns's freedom, even after Loring had granted the two-day delay. His rigid sense of professional ethics did not allow him to contact Burns directly, given that his offer of representation had already been refused. "I felt that it was improper for me to obtrude myself upon him," Dana wrote in his journal. "If any were to advise, it should be others than a lawyer who had once offered to act." On Friday morning, therefore, Dana asked Rev. Leonard Grimes, Deacon Coffin Pitts, and Wendell Phillips to visit Burns, in order to determine whether he wanted "to make a defence, or to have counsel at all."[22] Marshal Watson Freeman, however, had other ideas. Burns's capture was no longer even remotely a secret, and crowds had gathered around the now heavily fortified courthouse. Inflammatory hand-bills had been circulated throughout the city, announcing that kidnappers had imprisoned a man in the "Massachusetts Temple of Justice,"[23] and there was no telling what Boston's animated abolitionists had in mind. In that explosive atmosphere, the U.S. marshal intended to take no chances on a possible rescue plot, and he refused to allow the delegation to visit his prisoner. His obstructionism was obviously contrary to Judge Loring's intent—the continuance had been granted to allow Burns to consult with "friends and members of the bar"—but Freeman was adamant. There would be no visitors on his watch.

The three men returned to Dana's office, where it was decided that Phillips would try to obtain an order from Judge Loring, requiring that the marshal allow Burns to have at least some visitors. Dana wrote a note to Loring, explaining that he "scarcely felt at liberty to act as counsel for the man . . . [and] that the proper person to see him & ascertain his wishes had been refused admission."[24]

Phillips tracked down Loring in his office at Harvard, where he presented Dana's note and explained the need for someone to visit Burns. Loring was not sure that he could actually require the marshal to relent. As a mere commissioner, he did not exercise full judicial power and, in any event, the marshal's office operated independently of the courts in that era. After some discussion, however, Loring agreed to write a stern note, informing Freeman that Burns had a "right to see a few friends" so long as their names were "taken to him & their purpose stated to him."[25]

Phillips had only a moment to enjoy his success. As he was about to leave Loring's office, note in hand, the commissioner called him back with a word of advice. "Mr. Phillips," he said, "the case is so clear that I do not think you will be justified in placing any obstacles in the way of this man's going back, as he probably will." Phillips was dismayed by Loring's apparent prejudgment of the case, after having heard "only the disjointed story of a single witness," but the commissioner's comment really should have come as no great surprise.[26] Loring (and Phillips) had already seen the conclusive documents from the Virginia court and had heard Brent's positive identification of Burns. An effective defense was hard to imagine at that point, so Loring's advice was more in the nature of a caution than a rebuke. Perhaps the commissioner was even thinking of the prisoner's long-term welfare. Burns himself had recognized that extended proceedings might only make things worse for him, and Loring—unencumbered by idealism—may have understood the potential consequences better than did any of the antislavery attorneys.

In any event, Phillips soon presented Loring's order to Marshal Freeman, who reluctantly granted access to his prisoner. Phillips found Burns to be "intelligent & resolute," although deeply worried that his master would sell him on the New Orleans market. Burns denied that he had ever agreed to return to slavery, but he provided no information that might be useful to defeat Suttle's claim. Following "a little encouragement," Burns signed a power of attorney authorizing Phillips to engage counsel on his behalf, and to do "everything in [his] power to save him from going back to slavery." Adhering to all proprieties, Phillips then formally retained Dana, who in turn retained Charles Ellis to assist him.[27] The stage was now set for the rendition trial of Anthony Burns. The only thing lacking was a credible defense.

Marshal Freeman may have seemed unnecessarily callous when he turned away Grimes, Pitts, and Phillips on Friday, but the officer had good reason to be careful. Even as Dana sought a continuance before Judge Loring on Thursday morning, members of the Vigilance Committee were meeting at the office of the New England Antislavery Society to plan a militant course of action. Still seething over the rendition of Thomas Sims three years earlier, the abolitionists had little faith in the legal system and there was considerable sentiment in favor of organizing a forcible rescue. By the end of the day, the city was plastered with handbills that read:

KIDNAPPING AGAIN!!

A MAN WAS STOLEN LAST NIGHT BY THE

FUGITIVE SLAVE BILL COMMISSIONER!

HE WILL HAVE HIS

MOCK TRIAL

ON SATURDAY, MAY 27, AT 9 O'CLOCK

IN THE KIDNAPPER'S "COURT"

BEFORE THE HONORABLE SLAVE BILL COMMISSIONER,

AT THE COURT HOUSE, IN COURT SQUARE.

SHALL BOSTON STEAL ANOTHER MAN?[28]

It was obvious from the choice of language that the Vigilance Committee had no respect for any "kidnapper's court" or forthcoming "mock trial."

Marshal Freeman may not have known that Grimes and Phillips were members of the Vigilance Committee's executive committee, but he surely suspected that they were involved in something other than a strictly legal defense. Indeed, that very afternoon there was a closed-door meeting at Tremont Temple, where rescue plans were discussed by ardent abolitionists such as Theodore Parker, Samuel Gridley Howe, and Albert Gallatin Browne. Despite the attendees' resolve to "resist, defy, baffle, and nullify" the execution of the fugitive law, they were not able to settle upon a plan that day. They resolved instead to keep the courthouse under close surveillance all night so that Burns could not be spirited away under cover of darkness.[29]

By Friday morning hundreds of higher-law men had converged in central Boston, in anticipation of a meeting to be held that night at Faneuil Hall. Rev. Thomas Wentworth Higginson—who had organized the unsuccessful effort to have Sims jump to freedom from a courthouse window—hurried from his home in Worcester in response to a request from the utopian educator Bronson Alcott. Higginson had been active in the radical antislavery movement for years and had been dismissed from his position as minister of the Unitarian Church of Newburyport because of his radicalism. By 1854 Higginson had run unsuccessfully for Congress on the Free Soil ticket and had established himself as pastor of the Free Church of Worcester. His position on the Fugitive Slave Act was straightforward: "Disobey it . . . and show our good citizenship by taking the legal consequences." By either fate or coincidence, Higginson's Worcester congregation included a man "of remarkable energy" named Martin Stowell, who had been involved in the Jerry Rescue in Syracuse. Before he left for Boston, Higginson asked Stowell to recruit other parishioners who were "pledged to act that day for freedom."[30]

Meeting with the leaders of the Vigilance Committee, Higginson began agitating for a forcible rescue plan. Most of the committee members, however, believed it was too soon to take such an extreme action, fearing that a precipitous attempt would fail. True to his nature, Higginson insisted that immediate resistance was the only proper response. "Better a failure than to acquiesce tamely as before, and see Massachusetts henceforward made a hunting-ground for fugitive slaves."[31] Nonetheless, the committee would not approve his plan, opting instead to rally support at that evening's Faneuil Hall meeting, and then to wait for the commissioner's ruling before taking further steps.

Although outvoted at the meeting, Higginson was not willing to defer enforcement of the higher law until the government's law had run its course. Instead he caucused with Martin Stowell and a small group of militants, determined to launch an assault on the courthouse that very night, using the Faneuil Hall meeting as a distraction to cover their preparation. As Higginson later described it, the plan was to send a "loud-voiced" man into the gallery at the very height of the meeting, who would announce that a "mob of negroes [was] already attacking the Court-House." Higginson's expectation was that one of the speakers—preferably Wendell Phillips—would then call upon the "whole meeting" to run "pell-mell to Court Square ready to fall in behind the leaders and bring out the slave."[32]

While Higginson and Stowell were refining their plot, Dana was finally visiting Burns at the courthouse. He found the prisoner confined in a small room, guarded by some eight or ten men "of the rough, thief-catching order." Burns impressed Dana as "a very different man" from the frightened and exhausted fugitive of the previous day. Having had a night's rest and an opportunity to compose his thoughts, Burns now "seemed self possessed, intelligent [and] with considerable force both of mind & body." Burns told Dana something of his background and explained his fear of punishment at Suttle's hands, saying that his master was "a malicious man if crossed."[33] Dana did not record the conversation at length, but as a careful and accomplished lawyer it is certain that he probed for facts that might be useful in court. Later in the proceedings, Dana would rely on specific details of Burns's escape and his brief life as a free man in Boston, which he must have learned during his jailhouse interview on Friday evening.

Dana did not attend the Friday night meeting at Faneuil Hall, but thousands of other people did, packing the auditorium to standing-room capacity. The organizers had been imprecise about the purpose of the meeting, announcing only that they intended to "secure justice for a man claimed as a slave by a Virginia kidnapper."[34] They prudently did not say whether they sought justice in court or justice in the streets, thus drawing to the meeting those who would use legal means to defend a free man from kidnapping, as well as those willing to use any means necessary to liberate a captured slave.

The first few speakers were equally vague, linking the fugitive law to the Kansas-Nebraska Act, which just that day had been approved by the Senate. George Russell, the former mayor of Roxbury, began the meeting by denouncing "the boast of the slaveholder . . . that he will catch his slaves under the shadow of Bunker Hill." "We have made compromises," he declared, "until we find that compromise is concession, and concession is degradation." Samuel Gridley Howe continued the theme, telling the cheering crowd that "the South has decreed, in the late passage of the Nebraska bill, that no faith is to be kept with freedom." Then attorney John L. Swift turned the rhetoric up even further. "The compromises are no more—they were murdered by the Nebraska bill. . . . To-morrow Burns will have remained incarcerated [for] three days, and I hope to-morrow to witness in his release the resurrection of liberty."[35]

Everyone wanted Burns released, but nobody had yet said how that was to be accomplished. In fact, the leaders of the Vigilance Committee were divided, although more as to tactics than strategy. Higginson wanted a mid-meeting nighttime assault on the courthouse, and he had gone so far as to hide a crate of axes near an entrance to the building. But his plan had not been effectively communicated to the speakers on the podium, who might well have objected to it in any event. Wendell Phillips, whom Higginson had counted upon to lead the charge that night, instead called for the question to be settled "at the Court House to-morrow morning," when it would be determined "whether we shall adhere to the case of Shadrach or the case of Sims." Theodore Parker drew loud cries of "No! No!" when he addressed the assembly as "fellow subjects of Virginia," but the shouts of protest turned to cheers when he reported that twenty city policemen had refused "to lift a finger in support of the slave catchers." Lamenting that slavery had trampled the Constitution, Parker extolled the higher law. "It is in your hands and your arms," he told the crowd, "and you can put that in execution, just when you see fit." "There is a means, and there is an end," he exhorted the crowd. "Liberty is the end, and sometimes peace is not the means towards it."[36]

Then Parker called upon the meeting to "adjourn to meet in Court Square to-morrow morning at 9 o'clock," only to be interrupted by excited voices yelling, "No, to-night; let us take him out; let us go now."[37] Parker was distressed by the rash call to arms. Not realizing that the demand for immediate action was part of Higginson's plan, he tried to blunt the rebellion by calling for a show of hands, hoping that cooler heads would prevail. But half the audience raised their hands in support of each alternative, with angry cries now coming from both sides.

There was confusion among those on the platform and bewilderment in the hall. After some hesitancy, Wendell Phillips stepped forward again. "Do not balk the effort of to-morrow by foolish conduct to-night," he pleaded. "The zeal that won't keep till to-morrow will never free a slave." For a moment, it seemed as though the meeting would be able to proceed to an orderly conclusion, but then one of Higginson's allies shouted loudly from a position near the entrance to the hall, "Mr. Chairman, I am just informed that a mob of negroes is in Court Square attempting to rescue Burns. I move we adjourn to Court Square."[38] The hall dissolved in chaos, as men rushed to the door.

Higginson and Stowell had stationed themselves at the courthouse, along with Lewis Hayden and about twenty others. In addition to Higginson's axes, many of the men were armed with knives and pistols. They had also appropriated a stout timber from a nearby construction site, which they planned to use as a battering ram. Expecting numerous reinforcements at any moment, the small force waited nervously in the shadows near the eastern entrance to the building.

Surprisingly, the perimeter of the courthouse was not guarded, perhaps because the Massachusetts Supreme Court was holding an evening session and it was necessary to allow "ordinary visitors [to] pass freely." Inside the building, however, Marshal Freeman had posted a contingent of about fifty armed men, including a number of temporary deputies specially recruited for the purpose. Some of Freeman's guards were laborers and local police officers, but others were petty criminals, "bullies, blacklegs, convicts [and] fire-lighters." Freeman himself was also in the courthouse that night, conferring with Suttle and U.S. Attorney Benjamin F. Hallett about plans for the next day's hearing.[39]

At about 9:30 p.m., Higginson finally heard footsteps coming from the direction of Faneuil Hall. Then he saw a "rush of running figures, like the sweep of a wave [coming] round the corner of Court Square." At first he was elated. This was the time "for the trap to be sprung." Within moments, however, his excitement turned to disappointment. The crowd was much smaller than he anticipated, perhaps five hundred people in all, many of them looking far less than resolute as they meandered into the square. Worse yet, the leaders of the

Faneuil Hall meeting were nowhere to be seen. Instead, lamented Higginson, "we had the froth and scum of the meeting, the fringe of idlers on its edge."[40] Higginson did not realize it at the time, but a bottleneck at the door had prevented Phillips and Parker, and others on whom he could have depended for support, from even leaving the hall until the "idlers" from the back at the room had already reached the courthouse.

The arrival of even a feckless crowd was sure to alarm the guards, so Higginson and Stowell believed they had no choice but to begin the assault at once. Stowell distributed the axes, while Higginson and Lewis Hayden took hold of the construction beam and began battering at the courthouse door. After several blows, one of the hinges broke, leaving the door swinging loose. With only room for one man to squeeze through the doorway, Higginson looked over to Hayden, who "sprang in first." Higginson immediately followed his "black ally," as did Martin Stowell and another black man. They were met by several rows of deputies, under Marshal Freeman's personal command, swinging truncheons and waving swords.

The rescuers were driven against a wall by the deputies' fierce clubbing. Higginson was beaten about the head and face, sustaining a serious gash on his chin. Stowell and Hayden stepped back through the door, each firing a pistol shot to cover Higginson's retreat. One of the defenders—an Irish immigrant named James Batchelder, who worked as a truckman on the Boston wharf—fell to the ground with a wound in his groin.

Emerging through the doorway, Higginson attempted to rally his troops. "You cowards, will you desert us now?" he called to those who had held back.[41] But the courthouse door was now fastened shut, and the Boston police had arrived on the scene. Ax in hand, Stowell made one last assault on the door, but he was quickly arrested (along with eight others), leaving the rest of the crowd disheartened and dispirited. By then several of the Faneuil Hall leaders had arrived, but it was obvious that the attack had failed and there was nothing to do but go home.

All of Boston was grim on Saturday morning. James Batchelder had died in the hallway where he fell, causing grief to his wife and children and fury among local and federal officials. The mayor of Boston called out two companies of the state militia to defend the courthouse (in possible violation of the Latimer law, although preserving the peace and protecting public property probably did not fall under the law's prohibition against assisting in the return of fugitives). Marshal Freeman summoned two companies of U.S. Marines to join the guard.[42] By dawn Court Square had become an armed camp, with hundreds of officers and men standing watch.

As soon as the telegraph office opened, Freeman wired President Pierce, seeking authorization for his actions:

> In consequence of an attack upon the Court House last night, for the purpose of rescuing a fugitive slave under arrest, and in which one of my own guards was killed, I have availed myself of the resources of the United States . . . and now have two companies of troops . . . stationed in the Court House. Every thing is now quiet. The attack was repulsed by my own guard.[43]

Pierce quickly replied, "Your conduct is approved. The law must be executed." If it had not been clear before, it was now beyond argument that the Boston courthouse had become a federally protected slave pen. "The identity of interests between the Southern slave power and the national government could not have been more vividly exemplified."[44]

No one detested the Fugitive Slave Act more than Richard Henry Dana, and no one was more troubled to see Boston's courthouse under the control of the "hirelings of the U.S. marshal." Nonetheless, Dana was horrified when he learned about the riot, and he was especially shocked by Higginson's involvement. It was one thing for a crowd of blacks to rescue Shadrach Minkins—an action he had more or less approved three years earlier—but he had "hardly expected a married man, a clergyman, & a man of education to lead the mob."[45] It was far better, Dana believed, for gentlemen to resolve these matters in court.

~∽ **10** ∽~

THE HEIGHT OF CRUELTY

A nthony Burns was brought into court shortly after 9:00 a.m. on Saturday, May 27, 1854. His jailers had probably informed him of the previous night's skirmish, although none of his would-be rescuers had gotten within two stories of his makeshift cell. In any event, Burns surely realized that he was under even heavier guard than he had been two days earlier. He was still manacled, and now he was surrounded by "two or three brutal-looking men" on each side, with four or five more seated directly in front of him, "with pistols and bludgeons lurking in their pockets," only "half concealed from the offended eyes of the spectators." Suttle and Brent were there, accompanied by attorneys Edward Parker and Seth Thomas, both of whom were ostentatiously carrying guns.[1]

Burns's own counsel, Richard Dana and Charles Ellis, did not arrive for another hour. They were delayed first by a strategy meeting in Dana's office, and then by the series of blockades set up between the square and the courtroom. The two attorneys encountered guards at the doorway, in the lobby, at the foot of the stairs, and on two landings, each time being required to reestablish their right to proceed to the courtroom. Taking absolutely no chances with another rescue, Marshal Freeman had given strict orders to limit the number of spectators, issuing permits only to public officials, the press, and a few favored citizens. By the time court convened, there were still many empty seats in the small courtroom, although Theodore Parker, Robert Morris, and Leonard Grimes had been able to talk their way past the sentries.

Commissioner Loring called the proceeding to order, but Charles Ellis immediately requested another continuance. He and Dana had been formally retained only the previous afternoon, Ellis explained, which had not given them time to prepare a proper defense. In addition, Ellis also argued that the atmosphere of violence prevented reasoned deliberation.

> It is not fit that we should proceed while the courtroom is packed
> with armed men, and all the avenues to it are filled with soldiery,

making it difficult for the friends of the prisoner to obtain access to him.[2]

Ellis's implicit argument was that the extraordinary show of military force placed tremendous pressure on the court to rule in Suttle's favor. "He reminded the Commissioner that he acted as judge and jury in this case, and he ought to be able to say that he had given every chance for preparation [and] for reflection."[3]

Stepping forward for the first time in the proceeding, Seth Thomas belittled Ellis's request for additional time. The fugitive had already "admitted that he had no defence to make and only wanted time to think what to do," and counsel for the prisoner surely realized "that they had not any substantial ground of defence." It was obvious that Suttle's evidence could establish "property in this man," and therefore "the only duty of your Honor is to grant a certificate of removal to a place where the case is to be decided."

And then Thomas went much further, virtually accusing opposing counsel of responsibility for Batchelder's death. Referring to the "excitement last night and those engaged in it," he wondered whether Dana and Ellis did "not feel that the blood of a fellow man rests upon their heads." Another delay, he implied, might only lead to another attempt at rescue. "It is in effect an attempt to render this law invalid. It is no less treason to defeat the operation of this law than it would be to go to the other end of the court house and rescue a man convicted for murder."[4]

Dana was appalled by Thomas's accusation, and he rose immediately to the challenge. Of course there had been an earlier request for a continuance, he said, given the "facts of the arrest of Burns, at night, under false pretence, and his being hurried to the court house, which has not been kept as a jail, but as a slave pen." Point by point, Dana explained just how unfair and oppressive Burns's treatment had been. He had been terrorized by his arrest; Marshal Freeman had excluded visitors; Suttle had intimidated him in the courtroom; he now faced the possibility of sale in the New Orleans slave market. And yet the only question now before the court was "whether he shall be hurried into a trial now, or shall have reasonable time to prepare for it." Dana then decried Thomas's charge that delay might lead to another "disturbance." "That is an argument that can be addressed to no court, for it is a confession of weakness—that the law is not strong, and therefore the man must suffer."[5]

Commissioner Loring responded favorably, stating that he "looked upon Burns as one who is yet to be regarded as a freeman [because] he knew of no proof yet submitted that he was to be regarded as anything else." The requested delay was a short one, and there was no likelihood that important testimony would become unavailable over the next few days. He regretted the "excitement in the community," but he could not "consider it in this case." It was the court's sole duty to "look at the rights of the parties and see that justice is done," and he therefore granted a continuance until Monday, May 29, at eleven o'clock in the morning.[6]

Dana was extremely pleased with his morning's work, and contemptuous of opposing counsel's efforts to block the delay. He thought that young Edward Parker had seemed almost "ashamed of what he was doing" and Seth Thomas's manner had been "petty [and] mean." Never modest about his own talents, Dana believed that he had made a "magnificent speech" and had "never spoke[n] more to my satisfaction in my life."[7] Dana's argument had indeed been masterful, but it is hard to imagine that he had really presented the speech of a lifetime in support of a rather routine request for a continuance. In any case, Dana seems to have been so fully occupied with self-appreciation that he missed the most significant occurrence in court that day.

Toward the end of the session, Edward Parker had attempted to blunt the suggestion that Suttle intended to sell Burns in a distant slave market. In fact, "the claimant had consented to selling him here," he told Judge Loring. Neither Dana nor Ellis responded to that proposal but Rev. Leonard Grimes realized that Burns had been offered his freedom, if only at a price.

As soon as court recessed, Grimes approached Edward Parker and Suttle to find out whether they were serious about selling Burns. At Parker's urging, Suttle said that he was in fact ready to sell his slave. Commissioner Loring's adjournment, coupled with the court's description of Burns as a "freeman," indicated for the first time that Suttle might actually lose the case, which had become increasingly burdensome and conceivably dangerous (given the ever-present possibility of another rescue attempt). Parker thus informed Grimes that a sale could indeed be arranged, but only at the exorbitant price of $1,200, and only if it could be completed that very day. Grimes agreed to the terms. "Between this time and ten o'clock to-night, I'll have the money ready for you; have the emancipation papers ready for me at that hour."[8]

Grimes was being optimistic. As the minister of a poor black church, he had no easy access to such a great amount of money, so he set about raising the funds from wealthy white merchants and businessmen. Grimes encountered some resistance—especially from abolitionists who were unwilling to legitimate slavery, even if it meant freedom for a slave—but he eventually succeeded in obtaining pledges for the full amount. By earlier arrangement, he met attorneys Parker and Thomas at Judge Loring's office, where the commissioner drafted a deed of manumission.

By 11:00 p.m. all that remained was the actual payment and the release of Burns. To that end, the four men repaired to Marshal Freeman's office, where they expected to consummate the deal. Instead they found that Freeman was huddled with U.S. Attorney Benjamin F. Hallett, who vigorously protested the transaction. Hallett raised a series of specious legal objections to the sale— breaking off the hearing would jeopardize federal reimbursement for his expenses; a Massachusetts statute prohibited the sale of slaves—all of which were refuted by Loring and Grimes. But Hallett's real objection was political. One of his men had been killed trying to enforce the Fugitive Slave Act, and he was unwilling to see the law circumvented by a private contract. Once a certificate of removal had been granted, Hallett said, he might even be willing to contribute to the purchase of Burns. But he would not allow Burns to be freed without a hearing.

Loring and Grimes were unconvinced, but Hallett held a trump card. Gesturing toward a clock on the wall, the district attorney pointed out that it was now past midnight. No legal sale could take place, "as the Sabbath had already commenced."[9] Loring assured Grimes that the sale could be completed the following Monday morning at 8:00 a.m., but the disappointed clergyman probably realized that the opportunity had been lost.

Although he was aware of the negotiations, Dana had remained aloof throughout the day. He did not contribute to the fund, although he did remark to Grimes that the price seemed too high (he had learned in an interview with his client that Suttle had insured Burns for only $800). In a curious way, Dana's interest had aligned with U.S. Attorney Hallett's. Dana had undertaken Burns's representation in the hope of establishing that no fugitive could be legally removed from Massachusetts. Paying a ransom, however, would have conceded Suttle's lawful right to sell a human being in Boston. And worse, the availability of cash sales might actually encourage other slaveholders to

pursue their property. After all, it would be easier to sell a slave to abolitionists than it was to endure the cost and uncertainty of a prolonged hearing.
Theodore Parker and William Lloyd Garrison held the same view. Their goal
was to deter slave catching by making it risky and expensive, not to reward it
with payoffs.

Theodore Parker made the Burns case the subject of his Sunday morning
sermon, which drew the largest attendance in Boston. In front of four thousand people, Reverend Parker inveighed against the Fugitive Slave Act and
the Kansas-Nebraska Bill. Invoking the higher law, he castigated his fellow
citizens for standing by when Thomas Sims was returned to slavery in 1851. If
only Boston had said, "Thomas Sims shall not be carried off; and forcibly or
peacefully, by the majority of the great body of men had resisted it, no kidnapper would have come here again." Parker expressed no sympathy for the slain
James Batchelder, accusing him of assisting in the kidnapping of a fellow
man. "He liked the business of enslaving a man, and has gone to render an
account to God for his gratuitous work."[10]

Parker saved his harshest words for Commissioner Edward Loring, whose
only formal rulings thus far had been in favor of the defense. All of the confusion and excitement was Loring's fault, said Parker, presumably because
the commissioner had issued a warrant to Suttle in the first place. "He knew
the consequences of stealing a man in Boston." By Parker's lights, Loring had
acted immorally simply by holding the office of fugitive slave commissioner.
"Edward Greely Loring, Judge of Probate for the county of Suffolk, in the state
of Massachusetts, Fugitive Slave Bill Commissioner of the United States ... I
charge you with the death of that man who was murdered on last Friday
night. He was your fellow servant in kidnapping."[11]

Loring was made aware of Parker's harsh words and the thinly veiled demand for his resignation from the commissioner's position. The judge would
respond in due time.

—————

Dana had enormous confidence in his skills as an attorney, but he was far
from sanguine when the Burns hearing finally began in earnest on Monday
morning. Every aspect of the case seemed to favor the claimant. Dana's meetings with Burns had not disclosed any promising lines of defense, and the
hoped-for "flaw in the papers" remained elusive. Suttle's documents from the

Virginia court were conclusive under the Fugitive Slave Act, and there was virtually no hope that Judge Loring would keep them out of evidence. As Dana later reflected,

> We examined the record, and could find no flaw in it, on which we could rely with any confidence. . . . The Supreme Court of Massachusetts and the Circuit Court had pronounced the law constitutional, and sustained the jurisdiction of the Commissioner. On the point of identity, there was no hope of a defence. Col. Suttle and Mr. Brent were present, who had known him from a boy, and the latter was a competent witness. Burns had admitted the facts in the presence of Brent and the officers. . . . We had no reasonable hope of a successful defence.[12]

The great difficulty for the defense, of course, was the fact that the prisoner was unquestionably Suttle's slave, a reality that Dana and Ellis essentially conceded every time they referred to their client as Anthony Burns. Nonetheless, there was always the possibility that figurative lightning might strike, so Dana readied himself to take advantage of any errors in the claimant's case.

Before any witnesses could be called, however, Charles Ellis objected to Marshal Freeman's militarization of the courthouse. U.S. troops had blocked the hallways, he protested, barring friends of the prisoner and "pack[ing] the court room with friends of the law." Loring quickly brushed off the objection as an irrelevant delaying tactic. "The examination must proceed," he ordered.[13]

That was not good enough for U.S. Attorney Hallett, who jumped to his feet and "began to harangue the commissioner." Marshal Freeman's conduct had been unfairly maligned, fumed Hallett, and he felt bound to defend the "measures taken to preserve order in and around this court."[14] Loring was not interested in an extended debate on the issue. He interrupted Hallett and reminded the government attorney that the court had already denied Ellis's motion.

Hallett, however, had taken Ellis's comments quite personally. One federal deputy was already dead, and now the defense attorneys were objecting to security precautions. He angrily denied that the marshal had packed the courtroom. The soldiers were present only to preserve order and execute the laws.

Again Judge Loring interrupted. "Mr. Hallett," he said, "these remarks are irrelevant and entirely out of order."

And again Hallett refused to take his seat. His voice rising, he denounced "the men who committed murder that night" and those who continued to incite "riot and bloodshed." Some of the latter, he charged, were present in the courtroom and were "claimed by Mr. Ellis as his friends." How dare the defense question the necessity of armed guards? "The president of the United States has approved of this course."[15]

At that, Commissioner Loring realized that the wisest course was simply to allow Hallett to exhaust himself. He "sank back in his seat with a helpless air" and waited for the browbeating to end. Hallett, however, was not merely a blowhard. Formerly an antislavery man himself, he had now cast his lot with the pro-South Pierce administration. Still politically ambitious, he wanted to make sure his superiors in Washington recognized his efforts in the Burns case, and that meant making his presence known in court. Dana considered Hallett a petty despot whose "incredible ignorance of law [and] mock dignity" were an embarrassment to the bar, but he held his peace until Hallett relinquished the floor and allowed the trial itself to proceed.[16]

Edward Parker approached the bench and asked whether he needed to reintroduce the evidence that had been presented the previous week. Loring replied that it would be unnecessary, but Dana objected. That hearing had taken place when Burns was unrepresented and, in any event, defense counsel had no notes of the testimony. It was only fair, he argued, "that the examination should now commence as though the arrest had just been made." The court agreed, and directed Parker to re-read the complaint and warrant into the record.[17]

Dana was not just stalling for time. The entire defense strategy depended on locating a technical defect or inconsistency in the claimant's case, which in turn required extremely close attention to all of the details. He did not want to rely on his memory (or the court's) concerning the earlier testimony and, besides, it was at least possible that Suttle's key witness would contradict himself if required to tell his story twice.

In a full-dress trial, a plaintiff would ordinarily begin by presenting an opening statement. Suttle's attorneys passed up that opportunity as if to emphasize the summary nature of proceedings under the Fugitive Slave Act. Instead they immediately called William Brent back to the witness stand. Brent testified that he was a merchant in Richmond and that he had known Charles Suttle for many years. He identified "the black man in court" as Suttle's slave, Anthony Burns. For the previous two years, Brent had acted as Suttle's agent, hiring Burns to various employers in Richmond, most recently to Mr. Millspaugh. "There was no other Anthony Burns about the places resorted to by Suttle," and the fugitive could be recognized by the "scar upon his right cheek and a cut across his right hand." Brent had last seen Burns in Virginia on March 20, four days before "he was missing."[18]

All of the details were repetitive of Brent's earlier testimony, except the last one. The witness had not previously mentioned having seen Burns on March 20, either because he did not think it was important or because he did not think his testimony could possibly be challenged by the unrepresented slave. Claimant's counsel had not asked Brent to elaborate about the facts of Burns's disappearance, but Richard Dana took careful note of the dates, realizing—if no one else did—that the witness might have just given him exactly the opening he was looking for. For the time being, however, Dana remained silent. He would have to investigate the case more thoroughly before he could make use of Brent's promising slipup and, in any event, the witness had not yet completed his direct examination.

Brent's testimony then moved on to "the statements of the prisoner since his arrest." That was the point at which Dana had intervened in the first hearing, and defense counsel had no intention of allowing the evidence this time. Ellis objected on the ground that the Fugitive Slave Act expressly provided that "in no trial or hearing under this act shall the testimony of such alleged fugitive be admitted in evidence."

Seth Thomas replied that Burns's "admissions and confessions were a very different thing from testimony." Of course a fugitive could not testify under oath on his own behalf—and neither could the claimant, for that matter—because he was an interested party to the suit. But that rule did not exclude evidence of his admissions, any more than it would bar the confession of an accused criminal.

Dana was incensed by Thomas's argument. It was "the height of cruelty to the prisoner," he said, "to take advantage of the only power he had under this law, that of speech, to his detriment." Suttle should be limited to asserting his own rights, without appropriating for himself, through the use of "these alleged confessions, a portion of the prisoner's."[19] Furthermore, he argued, the court should consider the coercive nature of the interrogation. Any statement from an alleged slave to his master "is more likely to be deceptive, or wrongfully obtained or used, than of value to justice."[20]

Thomas retorted that a prisoner's admissions should always be admissible, "unless there is proof of some threat or promise."[21] He suggested that Brent's testimony should be accepted *de bene esse*—that is, provisionally—so he could show that Burns had spoken voluntarily and without coercion.

Loring agreed with Thomas's reasoning. The word "testimony" in the statute referred only to evidence given by a witness in court, and not to confessions or admissions. If there had been any coercion, Burns's own counsel could bring that out through cross-examination. Loring's crucial ruling may have been a correct reading of the law at the time but it was terribly unfair to Anthony Burns. Brent would now be permitted to put words in Burns's mouth without fear of contradiction, given that the defendant himself was barred from testifying. As legal scholar and historian Paul Finkelman has pointed out, Loring was committed only to procedural impartiality—the "forms of a fair hearing"—but not to substantive justice.[22]

Allowed to continue, Brent first related Burns's explanation of his presence in Boston. He had not intended to run away, but "being at work on board a vessel, and getting tired, fell asleep when the vessel sailed with him on board." Next Brent described the exchange when Suttle first confronted Burns on the evening of his arrest. Burns spoke first, according to the witness, as soon as Suttle entered the room:

"How do you do, Master Charles?"

Not bothering to exchange pleasantries, Suttle replied with a question of his own. "Did I ever whip you, Anthony?"

"No."

"Did I ever hire you where you did not want to go?"

"No."

"Did you ever ask me for money when it was not given to you?"

"No."

"Did I not, when you were sick, take my bed from my own house for you?"

"Yes," said Burns, as bidden. Then he recognized Brent and said, "How do you do, Master William?"[23]

Burns had also indicated his willingness to return with Suttle to Virginia, although Brent could not recall his exact words. At one point Dana objected to Brent's use of the word "slave" to describe Burns, arguing that it was a legal conclusion. Ever alert to procedural niceties, Judge Loring agreed and directed the witness "not to state any person to be a slave without corroborative legal evidence." As a consequence of the court's ruling, Brent described several circumstances that supported Suttle's claim of ownership (though straining to avoid using the prohibited word): Burns's mother and sister had lived with Suttle; Brent had given a bond to Suttle when he hired Burns; Suttle had once mortgaged Burns in order to raise money; Burns had had to display a written pass when he traveled to work in Richmond.[24]

Much of Brent's testimony had the ring of truth. For example, it was entirely likely that Burns had explained his escape by inventing a story about falling asleep, and the facts about Burns's family and employment were plainly accurate. On the other hand, some of his testimony was clearly contrived, or at least closely choreographed. It strains credulity to believe that Suttle had no harsh words for the captured fugitive, or that his only concern was to establish his kindness toward the runaway. Suttle had certainly done his best to extract a usable admission from Burns, acting no doubt on the sound advice of his attorney. But Brent had just as certainly omitted anything that suggested intimidation or pressure on the slave owner's part.

As was typical in nineteenth-century trial practice—when defense lawyers had no opportunity to obtain witness statements in advance—the cross-examination of Brent was "probing but unfocused." In the hope of uncovering something helpful, Charles Ellis began with a series of open-ended questions designed to draw out additional information from the witness. Did Brent own slaves himself? Yes, he had "acquired" some by marriage and had inherited others from his father. Had he ever traded in slaves? Not exactly; he had purchased several in 1841 or 1842 but had never sold any, and "further than that had never traded slaves." In response to other questions, Brent explained that Suttle had mortgaged Burns to John M. Tolson of Stafford County, Virginia, and that Burns had been leased to Millspaugh since January of the current year. Brent added that he had written to Suttle about three days after Burns was discovered missing.[25]

Ellis next asked Brent whether he had been paid to accompany Suttle to Boston, pressing him for details. The witness replied that Suttle had "said nothing about paying my expenses or remunerating me for coming" but had come "with him [as] a volunteer, as a friend." He had never before gone "on any similar expedition . . . on any matter of an alleged runaway." Taking one last stab at painting the witness as a mercenary, Ellis asked whether there had been any written agreement between Brent and Suttle. No, came the answer, "there has been no word or writing between us relative to any compensation."[26]

Ellis next turned to the confrontation between Suttle and Burns on the night of the arrest. Brent denied that Burns had been manacled that evening, and continued to claim that the prisoner had blurted out a greeting to "Master Charles." He denied that Suttle had warned Burns that he had "better consent to go back." In fact, Brent now added, Suttle had specifically advised Burns that "I make you no promises and I make you no threats." That last assertion was an obvious paraphrase of Seth Thomas's argument in favor of admitting Burns's "confession" so long as there was no proof of "some threat or promise." It is doubtful that Brent could have picked up on that point by himself, and more likely that Thomas had effectively coached the witness. In either case, Brent had succeeded in perfecting the foundation for Burns's admissions.

Dana took over the cross-examination at that point. He attempted to show that Brent—even if he was not being paid—was contractually obligated to assist Suttle in reclaiming his slave. The witness was evasive. He did not know whether the "bond between me and Suttle as to the hiring of Anthony is [still] in existence." He also insisted that he was "not responsible for Anthony's connection with Millspaugh, other than as an agent, which ceased when he escaped." Brent did admit, however, that he had not recounted the entire conversation between Suttle and Burns, but had only "answered the questions put to me."[27]

Brent was followed by Caleb Page, a teamster who had been employed in Asa Butman's posse when Burns was arrested. Page had been present in the jury room when Suttle interrogated Burns, and he was able to confirm the discussion "relative to the giving of money, flogging, [and] the use of the bed when sick." He was not close enough to hear all of the conversation, however, and he did not repeat Brent's claim that there had been "no promises or threats."

Page was the claimant's final witness. Once he left the stand, Edward Parker offered the record of the Virginia court, showing that Anthony Burns "owed service and labor" to Suttle and had "escaped from the state." As required by the federal law, the Virginia transcript also included a description of the missing slave, and Parker invited the commissioner to examine "the marks upon the prisoner, to see if they were at variance with those described in the document, to prove the identity." Loring said that he "perceived the scars on the cheek and hand, and took cognizance with his eye of the height of the prisoner." He asked whether defense counsel wanted to "have him brought to me for further examination," but Ellis declined.[28]

Dana did, however, object to the admissibility of the Virginia court record, as well as to a volume of the Revised Code of Virginia that Parker had offered as technical proof that slavery existed in Virginia. Loring overruled both objections, and Thomas rested the claimant's case, satisfied that his proofs were complete.

Attention now turned to Ellis and Dana. What could they offer in the way of a defense?

For the third time in as many court sessions, defense counsel asked the commissioner for a delay, this time on the ground that they needed time to confer about "the qualification of some expected witnesses." Because it was already nearing 3:00 p.m., Dana was hoping for an adjournment until the following day. Loring, however, was reluctant to grant any delay at all. Dana pressed the issue, citing his need to examine the legal authorities relied upon by Parker and Thomas, and Loring finally consented to a forty-minute recess, ordering court to reconvene at "half-past 3 o'clock."

Unlike the claimant's counsel, the prisoner's attorneys were not about to forgo making an opening statement to the court. Because their legal arguments were complex, built upon an intricate combination of natural law and strict statutory interpretation, they could not pass up a chance to explain their position to Judge Loring. They also had a broader audience to consider. Although courtroom oration was not much use to Charles Suttle—he would have been happy to return home with his slave, never to be heard of again—Anthony Burns had become the symbol of a movement (with or without his specific consent). There would never be a better opportunity to drive home the evils of the Fugitive Slave Act, the weakness of its constitutional foundation, and the necessity of political opposition to the intrusions of the slave power.

The most important consideration, however, was simply the need to occupy the rest of the day. As matters stood on Monday afternoon, the defense had no witnesses to call and no evidence to present. Burns himself was disqualified from testifying; nor could he have seriously challenged the gist of Suttle's evidence.

Fortunately, Brent had opened a fissure in the claimant's case that morning when he volunteered that he had seen Burns in Richmond on March 20. In fact, Burns had actually arrived in Boston on or about March 1—as he had earlier informed his lawyers—making Brent's sworn statement an impossibility. If that fact could now be proven, the discrepancy might be fatal to Suttle's claim. Although the Virginia court record was conclusive proof that someone named Anthony Burns was an escaped slave, Brent's in-court identification was the only evidence that the prisoner was indeed the person named in the warrant. Thus, undermining the reliability of Brent's testimony, especially on the accuracy of his identification, might well be the key to Burns's freedom.

But how could counsel establish Burns's presence in Boston at the beginning of March? Brent's dubious claim had first surfaced only late that morning, leaving little opportunity to locate any witnesses who could contradict him. Burns had no doubt provided his lawyers with the name of William Jones—the black man who had helped him find work washing windows—but it is unlikely that he knew the names of the men who had employed him at the Mattapan Works or at City Hall, much less whether his white bosses would remember or be able to identify him.

Consequently, the defense had considerable work to do before they could begin presenting their case. They had to locate and interview as many potential witnesses as possible and then, if Burns's story panned out, persuade them to testify in support of a fugitive slave. Nor could counsel tell Judge Loring why they needed an overnight recess—other than to explain elliptically that they had to explore "the qualification of some expected witnesses"—because that would have alerted Seth Thomas to the flaw in his case, which would have allowed him simply to recall Brent and remedy the mistake. Thus, the only solution was to temporize, extending the opening statement for the rest of the afternoon until the evening's real work could be done.

The assignment fell to Charles Ellis, and temporize he did. Ellis began his opening statement with yet another lengthy pitch for delay. "We need time," he pleaded. "The prisoner needs it, and has reason for it." Ellis complained that he had been given only a day to prepare for a trial that would "decide more than a man's life, when, if it involved only his coat, the wheels of justice could not be turned in months." Access to the prisoner had been denied, the law library had been locked, and it had been "next to impossible even for counsel to enter the Court Room, through the military forces." All of that was true enough, but it was not about to sway Judge Loring, who had in fact granted several delays (and had been subjected to some of the same indignities upon entering the building). Although the spectators may have appreciated Ellis's litany of grievances, the court was unmoved.

Ellis next sought to impress upon Loring the enormity of the judgment he was about to make. "We stand on the presumption, of which your Honor did well to remind [claimant's] counsel, of freedom and innocence." In such a case, "the instinctive feeling of common fairness and humanity" and the "plain principles of justice and law" require that presumption to apply "with multiplied force." Not quite willing to invoke the doctrine of higher law, Ellis implored Loring to weigh all questions of law and fact with "greater care" due to the greater "chances of error and the danger of its result," and to require the claimant to prove his case beyond a possible doubt."[29]

But only so much time could be devoted to high-minded generalities before Ellis would eventually have to address the specifics of the case. Everyone in the courtroom wondered whether there would be any factual substance to the defense, but Ellis did not yet know whether any witnesses would be available to place Burns in Boston at a time when Brent swore to have seen him in Richmond.

For the time being, he could only make an abstract promise: "Before proceeding with our evidence or stating it, we submit that, on their own showing, [Suttle and his lawyers] have no case." He disputed the validity of the Virginia court record, the adequacy of the warrant under which Burns was arrested, and even the proof—by way of a statute book—that slavery was legal under Virginia law. He also challenged the reliability of Burns's confession, and pointed out that it would have been inadmissible in Virginia under a ruling of the state supreme court:

> The master's will is the slave's will. All his acts, all his sayings are
> made with a view to propitiate his master. His confessions are made,
> not from a love of truth, not from a sense of duty, not to speak a

falsehood but to please his master. . . . We therefore more often get the wishes of the master, or the slave's belief of his wishes, than the truth.[30]

Defense lawyers are often compelled to take seemingly paradoxical positions, but Ellis's argument was more self-contradictory than most. He virtually admitted that Burns was a slave, in order to argue that the prisoner's confession of slavery should not be accepted by the court.

There was, however, a consistent underlying logic to the defense case. Ellis and Dana essentially conceded *sub silentio* that Burns was a slave, while arguing that the formal evidence of that fact was nonetheless insufficient to warrant sending him back into slavery. Moreover, they argued that the necessary quantum of evidence had to be "multiplied" many times over because of the moral weight of the court's decision. In other words, they were asking the commissioner to ignore or evade the undeniable purpose of the Fugitive Slave Act—which was to make renditions easier and more straightforward—in order to adhere to more fundamental considerations of freedom and justice (although they could not call it "higher law").

Thus, it was not mere obsequiousness that caused Ellis to praise Judge Loring's reputation for decency, which stood in sharp contrast to Commissioner George Ticknor Curtis's reputation as a slave hound. "We are thankful to have this case before your honor, rather than—before your honor . . . because we do feel that you judge as you would be judged." Decorum prevented him from criticizing Commissioner Curtis by name, but there could be no mistaking the meaning of his freighted pause. Ellis recognized that Loring faced a dilemma in deciding how strictly to enforce the fugitive law—"whilst holding a post, you feel bound to do its duties," he observed—but he promised to show the court a "way of escape, to see if any light can be thrown into this mass of blackness" created by the claimant's case.[31]

The commissioner's predicament, according to Ellis, was not caused by the defense, but rather by Suttle's attorneys, who sought to sully the court with the taint of slavery. In Boston fugitive rendition was the least part of a U.S. commissioner's job, which consisted almost entirely of accepting affidavits and attesting to documents in civil cases. Loring might easily have spent an entire career without once seeing a fugitive slave, if only Thomas and Parker had not imposed this case upon him. It was no surprise, said Ellis, that the notorious

Seth Thomas would appear for a slaveholder. "All expected to see [him] here." But Edward Parker was different. "The gentleman who for the first time appears in such a case, and whom it has been my privilege to call a friend, I did not think of meeting." As for himself, Ellis said "that sooner than lay my hand to the work of aiding in such a case, I would see it whither, and rather than speak one word for a slave claimant I would be struck dumb forever."[32]

That admonition was ostensibly aimed at opposing counsel, but it might just as well have been directed at Judge Loring himself. The most ardent abolitionists—William Lloyd Garrison, Wendell Phillips, Theodore Parker—called upon men of integrity to refrain from any involvement whatsoever with slaveholding. Just as they had declined to participate in ransoming Burns, they called upon judges likewise to refuse to preside over rendition hearings.

Ellis, however, was not about to approach that ideological precipice in his plea to Judge Loring, at least not directly. "Not only have I never opposed the [fugitive] law," he assured the court, "but I have done something to stay resistance to it. I stand here for the prisoner under and not against the law." Rather than demand that the commissioner resign his position or abort the hearing, Ellis proposed to provide him with a third way out. He could release Burns from Suttle's ownership while still formally adhering to the law as written. All it would take was sufficient humanity on Loring's part, and enough evidence to raise a nominal doubt.[33]

At the end of Monday's session, however, Ellis still did not know what he would be able to say, or do, the following day.

Even as Charles Ellis was concluding his remarks on Monday afternoon, others were busy tracking down witnesses who could support the claim that Burns had been living in Boston since early March. William Jones would not have been hard to find. He had attended the Friday-night meeting at Faneuil Hall and he had been in Court Square at some point following the riot. On Saturday he had attempted to attend the rendition hearing, but he was turned away by the marshal. Jones finally made at least visual contact with Burns on Sunday afternoon, when the prisoner was briefly allowed to lean out of the window and wave to his supporters.

Jones first spoke to the defense team at some point on Monday and he met again with Ellis or Dana on Tuesday morning. Jones also acted as agent for the defense lawyers. He contacted witnesses and supplied the attorneys with the names of three or four men who had seen Burns working at the Mattapan Works, several of whom also presented themselves at Ellis's office early Tuesday morning.

With Burns's alibi witnesses now in the fold, Ellis was able to complete his opening statement when court reconvened on Tuesday. Announcing that "the prisoner . . . has a case of his own," Ellis reminded the court that Brent had sworn "clearly and positively" that he had seen Burns in Richmond on March 20. Then Ellis dropped a bombshell:

> We shall call a number of witnesses to show, fixing as I think the man and the time beyond question, that the prisoner was in Boston on the first of March last, and has been here ever since up to the time of this seizure. . . . This is our defence.[34]

William Jones was called as the first defense witness. Suttle and his supporters had no reason to doubt Brent's testimony, and they had no idea that Burns had arrived in Boston several months before the date of his alleged escape. Suspecting an abolitionist conspiracy behind the prisoner's alibi, U.S. Attorney Benjamin Hallett made his skepticism known when Jones took the stand. "Here comes a witness that [Theodore] Parker has got to perjure himself," he whispered to a friend, although loudly enough to be overheard across the room.[35]

Jones's direct examination was brief and to the point. He described his first meeting with Burns on the street and their five days of window cleaning at the Mattapan Works. Jones had agreed to pay Burns 8 cents per window and had given him $1.50 at the end of the job. Burns complained that "I hadn't settled up with him right," so he "went to the clerk about it." Jones explained that he was able to remember the details of payment and the dates of employment because he kept a memorandum book. He handed his book to counsel so that the entry could be verified.[36]

Seth Thomas was unprepared for Jones's testimony, having only learned of Burns's proposed alibi earlier that morning. With no good way to contradict or impeach the witness, Thomas instead chose to question him at great length about the precise details of his story, hoping to catch him making inconsistent or implausible claims. Thomas therefore asked Jones to name the day of the week on which he'd first met Burns, to provide the exact place and time of the meeting, to describe Burns's clothing, to detail their itinerary as they searched for work, to describe the weather, and to name all the people to whom he introduced Burns. He also questioned Jones's involvement in the Faneuil Hall meeting and the deadly events at the courthouse on Friday night.

It was a rough grilling, lasting three times as long as the direct examination and marked by Thomas's conspicuous disrespect for the "colored witness" whose testimony he regarded "as the falsehood of a perjurer." Despite Thomas's bullying demeanor and his "fixed stare of contemptuous incredulity," Jones held up surprisingly well, rather adeptly turning away question after question. What was Burns wearing when they first met? "He had on lightish pants; can't describe his dress more particularly because it wasn't my business to examine his dress." What was the weather like that day? "It was a little cold; there might have been snow on the ground, but I don't recollect." What was Jones doing in Court Square on Friday night? "I stayed at the Court House all night Friday night, me and a watchman together, protecting the city property."[37]

For all his effort, Thomas managed to extract only one useful piece of evidence during the lengthy cross-examination. Jones testified that after they completed the window-washing job, he and Burns had looked for work at City Hall, where they met with a man named Mr. Gould. Although the information may have seemed insignificant at the time, Thomas would later use it to some advantage during his rebuttal case.

The prisoner's next witness was George Drew, a bookkeeper from the Mattapan Works. He recalled that William Jones and another black man had washed windows at the plant for several days in early March, and he was able to identify Burns as Jones's helper. He confirmed Jones's account of the dispute over Burns's payment, testifying that "Burns came up to me and asked me how much I paid Jones." He was able to fix the payment date as March 4 by looking at an entry in the "cash book."

This time the cross-examination was shorter, perhaps because Edward Parker felt constrained to show more respect for a white witness. Thomas asked Drew how he had come to testify, and whether he knew if Burns had any distinguishing marks. The witness answered that he had been requested to come to court by a "Mr. Stetson," who was not further identified and may have been an employee or friend of Dana's. He had "never noticed the scar" on Burns's right hand.[38]

Dana called three more witnesses from the Mattapan Works, each of whom identified Burns as having worked at the factory in early March. James Whittemore bolstered his own credibility by testifying that he was a member of the city council, a lieutenant of the Pulaski Guard, and a Hunker Whig (which is to say, not an abolitionist or a Free-Soiler). Thomas objected to Whittemore's political affiliation as irrelevant, but Dana persisted and the court ruled it admissible. Whittemore was able to recall seeing Burns specifically on March 8 or 9, because the window washing coincided with his return from a trip to Philadelphia.

H. N. Gilman, a teamster, recognized Burns by the scar on his face, having seen him in the "counting room" shortly after payday at the beginning of the month. Horace Brown had previously been a carpenter at the Mattapan Works but was now a police officer. He had seen Burns cleaning windows "some week or ten days before I left" on March 20. "I have not the slightest doubt about the man," he said, identifying Burns "by his general appearance and by the scar on his face."[39]

Thomas and Parker did their best to cross-examine the defense witnesses, dwelling largely on the manner in which they had come to testify. Two of the witnesses flatly denied being recruited or even approached by the defense. Whittemore insisted rather improbably that "no one asked me to come," although he admitted meeting with several other witnesses in Ellis's office that morning. Brown told much the same story. "I came here of my own accord," he testified. "I heard a rumor that the man in court was the man who cleaned windows with Jones, and I came in to see if I should know him." Only Gilman seemed completely candid, explaining that "Mr. Jones asked me yesterday if I didn't recollect the man who was in his employ last spring." Thomas was trying to show some collusion among the witnesses, so the minor evasiveness of Whittemore and Brown marginally advanced his case.

The defense called four other witnesses as well, but they were of limited value. William Culver, a Mattapan Works blacksmith, recalled that "Jones and his men" were cleaning windows "prior to the time we changed our hours of work, which was the first of April," but he did not identify Burns as part of the crew. Machinist Rufus Putnam testified to the same effect. He remembered "Jones and a colored man" working at Mattapan, and he could set the date because he commenced his own job at the same time. A carpenter named John Favor also said that Jones and Burns applied to him for work at the beginning of March, but he had "nothing by which I can fix the date definitely." Stephen Maddox, a black clothing dealer, testified that Burns asked him for a job in early March, but he could only estimate the date because he believed it was about two months before his "outside work" would commence in the beginning of May.[40]

Suttle's lawyers did not bother to cross-examine either Culver or Favor. Parker did question Rufus Putnam fairly closely, making slight headway when the witness acknowledged that he had gone to Ellis's office that morning with George Drew and James Whittemore.

As the court and spectators might have come to expect, Suttle's counsel concentrated their heaviest fire on the black witness, Stephen Maddox. Parker brought out that Maddox had not been born in Boston, intimating that the witness was a former slave or perhaps even a runaway. He challenged Maddox on trivial details. What was the address of his shop? Was Burns wearing an overcoat? What had he done after Burns departed? What did he mean by "outside work"? Upon learning that Maddox had been "summoned" to court by William Jones, Parker repeatedly accused the two men of colluding. Maddox denied ever speaking to Jones about Burns prior to Monday night, when they "talked about it two or three minutes." He did, however, admit talking "with Mr. Ellis about it this morning, in his office," and conceded that "Jones went there with me."[41]

The defense attorneys rested their case near the end of the day, well satisfied that they had damaged Suttle's claim. On short notice, they had produced nine witnesses who placed their client in Boston at a time when Suttle's slave was said to be in Richmond. Even discounting the two black witnesses (as Thomas would no doubt urge the court), and even allowing that several of the others were less than certain about important details, they could still rely on the unshaken testimony of Drew, Whittemore, Gilman, and Brown, all of whom were respectable white professionals with no known ties to abolitionism. Despite Benjamin Hallett's accusation of perjury, the defense case seemed promising—if only Judge Loring could be convinced to give Burns "the benefit of every error in law, and the benefit of every doubt."

Late Tuesday afternoon, Seth Thomas began the claimant's rebuttal case by calling a surprise witness of his own. During his lengthy cross-examination that morning, William Jones testified that he and Burns had looked for work at City Hall, where they met a man named Mr. Gould. Over the next few hours, Thomas's assistants had apparently succeeded in locating Cyrus Gould, who agreed to appear for the claimant. Gould testified that William Jones had indeed "worked on the 10th March for me, and on the 16th and 17th he worked on the City Building, which my brother has charge of." Jones's helpers, however, "had been one or two colored women." Burns was not there "at any time" and, in fact, there "was no man working" with Jones at all.[42]

There was no cross-examination, and the court heard no more evidence that day.

Thomas continued his rebuttal case on Wednesday morning, calling Erastus Gould to corroborate his brother's testimony that Jones's only assistants at City Hall had been women.

Then followed a heated exchange between Thomas and Dana over whether Constable Benjamin True would be allowed to testify about additional statements Burns had made while in custody. Dana objected on multiple grounds almost as soon as True took the stand, but Loring overruled him and allowed the testimony to begin. Thomas had asked only a few background questions, however, before the defense objected anew. Once again Loring ruled for the claimant. This time the witness managed to begin his story, explaining that he had been in charge of Burns since the night of the arrest. There had been a great deal of conversation between Burns and his guards, including talk "about Virginia, Massachusetts, and other matters." Although Burns at first "appeared terrified," he spoke freely with his jailors. True had never "threatened him or held out any promises" and in fact had treated his prisoner well, giving him "newspapers, oranges, oyster stews and candy when he wished them."[43]

Thomas was taking pains to show that Burns had not been coerced, and it appeared that he was building up to a stunning admission. Dana therefore objected again, arguing that any statements had been given "under circumstances which amounted to intimidation." As before, however, Loring ruled that "admissions by the prisoner, made either to Col. Suttle or any one else during his confinement, were competent testimony." After all that, True was finally allowed to complete his testimony, but it was anticlimactic at best. "I conversed with Burns about the length of time he had been here; he said he had been here about two months." Exactly two months earlier would have been the end of March, meaning that Brent could have seen Burns in Richmond after all. But True had been sufficiently imprecise that Dana decided against conducting any cross-examination.[44] Perhaps he was overconfident, but he was more likely saving his energy for the final argument.

Dana thought that Thomas and Parker had badly overplayed their hand. "If the claimant's counsel had merely put in his record & introduced evidence to prove that the prisoner was the person named in the record, we should have had no defence," Dana wrote in his journal. But instead they had allowed Brent to testify at unnecessary length, introducing superfluous information about Suttle's financial arrangements for his slave, as well as the details of Burns's alleged confession. Dana believed that he could use those additional facts to his own client's advantage, literally turning the claimant's case against him. As a trial lawyer, Dana's forte was a brilliant mastery of the facts. Charles Francis Adams said that Dana's technique exploited his "imaginative faculties and power of copious illustration," which enabled him to see things "clearly himself, and then mak[e] others see them as he saw them."[45] As the Burns case drew to a close, Dana was eager to practice his skills before Judge Loring.

Dana was renowned for his compelling eloquence, which came to him naturally. His father was among America's most famous poets and his grandfather had been chief justice of Massachusetts. Dana himself had written a best-selling memoir, *Two Years before the Mast,* at age twenty-five. The courtroom was crowded to capacity when he began to address the judge. For more than four hours Dana spoke almost extemporaneously, relying only upon a half page of notes he had written out that morning. He touched upon every substantive aspect of the case, from the sufficiency of the claimant's evidence, to the identity of the prisoner, to the technical provisions of the Fugitive Slave Act. He began, however, by skewering the extraordinary measures that had been undertaken to guard the courthouse.[46]

"I congratulate the commonwealth of Massachusetts," he said, anticipating that the case would soon be over, "that at length, in due time . . . her courts may be reopened, and her Judges, suitors, and witnesses may pass and repass without being obliged to satisfy hirelings of the United States Marshal and bayoneted foreigners." Given the unsavory nature of the marshal's guards, many of whom had criminal records, he remarked mordantly that the rest of Boston "has never been so safe as while the Marshal has had his posse of specials in this Court House."

Dana next took aim at U.S. Attorney Benjamin Hallett, who had gratuitously blocked the sale of Burns and then hectored the court in a proceeding where he had no official standing. He sarcastically congratulated the government of the United States "that its legal representative can return to his appropriate duties, and that his sedulous presence will no longer be needed here in a private civil suit, for the purpose of intimidation." Then with some sincerity Dana congratulated the "officers of the army and navy" who would soon be released from guarding "this fortified slave-pen," a service that "as gentlemen and soldiers they surely despise."

Those acerbic remarks had not been delivered merely for effect. Dana was in fact leading up to his main theme, which was the despicable nature of slavery itself. Why did it take the entire force of the federal government to guard a single slave? Why were only felons and thugs employed by the U.S. marshal? Why had the U.S. attorney shown so little respect for Judge Loring while intruding himself in a civil lawsuit? Dana answered that the court had already recognized the "presumption of freedom" at the beginning of the case and that only "fraud and violence" could succeed in consigning Burns to "perpetual bondage."

It was not exactly a ringing invocation of the higher law, but unlike the defense lawyers in the Christiana case, Dana was clearly unwilling to concede the legitimacy of slavery. Turning toward Seth Thomas—who had bested him in the Sims case—Dana heaped scorn on his adversary. "There are some in my sight now who care nothing for freedom, whose sympathies all go for despotism; but thank God they are few and growing less." Suttle may have had certain rights under federal law, but the court had no corresponding obligation of sympathy or indulgence for the slave owner's claim. Nor was it even necessary for the court to be evenhanded when deciding between "a few despised pieces of silver on the one hand, and on the other perpetual bondage of a man." Instead Dana demanded that Loring extend himself as far as necessary in order to rule in favor of freedom and against slavery:

> We have a right, then, to expect from your Honor a strict adherence to the rule that this man is free until he is proved a slave beyond every reasonable doubt, every intelligent abiding misgiving proved by evidence of the strictest character, after a rigid compliance with every form of law which statue, usage, precedent has thrown about the accused as a protection.

Dana proposed a novel standard of proof that would virtually negate the purpose of the Fugitive Slave Act. In effect, he had challenged the commissioner to nullify the law in substance, even while respecting it in form. Dana devoted the balance of his argument to explaining just how that could be accomplished.

First, there was the question of identity. Dana acknowledged that "there was a man in Virginia named Anthony Burns" whom Suttle claimed as a slave. But the commissioner did not have to accept Suttle's additional assertion that "the prisoner at the bar is that Anthony Burns." Instead Suttle had to prove the prisoner's identity to Loring's satisfaction, and only the court could determine whether the evidence was sufficient. "Let him fail in one point," counseled Dana, "let him fall short the width of a spider's thread, in the proof of this horrid category, and the man goes free."

No one could ever dispute a judge's finding of reasonable doubt, because all identifications were inherently unreliable. "On the point of personal identity, the most frequent, the most extraordinary, the most notorious, and sometimes the most fatal mistakes have been made." Dana provided examples, ranging from Isaac's misidentification of Jacob for Esau to Shakespeare's Comedy of Error. "Let us have no Tragedy of Errors, here," he implored the court. Suttle has "but one witness," Dana argued, "and the proof of identity hangs on the testimony of one man. It all hangs by one thread. That man is Mr. Brent."

But Brent's testimony was deeply flawed and inconsistent with the other evidence, or at least it could be viewed that way by a right-thinking judge. Brent's familiarity with Suttle's slave seemed scanty, based primarily on interactions in 1846 or 1847, when the slave was only a teenager, which would cause him to rely on the runaway's description in the Virginia court record. That description, however, was critically vague. Although it was obvious that "the prisoner at the bar is a full blooded negro," the Virginia court record had described the escapee only as "dark complexioned" without specifying his race. "It might as well have omitted the sex of the fugitive," argued Dana.

Even more significantly, the Virginia description said only that the fugitive had "a scar on his right hand." "A scar!" exclaimed Dana. "The prisoner's right hand is broken, and a bone stands out from the back of it, a hump an inch high, and it hangs almost useless from the wrist." No slave owner could have failed to specify such disfigurement in his description of a runaway. "This broken hand . . . is the most noticeable thing possible in the identifying of a slave. His right hand is the chief property his master has in him." And yet, "neither the record nor Mr. Brent say any thing about the most noticeable thing in this man. Nowhere in Mr. Brent's testimony does he allude to it, but only speaks of a cut."

The discrepancy was small and explainable—Brent, after all, had pointed out Burns in court and therefore had no need to describe him in detail—but Dana proceeded to magnify it several times over. There were only two possible explanations, he maintained, and both led inexorably to judgment for the prisoner. Perhaps Brent "does know intimately Anthony Burns of Richmond," in which case bias and a misplaced sense of duty had led him to identify the wrong man in court. Given the level of national "political excitement" and the "state of feeling between North and South," it was natural that a Southerner would tend to misidentify an alleged slave in a northern court. "No man could be more liable to bias than a Virginian, testifying in Massachusetts . . . with every powerful and controlling motive on earth enlisted for success." It was also possible, Dana allowed, that "Brent does not know Anthony Burns particularly well." In that case, it appeared that the witness had mistakenly, though in good faith, identified a convenient target.

In either event, the misidentification was underscored by Brent's testimony that "he saw this Anthony Burns in Richmond, Virginia, on the 20th day of March last, and that he disappeared from there on the 24th." Even after hearing from numerous alibi witnesses, Brent did "not go back to the stand to correct an error, or to say that he may have been mistaken." Thus, the court could only conclude that the witness did in fact see the true slave, Anthony Burns, in Richmond at a time when many other witnesses established that "the prisoner was in Boston, earning an honest livelihood by the work of his hands." That discrepancy alone, argued Dana, should provide sufficient doubt for the court to set Burns free.

Compared to Brent, the many defense witnesses were completely reliable and unimpeached. Knowing that Seth Thomas would soon attack William Jones as a perjurer, Dana took the bull by the horns. "Jones cannot be mistaken as to the identity," he contended. "The only question would be as to the truth of his story." Jones's testimony was "so full of details, with such minuteness of dates and names and places, [that it] must either stand impregnable or be shattered to pieces." But Thomas had cross-examined the witness relentlessly and had exposed no gaps. "The fullest test had been tried. The other side has had a day in which to follow up the points of Jones's diary, and discover his errors and falsehoods. But he is corroborated in every point."

Dana next described the testimony of his eight additional alibi witnesses. He urged Judge Loring to place his greatest faith in James Whittemore, who was "a member of the City Council." Other witnesses had been equally certain and even more detailed—George Drew, for example, had corroborated Jones's account of the dispute over Burns's pay—but Whittemore had the most important credential of all. Dana had asked the witness "whether he was under the odium of being either a Free Soiler or an Abolitionist," to which Whittemore replied that he was "a Hunker Whig." Dana assured Loring that he did not expect the witness's "political relations" to sway the court, but he pointed out that a Hunker Whig would have "no bias on our side." Quite revealingly, Dana then continued:

> I am anxious not only that your Honor should believe our evidence, but that the public should justify you in so doing. And there is no fear but that the press and the public mind will be perfectly at ease if it knows that your Honor's judgment is founded even in part, in a fugitive slave case, in favor of the fugitive, on the testimony of a man who has such a status . . . as a Hunker Whig.

The message was clear. Dana had shown Loring how to enter a judgment that could not be challenged or questioned by Boston's Whig establishment. The commissioner did not even have to prefer Whittemore's testimony over Brent's; he only had to conclude that the respectable Hunker Whig had raised some doubt about Burns's identity. If Loring was at all inclined for any reason to set the prisoner free, Dana had just provided him with an unassailable rationale for doing so.

The rest of Dana's points were makeweights, elegant legal arguments that had little or no chance of actually persuading Judge Loring. He renewed his motion to exclude Burns's statement on the night of the arrest, although he recognized that the court had already ruled against him. But if Burns's confession was to be credited, then the court had to accept all of the prisoner's statements as true—including the claim that he had fallen asleep while working on a ship and had never intended to escape. In that case, Dana asserted, the claimant's case failed because a slave's mere presence in a free state—as opposed to his "escape"—was insufficient to trigger the Fugitive Slave Act. That was a clever argument, perhaps even ingenious, but it rested upon an acrobatic distinction between two different sections of the Fugitive Slave Act and there was little reason to hope that stolid Judge Loring would be intellectually supple enough to follow it.

In much the same vein, Dana also argued that Suttle had insufficient standing to bring the suit, given Brent's testimony that Anthony Burns had been mortgaged to Tolson and leased to Millspaugh. For all the court could tell from the evidence, Millspaugh had authorized Burns to find work in Boston. Loring, however, had already participated in the aborted attempt to purchase Burns's freedom from Suttle, so it was hardly likely that he would now rule that some other Southerner had a superior possessory interest in the chattel.

Dana did not pursue the unconstitutionality of the Fugitive Slave Act, even though his cocounsel had railed against the Act in his opening statement. That issue had been decided emphatically by Justice Lemuel Shaw (and Commissioner George Curtis), so there was little to be gained by revisiting it in the Burns case. Given his background, Loring would naturally be loath to contradict his fellow Whig jurists, or to risk censure and rebuke by the establishment and lawyers whose opinions he valued most.

If Burns was to be released, therefore, it would not be on the basis of a purely legal construction or a creative reading of the Fugitive Slave Act. Rather, Burns's freedom hinged on the court's willingness to indulge his doubts—both moral and factual—about the sufficiency of Suttle's case. Dana could not quite ask the court simply to conjure up or imagine a reasonable doubt about the prisoner's identity, simply for the sake of denying Suttle's claim. That was too much to expect of Edward Loring, especially given the manifest certainty that Burns was truly Suttle's slave. But Dana could invoke the relationship between conscience and justice, cautioning the court to be wary of the "venomous beast that carries the poison to life and liberty and hope in its fangs." In closing, he quoted Loring's own earlier acknowledgment of the presumption of freedom:

> Hold to it now, Sir, as to the sheet-anchor of your peace of mind as well as of [the prisoner's] safety. If you commit a mistake in favor of the man, a pecuniary value, not great, is put at hazard. If against him, a free man is made a slave forever.... Sir, I implore you, in

view of the cruel character of this law, in view of the dreadful consequences of a mistake, send him not away, with that tormenting
doubt on your mind. . . . You are to do an act which will hold its
place in the history of America, in the history of the progress of the
human race. May your judgment be for liberty and not slavery.

Over the course of four hours, Loring had "paid great attention to all that
related to the identity" of the prisoner, taking notes whenever Dana reminded
him about the shakiness of Brent's testimony and the consistency of the alibi
witnesses. The judge put his pen aside, however, every time Dana ventured
into strictly legal arguments about the adequacy of the record or the validity
of Suttle's title. In all, that was a good sign for Burns, as the court seemed
most interested in the strongest aspects of the defense case.[47]

Now it was Seth Thomas's turn to seek a delay. Because it was already late afternoon by the time Dana concluded his argument, Thomas asked the court
to recess for the evening and to allow him to begin his summation the next
day. Dana objected, unwilling to extend even a small courtesy to opposing counsel, and Loring directed Thomas to start at once.

Thomas began his argument by openly mimicking Dana's round of con-
gratulations, though he substituted indignation for sarcasm. Thomas congratulated "the marshal, who had shown, in the discharge of his difficult and arduous
duty, firmness, decision, prudence, and kindness to the defendant." He congratulated the City of Boston for imposing order on a shameful mob. Pointing
at Theodore Parker, who was seated in the front row, Thomas reminded Loring
that the abolitionist minister had, in his sermon the preceding Sunday, virtually
accused the court of responsibility for Batchelder's death.[48]

Thomas asserted that the claimant's entire case could be summarized in
just two sentences: First, "that Burns owned service and labor" to Suttle. And
second, "that he escaped." Everything else was only obfuscation, raised by the
defense to avoid the obvious conclusion that Suttle was entitled to a certificate
of removal. As to both issues, Thomas argued that the Virginia court record
provided all of the required proof. "We have put in the transcript of a record.
It is duly authenticated, and is conclusive upon the court of the two facts
therein recited."

It was still necessary, Thomas agreed, to prove that the prisoner was the very person named in the record. But could there really be any doubt about identity? There was only one such Anthony Burns, "and nobody thinks of calling [the prisoner] anything else?" In an abundance of caution, however, the claimant had also offered the testimony of William Brent, "who had known Burns from a boy, had him in his own employ, and had leased him to others." Brent's testimony had been completely consistent with the fugitive's description in the Virginia documents: "a man of dark complexion, six feet high, with a scar on his face and another scar on his right hand, and about twenty-three years of age." That fit the prisoner so perfectly that "it would be difficult to find another person among the whole colored population of Boston who so well answers the description as the person at bar." Dana had made much of the prisoner's fractured hand, "but it is, nevertheless, a scar," explained Thomas. And most important, there was Burns's own "admission that Col. Suttle was his master."

Thomas turned next to the alibi evidence. It was true, of course, that "the man could not have been both here and in Virginia from the first to the nineteenth of March," but the defense case relied far too heavily on "the testimony of one Jones, a colored man." According to Thomas, Jones was simply a liar whose "story is manufactured for the case." "Jones undoubtedly did work at the Mattapan Works, and there was, no doubt, another colored there with him. But it was not Burns." The other black witness was also a perjurer, said Thomas. Stephen Maddox's testimony was "coined at the same mint, made up at the same factory" as Jones's.

Thomas could not so freely malign the white witnesses. Rather than call them liars, he explained that they were merely in error. "No doubt Whittemore saw Jones there, and perhaps on the day he named. . . . But he never saw Burns there. He is mistaken in the man. That is all." In fact, "neither Drew, nor Whittemore, nor Favor nor any one of all those called to support Jones, has seen Burns since, nor had they ever seen him before."

But why would so many otherwise reputable witnesses make the same serious mistake? According to Thomas, they had all been duped by a cunning black man:

> The truth is, Jones went to them and asked them if they did not
> remember the man he had with him cleaning the windows. . . .
> They came into court with this impression and made up their

minds that he was. That is the only theory consistent with their honesty.

But suppose that "Brent is wrong in testifying that he saw Burns in Virginia" on March 20 and that Whittemore and the others really did see him in Boston two weeks earlier. "The date is immaterial." Even if Brent had been confused, "the fact of owing service and escape remain," and Burns's identity had been amply shown by other means. Brent had identified the prisoner, whose appearance perfectly matched the description in the Virginia documents. "And then comes, besides, the defendant's admissions." The other witnesses—for both sides—might have been mistaken, "but this unfortunate man cannot be. He knows."

If Burns had not escaped from Virginia, asked Thomas, where had he come from? Why had there been no evidence about the man's origins or birth, or his life before he encountered William Jones on the streets of Boston? That argument seemed to invert the ordinary burden of proof, but in fact it was quite consistent with the principles of the Fugitive Slave Act. Suttle's prima facie case had been fully established by the Virginia court record and bolstered by Brent's testimony. In Thomas's view of the summary rendition proceedings, the burden of proof had in fact shifted to the prisoner to provide evidence that he was not a slave.

Therein lay the difference between enforcement of the positive law and Dana's appeal—albeit oblique and indirect—to higher values. For Thomas, all of Dana's intricate arguments were merely evasions aimed at thwarting execution of the law in circumstances where the facts were not really in dispute. The questionable alibi? The lease to Millspaugh? The attack on Brent? Those were all distractions from the court's duty under the statute. Slavery was an unpleasant reality, and some sympathy for the prisoner was unavoidable, but a judge had no choice but to retain a disposition of calm detachment.

Thomas believed that Dana's emotional appeal had been rude and unseemly, most especially his "extraordinary bitterness" toward the claimant's lawyers. "I am not conscious of having said or done anything in the course of the examination that need have provoked personal hostility," Thomas said. "My connection with the case has been strictly professional." The moral distance between the two lawyers was unbridgeable. To Dana, assistance to a slaveholder was unredeemably dishonorable, no matter the circumstances. To

Thomas, it was business as usual. It remained to be seen which approach the commissioner would choose.

Until then, Seth Thomas would have the last word: "I take leave of the case, confident in the proofs presented, confident in the majesty of the law, and confident that the determination here will be just."

Judge Loring adjourned court, announcing that he would deliver his opinion the following Friday morning.

∽ 11 ∽

JUDGE LORING'S PREDICAMENT

Dana returned to his office following the close of court on Wednesday evening, very optimistic about the outcome of the case. Never one to underestimate his own achievements, he wrote in his journal that the summation had been "entirely to my own satisfaction." For the second time in four days, he allowed that he just might have given "the best speech I ever made." This time he could have been right. Unlike his plea for a continuance the previous Saturday, his closing argument had addressed momentous issues with passion, coherence, and force. If there was any reasonable way to rule in favor of Burns, Dana had made it available to Judge Loring. On the other hand, Dana believed that "Thomas's argument was poor," as was to be expected from "a small pattern of a man in every way, moral & intellectual."[1]

Dana wrote nothing in his journal concerning the credibility of his own witnesses, although the weight of their testimony was certain to be a major element in Loring's decision. Perhaps he did not want to commit any doubts to paper, given that many of the defense witnesses had coordinated their testimony, just as Seth Thomas insinuated in his summation. In fact, there had been a meeting in Charles Ellis's office on Tuesday morning, involving at least William Jones, James Whittemore, Stephen Maddox, Rufus Putnam, and probably George Drew. Although Jones had good reason to recall working with Burns, it was improbable that the others had clearly remembered an anonymous black laborer whom they had briefly encountered nearly three months earlier. It is likely that at least some amount of memory jogging—if not outright suggestion—had taken place in the law office, although the level of Dana's own involvement is unknown.

Most of the defense witnesses had no particular reason to lie. Whittemore, Putnam, and Drew had nothing to gain by supporting a fugitive slave. As businessmen, they could only be harmed by alienating the Cotton Whigs who favored strict enforcement of the Fugitive Slave Act. Even if their testimony had been embellished, it was evidently sincere. As African-Americans, Jones and Maddox would have been naturally sympathetic to the plight of a run-away, and Jones had certainly extended himself on Burns's behalf. But Jones's story was well supported by documentation, and Maddox had carefully hedged his testimony so that nothing he said could be proven false. Although the extent of Burns's alibi was probably overstated, Dana apparently had no second thoughts about presenting it under the circumstances.

If there had been any outright perjury in the trial, it came from the other side. William Brent's account of Burns's alleged admissions seemed scripted, and Suttle's supposed admonition—"I make you no promises and I make you no threats"—was almost certainly invented to make the statement admissible. Brent had also probably lied about seeing Burns in Richmond on March 20, although not for the purpose of enhancing the case for rendition. As Suttle's local agent, he had been responsible for supervising Burns's employment, and yet he had evidently been unaware of the slave's escape in late February. Brent could not admit to Suttle that he had been so inattentive to his property, so he apparently claimed to have seen Burns only a few days before he turned up missing. What began as a relatively harmless (though false) excuse eventually became one of the central issues in a heated trial, and Dana no doubt felt completely justified in exploiting Brent's dissembling to the fullest extent.

In any event, Dana was not about to record any misgivings about the testimony as he waited hopefully for a favorable decision in the case.

———

With court in recess, Judge Loring spent the entire day Thursday composing his opinion. Knowing that his judgment would be closely scrutinized by both sides, he took care to address all of the relevant facts and issues. There would be emotional denunciations no matter how he decided the case, so it was essential that the commissioner provide a closely reasoned basis for his verdict.

Even as Loring worked on his text, others were making preparations as well. Abolitionist leaders called upon their forces to rally at the courthouse, ostensibly to prevent Suttle from secretly removing Burns in advance of the commissioner's ruling, but in reality hoping to be able to prevent the fugitive's rendition even if it was ordered by the court. Congressman Joshua Giddings arrived from Ohio to address a meeting of the Free Soil Party, where he recounted the story of a recent fugitive rescue near Cleveland. Giddings did not openly call for forcible resistance, as he had at a Christiana rally, but he condemned the entire proceeding as "concocted in Washington" for the benefit of slaveholders and left little doubt about the steps that ought to be taken if possible "in favor of liberty."[2]

Recognizing the dangerous situation, U.S. Marshal Watson Freeman paid a private visit to Judge Loring on Thursday afternoon. Freeman asked Loring for advance notice of his decision so he could take the necessary steps to defend the courthouse. Loring flatly refused, even though Freeman pressed upon him "the great responsibility he was under . . . and [the] risks of an alternative preparation." The marshal would just have to do his best, advised Loring, as "no man should know until it was pronounced."[3]

Fearing the worst, Freeman and the other authorities arranged for a maximum show of force. With the approval of Secretary of War Jefferson Davis, several columns of U.S. troops had been dispatched to Boston under the command of Major General Benjamin F. Edmands. By Friday morning fully twenty-two companies of Marines, infantry, cavalry, and dragoons were positioned about the city, with at least one thousand men under arms. The courthouse itself was guarded by an artillery brigade, whose heavy cannon was mounted on the steps and aimed menacingly at the square below. Burns was placed under a double guard of "bullies armed with bludgeons and pistols." Believing that the city faced "a tumult, a riot, or a mob," Mayor J. V. C. Smith issued a statement declaring that "military force is necessary to aid the civil authorities in suppressing the same." He proceeded to grant General Edmands and the chief of police "full discretionary powers to sustain the laws of the land" and he called upon "all well-disposed citizens" to clear the streets. The mayor's order amounted to a de facto imposition of martial law, as "soldiers with fixed bayonets filled all the avenues."[4] In addition to the federal troops, an additional 1,800 city police and volunteer militia were deployed.

The government's efforts at crowd control did not prevent Burns's supporters from gathering outside the courthouse. Some arrived as early as 6:00 a.m. on Friday, and their numbers gradually increased until the square was "thronged with people [including] females of every shade of complexion."[5]

Dana arrived early for court, where he found Burns already in the dock and Marshal Freeman supervising the guard. Freeman assured Dana that he had no additional warrants for Burns, meaning that the fugitive would be free to leave with his counsel in the event of a favorable decision. Burns himself was incongruously dressed in a "handsome suit" that had been given to him by Asa Butman and other marshal's guards. Some observers believed the deputies were sarcastically imitating the "ancient priests by adorning the victim whom they were about to sacrifice."[6] It is more probable, however, that the marshals were simply showing kindness toward a man with whom they had become friendly over the previous week. Indeed, a slave would have little use for a fine suit, so perhaps the guards were subtly expressing their hope for Burns's freedom.

Loring entered the courtroom promptly at 9:00 a.m., carrying his written judgment with him. The commissioner was obviously exhausted from his lucubrations, having worked late into the night on his opinion. Loring seemed hesitant and cautious as he spread his papers on the bench without even looking up at the lawyers and spectators. The entire room fell profoundly still, waiting to learn whether Anthony Burns would be released or enslaved that day.

The commissioner slowly began to read his decision. He turned first to the constitutionality of the Fugitive Slave Act, speaking at length about its purpose and history. Surprising no one, Loring held that the statute was constitutional in every respect. He affirmed his own authority as a commissioner to rule in the matter, holding that the matter before him was ministerial rather than judicial in nature. Because the only purpose of the hearing was preliminary—"extradition" rather than final adjudication—there was also no valid constitutional objection to the absence of a jury trial.[7]

Loring also noted that the statute had been held "constitutional by the unanimous opinion of the Judges of the Supreme Court of Massachusetts on the fullest argument and the maturest deliberation." In acknowledgment of his fellow Cotton Whig, Loring quoted extensively from the opinion of "our revered" Chief Justice Shaw in the Sims case, repeating the claim that the Fugitive Slave Clause had been "an essential element" in the formation of the Constitution.

The court had just ruled in favor of the claimant on a major point of law, but the defense had little cause for alarm. The thrust of Dana's argument had been based strictly on the facts of the case, so Loring's encomium to Justice Shaw did not necessarily mean an adverse ruling for Burns. The defense strategy, after all, had been to underscore the evils of slavery itself, while urging Loring to interpret the evidence in a way that allowed the court to set the prisoner free. The constitutionality of the statute was more or less irrelevant to that approach, so long as the commissioner was sufficiently sympathetic to the prisoner's alibi.

Dana might have been heartened as Loring continued to read his judgment. "It is said that the statute is so cruel and wicked that it should not be executed by good men," said the commissioner, clearly reacting to the position of the Garrisonian abolitionists. Neither Dana nor his cocounsel had ever raised such an argument in court, but Loring was obviously aware of the many calls for his resignation that had been made in meeting halls and churches. But if all good judges were to abstain from Fugitive Slave Act proceedings, Loring continued, "then into what hands shall its administration fall . . . and what is to be the protection of the unfortunate men who are brought within its operation? Will those who call the statute merciless commit it to a merciless judge?"

Loring had just identified himself as a merciful judge, whose job extended to "protection of the unfortunate men" imprisoned and enslaved under the fugitive law. He strongly suggested that his interpretation of the evidence—if not the Constitution—might be tempered by compassion. Burns had kept his eyes firmly on the judge throughout the reading of the opinion, and his hopes no doubt rose as Loring continued:

> If the statute involves that right, which for us makes life sweet, and the want of which makes life a misfortune, shall its administration be confined to those who are reckless of that right in others, or ignorant or careless of the means given for its legal defence, or dishonest in their use? If any men wish this, they are more cruel and wicked than the statute, for they would strip from the fugitive the best security and every alleviation the statute leaves him.

The sweetness of life? The right to legal defense? Security and alleviation for the fugitive? Those were the ideas on which the defense case had been premised, and here was the judge extolling those very same concepts. Dana must have smiled inwardly when he saw his final argument so closely reflected in the court's remarks.

With that introduction, Loring at last turned his attention to the facts of the case. The claimant, he noted, had to establish three propositions. First, "that Anthony Burns owed him service in Virginia; and second, "that Anthony

Burns escaped from that service." These two facts, he continued, had been proved by the Virginia court record, which had to be accepted as conclusive under the Fugitive Slave Act. But there was also a third proposition for the claimant to prove—"the identity of the party before me with the Anthony Burns mentioned in the record." On that issue alone, the court would weigh the evidence presented at trial. "This identity is the only question I have a right to consider."

That brought Judge Loring directly to Burns's alibi. "The question [is] whether the respondent was in Virginia or Massachusetts at a certain time." Brent had testified that "the Anthony Burns of the record was in Virginia on the 19th of March last," while "the evidence of the respondent has been offered to show that he was in Massachusetts on or about the first of March last, and thereafter till now."

The claimant had produced only one witness—William Brent—who had testified, Loring observed, "in circumstances which would necessarily bias the fairest mind." But apart from the fact that he was Suttle's friend and fellow slave owner, Brent's honesty had not otherwise been challenged. "His means of knowledge are personal, direct, and qualify him to testify confidently, and he has done so."

On the other hand, the defense had produced "many witnesses whose integrity is admitted." Loring apparently meant to exclude Jones and Maddox from the roll of honest witnesses, as their integrity certainly had not been "admitted" by Seth Thomas. But then again, Dana had invited him to take precisely that approach to the evidence, by relying only on the testimony of the reputable white witnesses. Their identification of Burns had also been based on "personal and direct" knowledge, continued the court, although somewhat "less full and complete than that of Mr. Brent."

Loring concluded that the testimonial conflict was "complete and irreconcilable," with credible witnesses on both sides. By Dana's logic, that should have ended the discussion. Even if the court rejected Dana's higher law–influenced standard of proof—"beyond any possible doubt"—Suttle still had to prove his case by some measure of evidence. Yet here was an irresolvable impasse. In that case, the "presumption of freedom," already accepted by the court, should have tipped the scales in favor of the defendant.

But Loring had not finished his analysis. "In every case of disputed identity," he opined, "there is one person always whose knowledge is perfect and positive, and whose evidence is not within the reach of error, and that is the person whose identity is questioned." In the case before him, that person was Anthony Burns. On the night of the arrest, Loring noted, Burns had greeted Suttle "by his *Christian name*—'How do you do, Master *William?*'" That was sufficient to establish that the two men knew each other. Loring added that he gave no weight "to the appellation 'Master,'" but he proceeded to recount Brent's entire testimony about the conversation between Suttle and Burns. Brent's story had been corroborated by Caleb Page, and that was good enough for Judge Loring. Burns's admission was sufficient to satisfy the court "beyond a reasonable doubt" that the respondent was "the Anthony Burns named in the record."

Just as Dana had feared, the court had appropriated from Burns "the only power he had under this law, that of speech" and used it to his detriment. Although the prisoner was compelled to remain silent in court, his own words were used as satisfactory proof to send him back into slavery. Dana had argued that the circumstances of the prisoner's confession had rendered it inadmissible, but Loring had two ready responses. First, he accepted Brent's dubious claim that Suttle had refrained from making promises or threats to the frightened Burns. But even if Burns had been "stupefied by circumstances and fear," Loring pointed out, his acknowledgment would still be admissible to prove his identity. The substance of Burns's statement—the absence of whipping; the giving of money—was not in issue, and thus the admission was not offered "to establish the truth of the matters to which [it] referred." Instead, Burns's exclamation had been offered only to show that he recognized Suttle, which in turn demonstrated that he was the very Anthony Burns who had escaped from Virginia. The court would not have accepted Burns's statement to prove that Suttle was a gentle or generous master, but it was nonetheless sufficient to send a man into slavery for life. So much for the good intentions of a merciful judge.[8]

Immediately following his ruling, Loring issued a certificate authorizing William Suttle to remove Anthony Burns "from the State of Massachusetts back to the State of Virginia." Suttle then executed an affidavit stating that he had reason to believe "that said fugitive will be rescued from me before he can be taken beyond the limits of this State."[9] Under the terms of the Fugitive Slave

Act, Suttle's stated apprehension—which was certainly well-founded, given the events of the previous Friday night—was sufficient to invoke the federal government's obligation to deliver Burns safely to Virginia. The formality of the affidavit was probably unnecessary. U.S. Attorney Benjamin Hallett expected "armed resistance" to the rendition, and the Pierce administration was fully committed to enforcing the law. The president himself had already authorized Hallett and Freeman to "incur any expense" necessary to "execute the process under the fugitive law on the United States." Hallett replied that he had "ample military and police force to effect it peacefully," adding that the "law reigns."[10]

While the commissioner completed his paperwork, Marshal Freeman's men began clearing the courtroom. Only Dana and Rev. Grimes were allowed to remain with Burns, who understandably had fallen into despair. For over an hour, the two men stayed at the prisoner's side, while Grimes offered prayers to keep "up his spirits as best he could." Now that the government had won the case, there was no reason for Hallett to continue to frustrate Burns's manumission, so Grimes was certain that a sale could be arranged as soon as Suttle returned with his slave to Virginia. Burns was cheered by that prospect, but he expressed his fear that he would soon be forgotten and then "sold down the river."[11]

At 11:00 a.m. Burns was returned to his makeshift cell in the marshal's office, still accompanied by Dana and Grimes. Informed that a U.S. Navy cutter was standing by to take Burns to Virginia, Dana told Marshal Freeman that he expected to accompany his client at least as far as the wharf. Freeman, however, denied Dana's request. For the first time in the entire proceeding, Dana lost his temper. Even a prisoner going to execution was always allowed the privilege "that his clergyman & counsel should go with him." He "strongly advised" Freeman not to stand in his way, but the marshal held firm, leaving Dana no choice but to make his good-byes in the cell. But now that he had been certified a slave, even the small consolation of privacy was denied to the prisoner. Constable Benjamin True—who had only days earlier testified against Burns—insisted on listening to the conversation. Dana objected, reminding the guard that he had been allowed in all previous interviews to counsel his client "without being overheard." Perhaps so, the guard replied, but Marshal Freeman had issued new orders. "All conversation with the prisoner must be within the hearing of the keeper."

That intrusion on confidentiality was unacceptable to Dana. "I shall hold no conversation in such company," he told the officer. "I shall not consent to hold any conversation with the prisoner on such terms." There was nothing further to be lost by allowing the guard to eavesdrop on their parting words—and Burns was desperate for sympathetic company—but Dana's professional pride overwhelmed his compassion. The lawyer took his client's hand and explained that he could not "in self-respect, converse with him on such terms." According to Dana, Burns thanked him warmly and said he "had no doubt all had been done that could be done." Rev. Grimes also said good-bye, bidding Burns to trust in God and presciently "giving him his address & that of Deacon Pitts, that he might write to them, if permitted."[12]

Outside the courthouse, General Edmands's men had been busy sweeping protesters out of the square. Through constant effort they managed to maintain a cordon sanitaire around the building's entrance, but only at gunpoint. As one observer noted, "It was the first time that the armed power of the United States had ever been arrayed against the people of Massachusetts."[13] The military, however, could not prevent the news of Loring's decision from spreading throughout the city, and there were not enough soldiers available to clear the streets of Burns's supporters. Thousands upon thousands of people lined every possible route between the courthouse and the wharf, often spilling into the square only to be pushed back by the assembled troops. For more than three hours, the crowd intermittently pressed forward and then retreated, while Hallett and Freeman tried to decide whether it was safe to begin the prisoner's march.

Finally, at 2:00 p.m., General Edmands declared the city secure. One hundred and twenty special officers, each man armed with "a short Roman sword & one revolver hanging in his belt,"[14] formed a hollow square in front of the courthouse, as Burns was escorted down the steps by Freeman and his deputies. Burns took his position in the middle of the cortege, while the crowd around him shouted their condemnation and anger. "Shame! Shame! Kidnappers! Kidnappers!" A company of Marines and another of infantry fell in at the head of the hollow square, while two companies of the National Lancers took positions on either side. The rear was guarded by another corps of Marines, as well as a small artillery detachment with a horse-drawn field cannon. Slowly the doleful parade began its advance toward the harbor.

Almost at once the crowd surged toward the procession, but the mounted lancers repelled them. Several more times it seemed as though the troops

might be blocked, or even attacked, by the angry mob, but the soldiers' bran-
dished bayonets were sufficient to keep the route clear. Jeers and hisses greeted
the troops at every turn, and a shower of bottles and "noxious substances"
rained down on them as they passed the office of the antislavery *Boston Commonwealth*. In return, the soldiers kicked and cuffed some of the cursing
spectators. At times it looked as though a second Boston Massacre might be
in the offing, but discipline held within the ranks and caution prevailed among
the mob. To one young observer, a British abolitionist named Richard Winsor, the city of Boston had become "a Roman altar, the sacrifice on which was
brightly burning." Though Winsor took no action that day, he would remember the scene four years later when, as a divinity student in Ohio, he had a
better opportunity to rescue a less heavily guarded fugitive slave.[15]

In slightly more than half an hour, the procession reached the wharf, where
a steamer waited to carry Burns to the cutter *Morris,* which was lying at an-
chor in the harbor. It took nearly an hour to complete the transfer, as the artillery detachment had considerable difficulty hauling their cannon on board.
At 3:20 p.m., with Burns hidden below deck, the steamer cast off.

Anthony Burns was successfully removed from Boston, but he was not forgotten. The Pierce administration had hoped that vigorous enforcement of
the fugitive law would quell the ardor of the antislavery movement, but the
spectacle of "a solitary black man walking down the middle of the busiest
street in Boston" turned out to be convulsive. President Pierce had signed the
Kansas-Nebraska Act only three days earlier, extending the slave power into
previously free territory. And now, with the excruciating rendition of Anthony Burns, it appeared that federal troops had indeed placed Massachusetts "beneath the feet of Virginia." In the space of less than a week, it seemed
that a line had been crossed, making the continuing accommodation of slavery nearly impossible. As Amos Lawrence put it on behalf of his fellow cotton
merchants, "We went to bed one night old fashioned, conservative, Compromise Union Whigs, and waked up stark mad Abolitionists."[16]

Beginning Saturday morning, June 3, with the *Morris* well on its way to Virginia, Benjamin Hallett was more concerned about James Batchelder than he
was about Anthony Burns. A federal officer had been killed in the attack on
the courthouse and Hallett was determined to bring the murderers to justice
in a federal court. Martin Stowell and eight others had been arrested by the

Boston police, acting under state law, but Hallett was out for bigger game. He was quite willing to allow the Massachusetts authorities to pursue the murder case against the men already in jail, but the federal prosecutor blamed the abolitionist movement itself for Batchelder's death. He set his sights on leaders such as Theodore Parker and Wendell Phillips.

It was Martin Stowell who had actually fired the fatal shot, and he still had his pistol in his waistband when he was arrested and taken to jail in the courthouse basement on Friday, May 26. Somehow Stowell managed to conceal the weapon from his jailers and he later smuggled it out of his cell with the assistance of a friend. Even without the murder weapon, however, there was sufficient evidence to hold Stowell and his colleagues for the murder of Batchelder, committed by "felonious assault . . . with firearms loaded with powder and ball."[17]

A coroner's jury was convened on Thursday, June 1, and it quickly reached the conclusion that Batchelder had been killed during the "assaults of a mob." Although the jurors were not able to name the person directly responsible— indeed, they were uncertain whether the victim's femoral artery had been severed by a knife wound or a gunshot—they identified nine men, including Stowell, as having engaged "in a greater or less degree in said riotous attack."[18] Under Massachusetts law, the role of a coroner's jury was limited to determining the cause and manner of death; it could not approve or initiate criminal charges. One month later, therefore, a grand jury was convened in the Commonwealth Court of Common Pleas, presided over by Judge E. R. Hoar.

Judge Hoar delivered a lengthy charge to the grand jurors, explaining that it was not necessary to identify the individual who actually shot or stabbed Batchelder. Rather, "each of the persons" engaged in the riot could be held "legally responsible for the death of that man," so long as their "common purpose were to rescue the prisoner by force."

> If the common purpose were to rescue the prisoner by force . . . and that led to the destruction of the life of one of the persons who had him in charge, or who was lawfully aiding the officers who had him in charge, that would render all responsible who were engaged in the common purpose.

"It has been said some times," continued Hoar, "that there are laws which it is the duty of citizens to disobey or resist." Perhaps the Fugitive Slave Act was one such law. In Hoar's own opinion, the Fugitive Slave Act was foul and reprehensible, "evincing a more deliberate and settled disregard of all the principles of constitutional liberty than any other enactment which has ever come under my notice." Anyone who accepted the "existence of a Most High" would naturally be called to "obey God rather than man."

No court had ever come closer to recognizing higher law, but Hoar was not yet finished with his charge. "Gentlemen," he said, "it is not a question of private conscience that determines our duties.... A man whose private conscience leads him to disobey a law recognized by the community, must take the consequences of that disobedience."[19] Whatever evil the Fugitive Slave Act had worked, the criminal law still had to be enforced. The grand jury responded by issuing indictments—on the charge of "riot and rout," rather than murder—against eight defendants, again including Stowell and, for the first time, Rev. Thomas Wentworth Higginson.[20]

Judge Hoar's grand jury charge implicitly acknowledged the shift in sentiment among Bostonians in the weeks following the Burns rendition. Although only a minority of citizens might have personally endorsed higher-law doctrine, many more had come to abhor the Fugitive Slave Act and to respect those who resisted it. It had taken some serious exhortation to obtain the indictment of the would-be rescuers, and it would be even harder to obtain convictions before a Boston jury. Recognizing the difficult task before them, the state prosecutors were notably unenthusiastic about bringing the matter to trial, deferring it time and again in favor of routine prosecutions under the state Liquor Act. Finally, in April 1855, the state charges were simply dropped without explanation.[21]

But while the state prosecutors dithered, U.S. Attorney Hallett doggedly pursued federal charges, convening his own grand jury on June 7 with Justice Benjamin R. Curtis presiding. The government's failure in the Christiana case made a treason charge impracticable, especially since the state murder case was still pending at the time. Consequently, the only offenses reasonably available to the court involved the misdemeanor of obstructing federal officers. U.S. Attorney General Caleb Cushing believed firmly that the antislavery movement tended "to promote disorder, sedition, and servile war." He therefore fully supported Hallett's plan to make an example of the speakers at "the recent seditious meeting at Faneuil Hall" by including Theodore Parker and Wendell Phillips among the defendants.[22]

Justice Curtis cooperated by charging the grand jury that guilt would attach to all who were "leagued in the common design," even if they had not been present at the riot, so long as they did "procure, counsel, command, or abet the substantive offence committed." Curtis allowed that "extradition of fugitives from labor is odious," but he cautioned the grand jurors against tolerating the "power of the mob." He concluded with the stern warning that "forcible and concerted resistance to any law is civil war, which can make no progress but through bloodshed, and can have no termination but the destruction of the government of our country."[23] The grand jury, however, adjourned for the term without issuing an indictment.

Undeterred, Hallett summoned another grand jury for the court's autumn term, hopeful that the citizenry by then would have reconsidered the wisdom of resisting the Fugitive Slave Act. This time he was rewarded with the indictment he sought against Parker and Phillips, perhaps because the grand jury members included Justice Curtis's brother-in-law. The defendants soon surrendered themselves—Parker was in fact elated at the opportunity to use his trial as a political platform—and the case was set to be heard in the federal circuit court the following April, before Justice Curtis and District Judge Peleg Sprague.

By spring, however, it appeared that Curtis was having second thoughts. In response to a defense motion, he surprisingly quashed the indictment on the highly technical ground that the underlying warrant for Burns's arrest had not accurately recited the statutory basis for Commissioner Loring's jurisdiction. Thus, the indictment of the rioters could "not show that the warrant was legal process, because it does not show that it proceeded from one having lawful authority to issue it."[24]

It seemed as though Justice Curtis was straining to find a basis to dismiss the case, rather than provide a stage for Parker's "torrential eloquence" or confront the strong likelihood that the defendants would be quickly acquitted by a sympathetic jury.[25] In fact, he admitted that his "objection to the indictment is technical" and that that the government's failure to include the necessary language had been of no "practical consequence" to the defendants. Nonetheless, he held to his strict reading of the law and all of the defendants were discharged.

Hallett was deeply aggrieved by the ruling, which he criticized as going off on "a point so remote and so nice" as to be unworthy of the court. "There is now no United States in Massachusetts," he complained, as federal law had become nearly unenforceable even to vindicate the death of a federal officer. Hallett made repeated efforts to renew the indictment, but Justice Curtis frustrated him at every turn, each time on the basis of a "remote" technicality. Finally Hallett met privately with Curtis, who flatly informed him of the "grave difficulties behind the indictments which in all probability no new indictment could cure." Because the "defect was in the warrant issued by the Commissioner," it would be pointless to attempt to redraft the indictment and it was therefore impossible to prosecute the defendants on the charge of obstructing federal officers.[26] Neither Curtis nor Hallett seemed to care that Anthony Burns had apparently been arrested and reenslaved pursuant to an invalid warrant—precisely the sort of "flaw in the papers" that Dana had hoped to find from the very beginning of the case.

Boston's abolitionists exulted in the victory. *The Liberator* referred to the ruling as the "end of a grand legal farce," and Samuel May crowed that the government had avoided "a contest" with Phillips and Parker because the prosecution was "clearly anticipating a defeat." One unapologetic conservative Whig recognized that there had not been any possibility of conviction and that a "trial would only have afforded the defendants a new chance to insult the Court and defy the law."[27]

It was true, of course, that Parker and Phillips would have turned their trial into political theater. Hallett was undeterred by that prospect, and it is impossible to know the extent to which Curtis—who hoped that he might someday be appointed chief justice of the Supreme Court—was motivated by the desire to avoid an extended controversy. But even without a platform in the federal court, Boston's antislavery community had other means of publicity.

Richard Henry Dana circulated a pamphlet titled *The Decision Which Judge Loring Might Have Given,* in which he explained precisely how the commissioner could have avoided ruling in Suttle's favor while still nominally respecting the positive requirements of the Fugitive Slave Act. In a masterpiece of understatement, Dana avoided direct condemnation of Loring while simultaneously demonstrating the many ways in which the court could have construed the evidence in favor of releasing Burns. Dana's argument was softly devastating, because it demolished Loring's claim that his decision had been compelled by obedience to the positive law. There had been ample room, Dana showed, to interpret even the Fugitive Slave Act in a manner consistent with natural law.

Theodore Parker had no similar use for indirection, and no need of politesse. He wrote a lengthy and scathing pamphlet detailing the defense he would have presented if the government had risked bringing him to trial. In "one of the most remarkable and flamboyant American books of the nineteenth century," Parker presented a "thorough treatise on the right of free speech, the wrong of slavery, and the nature of judicial tyranny." Published in November 1855, *The Trial of Theodore Parker for the "Misdemeanor" of a Speech in Faneuil Hall against Kidnapping* castigated the Curtis family—Benjamin, George, and their stepcousin Edward Loring—for their longstanding complicity with slavery, and argued that "barbarous laws must not be applied in a civilized age; nor unjust laws enforced by righteous men."[28]

The Trial of Theodore Parker was "eloquent and moving, irrefutable if you subscribed to the Higher Law, irrelevant if you did not." A few years earlier Parker might not have found many adherents. Following the Burns case, however, perhaps a majority of Bostonians had come to agree that righteous judges must forthrightly renounce "the wickedness of the statute" in order to effect the "Eternal Justice of God."[29] And not merely as an abstract principle.

Much of the blame for the Burns rendition was fastened tightly on the shoulders of Judge Edward G. Loring. Little had been expected of Benjamin Hallett, who owed his appointment to the proslavery administration of Franklin Pierce, and there was no use faulting Charles Suttle, who had behaved only as slaveholders were expected to behave. Loring, on the other hand, occupied positions of high esteem in Boston, as a judge of the Suffolk County Probate Court and a lecturer at Harvard Law School. As a U.S. commissioner, he had extended the promise of a fair and humane hearing to Burns, only to rule in favor of slavery and against freedom. For that offense he could not be forgiven.

Loring had become a pariah in Boston, scorned by his many former friends and colleagues and insulted by strangers on the street. Even his butcher was reported to have refused to serve him, loudly rejecting his "blood money." Loring was at least once hanged in effigy, and there was open talk of covering him with a "Revolutionary coat of Tar and Feathers."[30] Fortunately, calmer heads prevailed and Loring was never subjected to physical violence. (Suttle's supporters were not so reticent. On his way home to Cambridge on the evening of the Burns rendition, Richard Dana was attacked by a gang of toughs who beat him with an iron bar, breaking his glasses and drawing blood.)

In addition to suffering social opprobrium, Loring was also subject to professional retribution at the hands of his peers. The political climate in Massachusetts demanded some form of reckoning against the agents of the slave power, and Loring had the misfortune of being the largest and most available local target. "Of the obnoxious actors in the tragedy of Burns, no one was within reach of the power of the State but the Commissioner, Edward Greeley Loring."[31]

The first reprisal against Loring came at Harvard, where he had been teaching since 1852. At the time Harvard Law School had only two full-time professors, with Loring carrying a full teaching load in his less remunerative position as lecturer. Loring continued to teach until his position as lecturer came up for renewal in early 1855. By then petitions were already in circulation demanding his removal from the probate court, and Harvard was under great pressure to dismiss him from its faculty. On February 15, 1855, the Board of Overseers voted overwhelmingly against the renewal of Loring's contract, effectively terminating him that very day. There was no recorded debate and the Board of Overseers did not announce the reason for its decision, but "no one doubted that the Board had [acted] to express their disapprobation of Mr. Loring's conduct as Commissioner."[32]

Even more serious was the campaign to oust Loring from the Suffolk County Probate Court, to which he had been appointed in 1847. The movement was spearheaded by Wendell Phillips and Theodore Parker, who inspired more than twelve thousand citizens to sign petitions to the legislature demanding Loring's removal. Significantly, "many of [the signatories] were women, who, as being a class of persons deeply interested in the character of Probate Judges, very properly exercised their right of petition on this occasion."[33] The petitions were referred to the legislature's Committee on Federal Relations, which held hearings in February and March 1855. In effect, "Edward G. Loring was on trial for having been a slave commissioner."[34]

Before the hearings began, Loring filed a "Remonstrance" on his own behalf, asserting that he had done nothing more than abide by his "painful duty" to apply the Fugitive Slave Act in the case before him. "Magistrates do not make the laws, and it is not for them to usurp or infringe upon that high power." Much as he might prefer otherwise, "the extradition of fugitives . . . is within the provisions of the constitution of the United States."[35] Having administered the law fairly and evenhandedly, he had committed no misconduct. His removal from office, he argued, would therefore be an abuse of power.

Wendell Phillips presented the primary case against Loring, which was premised on the obligations imposed by natural law. Phillips carefully pointed out that he did not accuse the judge of "official misconduct,"[36] conceding that Loring had fulfilled his office faithfully, and in accordance with the law. It was not the content of Loring's ruling in the Burns case that Phillips found objectionable, but rather his very willingness to serve as a fugitive slave commissioner. Such service, standing alone, was sufficient to disqualify Loring from the probate court because it demonstrated his lack of moral fitness to preside over matters involving the welfare of widows and orphans.

Phillips argued that every fugitive commissioner was necessarily complicit in the evils of slavery, no matter how closely he adhered to the positive law. Consequently, Loring should have resigned from his office rather than preside over the rendition of Burns. "To consent actively to aid in hunting slaves . . . shows a hardness of heart, a merciless spirit, a moral blindness, and utter spiritual death, that totally unfit a man for the judicial office." Massachusetts could exercise no control over the federal government or the federal courts, but the Commonwealth could demand that its own judges prefer the higher law to the fugitive law, even if that meant abandoning their concurrent federal appointments. Loring having failed that test, "the hunting of slaves is, then, a sufficient cause for removal from the Massachusetts bench."[37]

Many of Burns's supporters were surprised when Richard Henry Dana became Loring's most eloquent defender in the removal proceeding. "Yielding to none" in his hostility to the Fugitive Slave Act, in his "condemnation of the rendition of Anthony Burns," or his "fidelity to the antislavery principle," Dana nonetheless argued that the impeachment of Loring would do great damage to the principle of judicial independence. Although he did not use the as yet uncoined term "slippery slope," he expressed his concern that the removal of a judge following one unpopular decision could lead to similar actions in the future. Should that happen, judges might become "mere tenants at the will" of the legislature." "If you remove Judge Loring because he executed the Fugitive Slave Law," cautioned Dana, "other judges, here or elsewhere, may be removed because they do not."

Dana had little good to say about Loring as either a judge or a person. Loring had decided the Burns case incorrectly, "from causes partly psychological, and partly accidental." The judge showed little understanding "of justice and humanity," and instead based his decision "chiefly [on] the interests of property." Even so, Loring's disastrous judgment had not been the product of misconduct or corruption. As Dana explained, the public is better served when judges—even those who make mistakes—are protected "against the great powers of Legislative and Executive authority." He admitted that Judge Loring was "wrong in acting as a commissioner [and that] his decision was wrong," and yet he argued that it would be a greater wrong to strip him of his office. In the end, the commissioner had done nothing more than enforce the positive law which, in Dana's opinion, could never justify his expulsion from the bench. "We must do justice even to our enemies."[38]

The Massachusetts legislature did not agree with Dana. On March 22, 1855, the Committee on Federal Relations recommended, by a closely divided vote, that Loring be removed from office by the process of Legislative Address. Provided in the state constitution, Legislative Address allowed the removal of a judicial officer by the vote of both houses. Unlike impeachment, Address required neither a supermajority nor a finding of misconduct, although it did require the governor's assent. By the end of April, both chambers had approved the committee report by overwhelming margins. The formal address to the governor read as follows:

> The two branches of the Legislature, in General Court assembled, respectfully request that your Excellency would be pleased, by and with the advice of the Council, to remove Edward Greely Loring from the office of Judge of Probate for the county of Suffolk.[39]

Governor Henry Joseph Gardner had recently been elected on an antislavery platform and it was expected that he would readily sign the order of removal. Instead, however, the governor shocked his supporters by denying the legislature's petition and retaining Loring in office. Specifically invoking Dana's argument, Gardner concluded that the case against Loring had been inadequate. "Let us grant Judge Loring that benefit of [the] doubt which he is accused of having withheld from the individual arraigned before his tribunal," he wrote in his message to the legislature. Then Gardner made it completely clear that he rejected using the higher law—especially the version that had gained so much popular support in Boston—as a basis for judicial action:

> It may be pertinent to ask what the duty of judges is. Are they to
> expound the laws as made by the law-making power; or are they to
> construe them in accordance with popular sentiment? When the
> time arrives that a judge so violates his oath of office as to shape
> his decisions according to the fluctuations of popular feeling, we
> become a government, not of laws, but of men.[40]

Public passion, however, was not so easily denied. Antislavery sentiment
had grown so strong in Massachusetts that the legislature repeatedly attempted
to secure Loring's ouster. Gardner denied a second petition in 1857, but in 1858
Nathaniel Prentiss Banks was elected governor as a Republican. The legislature
once again presented a joint address against Loring, and this time the governor acceded. Four years after Anthony Burns had been deprived of his freedom, Edward Loring was finally deprived of his office. He did not, however,
remain unemployed for long. Democrat James Buchanan had been elected
president in 1856, defeating John C. Fremont, the Republicans' first-ever nom-
inee. Buchanan was no less a doughface than Franklin Pierce—and he was
fully committed to the enforcement of the Fugitive Slave Act. Nor did he forget his friends. Within weeks of Loring's removal, Buchanan appointed him
to the Court of Claims in Washington, D.C., where he served until his death
in 1877.

Anthony Burns had been right to fear the consequences of challenging Charles
Suttle's claim of ownership. "I shall fare worse if I resist," he told Dana at the
outset of the case, acquiescing to representation only when Theodore Parker assured him that "it can do you no harm to make a defence." The slave, of course,
understood the nature of slavery far better than did the abolitionists.

Notwithstanding his claim of benevolence, Suttle treated his recovered
slave with extreme brutality once they were safely back in Virginia. Following
a brief stay in Norfolk, Burns was transferred to an infamous slave pen in
Richmond, where he was kept handcuffed and chained for more than four
months. Held in a squalid cell accessible only through a trapdoor, he was fed
only once a day and provided with a pail of fetid drinking water only once or
twice a week. As the most famous slave in America, he was exhibited to gap-
ing crowds almost daily for the first several weeks of captivity. He was not,

however, allowed any contact with the other slaves in the jail. "The taint of freedom was upon him, and infection was dreaded."[41]

Meanwhile, Leonard Grimes continued his efforts to purchase Burns's freedom, believing that Suttle was still committed to release his slave for the price of $1,200. Suttle, however, had reconsidered. He deeply resented the "violent, corrupt, and perjured opposition" he had encountered in Boston, which had insulted his dignity and multiplied his expenses. Accordingly, he upped the price to $1,500, which Grimes was not immediately able to raise.[42]

Burns himself proved remarkably resilient. Showing the same resourcefulness that had helped him escape earlier that year, he somehow managed to smuggle a number of letters out of the slave jail, including one that was addressed to "Lawyer Danner Boston Massachusetts." Burns informed Dana that he could be purchased for as little as $800, although Suttle would not make the sale to anyone from Boston. Dana is not known to have responded and, in any event, a reply would have been futile. Imprisoned slaves were not allowed to receive correspondence from the North.

In November 1854 Suttle sold Burns to a planter named David McDaniel for the low price of $910. As a cripple and a runaway, Burns had little value as a plantation slave, but McDaniel's "object was to speculate in him." McDaniel soon began correspondence with Burns's friends in the North, and in February 1855 he reached an agreement to sell his slave for $1,300. This time Leonard Grimes succeeded in raising the necessary funds, and he arranged to meet McDaniel at Barnum's Hotel in Baltimore to effect the transaction.

Grimes showed courage in traveling to Baltimore. He had earlier spent two years in a Virginia prison for the offense of aiding fugitive slaves, so he risked a great deal by venturing into Maryland.[43] Although he had been born free, Grimes had no guarantee that his papers would not be challenged once he was back in a slave state. The meeting went off as planned, however, and on March 1, 1855, McDaniel accepted the money from Grimes, at last making Anthony Burns a free man.

By the next day Grimes and Burns were in New York, where Anthony addressed the congregation of the city's largest black church. He expressed his thanks to be back in the North, "where men of my color could live without any man daring to say to them, 'You are my property.'"[44]

Burns arrived in Boston several days later, just as Dana was defending Judge Loring before the Massachusetts legislature. Although the legislative committee heard testimony from a number of witnesses about Loring's conduct of the fugitive trial, it does not appear that anyone thought to call Burns himself. The former slave did address a mass meeting at the Tremont Temple, where he "repeated his tale of outrage and suffering" but did not state any opinion about Loring's fate. Instead of demanding vengeance, he announced his intention to "preach the gospel" that had freed his soul many years ago and had now freed his body.[45]

Burns spent the next several weeks giving speeches in Massachusetts and New York. On March 30 he and Grimes met with Richard Dana. Characteristically self-absorbed, Dana wrote in his journal that Burns had come "to thank me for my defence & to pay his respects." Dana found Burns to be "in good health & spirits" and appraised him as "a modest, conscientious man [whose] story must be drawn from him." For several hours Burns told Dana about his return to the South—including his harsh imprisonment by Suttle and his relatively kind treatment by McDaniel. From the window of his office, Dana showed Burns "the Court House where he was confined" and pointed out the courtroom where the hearing had been held. For once, Dana did not see himself as the center of the story:

> What a change & what a life for an obscure negro! Now he visits the scene of his agony of trial, a hero, a martyr, with crowds of the learned & intelligent of a civilised community listening to his words! Who can tell what a day may bring forth!

His meeting with Burns did not cause Dana to reassess his support for Commissioner Loring. "I have every reason to be gratified & satisfied with the course I took in opposing the removal of Judge Loring," he wrote in the same journal entry. "The Committee have behaved shabbily," he continued, and the report favoring removal was "a wretched affair."[46]

Anthony Burns did not remain in Boston for long. Although he had several offers to earn a living on the antislavery lecture circuit—including one from P. T. Barnum!—he turned them all down. Burns had often expressed his desire to study for the ministry, and an anonymous "lady of Boston" generously provided him with a scholarship to attend Oberlin College for that purpose. By early summer Burns was in Ohio.

It was altogether fitting that he should attend Oberlin, which had been founded by abolitionists in 1833. If Boston was the intellectual center of antislavery theory, Oberlin was in many ways the heartland of abolitionist practice.

Located along the escape route from Kentucky to Canada, the town of Ober-lin prided itself on providing a safe haven for runaways, sheltering perhaps the largest black population by percentage of any municipality in the North. As Anthony Burns was no doubt instructed on his first day of class, there was no place in the United States more firmly devoted to the teachings of the higher law.

12

FREEDOM ON THE WESTERN RESERVE

In the early autumn of 1858, runaway slave John Price was living quietly in Oberlin, Ohio, while working intermittently as an agricultural laborer. He would soon become the focal point of the longest, and most radically politicized, fugitive slave trial of the antebellum era—a case that saw the first forthright invocation of higher law in a U.S. courtroom. Price himself knew little about politics, and surely less about abolitionist legal theory. He only knew that he wanted to be a free man. Nonetheless, his escape to the Western Reserve—an area in northeast Ohio noted for its militant antislavery sentiment—set the stage for a profound development in the legal struggle against the Fugitive Slave Act.[1]

Price had been born in northern Kentucky in the mid-1830s, the property of the well-to-do Bacon family of Mason County. In 1846 he was inherited by young John Parks Glenn Bacon, who operated a small farm about six miles from the Ohio River. John Bacon allowed Price a good deal of autonomy, entrusting him with management of the farm and sometimes leaving him unsupervised for several days at a time. As was typical among slave owners, Bacon believed he had always been generous to his slaves and had given them no cause for discontent.[2]

At some point, however, Price grew unhappy with his life in bondage, proximity to Ohio having no doubt exposed him to the possibility of freedom. Along with two other slaves—his cousin Dinah, who also belonged to Bacon, and Frank, who lived on a neighboring farm—he plotted an escape. An opportunity arose in mid-January 1856, when Bacon took his family on a short trip to visit his wife's father. Almost as soon as Bacon departed, John and Dinah stole two horses from their master's barn and rendezvoused with Frank. With Dinah riding double behind one of the men, they reached the Ohio River within a few hours. Although the river appeared frozen solid, it was impossible to be certain in the darkness. They released their horses and ventured onto the ice. Fortunately, the ice held and they were able to reach the other side.

Now on foot, the fugitives continued traveling north. Through either luck or prearrangement, they made contact with a family of abolitionists who provided them with food and shelter for the night, as well as directions to other safe houses along the underground route to Canada. At some point Dinah decided to go her separate way. Nothing more is known of her; she presumably either lived the rest of her life among the free black community in Ohio or she somehow found her way to Canada.

By late February or early March, John Price and Frank had settled in Oberlin, about forty miles southwest of Cleveland, apparently having abandoned any plans to reach Canada. The arrival of two more runaways would not have caused a stir anywhere in the Western Reserve, and it was even less unusual in Oberlin. The college had been founded on the principles of both coeducation and racial integration, and the village shared most of the school's attributes. Black and white citizens lived next door to one another, patronized one another's businesses, worshipped in the same churches, and attended the same schools.

At the time Oberlin was probably the most fully integrated community in the United States, and it was therefore often the destination of choice for free blacks. Frederick Douglass sent his daughter Rosetta to study at Oberlin, as did the benefactors of Anthony Burns. Harriet Beecher Stowe financed the Oberlin education of the former slaves Mary and Emily Edmonson, whose freedom had been purchased following their spectacular failed escape attempt from Washington, D.C., on the schooner *Pearl*. Sarah Margru Kinson, one of the slaves freed by the U.S. Supreme Court in the *Amistad* decision, also attended Oberlin before returning to West Africa as a schoolteacher.

The citizens of Oberlin also welcomed escaped slaves, often extending public assistance to destitute fugitives, who were cryptically referred to as "poor strangers" or "transient paupers" in the records of the town's expenditures. John Price was one such beneficiary of Oberlin's support, receiving $1.25 per week for his "board & keep" during times when he was unemployed. The payments to Price were authorized by the town clerk, John Mercer Langston, who was himself a free black man. An attorney and a graduate of Oberlin College, Langston was one of the first black public officials anywhere in the United States.[3]

Throughout the 1850s Oberlin earned a reputation as "one of the most notorious refuges of fugitive slaves in the North." Proslavery Democrats scornfully referred to the town's residents as "Ober-litionists," but students, faculty, and townsfolk accepted the would-be epithet with pride. The *Oberlin Evangelist* boasted that the town was "second only to Canada as an asylum for the hunted fugitives," and while that was probably an exaggeration, it spoke volumes about the community's commitment to racial equality and resistance to the Fugitive Slave Act.[4]

The highly visible presence of so many black people had the natural and unfortunate effect of drawing the attention of Kentucky slave hunters. Like slave catchers everywhere, the Kentuckians were not always scrupulous to distinguish between fugitives and free blacks, nor did the Fugitive Slave Act provide them any great incentive for care. Although Oberlin's black residents were certainly safer than those living closer to the Ohio River—where it was far easier simply to drag a captive back to Kentucky—they still lived in constant fear of kidnapping.

The theologians of Oberlin were not millenarians, but they knew they were living in remarkable times. Even if the battle against slavery was not yet an apocalyptic struggle, it was certainly a biblical confrontation between good and evil. In the years immediately preceding 1858, it must have seemed that the forces of slavery were winning.

The near civil war in Kansas had seen proslavery forces sack the abolitionist town of Lawrence while federal troops declined to intervene. Massachusetts's abolitionist Senator Charles Sumner was nearly beaten to death on the floor of the U.S. Senate by South Carolina congressman Preston Brooks, who was never prosecuted for the attack. Although the antislavery Republican Party was organized and made great strides in response to the excesses of the slave power, the proslavery Democrat James Buchanan soundly defeated John Fremont in the 1856 presidential election. The Democrats had run on a platform that endorsed "popular sovereignty"—meaning the spread of slavery into Kansas and other previously free territories—while denouncing the "Black Republicans" for their presumed sympathy toward enslaved, free, and fugitive "Negroes." Following his inauguration, Buchanan did not disappoint his southern allies. He urged Congress to admit Kansas as a slave state under the fraudulent Lecompton constitution, which declared that "the right of the owner of a slave . . . is the same and as inviolable as the right of the owner of any property whatever."[5] Although Congress narrowly defeated a resolution to admit Kansas as a slave state, border ruffians from Missouri renewed their violent attacks, murdering five free staters in May 1858.[6]

Perhaps most ominously, in March 1857 the U.S. Supreme Court had delivered its decision in the *Dred Scott* case, in which Chief Justice Roger Taney announced that no black person could be a citizen of the United States. Taney's most infamous statement described blacks as "beings of an inferior order, and altogether unfit to associate with the white race, either in social or political relations, and so far inferior that they had no rights which the white man was bound to respect." But the decision's consequences were in some ways broader and worse even than that. Taney's *Dred Scott* opinion had declared the Missouri Compromise unconstitutional on the ground that Congress lacked the authority to prohibit slavery in the federal territories. The Fifth Amendment, the chief justice held, guaranteed a slaveholder's right to own human property, including the right to travel and settle with his slaves in federal territories, and thus, even a duly elected territorial legislature could not enact laws prohibiting slavery. From that premise, Taney plausibly reasoned that Congress "could confer no power on any local government, established by its authority, to violate the provisions of the Constitution," which "distinctly and expressly" guaranteed the right "of property in a slave."[7] (Justice Robert Grier, who had presided over the Christiana trial, concurred with Taney; Justice Benjamin Curtis of Boston, however, dissented.)

Abolitionists and Free-Soilers everywhere were staggered by the *Dred Scott* decision, which appeared to many as the continuation of a "decade-long trend" toward the nationalization of slavery. If the Constitution protected slaveholding to the same extent as "property of any other description," then perhaps even the free states lacked the authority to prohibit slavery within their borders. As Abraham Lincoln cautioned the following year in his "House Divided" speech, "We shall *lie down* pleasantly dreaming that the people of *Missouri* are on the verge of making their state *free;* and we shall *awake* to the *reality,* instead, that the *Supreme* Court has made *Illinois* a *slave* State." Lincoln was dramatizing for political effect, but Taney's proslavery opinion definitely "lent credence to the fear of many northerners that an aggressive slave power was determined to extend its peculiar institution ... into the free states."[8]

By the summer of 1858 Oberliners had good reason to believe that slave power was indeed seeking to extend its reach deeply into the Western Reserve. Within just a few months there had been repeated attempts to capture fugitives in or near Oberlin.

In one instance, slave catchers tried to seize a black woman and her two children about a mile from the college. The mother's screams, however, alerted neighbors and caused the intruders to retreat. Undaunted, the slave catchers tried again a few days later, on the very night of Oberlin's annual commencement exercises. This time the response was even more forceful. Hearing the woman's cries, attendees at the commencement set off the town's fire bells. The entire fire company, including students and residents, then rushed to the black family's home and chased away the slave hunters. Also that summer, federal Deputy Marshal Anson Dayton led a midnight raid on the Wagoner family. Dayton's efforts failed ignominiously, however, when Mr. Wagoner met him at the door, shotgun in hand. Unwilling to risk their lives, Dayton and his posse fled into the night.

An attorney by profession, Dayton had once been fairly popular in Oberlin, having served for several years as town clerk and secretary of the board of education. In 1857, however, he had been replaced in both positions by John Mercer Langston, thus making him the first white man in the United States to be ousted from office in favor of an African-American. Dayton did not take well to his dismissal and he promptly changed his political allegiance from Republican to Democrat. He was rewarded for his defection with an appointment as deputy U.S. marshal, tasked by the Buchanan administration with enforcement of the Fugitive Slave Act. Still resentful over his loss of the clerk's position to Langston, Dayton accepted his new responsibilities with some determination but little success. In addition to the Wagoner fiasco, he had also failed on a foray into nearby Painesville, where he had been driven away by an armed mob. By September 1858 Oberliners considered Dayton "*persona non grata,* as he was suspected of espionage on the colored population and being in close touch with would-be captors."[9]

Despite the many attempts, there had been no successful slave seizures in Oberlin or its environs, every raid having been thwarted by the fugitives and their white protectors. Nonetheless, there were good reasons for the community to remain vigilant. Slave hunters were clearly abroad in the Western Reserve, and Oberlin appeared to be their prime target. Augustus Chambers—a freed slave who owned an Oberlin smithy—summed up the town's sentiment when he swore to resist any kidnapping, with arms if necessary. "As God as my judge," he said, "the man who tries to take my life will lose his own." Chambers scoffed at the possibility of a fair hearing under the Fugitive Slave Act. "When you pick up a negro worth $1,000 or $2,000, there is *money to divide among all concerned.* There is *nothing coming* to anybody if you sent him free."[10]

Chambers accurately described the mercenary nature of slave catching when he observed that "any white man who wants to make a few hundred dollars can swear away my rights." The business was quick, it was profitable, and it required very little in the way of capital or other resources. Any sufficiently bold and enterprising individual could set to work as a slave hunter, and in southern Ohio he could count on the assistance of federal marshals, U.S. commissioners, and much of the local citizenry. Things were more complicated, however, in such places as Oberlin, where it was relatively easy to locate fugitives but risky to capture them. And it would prove even harder still to carry a slave out of the Western Reserve.

Everyone who saw Anderson Jennings immediately recognized him as a fine "specimen of a Kentucky Slave Catcher." Tall, bearded, and powerfully built, he traveled well armed with a brace of revolvers and a bowie knife (which he proudly called his "Arkansas toothpick"). Jennings first arrived in Oberlin in late August 1858, on the trail of an escaped slave named Henry. The slave hunter sought the assistance of Deputy Marshal Dayton, but the two of them were unable to locate their quarry. Dayton did, however, provide Jennings with the descriptions of several other known fugitives, and the Kentuckian believed he could identify one of them as John Price, the property of his neighbor John Bacon. Jennings then sent a letter to Bacon, informing him that he had "discovered a nigger near Oberlin answering to the description of his runaway, John," and requesting written authority to capture Price.[11]

Upon receiving Jennings's letter, Bacon proceeded to the Mason County courthouse to obtain the necessary papers from the county clerk, Robert Cochran. Because Cochran was not available, the deputy clerk drew up a power of attorney appointing Jennings as Bacon's lawful agent "to capture and return [the negro, John] now at large in the State of Ohio." The document described the missing slave as "about twenty years old, about five feet six or eight inches high, heavy set, copper colored, and will weigh about 140 or 150 pounds." After Bacon executed the document, the deputy clerk signed Cochran's name and affixed the county seal. As Bacon was leaving the courthouse, Cochran suddenly returned to the building. Advised of the situation, Cochran asked Bacon to re-acknowledge his signature. For some reason, however, Cochran himself never signed the power of attorney, but instead left his deputy's signature in place.[12]

Once the documentation seemed complete, Bacon entrusted the power of attorney to another neighbor, Mason County slave catcher Richard Mitchell, with instructions to deliver it to Jennings in Ohio. Bacon gave Mitchell $50 for expenses and promised him an additional $500 for the return of his property. The two slave hunters rendezvoused in Oberlin on September 8, meeting at a hotel owned by Chauncey Wack, one of the few proslavery Democrats in town. The Kentuckians also conferred with Deputy Anson Dayton, seeking his participation in their mission. Dayton had no qualms about capturing Price, but he declined to assist in the arrest. Having twice recently been threatened at gunpoint, the deputy had apparently lost much of his enthusiasm for tracking fugitives. In lieu of his assistance, Dayton recommended that the Kentuckians obtain a warrant from a fugitive slave commissioner for the Southern District of Ohio, located in Columbus.

At first Jennings probably balked at Dayton's advice, as it involved considerable inconvenience and expense. A commissioner's warrant was unnecessary under the Fugitive Slave Act, which unambiguously permitted capture pursuant solely to a "duly authorized" power of attorney, so long as it was "acknowledged and certified under the seal of some legal officer or court" of any state. And even if a warrant was desirable as a backup measure, it would have been quicker and cheaper to seek it from the Northern District of Ohio in nearby Cleveland. Dayton, however, was familiar with conditions in Oberlin, and he realized that there was likely to be stiff resistance to the arrest of an alleged fugitive. The slave hunters would need all the legal authority they could muster, even if the warrant and power of attorney were technically redundant. And whatever the convenience of traveling to Cleveland instead of Columbus, it would be more than offset by risk that they might be recognized and intercepted by Cleveland's many abolitionists. In the end, Jennings accepted Dayton's counsel; he and Mitchell headed for the Southern District of Ohio.

Early on September 10, 1858, Jennings presented his power of attorney to acting U.S. Commissioner Sterne Chittenden, who held an impromptu hearing that was devoted more to formality than to substance. Based on nothing more than Jennings's word, and without questioning the bona fides of the slave catcher's documentation, Chittenden concluded that John was "a person held to labor in the State of Kentucky [who] has escaped into and is now a fugitive slave . . . in the State of Ohio." The commissioner then issued a warrant authorizing any federal officer to seize John and bring his "body before some United States Commissioner, within and for the Southern District of Ohio." Perhaps because he had never before issued a fugitive warrant, Chittenden inscribed a handwritten "scroll" following his signature, rather than affix the court's embossed seal.[13]

Jennings still needed to enlist reinforcements before heading toward the Western Reserve. His first recruit was federal Deputy Marshal Jacob Lowe, an experienced slave catcher with whom he had worked several times before. Lowe then suggested that they ask Samuel Davis, a part-time jailer and deputy sheriff, to join the posse. Davis needed very little convincing, especially after Jennings offered the two officers $50 apiece for their efforts.

With their business in Columbus concluded, the four men returned that evening to Chauncey Wack's hotel in Oberlin, there to plan the apprehension of John Price. They now had plenty of muscle, but they still lacked a local agent who could help them locate the fugitive without attracting too much attention. Wack suggested that Jennings might get the necessary help from General Lewis Boynton, a prosperous farmer who lived about two miles out of town (the military title was honorary, bestowed for service in the state militia).

On Saturday, September 11, Jennings and Lowe paid an unannounced visit to the Boynton farm. As it happened, Boynton was away on an errand, so the ever-cautious Jennings told the farmer's wife that he was interested in buying some dairy cows. Mrs. Boynton invited the two men to stay overnight so they could talk business with her husband the next morning. Jennings explained his mission to Boynton over breakfast on Sunday morning, but the old farmer was reluctant to participate in the slave-hunting plan. While the adults were still negotiating, Boyton's thirteen-year-old son, Shakespeare, joined the conversation. Jennings was so impressed by Shakespeare's energy and intelligence that he requested permission to make "an arrangement with the General's little boy to come and get the nigger out of town." The elder Boynton "made no objections" to his son's employment as a slave catcher and so, for a promise of $20, young Shakespeare agreed to lure John Price to a place where he could be captured without interference.

On the morning of Monday, September 13, the slave hunters made their move. Driving his father's horse and buggy, Shakespeare Boynton approached John Price at his home in Oberlin. As instructed by Jennings, Shakespeare offered Price temporary work digging potatoes on the Boynton farm. Price declined, however, because he had promised to help care for an injured friend. Thinking quickly, Shakespeare suggested that Price might still enjoy a short ride in the country. "Well, John," he said, "you've been cooped up there so long, the fresh air must feel good to you; and you may as well have a good ride while you're about it. I'll bring you back again."[14] Trusting the youngster, Price accepted the wagon ride, little expecting that he was being led into an ambush.

John Price and Shakespeare Boynton had traveled about a mile out of town when a buggy carrying Lowe, Mitchell, and Davis overtook them. The three slave catchers surrounded Price, seizing him and forcing him out of the farm wagon. Price resisted momentarily, but Mitchell threatened him with a pistol and the fugitive realized he had no choice but to surrender. "I'll go with you," he said, seemingly resigned to his capture. Having completed his part of the job, Shakespeare Boynton headed back toward Oberlin so he could carry the news of the successful mission to Anderson Jennings, who was waiting at Wack's Hotel.

With John Price seated securely between them, the slave catchers turned their buggy toward the nearby town of Wellington, where they planned to catch a late-afternoon train to Columbus. Deputy Lowe showed the commissioner's warrant to Price and informed him that he was being taken "back to his master." Mitchell, who had known Price in Mason County, made a point of shaking hands with the prisoner so he could later testify that Price had recognized him. Neither white man bothered to mention the necessity of a hearing under the Fugitive Slave Act. Of course, there was little reason at that point to talk of legalities. John Price had no rights that the white men were bound to respect, and the hearing was going to be a mere formality on the way back to Kentucky.

⸺⸱⸺

Mitchell, Lowe, and Davis were probably congratulating themselves as they proceeded toward Wellington. Shortly after they reached the halfway point, perhaps five miles and a little more than an hour's ride from Oberlin, they encountered another carriage headed in the opposite direction. Reckoning this to be his last chance at freedom, Price called out for help as the two wagons passed each other. It was a tense moment, but the two men in the Oberlin-bound wagon seemed to have ignored Price's cries.

It turned out, however, that one of those men was Ansel Lyman, an Oberlin student and militant abolitionist who had served with John Brown in Kansas. Lyman had not ignored Price at all; rather, he had realized that he would need reinforcements to challenge three armed slave hunters. Immediately upon arriving in Oberlin, Lyman raised the alarm—a black man had been kidnapped!—drawing dozens into the street. As word spread and the crowd grew larger, John Watson, a freed slave who ran a grocery store, was the first man to set off for Wellington. Many others—both black and white, male and female—followed on horseback and in wagons. Among them was Simeon Bushnell, a bookstore clerk, who shouted, "They have carried off one of our men in *broad daylight.*" "They can't have him," called others in response.

Hundreds of Oberliners set off to rescue John Price, even if they had to walk. The crowd was composed of students and faculty from the college, ministers, merchants, artisans, lawyers, laborers, and farmers. There were freedmen and runaway slaves, heedless of the potential risk to their own liberty. The rescuers included radical black men such as John Copeland and Lewis Sheridan Leary, who would later join John Brown at Harpers Ferry, but it also included many of Oberlin's pacifists and missionaries.[15]

Many of the men brought firearms, including Charles Langston, who tucked a pistol into his waistband. At age forty-one, Charles was twelve years older than his more famous younger brother, John Mercer Langston. Both Langstons (as well as their older brother, Gideon) had been born in Virginia, the sons of plantation owner Ralph Quarles, a Revolutionary War veteran, and his former slave, Lucy Jane Langston. Unlike the great majority of sexual encounters between white men and black women in the slave South—which were at best coercive and more accurately characterized as rape—the liaison between Ralph and Lucy was close and loving. Eventually their romantic relationship became "permanent and open," a marriage in all but name. Ralph Quarles raised his three mulatto sons as free persons, providing them with the "intellectual and manual training" necessary to manage his plantation and conduct their affairs. Quarles also provided for Gideon, Charles, and John Mercer in his will, leaving his substantial estate to the "children of Lucy, a woman whom I have emancipated." Presciently, Quarles arranged for his family to relocate to Ohio in the event of his death, which occurred in the spring of 1834, only six months after the execution of his will, when John Mercer was four years old and Charles was sixteen.[16]

Charles and John Mercer Langston both grew to adulthood in Ohio, keenly aware of their heritage as the children of a former slave and a Revolutionary soldier. Although he did not achieve his brother's prominence, Charles was not without accomplishments of his own. Among the first blacks to be educated at Oberlin, Charles worked primarily as a teacher and school principal, and occasionally as a journalist, while rising to a position of importance in Ohio's nascent black civil rights movement. He was appointed executive secretary and business agent of the Ohio State Anti-Slavery Society in 1853, and he served as an Ohio delegate to Frederick Douglass's National Black Convention in Rochester later that year. Charles Langston also played a behind-the-scenes role in organizing both the Free Soil and Republican parties, frequently consulting and corresponding with white leaders such as Joshua Giddings and Salmon Chase. Nonetheless, Langston had few illusions about the future of black Americans in the electoral system or the likelihood of peaceful change, having praised the "Christiana patriots" for their armed defense of liberty. Once, when touring the state on behalf of Douglass's newspaper, he was attacked by white thugs in the small village of Marseilles, managing to escape only by sneaking out of his hotel in the middle of the night.[17] Thus, it was not surprising that Langston would carry a gun on his mission to rescue John Price.

Lowe, Mitchell, and Davis arrived with their captive in Wellington sometime between noon and 1:00 p.m., completely unaware that they were being pursued. Anderson Jennings met them shortly afterward, having departed Oberlin before Ansel Lyman had raised the alarm. With more than four hours to spare before the departure of the train to Columbus, the white men and their black prisoner repaired for a meal to Wadsworth's Hotel, located just a few blocks from the railroad station. Jennings and Price recognized each other, having been neighbors in Mason County, and the two men shook hands. Jennings would later testify that Price expressed happiness about the prospect of returning to Kentucky, but the bewildered fugitive obviously had little choice about his destination.

The town square was unusually crowded that day because a fire earlier in the morning had drawn a large number of onlookers. Thus, the slave catchers did not immediately notice the growing crowd when, at about 2:00 p.m., the Oberlin rescuers began to reach Wellington. The first rescuers did not know where to find the slave hunters, so they simply gathered in the square, cheering as their numbers grew. Eventually Jennings and company realized what was going on. The shouts from the square had become loud and angry, and there was no mistaking the presence of black men with rifles. With the route to the railroad station completely blocked, and the posse's whereabouts sure to be exposed at any moment, Jennings turned to innkeeper Oliver Wadsworth for assistance.

Wadsworth's Hotel was hardly a fortress, but the owner was a slavery sympathizer who ordered his employees to guard the entrances and stairways. They moved John Price to an attic room, accessible only by a ladder, while Jennings and Lowe tried to figure a way out of their predicament. Although Wadsworth's guards might be able to keep the mob out of the hotel, there was no way to reach the railroad station without additional assistance.

Meanwhile, someone in the square discovered that the slave hunters were at Wadsworth's, and soon everyone was surging toward the hotel. Estimates of the crowd's size varied, but there were at least three hundred people—perhaps as many as five hundred, including both Oberliners and Wellington locals—more than enough to shut off every exit from the building. For the time being, there was a standoff, as the men on each side considered their options under the law, and otherwise.

John Watson, the black storekeeper, had been among the first rescuers to reach Wellington. Watson did not know that Price had been captured pursuant to legal documents and he almost certainly did not care. Along with the other Oberliners, he believed that the Fugitive Slave Act was invalid and that higher law rendered every slave catcher a criminal. It was Watson's idea to obtain an arrest warrant for kidnapping, so he headed for Wellington's town hall rather than join the growing crowd outside Wadsworth's. Based on Watson's sworn statement that John Price was a "freeman," Justice of the Peace Isaac Bennett issued a warrant and turned it over to Constable Barnabas Meacham for service of process.

That was not the first time Ohio abolitionists had attempted creative use of the criminal law as the means of foiling slave catchers. In January 1856—the same unusually frigid winter in which John Price fled from Bacon's farm—the Garner family had organized its own extraordinary escape from slavery. Robert and Margaret Garner had apparently devised the daring plan. They stole a horse and sled from Col. Archibald Gaines, their master on Maplewood Plantation, and used it to carry their four children, as well as Robert's parents, to the bank of the frozen Ohio River near Covington, Kentucky. Abandoning the sled, they crossed the ice on foot to Cincinnati.

Unfortunately, Gaines discovered the theft within hours, and he was soon on the trail of the missing slaves. A powerful and hot-tempered man, Gaines obtained a fugitive slave warrant from Commissioner John Pendery in Cincinnati and recruited several deputy federal marshals to his side. Somehow Gaines managed to learn—probably from an informant—that the Garners were hiding at the cabin of Margaret's cousin Elijah Kite, a free black man. After just "twelve hours as fugitives and perhaps only six or seven on free soil, the Garners found themselves surrounded by an armed posse."[18] Gaines called on the slaves to surrender and one of the deputies read out the warrant, but Robert Garner defiantly shouted back his refusal.

As a small crowd gathered, the federal officers decided to "force an entrance" rather than continue the siege. The deputies began to break down the cabin's front door, only to be met by gunfire from Robert. The desperate slave succeeded in severely wounding one of the slave catchers before he was wrestled to the ground and subdued.

Robert was able to hold off the posse for a few minutes, as Margaret retreated with her children to a back room. Realizing that she had no chance of escape, and no doubt recognizing her abusive master, Margaret determined that she would not allow her children to be returned to slavery. "Before my children shall be taken back to Kentucky," she cried, "I will kill every one of them." Taking a knife, she slit the throat of her three-year-old daughter, Mary, nearly decapitating the child. Margaret then turned to her other children—sons ages six and four, and an infant daughter—but the posse had by then fought their way into the cabin and the deputies restrained her.

News rapidly spread of the Garner family's tragedy. All across the country, newspapers carried the story of the black mother who had murdered her daughter to save her from slavery. Many of the accounts were freighted with sexual innuendo. Abolitionist Lucy Stone wrote about the "degradation [of] female slaves" and Margaret Garner's steely resolve "not to give her little daughter to that life." Other writers speculated—quite possibly accurately—that Gaines had been the father of some of Margaret's children.

In fact, the colonel had been emotionally devastated by Mary's death—he was seen sobbing over the child's corpse on the night of the raid—but that did not soften his insistence on reclaiming his other property. Pursuing his rights under the Fugitive Slave Act, Gaines demanded a commissioner's hearing so he could obtain the necessary certificates of removal for all of his slaves, Margaret included.

Lawyers rushed to Garner's defense, including John Joliffe, the acknowledged leader of Cincinnati's antislavery bar. But even with the help of a master advocate, there was little hope that Margaret could win her case. There was no doubt that she was Gaines's slave; her own actions had proved as much. The Fugitive Slave Act did not allow her to take the stand on her own behalf, so she could not testify to her exploitation by Gaines or her reasons for wanting to spare her daughter similar "cruel treatment on the part of their master." And in any event, the Act did not recognize any defenses. So long as Gaines's papers were in order, even the most sympathetic federal commissioner would have little choice but to commit Margaret and her children to slavery in Kentucky.

Joliffe, however, had a strategy in mind. He claimed that Garner was liable to be indicted for Mary's murder, which ought to subject her exclusively to the criminal law of Ohio. He then succeeded in obtaining a writ of habeas corpus from an Ohio probate judge, ordering that Garner be removed from federal custody and turned over to the Ohio courts. Joliffe believed that a homicide conviction would send his client "to an Ohio penitentiary, safely out of [her] master's reach." She could then be pardoned by Republican Governor Salmon Chase, who had been elected the previous year on an antislavery ticket.

As expected, the federal marshal refused to honor the habeas writ, which remained outstanding when Margaret's fugitive slave hearing began in front of Commissioner John Pendery. Midway through the proceeding, therefore, Hamilton County Prosecutor Joseph Cox obtained a grand jury indictment, officially charging Margaret Garner with murder. The prosecutor was acting in concert with Joliffe, in the hope that an actual indictment and warrant might carry more weight than the earlier writ. "I felt it my duty," said Cox, "to shield her as much as possible" from the fate of slavery.

Joliffe argued that the state's criminal charges took precedence over the fugitive slave case, which, after all, was only a civil claim for property. Commissioner Pendery, however, was unmoved. He refused even to receive a copy of the Hamilton County murder indictment before ruling on the rendition claim. The matter was strictly "a question of property" under the law of Kentucky, Pendery held, without addressing the pending criminal charges. He therefore ordered that Margaret Garner and her children should be "delivered into the custody and possession of the claimant, Archibald K. Gaines."[19]

Despite Ohio's competing demand for custody of Margaret Garner, U.S. Marshal Hiram Robinson acted immediately to enforce Commissioner Pendery's order. He and his deputies escorted the slaves to a ferry landing, where he personally delivered them to his counterpart from Kentucky. There had been public calls for Governor Chase to intervene, with the state militia if necessary, in order to defend Ohio's sovereignty. But Chase had no appetite for conflict with the federal government, and he took no action. The ferry departed without incident, and Margaret Garner was soon back under the control of her master.

Having failed to enforce Ohio's jurisdiction before Garner was taken from his state, Salmon Chase later attempted to obtain her extradition from Kentucky. Chase's belated efforts were thwarted, however, by the stalling tactics of Kentucky Governor Charles Morehead, who temporarily prevented the service of Chase's writ of extradition. That delay allowed Archibald Gaines sufficient time to take Margaret Garner aboard a riverboat bound for Arkansas, well beyond the effective reach of Ohio's legal process. Abolitionists took Chase to task for his failure to act more decisively when he had the chance. Theodore Parker, who had long been Chase's ally and friend, issued a stinging denunciation of the governor's refusal to use force. "It had been foolish to rely on an arrest warrant," said Parker. After all, the only law that "slave-hunters respect is writ on the parchment of a drumhead." Chase was so troubled by the criticism that he never spoke publicly about the Garner case, even when he was confronted by a similar state-federal conflict following the seizure of fugitive John Price.

———◦•◦———

Constable Meacham was no doubt well aware of the Garner case when he attempted to serve the kidnapping warrant at Wadsworth's Hotel. The officer had no trouble reaching the room where John was held, where he announced that "he had a warrant for three men who had the negro." He was sharply interrupted by Jacob Lowe, however, who told the constable that "he had better not be too fast." Displaying the federal warrant, Deputy Lowe informed Meacham that the slave catchers had no duty to obey the orders of an Ohio court. Lowe also threatened that Meacham himself would be liable for damages under the Fugitive Slave Act "if the negro was lost." Lowe's warning was well taken: the Fugitive Slave Act did indeed prohibit "all molestation" of the slave catchers "by any process issued by any court, judge, [or] magistrate," and it also imposed a $1,000 fine upon any person "who shall knowingly and willingly obstruct, hinder, or prevent" the delivery of a fugitive to his master. With little confidence in his own authority, and without any solid reason to believe the Ohio authorities would back him up, Meacham retreated from the hotel.[20]

Meacham would hold on to the warrant for the rest of the afternoon, but he refused to serve it despite the urging of Charles Langston and others. Confused about the contradictory requirements of state and federal law, Meacham tried to obtain a written guarantee of indemnification from several Wellington lawyers—most of whom prudently turned him down.

Lowe had succeeded in intimidating Meacham, but the surrounding crowd had only grown more militant in the meantime. Anxious to avoid violence, Jennings and Lowe agreed to meet with a series of the rescuers' representatives in the hope that they could negotiate some sort of compromise. The slave catchers showed their documents to everyone who was willing to look at the papers, proposing at one point that a delegation of rescuers accompany them to Columbus to ensure that Price received a fair hearing. Nobody was willing to accept the offer, however, and it is unlikely in any event that anyone could have persuaded the leaderless crowd to disperse.

As the Kentuckians' dilemma worsened, Jennings decided to appeal directly to the crowd. Stepping out onto a hotel balcony, Jennings declared he wanted "no controversy with the people of Ohio." Nonetheless, he said, "this boy is mine by the laws of Kentucky and the United States." Jennings had badly misjudged his listeners. His appeal to the laws of Kentucky only made the crowd angrier. "There are no slaves in Ohio," someone shouted back. "The boy is willing to go to Kentucky," Jennings replied. That made the crowd angrier still, and they called for the slave to be brought to the balcony.

Surprisingly, Jennings complied, bringing Price out to speak for himself. Earlier, in the hotel attic, surrounded by four armed men, Price had attempted to placate his captors by agreeing to return to his master. Out on the balcony, however, the frightened slave was more evasive, saying only that he "supposed" he would have to return because Jennings "had got the papers for him."

Reacting to Price's obvious equivocation, people in the crowd called for him to jump from the balcony, with one man shouting that "all hell" could not force the captive to Kentucky against his will. Before anything more could happen, however, John Copeland started waving his pistol at Jennings. Copeland had few qualms about killing in the name of freedom—as he later proved at Harpers Ferry—although it was unlikely that he intended to fire a shot at such close quarters. But the mere sight of an armed black man was enough to panic Jennings, who hastily dragged Price back into the hotel.

Not every Oberliner was ready to use force. Charles Langston thought that a writ of habeas corpus—to be obtained from the county judge in nearby Elyria—might be more useful than Constable Meacham's feeble warrant (which had been issued by a mere justice of the peace). As Langston crisscrossed the square trying to borrow a horse for the trip to Elyria, Lowe happened to see him from the hotel window. Lowe and Langston had known each other in Columbus—where Langston had once worked—and the deputy believed that the schoolteacher "was a reasonable man." Lowe sent for Langston, in a last-ditch effort to resolve the impasse. To his misfortune, Langston would be one of the last Oberliners to negotiate with the posse.

The discussion between Lowe and Langston was cordial, though unproductive. Langston attempted to persuade the deputy to release his prisoner, pointing out that the crowd was "bent upon a rescue at all hazards." Lowe countered by renewing the offer to have a committee of Oberliners escort him to Columbus. Acknowledging the apparent legitimacy of Lowe's papers, Langston agreed to present the proposal to the crowd, although he assured the deputy marshal that the rescuers would have none of it. To emphasize his point, Langston spoke one last time to Lowe, saying either "*We* will have him anyhow," or "*They* will have him anyhow." The disputed pronoun would have great significance later, when Langston was prosecuted for violating the Fugitive Slave Act.

Not long after Langston emerged empty-handed from the hotel, members of the crowd decided that the time for talk had ended. Separate groups stormed the building from all sides, entering almost simultaneously through the front and back doors. The charge up the front steps was spearheaded by Ansel Lyman and Oberlin student William Lincoln. The assault on the back door was led by John Copeland and several other black men from Oberlin. The two groups of rescuers struggled past Wadsworth's employees, making their way up an interior staircase until they reached the door of the attic redoubt. They called on Jennings and Lowe to release Price, but the deputy marshal refused. He was personally responsible for Price's custody, and he would not surrender his prisoner no matter how hopeless the situation appeared.

Taking advantage of a hole in the wall, Lincoln managed to force open the attic door, knocking Jennings to the ground in the process. Other rescuers, including John Copeland, pushed through the doorway, causing confusion among the slave catchers. Richard Winsor, an Oberlin theology student, grabbed Price by the arm and hurried him out into the hall. Winsor had waited more than four years for just that moment. In 1854 the young Englishman had been in the crowd that stood by as Anthony Burns was marched in chains to Boston Harbor for his rendition to Georgia. Winsor had silently vowed never to watch another black man delivered to slavery, and he joyfully took the opportunity to make good on his pledge.

The rescuers carried John Price out of the hotel, bearing them on their shoulders into the public square. The crowd let out a cheer of victory as Price was thrown into the back of Simeon Bushnell's wagon, which the bookstore clerk then furiously drove back to the safety of Oberlin.

John Price would be hidden in Oberlin for a few days and then spirited across Lake Erie to Canada, where he was able to live the rest of his life in freedom. Although no word of him ever came back to Oberlin, John Mercer Langston would later remark confidently that "John Price walks abroad in his freedom, or reposes under his own vine and fig tree with no one to molest him or make him afraid."[21]

For the rescuers, however, there would be another chapter in the story.

13

THE SON BETRAYS AND THE FATHER INDICTS

John Mercer Langston had missed the rescue—he was out of town on business that morning—but he arrived home just in time to greet "the returning hosts, shouting, singing, rejoicing in the glad results of their brave, defiant, successful enterprise." Later that evening there was a grand rally in the Oberlin town square, featuring "speeches in denunciation of slavery, the Fugitive Slave Law, slaveholders, and all those who sympathized with and would aid them." John Mercer Langston, in a self-described attempt to make up for "what he had failed to accomplish in deeds on that eventful day," delivered a "fiery" speech condemning the "dark and frightful methods" of the slave hunters.[1]

The crowd appreciated John Mercer's oratory, but they were anxious to hear from the rescuers. "Charlie, Charlie, Charlie Langston," they shouted, until the younger man called upon his older brother to speak. Charles Langston then described the events, beginning with his own parley with Deputy Lowe in the attic of Wadsworth's Hotel. According to one observer, Charles claimed that he had refused Lowe's request for assistance and warned the slave catcher against trying "to keep John, for *they* would have him anyway." The rally continued until late at night, concluding with the community's solemn pledge that "no fugitive slave should ever be taken from Oberlin and returned to his enslavement."[2]

Elsewhere the reaction to the rescue was hostile, especially in Washington, D.C. The Oberliners had physically intimidated a federal marshal, who was acting under the authority of a federal warrant, by making threats and brandishing firearms. Although no one was seriously injured in the rescue—unlike the earlier events in Boston and Christiana—it had been a challenge that the proslavery Buchanan administration found impossible to abide. Elected in 1856, Pennsylvanian James Buchanan was a classic doughface. As early as 1851 he had stated his support for the Fugitive Slave Act in no uncertain terms, writing to a fellow Democrat that "the Fugitive Slave law must be sustained;

because I believe it is right in principle & in sustaining it we sustain the Union."[3] Now, as president, he had the opportunity to act on his beliefs.

By mid-October a federal grand jury had been convened in Cleveland. Every member of the grand jury was a Democrat—and therefore presumably ill-disposed toward the radical abolitionists of Oberlin—even though northern Ohio was overwhelmingly Republican and antislavery at the time. In an era when grand juries were hand-chosen by the clerk of the court, it was far from surprising that a Buchanan appointee would select only fellow Democrats in a highly politicized case. But even under those circumstances, it was shocking that one of the grand jurors was Lewis Boynton, who had colluded with the slave hunters and had permitted his son Shakespeare to serve as a decoy in John Price's capture. As John Mercer Langston put it, "The son betrays, and the father indicts!"[4]

The grand jury began hearing testimony in early November, having been provided with a list of witnesses by Anson Dayton and other informers. There was never any real doubt about the outcome, as Judge Hiram Willson's charge left little or no room for leniency. Deriding the rescuers' motives for violating the Fugitive Slave Act, the court belittled their "declared sense of conscientious duty." Scoffing at the very idea of higher law, the judge continued,

> There is, in fact, a sentiment prevalent in the community that arrogates to human conduct a standard of right above, and independent of, human laws; and it makes the conscience of each individual in society the test of his own accountability to the laws of the land.
>
> While those who cherish this dogma claim and enjoy the protection of the law for their own lives and property, they are unwilling that the law should be operative for the protection of the constitutional rights of others.

The "dogma" of the higher law, cautioned Judge Willson, "is almost invariably characterized by intolerance and bigotry," and it should "find no place or favor in the Grand-Jury room." Even those who opposed the Fugitive Slave Act were bound to execute it, Willson said, as a condition of guaranteeing the protection of property for all citizens "whether residing north or south of the

Ohio River." That was an advance warning to the eventual defendants, virtually daring them to assert a "higher law" defense at trial.

—————

The grand jury issued its predictable true bill on December 6, 1858, indicting thirty-seven men for violations of the Fugitive Slave Act. Twenty-five of the defendants were closely associated with Oberlin—either as students, faculty, residents, or graduates—and the remaining twelve were from Wellington. Of the Oberlin defendants, twelve were black men, including Charles Langston, John Copeland, John Watson, and the Langstons' brother-in-law Orindatus S. B. Wall. The white defendants included key figures in the rescue such as Simeon Bushnell, William Lincoln, Ansel Lyman, and Richard Winsor, but three of the indictees had never even been present in Wellington. James Fitch, Henry Peck, and Ralph Plumb, all leaders of the Oberlin community, were charged with "aiding and abetting" the rescue, meaning only that they had encouraged others to resist the Fugitive Slave Act. The inclusion of Fitch, Peck, and Plumb made it painfully obvious that the Buchanan administration was taking political aim at the abolitionist movement, hoping to use the mass prosecution as a means of suppressing resistance in the North and currying favor in the South.

The rescuers were anything but intimidated. They loudly rejoiced in their indictment, recognizing that it provided them with an unprecedented opportunity to publicize the struggle against slavery. On January 7, 1859, they held a "Felons' Feast," a great public banquet at which they gathered to plan their strategy and declare the righteousness of their cause. As reported in the antislavery press, numerous speakers proclaimed their dedication to human freedom and their hatred for the Fugitive Slave Act. One speaker announced that the "detested law never could be enforced" in the Western Reserve, concluding that "no fines it can impose or chains it can bind upon us, will ever command our obedience to its unrighteous behests."

Many supportive letters were read aloud, including one from John Brown Jr., who had served as second in command to his father in Kansas. The Brown family had a deep religious and institutional connection to Oberlin. Owen Brown—the father of John Brown Sr.—had been a trustee of the college, and John Brown Sr. himself had worked for a time as Oberlin's agent and surveyor. The younger Brown's message was greeted with great applause, as he articulated the higher law justification that would soon be presented in Judge Willson's court and that would, by the end of the year, become a rallying cry for the violent overthrow of slavery: "Step by step the Slave Power is driving us on to take one or the other horn of the dilemma, either to be *false* to *Humanity* or *traitors* to the *Government*."

In the weeks that followed, supporters of the defendants held numerous public meetings for the purpose of generating both funds and sympathy. These events were well covered in the press, as the rescuers realized that publicity was the greatest counterweight to government power. Henry Peck wrote in *The Liberator* that "the fire which this outrage has kindled in Lorain [the Ohio county of both Oberlin and Wellington] will not go out till an effort has been made to teach these arbitrary and insolent officials that freemen know what their rights are."[5]

As the spring trial date approached, the defendants retained four of Ohio's most prominent attorneys, all of whom served pro bono. Lead counsel Rufus Spalding was a former speaker of the Ohio House of Representatives, and he had also served on the state supreme court. Although nominally a Democrat, Spalding had supported Republican Salmon Chase's antislavery campaign for governor. The other defense lawyers were Albert Gallatin Riddle, a former county prosecutor; Franklin Backus, also a former prosecutor and member of the Ohio legislature; and Seneca O. Griswold, the youngest of the three, who was an Oberlin graduate.[6]

It is impossible to know why John Mercer Langston did not join the defense team. Many decades later John Mercer would write in his memoir that he "would have taken part as one of [the] attorneys in the trial" but he had agreed with his brother that Charles "was the best qualified man of his race" to speak in court. That convoluted explanation is highly questionable. There was no reason that two black men could not address the court and, in any event, there was no guarantee *ex ante* that the judge would even allow Charles Langston—who was not a lawyer and who was prohibited from testifying by the interested party rule—to speak at trial. It is conceivable that some of the white defendants were unwilling to be represented by a black man in front of an already hostile judge and jury. Or perhaps Charles Langston himself preferred other counsel; he would not have been the first or last man to reject the help of an overachieving little brother. Alternatively, John Mercer may simply have been unsure of his own skills as an advocate, given that his practice was mostly devoted to business accounts and collections. In any event, the case went to trial without him, and John Mercer later expressed great satisfaction with the work of the "learned attorneys" who did represent the rescuers. He complimented Spalding and company for demonstrating the "highest moral tone [and] the spirit of the deepest and broadest sentiments of right," and he praised the lawyers for their "touching diction, appeal and eloquence [and their] captivating, attractive style and manner."[7]

The prosecutor was U.S. Attorney George Belden, a staunch Democrat and resolute supporter of the Fugitive Slave Act. Belden sincerely believed that the rescuers were guilty of treason—in keeping with Daniel Webster's earlier formulation of the crime—even though there was little precedent for bringing a capital charge in a case where no one had been seriously injured. Despite Belden's view of the offense, a treason prosecution was not approved by U.S. Attorney General Jeremiah Black. A stern advocate of law and order, Black had no sympathy for fugitives or abolitionists, but he had been a justice of the Pennsylvania Supreme Court during the Christiana trial and he well understood both the difficulty involved in proving treason and the pitfalls inherent in overcharging a case. When it came to enforcement of the Fugitive Slave Act, Black was unyielding.[8] He instructed Belden to prosecute the rescuers to the fullest extent of that law, and he authorized the U.S. attorney to engage another lawyer as associate counsel. Belden retained George Bliss, a former judge and Democratic congressman, to assist him at trial.

On March 8, 1859, Belden and Spalding met to resolve pretrial issues and begin selecting a jury. Belden was determined to try the rescuers individually rather than as a group, a decision the prosecutor would eventually regret. At the time, however, the strategy seemed reasonable enough. The events at Wellington had been chaotic, and it had not yet become clear how each of the individual rescuers had participated (if at all). By bringing his strongest cases first, Belden could clarify the issues and the specific details of the crime. It also seems likely that he intended to separate the Oberlin defendants (whom he despised) from the Wellington defendants (who could plausibly claim to have been bystanders). Belden informed Spalding that Simeon Bushnell—the accused getaway driver—would be tried first, with the others following as their names appeared on the indictment.

The two attorneys next turned to jury selection for the first trial. The venire consisted of forty men—again hand-chosen by the Buchanan-appointed court clerk—none of whom were from Lorain County. Although the panel included ten Republicans, each side was allowed twelve strikes, which Belden promptly used to reduce the venire to twenty-eight proslavery Democrats. Spalding then exercised the twelve defense strikes, leaving a pool of sixteen, from which the eventual jurors would be chosen at the opening of trial. The final selection would not really matter, as it was clear that the defendant would have no sympathizers on this jury.

Belden had good reasons to begin the prosecution with Bushnell. Numerous witnesses could testify to the bookstore clerk's participation in the rescue, and it appeared that the defendant had no valid defense. Every prosecutor always wants to start strong, and Bushnell seemed like the easiest target for a certain conviction.

The defense attorneys also had ambitious goals for the Oberlin cases. In addition to representing their clients, they hoped to use the courtroom as a political platform to expose the iniquity of slavery itself. If possible, they planned to call upon both the judge and jury to follow the higher law, without regard to the demands of the Fugitive Slave Act.

The defense lawyers in the Hanway and Burns cases had shied away from such overtly political tactics. Thaddeus Stevens had conceded the legitimacy of slave hunting, and Richard Henry Dana had strained to fit his moral arguments into the uncomfortable confines of the Fugitive Slave Act while simultaneously distancing himself from rescue attempts. But much had changed in the ensuing years. Public opposition to the extension of slavery had matured from a moral and religious sentiment into a full-fledged political movement under the leadership of the Republican Party. The party's most prominent national figure, Senator William Seward of New York, had declared only a few weeks after the Oberlin rescue that the nation was in the midst of an "irrepressible conflict" between slavery and freedom. It was Seward who had also—in 1850—first announced that there was a "higher law than the Constitution." It was therefore a relatively small step for Republican lawyers in the spring of 1859 to conclude that there was also an irrepressible conflict between higher law and enforcement of the Fugitive Slave Act.

As a theological ideal there was nothing novel about preferring the law of God to the law of man, but the Oberlin rescue lawyers wanted to assert the same principle as a legal defense. That was a new and untested strategy. Historian and Oberlin native William Cochran, who had been ten years old at the time of the rescue, would later criticize the defense lawyers for placing their political aspirations ahead of their clients' interests.[9] Although it is true that two of the four attorneys were later elected to Congress as Republicans, there is every reason to believe that Bushnell and the other defendants were themselves strongly committed to the higher law defense.

Simeon Bushnell's trial began on the morning of April 5, 1859, in Cleveland's new Cuyahoga County courthouse, where quarters were also provided to the U.S. District Court. It was an unusually cold spring day, with occasional light snow and a persistent chill in the air. The building, only recently completed, still lacked stoves for heat, and even some necessary furniture. But the federal prosecutors had a huge stake in the trial, and they were determined to press forward, no matter how uncomfortable or inconvenient the facilities.

The courtroom was crowded to capacity. In addition to Bushnell and the four defense attorneys, nineteen of the other defendants also attended the trial. Although they had been released on their own recognizance and were not required to be in court, Bushnell's Oberlin colleagues were determined to show their support for their codefendant and their disdain for the government's case. The Wellington defendants, however, were mainly conspicuous by their absence. Belden had excused their attendance, and most of them took advantage of the opportunity to remain at home.[10]

Friends and supporters of the defendants filled the spectators' gallery, while journalists from dozens of newspapers and magazines competed for front-row seats. The correspondent for the staunchly Republican *New York Tribune* was John Kagi, one of John Brown's chief lieutenants. Kagi himself had participated in a slave rescue in December 1858, when Brown's men crossed from Kansas into Missouri on a raid that freed eleven slaves, while killing a slave owner who attempted to defend his "property." When he was not reporting on the trial, Kagi used his visit to Cleveland to raise funds and recruit troops for Brown's coming attack on Virginia.

Belden and Bliss sat alone at the prosecution table. They would eventually call nineteen men to testify against Bushnell, but the witnesses were sequestered in an adjoining room during most of the proceedings.

The first order of business was the final selection of jurors. The clerk read out the names of the first twelve men on the list. Only one of the twelve jurors was from the Western Reserve, the other eleven coming from more conservative towns and villages elsewhere in northern Ohio. The *Oberlin Evangelist* sarcastically called the panel's composition a "political singularity," given that Cleveland was by far the largest population center in the court's district. Judge Willson allowed Spalding to ask each juror whether he had "formed any opinion of the guilt or innocence of the accused," and each man duly denied any biases or partiality. Spalding had no further strikes at his disposal and he was compelled to accept a jury consisting entirely of "Taney Democrats" (as one newspaper described them).[11] With that accomplished, the court adjourned for the morning.

The afternoon session began with the prosecution's opening statement. George Belden read at length from the indictment, informing the jury that the "negro slave called John," the property of John Bacon, had been a person "held to service and labor in the state of Kentucky" who had escaped into Ohio. "Anderson Jennings," the indictment continued, "duly authorized for that purpose by power of attorney . . . did pursue and reclaim the said negro slave." The jurors could not have noticed that the indictment—and therefore Belden's opening statement—made absolutely no mention of the fugitive slave warrant that Jennings had obtained from Commissioner Chittenden in Columbus. That glaring omission did not escape Spalding's notice, however, and defense counsel would make much of the disparity during the trial.

Belden himself understood that the warrant was the weakest link in his case. Following Anson Dayton's sly advice, Jennings had obtained the warrant in Columbus, rather than Cleveland, but the ploy had been more devious than effective. Commissioner Chittenden—who was new on the job—apparently had not realized that the fugitive would be apprehended in Oberlin, which lay in the Northern District of Ohio and therefore outside the geographic jurisdiction of his court. By the time the indictment was drawn, however, Belden had identified the potential defect in the warrant. The prosecutor feared that such a technicality could be used to argue that the warrant had been wholly invalid—and that John Price had never been legally in the custody of Deputy Lowe—thus undermining the charge that the rescuers had violated federal law.

In his opening statement, Belden therefore attempted to cure the discrepancy by asserting that Lowe had only been "lawfully assisting" Anderson Jennings, who was operating under the authority of the clearly valid Kentucky power of attorney. The extremely fine point must have sailed far over the jurors' heads, but it would become a matter of great contention in the days that followed.

Belden next turned to the details of Bushnell's involvement. Still reading from the indictment, the prosecutor asserted that the defendant, "with force of arms, unlawfully, knowingly, and willingly . . . did rescue the said negro slave . . . well knowing that the said negro slave called John, was then and there a fugitive person held to service and labor."

Finally the prosecutor addressed the jury in his own words. He said he would prove that Price had been rescued "not only to the great detriment of his owner," but even "against the earnest wishes of the *negro himself*, who expressed himself anxious to return to the service of his master." Perhaps Belden actually believed the great lie that slaves were happy in bondage, or perhaps he only hoped the jury would find it easier to convict the defendant if they believed that Bushnell had violated Price's wishes as well as Bacon's rights. In either event, the prosecutor went on to paint Bushnell as one of the ringleaders of the crime. The defendant, he alleged, had been instrumental in stirring up "a great deal of excitement in the town of Oberlin" prior to the rescue. He had called "for volunteers to go to Wellington [but] rejected some, saying that he wanted *men* not boys, as there would most likely be a fight." That accusation would have drawn a laugh from anyone who glanced at the defense table. Bushnell was short, slight, and quite youthful in appearance. He looked much more like a bookseller than a fighter, and nothing at all like someone who would plausibly reject volunteers for insufficient masculinity.

Following Belden, defense lawyer Rufus Spalding opened briefly on Bushnell's behalf. Without addressing the actual evidence, Spalding argued that the prosecution was barred because a higher law rendered slavery a nullity. He conceded that a black man had been captured and subsequently rescued, and he did not explicitly deny that Simeon Bushnell had played a part. But, he continued,

> by no law, human or divine, did the negro rescued owe service to any man living; that his arrest was kidnapping, procured by the use of the most scandalous and fraudulent deceit, and that whether the defendant aided to rescue him or not, he was amenable to no criminal statute whatsoever.

Spalding and his colleagues would also raise a conventional defense, challenging many of the specifics of the prosecution case. In fact, the defense lawyers barely alluded to the higher law theme for the first five days of the trial. But of course, they were operating in uncharted territory, and it proved far easier to plan their radical case than to present it.

———

The first prosecution witness was John Bacon. Even though he was the aggrieved slave owner, Bacon was not a formal party to the criminal prosecution and thus the interested party rule did not prohibit him from testifying. Bacon swore that he owned John Price—"bone and flesh"—but the slave had run off without consent. To retrieve his property, Bacon had executed and delivered to Anderson Jennings a power of attorney that described Price as "about twenty years old, about five feet six or eight inches high, heavy set, copper colored, and [weighing] about 140 or 150 pounds." Price had never been returned to Bacon, his lawful owner.

Franklin Backus conducted a long cross-examination of Bacon, attempting to expose a flaw in his claim of ownership. Bacon, however, was unshakable in his account. "The boy's mother was held by my father as a slave from my earliest recollection," Bacon testified, and in fact, he had been present when Price was born. Only at the very end of the cross-examination did Backus obtain any useful information.

"What was the arrangement between you and Jennings?" he asked. "What was you to give him if he got John back for you?"

The prosecution objected, fearing that Jennings's financial incentives would provide evidence of bias. The court, however, directed the witness to answer.

"If he brought him back," replied Bacon, "he was to have one half of what the nigger would sell for."

There was nothing unusual about paying a commission to a slave catcher. But Bacon's admission—that Price was to be sold following his capture—undermined Belden's earlier claim that the rescuers had prevented the happy reunion of owner and slave.

The next witness was Robert Cochran, the clerk of court in Mason County, Kentucky. Cochran did not know "the negro, John," and had no information about the escape, but he was able to identify the official seal on the power of attorney that had authorized Jennings to seize the runaway. Cochran explained a discrepancy in the document—the papers had been drawn up and signed by his deputy—but assured the court that the official acknowledgment was in order. The power of attorney was admitted in evidence without cross-examination.

The first two witnesses established that a certain slave named John had escaped from Kentucky, but they could not provide a link between the wanted slave and the man who had been rescued in Wellington. That would require an eyewitness.

The prosecution then moved on to the heart of the case. Anderson Jennings testified that he had "known John two or three years before he ran away." Without prompting, Jennings added that he had taken custody of Price "at Wellington."

"Did he recognize you?" asked Belden, knowing that John's admission would establish that the captive was indeed the runaway named in the power of attorney.

Backus jumped to his feet, objecting sarcastically that the words "of this piece of property, this chattel, this *thing*" could not be admitted as evidence against the defendant. "The recognition of his master's agent by this chattel," he continued, "was no more than the recognition a dog might make by the wagging of his tail."

Belden shot back that the slave's own words were competent "for the purpose of identifying this piece of property."

That was just the response Backus wanted. The purpose of the objection had not been to belittle Price by comparing him to a dog, but rather to emphasize the moral incongruity inherent in slavery. The government had recognized the fugitive's humanity by offering his statement as evidence, even as it denied his humanity by making him a slave. The irony was inescapable, and it was only accentuated by Belden's stiff reply. Backus expected that the evidence would nonetheless be allowed, thus making the larger political point that Price was a human being and therefore entitled to human rights. Judge Willson, however, did not take the bait, sustaining the defense objection without comment.

Jennings then described the events of the rescue in considerable detail, including the retreat with his prisoner to the attic room at Wadsworth's, the negotiations with Constable Meacham and others, and his brief foray onto the balcony where Price addressed the crowd. "Purty soon they come up the stairway and begun to pry at the door," he said. The spectators laughed rudely at his country drawl, which was so thick that it was transcribed phonetically in the record. "Then the next I know'd I got a punch on the side o' my head, which went through my hat, and knocked me over." After Jennings's "wounded hat" was admitted in evidence, he finished his story:

> The next I see of the nigger he was a paddlin' downstairs over the heads of the crowd, as it seemed to me. Then I went to the window, and saw 'em puttin' him into a wagon that stood in the middle of the square.... Have never seen John since.

Jennings could not identify the driver of the wagon. He closed his direct testimony with the complaint that there had been "twenty niggers in the crowd."

The cross-examination was conducted by Backus, who mocked Jennings by imitating his backwoods accent. Backus spent several hours asking Jennings to recount the events surrounding Price's capture and rescue, in the hope that the slave hunter would stumble or contradict the other witnesses. The first contradiction came quickly, as Jennings flatly denied that he had ever "made any arrangement with Bacon about pay for ketchin' the nigger." Far from "havin' one half of what the nigger would sell for," Jennings insisted that he had undertaken the mission "out of pure neighborly regard."

Backus next tried to shake the witness's identification of the fugitive. Bacon's power of attorney had described the runaway as "copper colored," but other witnesses would testify that John Price of Oberlin had been decidedly black. Had the slave hunter captured the wrong man? Jennings had an extended answer:

> We have different names for different colored niggers at the South. Some we call black, some yellow, and some copper-colored. Yellow is part white and part black blood, usually about half-and-half. Copper color is between black and light mulatto. Black is black— pure African. Some would call John copper color, but I should call him black. Have seen blacker niggers than him.

There was at least some ambiguity in Jennings's description of his prisoner, so prosecutor Belden attempted to repair the damage on redirect examination by asking for yet another description. "John was a full blooded negro, not a drop of white blood in him," the witness confidently replied. Belden had worse luck, however, when he tried to clear up the inconsistency over Jennings's expected payment. "There was no arrangement between me and Bacon about compensating me for fetching the nigger back," Jennings insisted.

Jennings was followed to the stand by numerous additional witnesses who underscored the most important details of the prosecution case. Richard Mitchell, Jennings's slave-hunting partner from Kentucky, testified that he had shown the power of attorney to the crowd in front of Wadsworth's, which presumably included Simeon Bushnell. Norris Wood, an Oberliner but not a rescuer, described John Price's appearance on the balcony. According to Wood, Price told the crowd that the Kentuckians "had the papers, and he s'posed he'd have to go."

Jacob Wheeler, the postmaster of a nearby town, had gone to Wellington that day "to see about the fire." Perhaps because of his official position and seeming neutrality, he had been allowed into the attic room where John Price was held prisoner, and he stayed there for almost the entire afternoon. Wheeler confirmed that Deputy Marshal Lowe had shown the power of attorney to eight or ten men, including Charles Langston and Constable Meacham, in the various deputations that attempted to negotiate Price's release. Wheeler himself had questioned Price—he described it as "catechizing" the fugitive—in detail. When Wheeler began to describe the conversation, however, the defense again objected "to testimony as to what this piece of property said." This time the court overruled the objection, again without explanation.

According to Wheeler, Price admitted that he was the property of "a man by the name of Bacon" in Kentucky. Wheeler questioned whether Price had ever been mistreated by his master, to which the slave "hesitated and appeared to hang back, as if he thought he was abused sometimes." Wheeler persisted, pointing out that it was necessary for "white folks to correct their own children, sometimes for their own good." Price compliantly agreed that he had not been treated more harshly "than some white folks punish their children," adding for good measure that "he had started to go back to Kentucky once; got so far as Columbus, and the folks from Oberlin overtook him and brought him back." The audience laughed out loud at Wheeler's gullibility. The far-fetched story was obviously a frightened slave's attempt to soften his punishment, but the witness appeared to have taken it seriously.

Most important, the prosecution produced a half dozen witnesses who testified to Simeon Bushnell's direct involvement in the rescue. Seth Bartholomew, an Oberlin ne'er-do-well and petty criminal, testified to the "excitement" in town following Ansel Lyman's report of the kidnapping. He claimed to have seen the defendant conversing with James Fitch, Henry Peck, and Ralph Plumb, one of whom told Bushnell to "go out and get 'em ready." Shortly afterward, Bartholomew saw Bushnell driving a wagon headed for Wellington, accompanied by the black man Orindatus S. B. Wall, who was holding a rifle. According to Bartholomew, Bushnell told an unarmed student to get out of the wagon because "he had no business in there."

Artemas Halbert backed up most of Bartholomew's account, testifying that he had overheard Bushnell and Wall agreeing to obtain a gun before driving to Wellington. Halbert had also gone to Wellington himself, where he saw Bushnell sitting in a buggy. He asked the defendant "if that was the buggy which was to carry the nigger off, and [Bushnell] said, 'it was.'" A few minutes later Halbert saw Price "put into the wagon," which started off toward Oberlin with Bushnell driving. Halbert was followed by Bela Farr, who testified that the defendant had bragged about his exploits the following day. "If taking him and bringing him from Wellington is a crime," said Bushnell to Farr, "I suppose I am guilty."

Belden and Bliss presented nineteen witnesses over the course of five court days, but they did not call Jacob Lowe to the stand. The Columbus deputy marshal knew more about the sequence of events than any other person: he had dragged John Price at gunpoint from Shakespeare Boynton's wagon, driven the fugitive to Wellington, and helped barricade the prisoner at Wadsworth's Hotel. Lowe had been present during all of the failed negotiations, and he had struggled with the rescuers who freed the slave. Several witnesses described Lowe's display of the warrant and his promise to ensure a fair hearing for John, but the deputy himself never testified.

The prosecutors had obviously made a tactical decision to shield Lowe from cross-examination, fearing that he would be severely questioned about the alleged flaws in the federal warrant. A vigorous cross-examination of Lowe might have suggested that Price had indeed been seized from Boynton's wagon without valid authority. Belden took the position that Lowe had always been acting as Jennings's lawful assistant, but he prudently chose to avoid exposing the deputy to questioning on the issue.

The final prosecution witness was Oberlin tavern owner Chauncey Wack. A slavery sympathizer and confidant of Anderson Jennings, Wack had followed the rescuers to Wellington strictly out of curiosity. He testified that the crowd outside Wadsworth's had been repeatedly assured that the papers for John Price were lawful. Someone in the crowd had shouted that they "didn't care for papers" and that "they'd have [Price] anyhow." Others said "they'd tear the house down" because they were "Higher Law men."

Only at the very end of the testimony—with Wack's taunting reference to the higher law—had Belden and Bliss allowed their case to stray into politics. It was not that they had any reservations about politicizing the prosecution, but only that they saw no reason to muddy the otherwise uncomplicated case against Bushnell. In effect, the prosecution was saving its political fire for a bigger prize.

Facing overwhelming evidence of Bushnell's involvement in the rescue, the defense lawyers had done the best they could on cross-examination. They raised jurisdictional issues: had the power of attorney been properly displayed? They raised evidentiary issues: were the fugitive's admissions voluntary and reliable? They raised the question of identification: was John Price black or copper colored? They missed no opportunity to show that many of the witnesses had never seen Bushnell in Wellington. They made Seth Bartholomew admit that he had once stolen "half a cheese," and they accused Anderson Jennings of paying his bar tab with a counterfeit $10 bill. The cross-examiners challenged every aspect of the prosecution case, but they evidently found no occasion to pursue Spalding's opening theme—that the higher law precluded a conviction—even when openly goaded by the oleaginous Chauncey Wack. They would become increasingly more assertive, however, once the defense began its case in chief.

There was a murmur of surprise in the courtroom when Lewis Boynton took the stand as the first witness for the defense. The "General," after all, had connived with Jennings and Lowe over the capture of John Price, and he had served on the grand jury that indicted Bushnell and the other defendants. The apparent purpose of calling Boynton was to emphasize the slave catchers' devious tactics, implying that there had been something underhanded about their pursuit of the fugitive. If their papers were in order, why did they have to use a child to lure their victim out of town?

It was risky to begin with such an openly hostile witness, and Lewis Boynton was uncooperative right from the start. He sarcastically volunteered that he should "not be driven out of the Court House if I say I [was] a delegate to a Democratic convention."

"Not out of *this* Court House, certainly," came Albert Riddle's quick retort. That was the last point the defense would score with their opening witness. Riddle began to ask Boynton about his meeting with Jennings and Lowe, but Judge Willson sustained a prosecution objection and the witness was excused from the stand.

The defense lawyers got better answers from Shakespeare Boynton, whom they called next. The teenager proved to be appallingly callous, treating the trial like a vulgar joke. *"Expect* I am a son of last witness," he said, "but it's hard telling now-a-days." Shakespeare explained his role as a decoy, lying to John and leading the unsuspecting black man into an ambush. He was proud to have received $20 for his work and he regretted only that he had not been able to earn even more by catching other slaves. Abolitionists were outraged at the very idea of employing a child in such a scheme of betrayal. Perhaps the jurors were also as shocked as defense counsel hoped. The court, however, ruled that the circumstances of the initial arrest were "utterly immaterial" to the charge against Bushnell, and the prosecutors therefore did not bother to cross-examine young Boynton.

The defense then called three of Bushnell's codefendants—Henry Peck, Ralph Plumb, and James Fitch—who had been derided in the proslavery press as the "saints of Oberlin." Of all the defendants, Peck, Plumb, and Fitch were the most closely associated with higher law doctrine. None of the three men had actually gone to Wellington, and their indictment was understood as a well-aimed blow against abolitionist organizers. Putting them on the stand, therefore, was in good part a counterstatement by the defense. Bushnell was not afraid of associating himself with Oberlin's most visible and controversial leaders, and the "saints" were equally ready to stand up for the driver of the getaway wagon.

Although calling the witnesses was a bold decision, their actual testimony was relatively mundane. All three contradicted Seth Bartholomew's claim that they had huddled with Bushnell—presumably giving him instructions— immediately before the rescue. They did not deny speaking with one another— providing admissions that the prosecution might be able to use when the saints themselves faced trial—but they were adamant that Bushnell had not participated in their discussion. In addition, Henry Peck supported the defense claim of misidentification, testifying that John Price "was a decidedly black man."

The cross-examinations were conducted by George Bliss, who emphasized the Oberliners' open "indignation" at Price's capture and the fact that they had all been charged with "aiding and abetting the rescue." Bliss threateningly asked Peck if he knew anything of Price's whereabouts following his return to Oberlin, but the witness denied all knowledge and the prosecutor did not pursue the point.

Following the saints, various defense witnesses testified about the technical jurisdictional issue. Joseph Dickson, a Wellington attorney who had negotiated with Lowe, said that the deputy "showed me his warrant—no other papers." Law student Lysander Butler said the same thing, denying that the Kentucky power of attorney had ever been displayed. James Patton testified that only the warrant had been read to the crowd when Jennings brought Price onto the hotel balcony. Patton's testimony somewhat backfired on the defense, however, when George Bliss forced the witness to admit that "the crowd responded to the reading of the warrant by saying that they cared nothing for papers; they would have the boy anyhow."

More significantly, four witnesses testified about John Price's appearance, contradicting the description of the "copper colored" runaway in Anderson Jennings's power of attorney. Among them was John Cox, who said that Price was "very black, so black he shone." Misidentification of the fugitive, however, was not really a defense to the charges against Bushnell. Even if Jennings and Lowe had arguably seized the wrong man, it should have been up to Commissioner Chittenden in Columbus to determine whether "very black" John Price of Oberlin was the same person as "copper colored" John Price of Mason County. To the prosecution, it was obvious that Bushnell and the other rescuers had criminally prevented any such hearing from ever taking place.

But what if the defense could show that the Fugitive Slave Act did not provide an opportunity for the fair resolution of a prisoner's identity? What if the chance of misidentification was so great, and so irremediable, that free men were certain to be dragged arbitrarily into slavery? Even the Buchanan administration could not justify the willful enslavement of free men. That would constitute kidnapping under the laws of Ohio and every other free state, perhaps implying an attendant moral right for citizens to intervene.

The final defense witness, emancipated slave Orindatus S. B. Wall, drove home that point in a uniquely compelling way. Wall placed himself in significant jeopardy by taking the stand. He was a defendant in the case, and he had been identified as carrying a rifle at the scene of the rescue. On the other hand, he also created a problem for the prosecution and the judge. Under federal law at the time, the court had discretion to exclude non-white witnesses. Judge Willson, therefore, had to determine whether Wall would be permitted to testify for the defense. That presented an exquisite dilemma for the prosecution. An objection, if sustained, would emphasize the inadequacy of the courts to hear the claims of black men. Allowing Wall to take the stand, however, would imply that black men indeed had rights, again bolstering the defense.

Belden did object to Wall's testimony, although his argument was not preserved. Judge Willson overruled the objection, declaring Wall "to be a perfectly competent witness."[12] The black man was, however, the only witness in the entire trial who affirmed his testimony rather than take the usual oath. The record does not disclose whether that departure was related to his race.

Wall was the mulatto son of a North Carolina plantation owner, and he proceeded to provide the jury with a taxonomy of the complexions "by which people of color were classified." He explained that "there were black, blacker, blackest. Then copper color, which is about the color of hemlock tanned sole leather. Then there are dark, lighter, and light mulatto." Wall knew John Price very well, and there was no way that any Southerner would have described him as copper colored. "He was a decidedly black negro."

After nearly seven days of trial, the testimony was now complete. Judge Willson recessed the proceeding for several hours so the attorneys could prepare their final arguments.

———

There was standing room only when the trial reconvened that afternoon. "Every available spot was occupied by spectators," according to the *Cleveland Evening Herald,* "and nothing save the admirable ventilation and the lofty ceiling, rendered the air of the room tolerable."

Assistant Prosecutor George Bliss argued first for the government, and he made it immediately clear that the trial was as much about Oberlin as it was about John Bacon's runaway slave. The case was exceptionally important, he told the jury, because some people "desire to be permitted to pursue their rebellion against the laws of the country." He warned that concerted resistance to the Fugitive Slave Act could only lead to "a dissolution of the Union."

"When these Oberlin men went down to Wellington," inveighed Bliss, "they proclaimed that they did so under the Higher Law, for they knew they were outraging the law of the land." There could be "no need of Higher Law," said the prosecutor, and especially "no need of the rallying of the children of God . . . in the shape of a riot." The Fugitive Slave Act itself was sufficient to protect the rights of "the free negro men of Ohio." "It is a pity," he said sarcastically, "that all the good people of Oberlin" had not behaved according to law.

Addressing the specifics of the case, Bliss argued that Jennings's testimony was more than adequate to establish that Price had been Bacon's slave in Kentucky. But if more evidence was needed of Price's escape, it was provided "by his being found in the common resort of fugitive slaves, to wit, in Oberlin." Bliss conceded that the government was required to prove that Bushnell had "some notice as to the character of John as a fugitive from justice," but that was amply shown simply by the defendant's presence in the crowd. "The Oberlin people who came to the rescue of John, knew he was a fugitive, their language showed it."

It seemed as though the entire prosecution case could be summarized in a single word: Oberlin. Bliss touched only briefly on other matters. He refuted the defense contention that Jennings had never displayed his power of attorney; he dismissed as quibbling the dispute over the fugitive's complexion; he reiterated the claim that Price really wanted to return to Kentucky. But only near the end of his two-and-a-half-hour argument did the prosecutor even mention Bushnell by name. The defendant, Bliss argued, had been an instigator of the rescue, having "induced persons to go there armed," and later he was in "the buggy in which the negro was placed."

But enough about Simeon Bushnell, who had never been the real target of the prosecution. Bliss concluded by again taking square aim at Oberlin:

People around Oberlin think so little of their government and the statutes of the Federal Government, when they interfere with their sympathies with negro men and women, that they consider their violation a good joke.

"Is it right," the prosecutor asked the jury, that "any people should impugn the laws of the land, knowing no law but their own consciences?"

————•••————

The defense lawyers would address the jury for nearly two full days. Albert Riddle spoke first, and he was not at all intimidated by Bliss's harsh accusations. Rather than avoid the higher law or approach it obliquely—as earlier lawyers had done in comparable cases—Riddle flatly announced that it should form the very basis of the jury's decision:

> And now, as to the matter referred to, the so-called dogma of the Higher Law . . . I am perfectly frank to declare, *that I am a votary of that Higher Law!*
>
> *Right,* and its everlasting opposite, *Wrong,* existed anterior to the feeble enactments of men, and will survive their final repeal—and must ever remain Right and Wrong, because they are such, unchanged and unqualified by your acts of Congress, and statutes of your Legislatures.
>
> You may erase, expunge, exile and outlaw this thing, Right, from your statutes, and denounce it as wrong, and still it is Right.

From the outset of his argument until its very end, Riddle placed the focus of the defense on morality rather than law, calling slavery and the Fugitive Slave Act the "sum of all villainies." Riddle mocked Bliss's call to punish the rescuers in the name of the law. Instead of enforcing the Fugitive Slave Act, he told the jurors, they should congratulate John for running away and salute the rescuers for "following the path of conscience."

Riddle admitted that John Price had been a slave in Mason County—"that thing which all the laws of God declare cannot exist"—and that Bacon exercised the "felon right" to hold him in bondage. Riddle even conceded that the rescuers knew that Price was a slave.

> The defendant and his associates approached; and, knowing John
> was a slave in Kentucky . . . they put forth their strong hands and,
> wrenching John from the grasp of his captors, consigned him to
> the boundless realm of freedom!

But none of that should matter, argued defense counsel, because Bushnell and the rescuers "obeyed the laws of God, as written in revelation, as written in the free creation, and stamped in the nature and instincts of man."

Riddle did not entirely ignore Bushnell's legal defense. He raised the same technical arguments that had surfaced throughout the trial. The indictment was insufficient because it did not follow the precise wording of the Fugitive Slave Act; Bacon's title to Price had not been sufficiently established; Jennings's Kentucky power of attorney conflicted with Lowe's Ohio warrant; the "illegal and useless" warrant itself lacked a seal, and it had been issued by the wrong court.

But those arguments were secondary to the thrust of the defense, which was a scorching attack on the Fugitive Slave Act. Riddle used by turns the language of religion and the language of scorn. Deputy Lowe had consented "to play pimp and pander to this bawd of American Slavery." The "unfortunate Shakespeare Boynton" was an "alarmingly precocious little deceiver," while Anderson Jennings was "the evil genius of this disgusting transaction." The betrayal of John Price was "a treason so measureless and profound, that the years of God's eternity will be strained to punish it!"

Above all, Riddle exalted the righteousness of the Oberlin rescuers. He likened them to a Pilgrim band, whose "teaching has gone forth an influence for good, and for good alone." Only in Oberlin, he said, do the "fleeing, the hunted, and the oppressed . . . find all the beautiful charities of benignant Christianity awaiting them with beckoning hands." Rejecting all of Bliss's charges against Oberlin, Riddle replied, "That which is charged upon her as her crime, is her chiefest crown."

The jury remained silent during Riddle's argument, but the spectators often interrupted the proceeding with laughter and applause. At one point District Attorney Belden objected to the "disturbances," asking that the disturbers "be taken into custody" if they continued their outbursts. Rufus Spalding responded that the spectators had every right to applaud.

"*What, sir!*" shouted Belden. "Do you mean that *you* sanction such manifestations?"

"I do, sir," retorted Spalding.

"Well, sir," threatened Belden, "you will doubtless have an opportunity to leave with the rest then."

The court interceded before the two men came to blows, and no spectators were removed from the courtroom. Belden's bluster had no effect on Riddle, who continued his argument as before.

After more than eight hours, Riddle finally reached his conclusion. He asked the jury to save "the free citizens of Ohio" from turning into "baying dogs at the bidding of Southern despots," and he all but called upon them to disobey "this unutterably loathsome [and] wicked Act of 1850."

Today it may seem that eight or nine hours of closing argument would be more than sufficient in a relatively simple case, but mid-nineteenth-century audiences were accustomed to listening to oratory at great length. Consequently, it was only natural that senior counsel Rufus Spalding would also argue on behalf of the defendant, continuing for yet another full day. Not to be outdone by his younger colleague, Spalding indulged his own rhetorical flourishes. Referring to Shakespeare Boynton as an "unfortunate child," he bemoaned,

> How readily he consented to play the Judas, and how well satisfied he was with the reward of his treason—the twenty—it should have been thirty—pieces of silver.

Spalding delivered a dire warning that even free white citizens might someday be apprehended under the Fugitive Slave Act. Dramatically pointing to a child in the gallery, he raised his voice,

> Gentlemen of the Jury, is there one of you who would not be proud to reckon that "flaxen haired" little boy yonder among your children? His skin is whiter than the District Attorney's, and his hair not half so curly! And yet, less than six months ago that child was set free in the Probate Court in this city, having been brought a *slave* from North Carolina.

In keeping with the overall defense strategy, Spalding also assailed the technical defects in the prosecution case, though always returning to his main theme. He defended the rescuers' commitment to abolition, admitting "that Oberlin is an asylum for the oppressed of all God's creation, without distinction of color." Repudiating Chief Justice Taney's *Dred Scott* decision, Spalding asserted that there could be no such thing as lawful "property in a slave."

Three days earlier George Bliss had cautioned the jury that disrespect for the Fugitive Slave Act might lead to dissolution of the Union. Spalding accepted that challenge, as perhaps no attorney had done before. The rescue of slaves, he said, was worth endangering the Union, because the encroachment of slavery and slave catchers meant the end of liberty in the North:

> I have said that slavery is like a canker . . . and I now say that unless the knife or the cautery be applied to the speedy and entire removal of the diseased part, we shall soon lose the name of freedom, as we have already lost the substance, and be unable longer to avoid confessing that TYRANTS ARE OUR MASTERS.

Spalding saved his most audacious plea for last. He openly called for Judge Willson to declare the Fugitive Slave Act unconstitutional, notwithstanding the controlling precedent to the contrary. That was nothing short of a demand for civil disobedience by the court itself. Five years earlier Richard Henry Dana had been unwilling to go that far when he argued the Burns case before Commissioner Edward Loring in Boston. But times had changed, and abolitionist lawyers had become far more aggressive. "Had I the distinguished honor to occupy the seat which is so eminently filled by your honor," said Spalding,

> I should feel bound to pronounce the fugitive law of 1850 utterly unconstitutional, without force and void; though in thus doing I should risk impeachment before the senate of my country; and, Sir, should such an impeachment work my removal from office, I should proudly embrace it as a greater honor than has yet fallen to the lot of any judicial officer in these United States.

"This act *can bind no one*," exhorted Spalding. Not the court, not the jury, and least of all the defendant.

Riddle and Spalding had together developed a new and daring legal strategy of civil disobedience. They challenged the moral legitimacy of the Fugitive Slave Act and called upon the judge and jury to defy the law itself. William Lloyd Garrison and Theodore Parker had delivered similar arguments in print and from the pulpit, but no lawyers had yet risked making such a demand in court.

With no tradition of comparable advocacy to build upon, Riddle and Spalding were working virtually from scratch, creating a new line of defense before a hostile court. Their case was not fully cohesive—they presented their main themes only in final argument, somewhat inconsistently with the testimony of their own witnesses—but they deserve great credit for exploring such a radical approach to the trial, even if they did not perfect it. Where other lawyers would have simply defended the rescuer, Spalding and Riddle justified the rescue itself.

District Attorney Belden understood that the defense lawyers were speaking to an audience beyond the courtroom. He began his rebuttal argument by fuming that "for three days has the crowd been addressed; not the court, not the jury." "Are we in a dream," he asked, "or are we in a political hustings?"

Belden had more harsh words for "the Saints of Oberlin, Peck, Plumb, Fitch, to which are to be added Saints Spalding and Riddle, and *sub-saint* Bushnell—all Saints of the Higher Law." Although he drew "unmistakable hisses" from the spectators, Belden argued that "slaves were not fit for freedom" and that slavery itself was sanctioned by the Bible: "Christ denounced idolatry, polygamy, but not a word against slavery. He did not tell them of a Higher Law as against the laws of the land."

Like the defense lawyers, Belden spoke only briefly about the actual facts of the case. He cautioned the jury to "take no account of the quibbles and technicalities which might stand in the way of a conviction," and he said that the case could be resolved by making one simple observation: If John "had not been known to be a slave, there would have been no mob to rescue him."

Following Belden's rebuttal, the court proceeded to instruct the jury. Willson informed the jurors that Bushnell could not be convicted unless they were convinced that he "knew the negro was a fugitive from labor." That instruction heartened the defense, although it was undermined by Willson's further clarification, "that dark complexion, woolly head, and flat nose, with possession and claim of ownership, do afford *prima facie* evidence of the slavery and ownership charged."

Willson also backed up the prosecutors on the question of Jennings's authority. "Although the slave might have been taken in the first instance upon a void warrant, it was nevertheless competent for [Jennings], by virtue of his power, to take and control him at any time." At the prodding of defense counsel, however, Willson added that the prosecution had to prove "that the fugitive was held by virtue of the power of attorney" at the time of the actual rescue.

That left only the higher law to be addressed. Willson disposed of it by informing the jury that the case was "to be divested of everything that is extraneous" and to be decided strictly "according to the law and testimony as delivered to you in Court." Then he added sharply,

> Much has been eloquently said by learned counsel that would be entitled to great weight and consideration if addressed . . . to an ecclesiastical tribunal, where matters of casuistry are discussed and determined.

Notwithstanding Willson's mostly stacked instructions, the defense lawyers were optimistic about the outcome of the trial. They had unnerved District Attorney Belden, whose sputtering rebuttal had been forced to take their higher law arguments into account. The jury charge had also given them some hope, requiring proof "that the fugitive was held by virtue of the power of attorney." That was clearly the weakest aspect of the prosecution case. Whoever else had seen the Kentucky document, there was no evidence that it had ever been displayed to Simeon Bushnell. The defense team's optimism increased as the jury continued to deliberate for more than three hours—an unusually long time in that era.

Finally court reconvened. "Gentlemen of the Jury, have you agreed upon a verdict?" asked the judge.

"We have, your Honor."

"What is your verdict, Mr. Foreman?"

The lawyers and the defendant stood and held their breaths.

The jury foreman spoke only one word: "Guilty."

The rescuers looked as though they had been struck "by a thunderbolt." They cast "quick, uneasy glances at one another," showing sympathy for Simeon Bushnell and concern for their own futures.[13]

The lawyers, however, had little time to express their disappointment. Bushnell's case had been only the first of many, and although it was late Friday afternoon, the next trial was already about to begin.

∽ 14 ∽

VOTARIES OF THE HIGHER LAW

S everal weeks before Bushnell's trial, attorneys Belden and Spalding had agreed on the order in which they would take up the subsequent cases. Based on their understanding of that agreement, the defense lawyers had prepared to defend Henry Peck, an Oberlin professor of sacred rhetoric, against the charge of "aiding and abetting" the rescue. Both Belden and Bliss had railed mightily against "Saint Peck" in their closing arguments, so it made sense that the second prosecution would be against one of the spiritual ringleaders of abolitionism on the Western Reserve. The defense lawyers were therefore shocked when Belden announced that the next trial would be against Charles Langston.[1]

Whether there had been an honest misunderstanding or a doublecross, Spalding and company objected to what they saw as a troubling switch in the prosecution agenda. Charles Langston had been present throughout the afternoon in Wellington, although his involvement had mostly been as a negotiator. Deputy Jacob Lowe had appealed to Langston for assistance, and Langston had promised to convey Lowe's suggested compromise to the crowd outside Wadsworth's hotel. The prosecution of Langston, therefore, had a touch of vindictiveness about it, and perhaps a touch of racism. Langston was the most prominent black man among the defendants, and advancing him to the head of the prosecution queue served as a stark warning to Ohio's other black leaders.

Despite Spalding's protest, Belden held firm. It was his right to determine the order of the prosecution, no matter how that disadvantaged the defense. Realizing that he was powerless, Spalding allowed that he might be ready for Langston's case by the time a new jury was chosen.

Now it was Judge Willson's turn to blindside the defense. Willson announced that there was no need to choose a new jury. "The present jury was one struck and selected for the term . . . and it was proper that they should try all the cases."

That brought defense lawyer Franklin Backus angrily to his feet. It was impossible for the "present jury" to be impartial, he argued, because it had already heard and determined the most important issues in the case—Bacon's ownership, John Price's identity, and the legitimacy of Jennings's power of attorney. It could not be "pretended that they would come to another trial with no opinions formed in their own minds." The court's proposal, Backus fulminated, "was an unheard of and most villanous [sic] outrage on the sense of the civilized world." Not one to temper his words, Backus declared that Willson had embarked on "a monstrous proceeding, the like of which had never been known since courts were first in existence."

Even in the mid-nineteenth century, when ornate declamation was part of a lawyer's stock in trade, Backus's accusations were extreme, and hardly calculated to persuade the judge to change his mind. Willson cautioned the defense lawyer against his "intemperate zeal" and ruled that Bushnell's jury would continue to sit.

Rufus Spalding was no less dismayed at the prospect of trying successive cases before the same conviction-prone jurors. Without taking time to consult his numerous clients, Spalding announced that the defendants would all refuse to "appear by attorney before such a jury." Spalding had played the only card in his hand—the threat of boycotting the rest of the proceedings—but the prosecution simply called his bluff. "Very well," said Belden. If the defendants would not participate in their own trials, "then I ask the Court to order these men all into the custody of the marshal."

Judge Willson immediately complied with Belden's request, directing the marshal to take all of the defendants into custody, and also instructing him to apprehend "such of the indicted as were not in the Court-Room."

For reasons that he later attributed to the court's confusion, Spalding next asked that the defendants' recognizances—upon which they had been released without posting bail—be canceled. Belden remarked that the defendants could subsequently be freed only upon supplying sufficient "sureties," with Judge Willson adding cryptically that "personal recognizances in the sum of $1000 each" would be sufficient. The situation was indeed confusing. Had the defendants been ordered into custody on the prosecutor's motion, or had they surrendered themselves in protest? That question would assume great importance as the cases progressed, but for the time being it was only certain that the defendants had suddenly been committed to jail. Judge Willson then adjourned court until Monday morning, leaving others to resolve the meaning of his order.

Federal Marshal Matthew Johnson was no friend of the rescuers—as a loyal appointee of the Buchanan administration he had assisted in assembling the proslavery grand jury—but he had no available facility in which to place so many new prisoners. Johnson therefore offered to let all of the defendants go home for the weekend—with the exception of the recently convicted Bushnell—if they would promise him to return on Monday morning.

By then the defendants had taken the time to caucus. Seizing Judge Willson's peremptory order as an opportunity to demonstrate the encroachments of the slave power—and the tyrannical nature of the federal courts—they refused to cooperate with Marshal Johnson's reasonable request. Instead the defendants announced that they would remain in jail "until relieved by due course of law." They were resolved to remain in custody, sharing "Bushnell's fortunes as long as possible," unless Judge Willson "should amend the wrong" he had done. They would "give no bail, enter no recognizance, and make no promises to return to the Court."

The defendants' intransigence left Marshal Johnson with a dilemma. Lacking a federal jail, and with too many prisoners to lodge in the courthouse, he was dependent on Cuyahoga County Sheriff David Wightman for access to the county jail. But Wightman was a staunch Western Reserve Republican, and it was not obvious that he would provide any assistance to the Buchanan administration. With no alternative at hand, however, Johnson escorted his charges to Wightman's Castle (as it was called), which was just down the street from the courthouse.

As expected, Sheriff Wightman was reluctant to assume custody of the federal prisoners, but he finally agreed to admit them. "Gentlemen," he said to his new inmates, "I open my doors to you, not as criminals, but as guests. I cannot regard you as criminals for doing only what I should do myself under similar circumstances."[2]

George Belden was definitely pleased with his work. In a letter to Jacob Thompson, Buchanan's secretary of the interior, the prosecutor boasted of his "great triumph" in the Bushnell trial, noting that he had accomplished the victory in a Republican stronghold.[3] Belden had every good reason to believe that he would be equally successful in the case against Charles Langston.

When court reconvened on Monday morning, Rufus Spalding had his first opportunity to examine the official court journal from the previous Friday's contretemps. To his astonishment, he saw an entry reading that each defendant had "given up his recognizance, on his own free will and pleasure." Spalding moved for a correction of the record, asking that it be emended to state that the defendants had been taken into custody "on the motion of the District-Attorney" and had requested the cancellation of their recognizances only once the court had granted the order. The distinction was not trivial, as it governed whether the defendants would simply be released once the proceedings resumed that day, or would instead be required to post cash bail.

For reasons of honor—and publicity and politics—the defendants were not willing to admit that they had been guilty of such "folly and indiscretion" as to voluntarily surrender themselves. They insisted that the court admit that the record was mistaken. Willson was equally unwilling to concede error, ruling that the "entry was correct according to [his] recollection." Spalding persisted in pressing the point, causing Willson to rebuke him for his "insolence." If defense counsel continued in that manner, said the court, his name would be "stricken from the bar." Spalding dared the judge to make good on the threat, to which Willson replied that "it probably would be done." Tempers eventually cooled, however, and both Willson and Spalding backed away from the confrontation.

But even though Spalding avoided a finding of contempt, his clients remained in custody. They were, as they expressed in a joint statement, "not willing to have *even an appearance of submission* to a tyrannical power" lest that be misinterpreted as obedience to the "diabolical Fugitive Slave Act." On the basis of that principle, the Oberlin defendants would remain in jail for nearly twelve weeks.

Spalding got better results when he renewed his challenge to the jury array. "It would be a farce to go before them again for justice," he argued. Surprisingly, Willson relented, ruling that the evidence against Langston was essentially "the same as that against Bushnell," thus requiring a new jury. He ordered Marshal Johnson to assemble a new panel, and recessed court for several hours for that purpose.

Johnson returned to court in the afternoon with twenty or so potential jurors. The attorneys were allowed to question the panel, with District Attorney Belden first establishing that none of them had any "objection to the enforcement of the Fugitive Slave Law." Spalding then asked the jurors whether they had formed any opinions about the Bushnell case. One man answered that he thought "the boy [John Price] was a slave," but the court decided that was not sufficient to disqualify him. Only those jurors who already believed that Price had been "illegally rescued" were removed for cause, resulting in a jury comprising "nine Administration men, two Fillmore Whigs, and one Republican who had no objection to the Fugitive Slave Law."[4]

Bushnell's conviction, and the incarceration of the other defendants, had rallied abolitionist opinion even more strongly behind the rescuers. William Lloyd Garrison now predicted that Langston's prosecution would "give a fresh impetus to our noble cause." Ohio Congressman Joshua Giddings recognized that the defense of the rescuers could serve as a call to greater resistance to slavery and slave hunting, declaring that Cleveland in 1859 had become similar to "the Boston of 1775," the cradle of resistance to tyranny.[5]

In light of Giddings's comparison of abolitionist Cleveland to revolutionary Boston, it was noteworthy that Charles Langston's trial commenced on April 18, 1859, the eighty-fourth anniversary of Paul Revere's ride through Lexington and Concord. That symbolism, however, appears to have been missed, or at least not remarked upon by the court.

A transcript of the opening statements did not survive in the records of the Langston case. We know only that the attorneys' remarks were relatively short, lasting not more than a couple of hours in total. George Belden read aloud the indictment against Langston, who, in contrast to Bushnell, was charged with interfering with the execution of a federal warrant. Albert Riddle briefly set forth the defense. Unlike Bushnell, who faced trial with nearly all of his codefendants present for support, Langston was accompanied only by Henry Peck and Ralph Plumb, who had been brought to court by special order. The other defendants were required to remain in jail.

Much of the prosecution case simply repeated the evidence from the earlier trial. The first witness was John Bacon, who again testified to the ownership of his escaped slave. He was followed by Robert Cochran, the Mason County clerk, who testified to the validity of Jennings's power of attorney and supported Bacon's claim of undivided ownership.

Anderson Jennings was the first witness to provide any evidence that Langston had participated in the rescue, stating somewhat equivocally that he thought the defendant was nearby when the crowd stormed the attic room to free John Price. Jennings also provided the details of his arrangement with Shakespeare Boynton, and he insisted that he had "directed the seizure of John at Oberlin [and] had charge of him at Wellington." Jennings testified to Price's alleged desire to return to Kentucky, characteristically refusing to allow that a runaway would show the least reluctance to return to bondage. The defense lawyers continued to object to the admission of statements from "property." This time the court entered a compromise ruling: Price's "*acts* but not the words were evidence."

Jennings's most damaging testimony involved an exchange with Langston that occurred about thirty minutes before the rescue. Jennings said that Langston came into the attic room to participate in a round of negotiations. Langston was asked to help persuade the crowd to disperse, but "he refused to do it, and said we might just as well give him up, as *they* were determined to have him." Then, apparently realizing that he had attributed a less incriminating pronoun to the defendant, Jennings quickly corrected himself: "He said, *we* are determined to have him." The point of this was to establish that Langston had not merely described the crowd's intentions ("they" were determined) but rather delivered a first-person threat ("we" will have him).

In a very lengthy cross-examination, defense counsel required Jennings to repeat nearly all of the details he had covered on direct examination. The tactic was intended to search out inconsistencies, but for the most part it had little effect. Jennings stuck to the basics of his story, adding several times that "everybody was shown the power of attorney and warrant both." Only at the very end of the cross-examination did the witness slip. Asked once again for Charles Langston's exact words, Jennings quoted the defendant as saying, "You might as well give the negro up, as *they* are going to have him any way." This time the slave catcher was not given an opportunity to correct himself.

Richard Mitchell was the fourth Kentuckian to testify. He stated that he knew John Price—"a full-blooded Negro"—and recognized him as the captured runaway he seized in Ohio. Once again there was an objection to the admission of the fugitive's statements. This time the court specifically ruled, without any appreciation of the irony, that "for the purposes of testimony, all persons whether black or white must be regarded as persons."

On cross-examination Franklin Backus compelled Mitchell to admit that he could not identify Langston as a participant in the rescue. The most contentious moment in the cross-examination came when Belden rudely interrupted Backus to threaten that "unless Prof. Peck desisted from suggesting questions to the opposite counsel he should order him back to jail." In reply, Backus chided the prosecutor for his "sensitiveness." It made no matter whether Peck had proposed any questions, he said, and in any event, the theology professor had "suggested no questions at all."

Mitchell's testimony was followed by an interlude of even higher drama, when Sheriff Richard Whitney of Lorain County stepped to the front of the courtroom and announced that Jennings and Mitchell had been indicted on a charge of kidnapping. Accompanied by a lawyer and several assistants, Sheriff Whitney produced a warrant issued by the Lorain County Court of Common Pleas and attempted to take the two slave catchers into custody. The federal authorities, however, apparently had advance notice of the indictment of the prosecution witnesses. A deputy U.S. marshal—his boss, Matthew Johnson, was evidently out of the room—promptly produced a bench warrant that committed the Kentuckians to federal custody as material witnesses. Asked to rule on the priority of the competing warrants, Judge Willson held that Whitney's attempted arrest was "an unheard-of proceeding and a contempt." The witnesses would remain safely in federal custody for the duration of the trial.

The indictment of Jennings and Mitchell had been engineered by Western Reserve abolitionists. The Lorain County charge was part of what John Mercer Langston called "a counter proceeding which would open the doors of the state penitentiary to the perpetrators of such kidnapping."[6] Although the arrest of Jennings and Mitchell had been thwarted for the time being, the renewed invocation of Ohio's criminal law would have profound consequences in the months to follow.

As things stood, however, Charles Langston was still on trial. The next witness for the prosecution was the ever-compliant Chauncey Wack, who had little trouble placing Langston in the center of events. According to the Oberlin hotelkeeper, the defendant had been on the balcony at Wadsworth's less than five minutes before the "rush" of the crowd that escorted Price down the stairs. No other witness claimed to have seen Langston on the balcony—and Wack was forced on cross-examination to concede that he might have had the timing confused.

Wack's cagey exaggerations were fairly easily discounted. He was followed, however, by a series of witnesses who testified far more damagingly to Langston's allegedly threatening statements. Norris Wood testified that Langston said "*we* will have him any way," displaying a gun as he spoke. Charles Wadsworth testified that he and Langston discussed the legality of Price's capture. "I asked him if the papers which the slaveholders had were all right. He said it made no difference whether they were right or not, they were bound to have John any way." N. H. Reynolds saw Langston in the hotel hallway, and heard him say "that they had got to have him before the train [to Columbus] came in, or they would not succeed in getting him." Posse member Samuel Davis put it the same way. Langston "turned round and said, 'We will have him any how.'"

Deputy Marshal Lowe, who had not taken the stand in the Bushnell case, testified about his negotiation with Langston, which occurred about an hour and a half before the crowd's assault on the attic room. Lowe had known and respected Langston for several years, and at first his testimony seemed to exonerate the defendant by characterizing him as a peacemaker:

> I told him that I would like to have him go down and explain to the crowd how things were. He expressed himself satisfied that the negro was legally held, and said he would go down and tell the people so.

Langston departed, returning in about twenty minutes to inform Lowe that "they were determined . . . on having the boy." The two men, sitting together on a bed, then discussed Lowe's proposal to set up a committee to accompany the posse to Columbus, "and see that John had a fair trial." Langston said he wanted to avoid trouble and was therefore "very anxious to have [Lowe's proposal] carried out. But the people below would not agree to, or to hear of it."

At this point, it still seemed that Langston's role might be innocent, but then Lowe threw a bombshell, contradicting every statement he had already attributed to the defendant. Langston got up at the end of their conversation, said Lowe, "and just as he was about to go down stairs he said 'we will have him any how.'"

The defense attorneys cross-examined Lowe about the validity of the federal warrant. Lowe countered, however, that he had acted on the authority of the federal papers only when he apprehended Price near Oberlin. Upon arriving in Wellington he had turned custody of the fugitive over to Jennings, the holder of the power of attorney, and he thereafter acted only as the Kentucky slave hunter's assistant. Lowe agreed that he considered Langston a reasonable man, but then the cross-examiner made a classic mistake.

"Didn't he say 'I won't interfere any way?'" asked the defense lawyer.

"He did not—am *sure*," replied the witness, who then took the opportunity to repeat his most damaging testimony. "As Langston rose from the bed he said, '*we* will have him any how.'" Then Lowe added for good measure that "I felt disappointed when Langston said what he did."

The testimony against Langston was well orchestrated. The identical statement, or nearly so, was ascribed to him by witnesses who saw him at various times in different locations. It was as though Langston had spent the entire afternoon telling all listeners that "we will have him anyhow," with only slight variation. One witness even had Langston repeating those same words at a post-rescue rally in Oberlin. According to Philip Kelly, Langston bragged of warning Lowe "that it was no use for them to try to keep John, for they would have him anyway." One would think that a well-educated man such as Charles Langston might have varied his verb choice now and then—claiming at least once that they would free, rescue, liberate, take, or perhaps release the prisoner. But no. According to the prosecution witnesses, Langston stuck to the oddly passive "we will have him" on every occasion.

However much the suspicious uniformity of the prosecution testimony might have diminished its credibility, one witness delivered a surprising and devastating blow to the defense. Wellingtonian William Sciples, himself one of the indicted rescuers, made a deal with the prosecutors to testify against his codefendant. Sciples claimed to have seen Langston in the hotel hallway, outside the garret where Price was imprisoned. Speaking with a group of "*mixed* men; three or four were colored," Langston assured his fellow rescuers that "we will have him at any rate before he shall go South." In exchange for his cooperation, Sciples was immediately released from jail without bond and the charges against him were later dismissed.

Among the last witnesses for the prosecution was Sterne Chittenden, the fugitive slave commissioner who had issued the warrant for Price's capture. He verified his authority and authenticated the warrant. Shortly after Chittenden's testimony, the prosecution rested.

The defense began with a string of witnesses who testified to the supposed defects in the posse's papers. Joseph Dickson, a Wellington attorney, said that he had examined Lowe's warrant and observed that it had no seal, and that Jennings had never even mentioned holding a power of attorney. Justice of the Peace Isaac Bennett and Constable Barnabas Meacham likewise testified that there was no seal on the warrant and that the power of attorney had not been displayed to the crowd.

The defense objective was to show that John Price had been held illegally, thereby justifying the rescue or at least negating the charge of intentionally interfering with the execution of a federal warrant. But the technical points were both complex and abstruse; the defense would still have to explain why that issue should not have been presented to a federal commissioner, as Lowe had proposed and the rescuers refused. The question of Price's identification— was he black or copper colored?—was not raised at all by the defense witnesses at Langston's trial. In any case, that too was a question that could have been presented at a commissioner's hearing, but for the rescuers' intervention.

A more promising line of defense was introduced by witnesses who testified to Charles Langston's efforts to resolve the situation peacefully, either through negotiation with the slave catchers or by invoking Ohio law. Langston had been involved in obtaining the first kidnapping warrant, which was issued by Justice of the Peace Isaac Bennett on the dubious theory that Ohio law superseded the Fugitive Slave Act. The defendant had also urged Constable Meacham to serve the warrant, and he had attempted to organize a trip to Elyria for the purpose of securing a writ of habeas corpus from the probate court. Constable Meacham had refused to serve the warrant, for fear that he would be sued, and nothing ever came of Langston's efforts to obtain a writ. Nonetheless, Langston's attempts to use legal means severely undercut the prosecution claim that he was an instigator of the forcible rescue.

At the risk of implicating themselves, three of the indicted rescuers testified that Langston had not been on the hotel staircase during the assault on the attic room, thereby contradicting the unreliable Chauncey Wack and the perfidious William Sciples. Henry Evans, for example, testified that he had been immediately outside the attic door "at the time of the Rescue" but that Langston was not present when Price was "passed out" of the garret. Seizing an opportunity, the cross-examiner asked whether the witness himself had been armed at the time. Spalding objected to the question, arguing that Evans should not be forced to incriminate himself or to provide evidence that could be "used by the District-Attorney when the witness was put on his own trial." Judge Willson agreed that the witness could refuse to answer the question, "but if he did his whole testimony would be ruled out." Evans unselfishly jeopardized himself for Langston's sake, admitting that he "had a small rifle."

The defense could not fully contradict the testimony regarding Langston's alleged threats that "we will have him any way." Several witnesses testified that they had not heard Langston say any such thing, but it was impossible actually to prove the negative—that the defendant had never made any incriminating statements to anyone—especially given that the most serious threats had purportedly been made directly to Lowe and Mitchell.

Langston himself could have denied making the damning statements, but as the defendant he was disqualified from testifying on his own behalf. Thus, Langston was prevented from taking the stand—not because he was a black man, but because he was the defendant—and the jury was not allowed to hear the most probative evidence regarding his alleged threats to Jennings and Lowe.

After the defense rested, Belden announced that four of the Wellington defendants wanted to withdraw their pleas of not guilty and enter pleas of nolo contendere. In what was evidently a continuation of the divide-and-conquer strategy that led to the deal with William Sciples, Belden explained that the Wellingtonians had acted only "from impulse," which placed them in a far "different light from those who came ten miles for the purpose of rescuing John." The four defendants then distanced themselves from the abolitionist defense lawyers and threw themselves upon the mercy of the court. Belden asked the court to make the "punishment as light as possible," and Judge Willson agreed. He imposed a fine of $20 on each of the Wellington defendants and sentenced them to imprisonment for twenty-four hours. The jail time, however, was to be served comfortably in the Forest City Hotel, and all four defendants were freed by nightfall.

Belden then presented his rebuttal case, recalling Sciples, Lowe, and Jennings, who reiterated key points from their earlier testimony. That was probably a mistake on the part of the prosecution, as the three repeat witnesses offered very little in the way of clarification. The presentation of rebuttal testimony, however, allowed the defense to present a surrebuttal case, which Spalding used to mount a furious attack on the defector William Sciples.

Four witnesses testified about Sciples's poor reputation for truth and veracity. The mayor of Wellington, who had known Sciples for ten years, said flatly that he would "not believe him under oath," and Wellington's justice of the peace and constable each said the same. Indicted rescuer Matthew Gillet swore that Sciples was "not a man of truth." Gillet's testimony caused a "sensation in court," and not only because he was, at seventy-four years of age, one of the most revered and "respectable citizens of Lorain County." Gillet was a Wellingtonian who had refused to bargain for his freedom with the district attorney, choosing to stay in jail rather than betray his friends. His stalwart testimony on behalf of Langston stood in sharp contrast to his timorous nolo-pleading neighbors.

With that display of courage and fidelity, the evidence closed.

District Attorney George Belden argued first for the prosecution, presenting a stern summary of his case. It was plain that John Price was a slave of Bacon's who had escaped to Ohio. It was surely within the power of the master to retake his slave, either personally or through an agent. Jennings had therefore acted lawfully at every turn—both planning Price's seizure in Oberlin and holding him in Wellington—pursuant to a good power of attorney and a valid federal warrant. The jury should disregard the "impotent and miserable" attempts to discredit Bacon's claim and to challenge the authority of Jennings's papers.

Belden next turned to the "agency Langston had in the rescue," describing the defendant as "very cunning and very hypocritical, very shrewd, but very deceiving." The evidence, said Belden, showed that the entire crowd had acted with "common intent" and that Langston's own acts were calculated not to keep the peace, or even to punish the kidnappers, "but to rescue the negro." Such an attempt to defeat the enforcement of a federal law came perilously close to treason, argued Belden. Although his superiors had not authorized him to bring a capital charge against the rescuers, Belden still wanted to make sure everyone understood the potential cost of exalting the higher law.

At that point Belden began to "read some law" to the jurors—no doubt to remind them of their duty to follow the federal statutes rather than their own consciences—but he was interrupted by Franklin Backus. The defense lawyer sarcastically asked whether Belden was aware of a recent case from South Carolina, in which a "Federal Court held that the jury were the judges of the law." Belden became visibly angry—one observer wrote that "he grew as black in the face as the devil is painted"—and he loudly denounced Backus as "a demagogue." The two men continued to exchange insults while the jurors watched in amazement. Even Judge Willson was apparently speechless, as he did nothing to intervene. Perhaps it was just as well to allow the attorneys to shout themselves out, as Belden eventually "cooled down and came back to the case."

The prosecutor had saved his most devastating argument for last. Langston would be guilty, Belden told the jury, even if he had done nothing more than attempt to have a state court warrant served against Lowe. Because federal law is supreme, Belden reasoned, interference with the deputy marshal "under legal process" was every bit "as unlawful as the interposition of violence." From a legal perspective, that was potentially a crushing blow, as it transformed Langston's best defense—that he had only tried to free Price through legal means—into a virtual admission of guilt. It was true that the Fugitive Slave Act prohibited "all molestation" of slave catchers "by any process issued by any court," but no prosecutor had previously argued that it was a crime for a fugitive's sympathizers to seek habeas corpus relief from a state judge. Only two months earlier, the U.S. Supreme Court had ruled that state courts could not interfere with enforcement of the Fugitive Slave Act, but even that unanimous opinion—written to no one's surprise by Chief Justice Taney—did not hold that the act of petitioning a state court could itself constitute a separate crime.

It was not hard to grasp the implications of Belden's argument, which threatened to criminalize even peaceful—and otherwise seemingly lawful—

resistance to the Fugitive Slave Act. At a time when federal courts were few and far between, and not always in session, recourse to a county judge was often the only way to slow down slave catchers on their way south with a captive. Indeed, the crowd outside Wadsworth's Hotel in Wellington had good reason to believe that Jennings and his prisoner were about to board a southbound train, and there was no guarantee that they would stop in Columbus as they had sometimes promised. A locally issued writ or warrant was therefore the only available legal means to ensure that the slave hunters did not head directly for Kentucky. Thus, when Belden insisted that Langston should be convicted simply for "interposing" legal process, it was interpreted as yet another step in the Buchanan-Taney cabal's policy of nationalizing slavery. One observer said that Belden's proposition was "as monstrous a doctrine as that of the Dred Scott decision."

Arguing first for the defense, young Seneca Griswold did not explicitly refer to the higher law as Albert Riddle had done two weeks earlier on behalf of Simeon Bushnell. Perhaps Griswold believed that Langston's case was stronger than Bushnell's and there was no need to resort to metaphysics, or perhaps he feared that it would be too provocative to invoke higher law on behalf of a black man. As it was, his argument was controversial enough.

Griswold directly confronted the issue of race. Despite the theoretical guarantees of the Constitution, he explained to the jury, Langston could have no jury "of those who are his peers." Referring to the most damaging holding of the *Dred Scott* decision—that even free black men could not be citizens of the United States—Griswold continued: "Not only is he an alien, but in the view of the law which governs this Court, he is an outcast. He has no equality, no rights, except in being amenable to the penal statutes."

Such treatment was intolerable, said Griswold, especially concerning someone as accomplished and well educated as Charles Langston. The defendant was "in every attribute of manhood . . . incomparably superior" to the vulgar slave hunters who testified against him, and yet the Kentuckians had crudely referred to Langston as "only a nigger." Surely a jury of northern Ohioans would be more enlightened than a couple of buffoons from the backwoods.

Defense counsel implored the jurors to "lay aside all political bias and prejudice" and to "forget his race and color, and try his case as though he were one of your equals." It was the jury's duty to take special care in judging Langston's case, in order to compensate for the wrongs of slavery and the insult of race prejudice.

During a full day of argument, Griswold touched on fine technicalities and larger themes. He contended that both Lowe's warrant and Jennings's power of attorney had been defective, and he pointed out numerous small inconsistencies among the many prosecution witnesses. More convincingly, Griswold argued that Langston had not been "identified with the crowd who effected the rescue" and that his mere presence at Wellington was not a crime. After all, Langston had only "counsel[ed] peace and a resort to legal measures," and he could not be held accountable for others' acts of violence. Griswold acknowledged the prosecution's claim that "calling for a legal investigation" constituted a crime, but he derided that position as worse than any known even "in the darkest ages of English tyranny."

It was still necessary to deal with Langston's supposed threats to Jennings and Lowe. If Langston had indeed made the statement "*we* will have him," Griswold conceded that would tend "strongly to connect the defendant with those engaged in the rescue of John." But Griswold quickly discounted Jennings's account of the conversation. The Kentuckian's rustic accent and speech pattern made it impossible to fasten "any tolerable degree of accuracy in his statements."

It was more difficult to dismiss the testimony of Jacob Lowe. Griswold argued that a conviction could never rest solely on "Lowe's recollection of a particular word," especially since the word—"we" rather than "they"—was "at variance with the defendant's whole conduct" that afternoon. It was far more likely that Langston had been referring to the crowd outside the hotel, as opposed to his own intentions, when he cautioned Lowe to release his prisoner because "*they* will have him anyhow." Griswold reminded the jurors that witnesses frequently "alter a few expressions really used," whether intentionally or not, and the liberty of a man should "not be staked upon the recollection by a witness of a single word." Stepping beyond the rules of evidence, Griswold maintained that Langston would have denied the accusation if he had not been "debarred from testifying." That assertion was probably impermissible, but Belden (and the court) allowed it to pass.

In closing, Griswold made his strongest moral claim. Rather than punish Charles Langston, the judge and jury, if they had "any spark of humanity left in [their] bosoms," should rejoice "over the escape of a brother man from bondage." Calling almost for the annulment of the Fugitive Slave Act, Griswold insisted that "no higher power nor greater right than brute force" could make a man a slave, even if the law said otherwise. "Laws, to claim the respect of good men, must be good," he said. "And let us thank God if the noblest impulses of the human heart are so strong that no cruelty of law itself can chain them down."

Franklin Backus picked up where his junior colleague left off, with a ringing defense of civil disobedience:

> The offence here charged, then, is a political offence. The defendant is charged not with the breach of a moral, but with a legal rule. . . . He does not stand before you accused of the commission of any thing which is within itself a crime, but with an act which is only a crime because the law declares it is.

Langston could not be considered a criminal, argued Backus, because he was "inspired by the noblest of motives, such as all good men approve." That was a call for jury nullification, which Backus amplified with a further emotional appeal. The defendant, he told the jury, "could count a long line of ancestry on one side *not* of African blood, but wealthy and respectable Anglo-Saxon sires." Langston's background—the son of a Revolutionary War veteran—had not been offered in evidence, but it must have been so well-known that there was no objection from the prosecution. In light of the defendant's parentage, Backus continued, the jury's "reluctance must be tenfold greater by your verdict to shut out this man—emphatically a MAN—from the few privileges yet allowed him in this 'land of the free.'" That argument was a non sequitur—given that the premise of the abolitionist movement was that white ancestry should confer no special rights—but it was obviously designed to appeal to the sympathies, or biases, of the jurors.

Then defense counsel presented a remarkable argument premised on both (strongly) philo-Semitic and (somewhat) anti-Catholic themes, no doubt reflecting the prophetic Protestantism then prevalent in northern Ohio. Backus invoked the case of Edgardo Mortara, a six-year-old Jewish child in Italy who had been seized from his family by the papal police. The boy had been secretly baptized by a domestic servant, thus becoming—although unknowingly and without the consent of his parents—a Christian who could not legally be raised in a Jewish home. The kidnapping of Edgardo, which had occurred less than a year earlier, caused international outrage, as liberal Western governments protested the Papal State's cruelty toward Jewish families. The Buchanan administration presented a formal protest to the Vatican, but Pope Pius IX was unyielding. The seizure was completely lawful under canon law, all procedural steps having been closely followed, and a Jewish family could not be allowed custody of a baptized child.

The American public showed great sympathy for the Mortaras, and Backus attempted to turn that to his own client's advantage. There was a poignant symmetry between the pope's action and enforcement of the Fugitive Slave Act. In both cases, a seemingly immoral law was used to seize an individual and tear him away from either his parental home (as in Edgardo's case) or his adopted home (as in the case of John Price). No amount of procedural regularity, in the form of a papal decree or a commissioner's warrant, could justify such a kidnapping—or so defense counsel hoped the jury would conclude.[7]

Backus did not rest on generalities. Though all Americans were shocked by Edgardo's kidnapping, he explained that Jews would naturally "feel themselves more outraged" by the event:

> You and I condemn the act in the abstract as heartily as can any one belonging to the outraged race, yet at the same time we well know that it does not *take hold of us* as it does—and naturally does—of them. . . . Why? Because of this bond of kindred.

If American Jews were specially affected by the kidnapping of Edgardo Mortara, then it should certainly follow that Charles Langston would react strongly to the seizure of John Price:

> Well then, when one thus allied to this *defendant* . . . is pursued, decoyed, and seized, and is about to be hurried back to a deeper and more hopeless bondage . . . do you not understand that the feelings of this defendant would naturally be affected to a degree

to which you would not expect those of one of the dominant race here to be stirred?

In other words, Langston's race alone was reason enough to nullify the Fugitive Slave Act, at least in his individual case. Whatever the defendant's involvement in the rescue, he could not have been expected to act otherwise. Who would not take similar action in similar circumstances? How could the jury fail to understand and excuse Langston's instinctive sympathy for a runaway slave?

That was powerful rhetoric, although it was somewhat inconsistent with many other key aspects of the defense case—that the slave status of John Price was unproven, that the court papers had been defective, and that Langston had neither encouraged the crowd nor participated in the rescue. Over the course of his six-hour speech, Backus addressed all of the technicalities at great length, but he concluded with one final plea that the jurors turn to their consciences and provide the defendant with "in this *one* instance, equal justice, as you would to a man whose complexion was of another hue."

George Bliss delivered the prosecution's blistering rebuttal, shorter by orders of magnitude than the extended arguments of the defense. It was immaterial, he said, whether Langston's offense "was one against moral ideas or simply against the civil statute." Defense counsel's proposed preference for conscience over law would "tear down and annihilate the Government of these United States."

Taking advantage of Backus's "blood sympathy" argument, Bliss referred the jury to the testimony that Price had been eager to return to his master. Thus, it was not "a feeling of sympathy for John that prompted Langston and his associates to rescue him from the hands of the party which was taking him back to the South." Rather, Bliss claimed, the defendant's true "purpose, fixed and determined, was to violate and set at defiance one of the laws of the land."

The prosecutor was not reluctant to address the issue of civil disobedience, urging the jury to reject the idea that citizens may elect to challenge the law. The crowd in Wellington "did not care for the law" but instead "made their own laws." Although the "right of a portion of our inhabitants to hold property in slaves may be an unpleasant one to contemplate," he said, the rights of the "residents of Kentucky [cannot] be broken down by such men as Charles Langston."

Nor did Oberlin escape Bliss's scorn. The town was a "buzzard's nest . . . where negroes who arrive over the underground railroad are regarded as dear children." And worse, "the students who attend that Oberlin College are taught sedition and treason . . . and they graduate from that institution to go forth and preach opposition and treason."

Langston should be convicted simply because he had been in the crowd that freed the fugitive. The defendant had, after all, threatened Lowe that "we will have him any way." But Langston had done more than that. "Through the scheme of the warrant which [Constable] Meacham held . . . Langston was so connected . . . as to make him one of the rescuing party."

Judge Willson again delivered a jury charge highly favorable to the prosecution, repeating many of the instructions he had given in Bushnell's case. The court also instructed the jurors "to divest . . . any and all prejudices" against the Fugitive Slave Act, cautioning them that all "acts of Congress, placed upon the statute book, should command obedience."

Concerning Langston's technical defenses, Willson informed the jury that Jennings's power of attorney was perfectly valid, even though it had not been "sealed" by either Bacon or the Mason County clerk. An official seal was required only for the purpose of conveying real estate, he ruled, but it was an unnecessary formality for the evidently less solemn purpose of enslaving a human being. Worse yet for the defense, the court charged the jury that Langston's presence in the crowd, even if wholly nonviolent, made him "a party to every act which may afterward be done by any of the others, in furtherance of such common design."

Worst of all, the court accepted the prosecution's theory of unlawful rescue-by-writ. "When a fugitive from labor is captured and held by any of the modes [specified in the Fugitive Slave Act], any interference by the State authorities has no justification." Because Langston had "urged the execution of [Meacham's] warrant for the purpose of liberating the fugitive, his conduct in this particular implicated him as much in the common design of the mob, as if he had given his aid to the rescue by physical force."

After twelve days of testimony and an additional three days of argument, the case was finally in the jury's hands. There was much for the jurors to review. The prosecution relied on a novel theory of crime-by-warrant, and Langston had presented an unusually powerful defense—both legally and emotionally. But to everyone's surprise, it took the jury only thirty minutes to render a verdict of guilty. That, however, turned out to be far from the last word in the case.

➣ 15 ➣

AN IRREPRESSIBLE CONFLICT

Bushnell's sentencing had been deferred following his conviction, so the two defendants came together before the court on Wednesday, May 11, 1859, more than five weeks after the start of the first trial. Bushnell would face the bench first, but it was Langston's subsequent sentencing that created a dramatic new precedent for American courts.

Willson opened the morning session by asking Bushnell whether he had anything to say. With his wife and young child at his side, the prisoner remained silent, shaking his head to indicate that he declined to speak. Annoyed at the defendant's response, Willson prodded him to make a statement. Did he have *"any regrets* to express for the offence of which he stood convicted?" "No," replied Bushnell, he had no regrets.[1]

It soon became obvious that Judge Willson had intended to trap the defendant into precisely that answer, as the court immediately began to read aloud from a prepared manuscript. Willson castigated Bushnell for thinking "a praiseworthy virtue to violate the law . . . with exultation and defiance." The court continued to excoriate both the defendant and the higher law:

> A man of your intelligence must know that the enjoyment of rational liberty ceases the moment the laws are allowed to be broken with impunity. . . . You must know that when a man acts upon any system of morals or theology which teaches him to disrespect and violate the laws of the Government that protects him in life and property, his conduct is as criminal as his example is dangerous.
>
> The good order and well-being of society demand an exemplary penalty in your case. You have broken the law—you express no regret for the act done, but are exultant in the wrong.

The sentence was harsh—sixty days' imprisonment and a fine of $600 plus costs. Although it was less than the maximum under the statute, the fine was an impoverishing amount for a bookstore clerk. Bushnell collapsed into his seat. A pure heart and a clear conscience provided no ground for mitigation in Judge Willson's court.

When it came time for Charles Langston's sentencing, Willson instructed the defendant to rise and asked whether there was any reason "why the sentence of the law should not now be pronounced upon you?" Unlike Bushnell, Langston did not decline the court's invitation to speak on his own behalf. He had much to say, and he was well prepared to say it. He then delivered a speech that his brother would later describe as "beautiful and powerful," and perhaps "the most remarkable speech that has been delivered before a court by a prisoner since Paul pleaded his own case before Agrippa."[2]

"I know that the courts of this country," the defendant began, "are so constituted as to oppress and outrage colored men." "I cannot, then, expect, judging from the past history of the country, any mercy from the laws [or] from the Constitution." Nonetheless, there were issues that had to be addressed and an audience to be reached well beyond the courtroom.

Langston recounted the many reports of slave hunters in Lorain County, "lying hidden and skulking about, waiting for some opportunity to get their bloody hands on some helpless creature to drag him back—or for the first time—into helpless and life-long bondage." Thus, a great fear affected all of the black people in and around Oberlin, some of whom had earned their freedom "by long and patient toil," and some of whom had been freed through the "good-will of their masters." But Langston did not speak only on behalf of those who had been lawfully manumitted:

> And there were others who had become free—to their everlasting honor I say it—by the exercise of their own God-given powers—by escaping from the plantations of their masters, eluding the bloodthirsty patrols and sentinels so thickly scattered all along their path, outrunning bloodhounds and horses, swimming rivers and fording swamps, and reaching at last, through incredible difficulties, what they, in their delusion, supposed to be free soil.

It was for these "three classes"—pointedly including fugitives—that Langston had intervened against the manhunters who had "by lying devices" gotten their hands on John Price. It was Langston's moral duty to "to do what I could toward liberating" the captive. "I will not say [he was] a slave, for I do not know that," explained Langston, calling Price instead "a *man, a brother,* who had a right to his liberty under the laws of God, under the laws of Nature, and under the Declaration of Independence." It was higher law, not the Fugitive Slave Act, that Langston had felt himself compelled to obey.

Invoking his own ancestry, Langston added that "my father was a Revolutionary soldier; that he served under Lafeyette, and fought through the whole war; and that he always told me that he fought for *my* freedom as much as his own." Yet the Fugitive Slave Act threatened to return even free men to slavery, because under its terms "BLACK MEN HAVE NO RIGHTS WHICH WHITE MEN ARE BOUND TO RESPECT." As Langston loudly quoted the despised *Dred Scott* decision, the spectators burst into loud applause (and the reporter recorded his resounding words in capital letters).

Langston declared that he never believed that the Kentuckians had any legal right to seize Price, and that he had only attempted to secure access to "justice for my brother whose liberty was in peril." Even a black man, although considered by virtue of his race *"an outlaw of the United States,"* should have the right to challenge a slave hunter's warrant without subjecting himself to the "pains and penalties of the Fugitive Slave Act." Again the spectators cheered, but Langston had not yet finished his point. *"Whatever more than that has been sworn to on this trial, as an act of mine, is false, ridiculously false."* As to the claimed threat—"we will have him"—Langston was so adamant that his words were recorded with double emphases: *"This I* NEVER *said."*

The defendant asserted his innocence and condemned the Fugitive Slave Act as an unjust law made to "crush the colored man." And then he added,

> I have another reason to offer why I should not be sentenced. I have not had a trial before a jury of my peers. . . . The colored man is oppressed by certain universal and deeply fixed *prejudices.* Those jurors are well known to have shared largely in these prejudices, and I therefore consider that they were neither impartial, nor were they a jury of my peers.

But Langston was not done yet. He concluded with a call for future civil disobedience:

> If ever a man is seized near me, and is about to be carried South-
> ward as a slave . . . [and] if it is adjudged illegal to procure even
> such [a legal] investigation, then we are thrown back upon those
> last defences of our rights, which cannot be taken from us, and
> which God gave us that we need not be slaves.

There was little doubt about the nature of the "last defences" Langston had
in mind. He informed the court that he stood "unjustly condemned, by a tribunal before which he is declared to have no rights," and from which he expected neither justice nor mercy. Then he added without apology, and leaving
no uncertainty about his intentions,

> I must take upon myself the responsibility of self-protection; and
> when I come to be claimed by some perjured wretch as his slave, I
> shall never be taken into slavery. . . . I stand here to say that I will
> do all I can, for any man thus seized and held.

The gallery broke into "great and prolonged applause," which the bailiff
could not quell until the judge threatened to clear the courtroom. It had obviously been a momentous occasion. Perhaps no convicted prisoner—and certainly no black man—had ever before so thoroughly rebuked a judge, challenged a criminal statute, and announced his intention to continue violating
the law in the future.

Then the judge spoke, this time extemporaneously. If Willson had prepared a reprimand in advance, as he had done in Bushnell's case, he put the
manuscript aside to respond directly to Langston. He had clearly been moved
by the defendant's forceful address:

> You have done injustice to the Court, Mr. Langston, in thinking
> that nothing you might say could effect a mitigation of your sen-
> tence. You have presented considerations to which I shall attach
> much weight.
>
> I see mitigating circumstances in the transaction which should
> not require, in my opinion, the extreme penalty of the law. This court
> does not make laws. . . . We sit here under the obligations of an
> oath to execute them, and whether they be bad or whether they be

good, it is not for us to say. We appreciate fully your condition, and while it excites the cordial sympathies of our better natures, still the law must be vindicated. On reflection, I am constrained to say that the penalty in your case should be comparatively light.

In what may have been the first time a federal court even partially recognized the legitimacy of civil disobedience in resistance to the Fugitive Slave Act, Willson sentenced the defendant to twenty days in prison and a fine of $100, plus costs. It was a far less drastic sentence than the one imposed on Bushnell, although Langston had been far more defiant.

One small victory for the higher law.

Emotions ran high in the course of the sentencing hearings, and the situation was not helped when George Belden angrily announced in the midst of the proceedings that Lorain County Sheriff Herman Burr had just arrested Anderson Jennings, Jacob Lowe, and Richard Mitchell on the charge of kidnapping. Belden was furious that his witnesses had been jailed. He believed that the arrest had been the "work of the defendants," whom he accused of "delaying and hindering" the trials before Judge Willson's court. Belden claimed that the incarceration of his witnesses would make it impossible for him to bring the next of the rescuers' cases to trial, meaning that the remaining defendants would have to remain indefinitely in custody.

Rufus Spalding ridiculed Belden's request for a continuance, and he demanded that the next trial begin immediately after the two sentencings. The federal prosecutor, he said, could easily arrange for the attendance of the three witnesses by obtaining a "writ of *habeas corpus ad testificandum*." In any event, the defendants would not agree to a continuance unless Belden filed a written motion with supporting affidavits submitted under oath.

Belden was offended that the defense attorney had refused to accept his word. He replied that his "official character"—meaning his position as U.S. attorney—should "give power enough to the bare motion to postpone."

"Your official character can add nothing to the statement," retorted Spalding.

"Nor your blackguardism," Belden shot back.

"And your private character still less," said Spalding, who appeared to get the last word.

Weary of the bickering and anxious to proceed, Judge Willson agreed for once with the defense position. He ordered Belden to present his request in writing and, in a gesture to the prosecution, requested affidavits from both sides. Court adjourned for several hours to allow the attorneys to prepare the necessary papers.

Tempers did not fade during the recess.

Belden's written motion began by reciting the same grounds for a continuance that he had urged earlier. His key witnesses had been arrested and were not readily available to testify. What's more, Belden continued, it was well known that Bushnell and Langston were about to apply to the Ohio Supreme Court for writs of habeas corpus, which would "require the immediate attention of the District-Attorney." In sum, Belden concluded, any delays were attributable to the rescuers themselves, who, in any event, were held in custody only because they had voluntarily surrendered their recognizances and thereafter refused to post bail.

The defense motion denied all of Belden's claims, asserting that none of the defendants had voluntarily surrendered themselves and that the revocation of their recognizances had been due to an error in the court record.

Judge Willson was more than familiar with the dispute about the court record, having repeatedly ruled against the defense on that very issue. He announced that the continuance would therefore be granted and that he did not want to hear any argument on the question.

Defense counsel Albert Riddle nonetheless began to harangue Willson on the injustice of his ruling. The entry on the court journal had been in error, he insisted, due to the clerk's "hurry and perhaps excitement of the occasion." His clients could not "go forth honorably" until the mistake was corrected.

Belden replied that the court had shown "unparalleled leniency" by initially releasing the defendants without bail, and that it was wholly the fault of the "learned counsel for these defendants" that they had petulantly surrendered themselves into custody as a protest against one of Judge Willson's rulings.

"That's false, utterly false," snapped Riddle. "That's a lie," added Spalding.

That attack prompted an angry retort from Belden. "Much as I have been abused and charged with all manner of unworthy motives," he said, "I have not taken one step which I thought in my own mind would *even look* like unkindness, severity, or unfairness." The defense lawyers, in contrast, he told the court, always insist "that your Honor is wrong, that the Clerk is wrong, that I am always wrong," and they never show a "respectful attitude" toward the court.

Riddle attempted to speak yet again, but the court told him that "further remarks are quite unnecessary." Riddle persisted and the judge repeated himself with additional emphasis. "Further remarks are quite unnecessary, sir." Having finally succeeded in silencing the determined defense lawyer, Judge Willson once again announced that he would grant the prosecution's request for a continuance, that the court journal was correct and would not be amended, and that the defendants would be released from custody only upon posting bail.

The next trial, for John Watson, was set for the court's July term. That was two months away, but Willson expressed his confidence that the incarcerated defendants would not "be particularly incommoded by so brief a delay."

Albert Riddle had claimed that he and his imprisoned clients had no "morbid relish for self-inflicted martyrdom," but disinterested observers might well have doubted his words. The attorney had adopted an antagonistic style of advocacy that must have seemed more likely to harm his clients than to help them, as he insulted the prosecutor and hectored the court. With so many defendants yet to face trial, why had Riddle—with his colleagues' obvious approval—risked alienating the very judge before whom they would have to argue all of the remaining cases? At least part of the answer is that the defense lawyers had no intention of staying in Judge Willson's court. Rather, they planned to challenge Willson's rulings by seeking writs of habeas corpus in the Ohio Supreme Court. That action would raise profound issues regarding the intersection of state and federal authority, potentially placing the free state of Ohio in direct conflict with the government of the United States.

Only a few days after Langston's conviction and sentencing, the rescuers' attorneys filed their petition before the Ohio Supreme Court. The high court was in recess at the time, with only Justice Josiah Scott then sitting in Columbus. Scott immediately scheduled the matter for a hearing before the full bench, summoning his colleagues by telegraph to convene in a special session eight days later. Although the application for the writ formally sought only the release of Langston and Bushnell, it was obvious that the court's ruling would apply to all of the defendants. Nonetheless, only the two named prisoners were legally entitled to appear in person at the proceeding, and Justice Scott issued an order to Cuyahoga County Sheriff Wightman commanding him to "produce their bodies" pursuant to the writ.

As an antislavery Republican, Sheriff Wightman was eager to cooperate with the defendants' counsel, but federal Marshal Matthew Johnson had other ideas. Even though Langston and Bushnell were lodged of necessity in the county jail, they were legally in federal custody following their convictions under the Fugitive Slave Act, and Johnson was reluctant to concede any state court's jurisdiction to order even their temporary release. Johnson wired U.S. Attorney General Jeremiah Black for instructions, and Black replied emphatically: "*Under no circumstances* was the order of the [Ohio] Supreme Court" to be "obeyed in the production of the bodies" of Langston and Bushnell.

Marshal Johnson dutifully instructed Sheriff Wightman to refrain from bringing the federal prisoners to Columbus, and Wightman just as dutifully responded that he intended to comply with the order of his own state's highest court. For a brief time, it seemed as though there might be some sort of confrontation between the two officials. Marshal Johnson, however, backed down. He tacitly agreed that the sheriff could take the defendants to the hearing in Columbus, so long as he could accompany Wightman on the train.

Attorney General Black was deeply unhappy about the compromise in Cleveland, fearing that it might set a precedent for requiring federal officials to comply with orders from state courts. It would be intolerable for the Ohio Supreme Court to order the release of federal prisoners, and the attorney general was determined that no such ruling should ever be enforced. Black therefore contacted federal officials throughout Ohio, informing them that the Ohio courts had "no authority to meddle in this business" and repeating that "under no circumstances" were Langston and Bushnell to be released no matter how the Ohio Supreme Court ultimately ruled. Black authorized the use of military force if necessary to hold the federal prisoners, instructing his subordinates to "maintain the rights of the United States against all lawless aggressions," including those that originated in the Ohio courts.[3]

The defendants and their supporters were not aware of Attorney General Black's direct involvement in the case, but they were certainly ready to resist the Buchanan administration. Abolitionists and Republicans across northern Ohio united behind the imprisoned rescuers, and a massive rally was scheduled to be held in Cleveland on Tuesday, May 24, only one day before the Ohio Supreme Court would hear argument in the case.

On the day of the event, many thousands of people poured into Cleveland by wagon and railroad. A special train of thirteen cars was chartered from Oberlin, and the scheduled trains from Elyria, Columbus, Cincinnati, and many other communities all arrived with their coaches filled to capacity. The crowd first gathered in the Public Square, with banners waiving and a brass band playing the "Marseillaise," but before the rally could even begin, a large contingent marched several blocks to the county jail, where they demanded to hear from the rescuers.

Sheriff Wightman willingly obliged the antislavery crowd, allowing his prisoners to step into the jail yard in order to address their supporters through the gate. Charles Langston spoke first, shouting to be heard. "I am a felon," he called out, "tried convicted and sentenced for willful and malicious violation of the laws of this country." There was not the slightest repentance in his voice as Langston continued, declaring that he and the others had been "imprisoned for breaking the bonds of the oppressor, giving liberty to the captive, and letting the down-trodden . . . go free."

"Shall we submit to this outrage on our rights?" demanded Langston of the crowd.

"No," they shouted in reply.

"Are you here to-day to obey the Fugitive Slave Law?"

"No!"

"Are you here to sustain the dicta of the Dred Scott decision? Are you here to support the decision of the United States Court of the Northern District of Ohio? Will you tamely submit to this tyranny and despotism?"

"No," they thundered, raising three cheers for Langston.

Defendants Henry Peck, James Fitch, and Ralph Plumb—the celebrated "Saints of Oberlin"—also spoke from across the jailhouse fence, condemning the "armed villains" who had assaulted and seized John Price and exhorting the crowd to join their "great political revolution." This "irrepressible conflict" would continue, said Ralph Plumb, until the "greater question of personal freedom is settled." Calling for continued resistance to the Fugitive Slave Act, James Fitch added that "we have trampled on this infamous enactment many a time in our day, and never while God shall spare us, will we yield obedience to its wicked demands."

The crowd then headed back to the Public Square, where the rally's formal program was about to begin. By some estimates, as many as twelve thousand people filled the square, listening to defense counsel Rufus Spalding, Ohio Congressman Joshua Giddings, and John Mercer Langston.

Spalding was the most moderate of the scheduled speakers, mindful of the fact that he was due to appear in court the following day. He commended the rescuers for "obeying the natural instincts and dictates of our nature," but he counseled the crowd that objections to the Fugitive Slave Act should be made "in a peaceful and constitutional manner."

Giddings was far more inflammatory. The Republican congressman had applauded the shootings at Christiana and demanded the liberation of Anthony Burns, and he was no less confrontational when speaking closer to home. He asked his constituents whether they were ready "to resist the enforcement of this infamous Fugitive Slave Law" and instead to obey "the high behests of Heaven's King." Calling upon the crowd to join him in declaring a commitment to "forcible resistance," he added that "I would have this voice sound in the mouth of the cannon."

Not to be outdone, John Mercer Langston provocatively declared that he "hated the Fugitive Slave Law as he did the Democratic party." The only black man and the only Oberliner on the platform, John Mercer "trampled the Fugitive Slave Law under his feet, for it incarcerated his own brother, and his friends and neighbors for disobeying its bloody commands." As he swore "eternal enmity to this law," he expressed little confidence in judicial remedies. Let us "fall back upon our own natural rights, and say to the prison walls 'come down' and set those men at liberty."

Governor Salmon Chase had never spoken publicly about the Oberlin rescue, just as he had maintained silence on the Margaret Garner case three years earlier. Although he had long been a leader of the antislavery movement in the United States, he had been careful not to associate himself with open resistance to federal law. As an attorney, Chase respected the supremacy of the federal courts; as a politician, he did not want to jeopardize his prospects for the 1860 presidential election.

It was therefore a surprise when Chase stepped forward unannounced to the podium. Delighted to see that their governor had decided to take a stand, the crowd responded with "hearty and tremendous cheers." Only "a few hours ago," the governor announced, "he was sitting in his office at Columbus, not expecting to be present" at the rally in Cleveland. At the last minute, however, "he had felt it his duty" to speak.

Chase did his best to walk a fine line. He denounced the Fugitive Slave Act as "a symbol of the supremacy of the Slave States, and the subjugation of the Free" and declared that the convictions of Bushnell and Langston should be considered "null and void" under the Constitution. The seizure of "the negro boy John under a power of attorney" had been nothing less than "war against a citizen of Ohio." Nonetheless, he "did not counsel revolutionary measures" and he warned the crowd against undertaking further acts of violence. The great remedy for injustice, he said, was "at the ballot box," and he urged the citizens to "see to it, too, what President you elect." No one doubted which potential candidate he had in mind.

For all his temporizing, however, Chase realized that he had to take a stand. What would happen if the Ohio Supreme Court issued a writ for the release of the federal prisoners? Would the U.S. marshal respect the order? And if not, would the Ohio authorities be able to enforce it? Summoning his resolve, the commander in chief of the state militia took a step toward the abyss:

> If the process for the release of any prisoner should issue from the Courts of the State, he was free to say that so long as Ohio was a Sovereign State, that process *should be executed*.

Southern fire-eaters had issued ultimatums to the federal government for decades, but it was stunning to hear a northern governor assert a state's right to use force against U.S. authorities over the issue of slavery. Pennsylvania's government had assisted in the Christiana prosecutions during the Fillmore administration, and Massachusetts's government passively endured the humiliating rendition of Anthony Burns at the direction of President Pierce. But now there was no mistaking Salmon Chase's direct challenge to President Buchanan. "When the time came," he said, "and his duty was plain, he, as Governor of Ohio, would meet it as a man."

Chase's public challenge to federal authority was audacious, but it was not quite unprecedented. For the previous five years, the state of Wisconsin had been locked in a similar struggle with the federal government over the rescue of a fugitive slave.

In early March 1854 a Missouri runaway named Joshua Glover was living in a rural cabin about four miles from Racine. Glover had escaped two years earlier from his master, Benammi Garland of St. Louis, and he was now supporting himself as a carpenter and mill hand. Garland had somehow learned of his missing slave's whereabouts and the slave owner traveled to Wisconsin, where a federal judge issued a warrant for Glover's arrest.[4]

On the afternoon of March 10, Garland and six other men, including two deputy U.S. marshals, barged into Glover's cabin. After a brief but violent struggle, the posse succeeded in arresting Glover, as two of his friends escaped into the surrounding countryside. The slave hunters manacled their captive and brought him by wagon to Milwaukee, where they expected to obtain a certificate of removal from a federal commissioner. Arriving in the night, Garland arranged for his prisoner to be secured in the county jail until he could be brought to court the next day.

By morning, however, Glover's friends had spread word of the kidnapping, alerting abolitionists in Racine who quickly wired their confreres in Milwaukee. The first Milwaukee abolitionist to receive the telegram was Sherman Booth, a printer and publisher who originally hailed from New England. A Yale graduate who had been involved in the defense of the prisoners from *La Amistad* fifteen years earlier, Booth immediately began preparing handbills to distribute throughout the city. "Citizens of Milwaukee," he wrote, "shall a Man be dragged back to Slavery from our Free Soil, *without an open trial of his right to Liberty?*"

When Booth demanded an "open trial" for Glover, he was not calling for a hearing under the Fugitive Slave Act. Like all abolitionists, he had only contempt for the truncated proceedings in which a fugitive was not even allowed to speak. Booth and his allies therefore applied for a writ of habeas corpus from a Wisconsin judge, which led to the familiar drama of dueling writs and warrants between state and federal officials. When it became obvious that federal Deputy Marshal Charles Cotton was determined to maintain custody of Glover, a crowd stormed the county jail. Breaking down the door with pickaxes, they freed the prisoner and hid him until arrangements could be made to take him to Canada. Booth's role in the actual rescue was unclear, but he was seen riding a horse next to the wagon that carried Glover to freedom.

Sherman Booth was subsequently indicted, tried, and convicted for violating the Fugitive Slave Act (as was another man, John Rycraft, who had been more directly involved in the assault on the jail). The case had a complex procedural history, but it eventually reached the Wisconsin Supreme Court pursuant to a writ of habeas corpus directed against U.S. Marshal Stephen Ableman, who had formal custody of Booth and Rycraft following their convictions. Booth and Rycraft were represented by Byron Paine, a young attorney with deep roots in the abolitionist movement. Paine called the Fugitive Slave Act a "monstrous moral deformity," but he premised his legal position on more commonplace arguments. The Act could not be enforced against the defendants, he contended, because it violated constitutional guarantees of due process to the fugitive and conferred judicial power on low-level commissioners. The U.S. attorney replied that the Wisconsin court lacked jurisdiction over federal officers, no matter the infirmities in the federal law, and that any order regarding Booth and Rycraft would therefore be "erroneous and unlawful."[5]

The Wisconsin Supreme Court swept aside Ableman's objections and declared the Fugitive Slave Act unconstitutional, voiding the indictments and convictions of Booth and Rycraft and ordering their discharge from custody. Marshal Ableman complied with the order, releasing Booth and Rycraft in a "crowning, if fleeting achievement" in the legal struggle against the Fugitive Slave Act.[6] Attorney General Caleb Cushing promptly appealed the matter to the U.S. Supreme Court.

The appeal, now captioned *Ableman v. Booth,* was delayed for several years, in part because the uncooperative Wisconsin Supreme Court refused to provide the clerk of the U.S. Supreme Court with a certified record of the proceedings. The case was finally reached for argument in early 1859, by which time James Buchanan had become president and Jeremiah Black had succeeded Caleb Cushing as attorney general. Recognizing the case as a potentially fatal challenge to enforcement of the Fugitive Slave Act, Black himself appeared before the Supreme Court. The attorney general argued that the Wisconsin Court's ruling threatened to "overthrow Federal authority" and that unless it was reversed, "the Union of the States will become a rope of sand."[7] Booth was not represented at the oral argument, having declined either to file a brief or to appear by counsel, although he had submitted several printed pamphlets at an earlier stage of the proceeding.

On March 9, 1859, Chief Justice Roger Taney delivered a unanimous opinion overruling the decision of the Wisconsin Supreme Court. "No state," said Taney, "can authorize one of its judges or courts to exercise judicial power" over an officer of the United States. Thus, "no state judge or court could ever order the release of a federal prisoner." Taney also took advantage of the opportunity to declare the Fugitive Slave Act constitutional "in all of its provisions," although he did not deign to provide the bases for his holding.[8]

The decision in *Ableman v. Booth* had been reported in Ohio newspapers, but the full opinion itself had not yet been published at the time of the May 24 rally in Cleveland. Thus, Governor Chase may have been unaware of Taney's stern warning to state officials who endeavored to free federal prisoners. Any such attempt, wrote the chief justice, would require the federal marshal to "call to his aid any force that might be necessary to maintain the authority of [federal] law against illegal interference."

There had been no physical confrontation between state and federal authorities in Wisconsin; Booth had been released from jail long before the U.S. Supreme Court upheld his conviction, and there would be no attempt to rearrest him until the spring of 1860.[9] But the situation was different in Ohio in May 1859. The Oberlin rescuers were still in jail and Governor Chase had all but promised to deploy the state militia on their behalf.

With the governor of Ohio and the chief justice of the United States separately issuing implicit calls to arms, the Ohio Supreme Court took up the cases of Simeon Bushnell and Charles Langston.

On the morning of Wednesday, May 24, 1859, the Ohio Supreme Court convened in special session to consider the habeas corpus petitions of the convicted Oberlin rescuers. Simeon Bushnell and Charles Langston were present with their attorney Albert Gallatin Riddle. They were joined at the defense table by Christopher Wolcott, the attorney general of Ohio, who had been specially assigned to the case by Governor Chase. Chase himself was seated in the courtroom, along with U.S. Senator George Pugh, in a strong show of political support for the prisoners. George Belden was there on behalf of the Buchanan administration, along with attorney Noah Swayne, who had been separately appointed to represent U.S. Marshal Matthew Johnson.

Chief Justice Joseph Swan called the court to order, inviting Albert Riddle to present the opening address. Riddle argued first that imprisonment of his clients was illegal, and their conviction a nullity, due to the unconstitutionality of the Fugitive Slave Act. Realizing that the federal courts had almost invariably upheld the rights of slave owners, Riddle asserted that those decisions— including *Prigg* and *Dred Scott*—had been based on a "judicial falsification of history" and should therefore carry no weight. Riddle also contended that *Ableman v. Booth* should simply be ignored because the decision had "not yet been given to the courts in such a form that can be treated . . . as authority." In any event, Riddle added, the Ohio Supreme Court stood as the "exclusive court of last resort" in the *"protection of the rights of the citizen,"* and it was therefore "not bound . . . by the decisions of any other tribunal."

Riddle's second argument was even more radical. The Fugitive Slave Act, he told the court, was invalid because it contravened the "inviolable right of persons to personal liberty." Kentucky's law might establish slavery, but Ohio's law presumed that "every man is a freeman." Therefore, "a slave cannot be claimed as *property*" anywhere in Ohio, even when an owner's agent appears to be armed with legal process from a neighboring state. Any other ruling, Riddle continued, would effectively turn slavery into "an institution of Ohio." Such a "dark stain [and] horrid contingency" should never be countenanced by the court. Notwithstanding the rulings of the U.S. Supreme Court, a claim of "property in man" had no standing in Ohio.

Riddle spoke for the entire morning session, concluding what he referred to as his "brief presentation" with an appeal for the court to consider all of the case's "grave and great considerations." He did not expand on the implications of that request.

Following the noon recess, Noah Swayne announced that neither he nor District Attorney Belden would present oral argument on behalf of the federal government, preferring instead to rely "on the authorities presented in [their] printed brief." The brief made a single, simple point: the federal conviction could not be "collaterally questioned" in the Ohio courts. Under *Ableman v. Booth*, "the adjudications of the Supreme Court of the United States, upon all questions within its jurisdiction, are binding upon the State Courts, and conclusive."

Attorney General Wolcott was offended by Swayne's waiver of oral argument. Taking the lectern on behalf of the State of Ohio, Wolcott suggested that a respectful discussion of the relevant issues could occur only when "voice responds to voice, and eye looks into eye." In the absence of his adversaries' oral argument, the court had been left "utterly in the dark as to the grounds on which they rest their resistance" to the application for habeas corpus, and forced to rely on a "skeleton" brief.

Wolcott's own argument was anything but skeletal. He spoke for more than a full day, insisting that the state court's right to grant habeas corpus "stands on grounds as firm as the earth itself." The Fugitive Slave Act, he said, was the "depth of atrocity" and a "flagrant usurpation by Congress of wholly undelegated powers." Enforcement of the Act would impose slavery itself upon Ohio, to which the attorney general loudly said, "NEVER! We *won't* have the whipping-post in Ohio. We won't have the knife and the branding iron. . . . We won't have the barracoon here."

The U.S. Supreme Court, argued Wolcott, was "a sectional court," dominated by five justices who were "themselves slaveholders, and therefore directly and personally interested in all these questions." Therefore, he said, the Ohio courts were not bound by *Prigg* or *Ableman* or any other decision that denied "the natural birthright of man to his freedom."

Picking up where Governor Chase had left off at the previous day's rally, Wolcott raised the specter of a "collision between the state and the Federal Government." "What then?" he asked rhetorically. "Are we children; are we old women that we should be frightened from duty by this menace?" He provided his own bold reply: "If collision can be avoided only by striking down every safeguard which the Constitution had hedged about the liberty of the citizen, LET COLLISION COME."

Sounding very much like a northern secessionist, the attorney general of Ohio had repudiated the Supreme Court of the United States, castigated Congress, and denounced the "absolute despotism of the Federal Government." Only at the last moment did he back away from the most extreme implications of his argument. "But there will be no collision," he reassured the Ohio justices, predicting instead that "the Federal Government will acquiesce" in any judgment that ordered the release of the defendants.

Wolcott had good reason to believe that the Ohio Supreme Court would be willing to challenge the authority of the federal government. All five justices were Republicans, and Chief Justice Swan was a known abolitionist, having once served as vice president of the antislavery Kansas Emigrant Aid Society.

Thus, expectations were high when the court retired to deliberate at the end of the day on Friday.

The justices conferred over the weekend and returned to announce their decision on Monday afternoon. As soon became apparent, the court was split 3–2, and Chief Justice Joseph Swan held the deciding vote. From the moment Swan started to read aloud from his majority opinion, the outcome of the case was clear.

The Constitution, began Swan, "guarantees to the owner of an escaped slave the right of reclamation," and any citizen who knowingly interferes has committed a violation of "the fugitive slave laws" that had been validly enacted to vindicate "the constitutional right of the owner of slaves." Thus, there was no such thing as a right "to rescue escaped slaves from their owners," as was evident from an "unbroken current of decisions" from the Supreme Court of the United States and the courts of the other free states.

Swan was a Republican, and perhaps in some ways he was even a radical, but he drew the line at judicial insurrection. The Fugitive Slave Act may have been noxious, but that alone "did not demand of this court the organization of resistance" to the federal government. It was the job of legislatures, not judges, to rid the people of offensive statutes. While Swan's conscience was troubled by the result of his decision, he was not willing to place his "private personal views" above the law. Rejecting the defense appeals to the higher law, he said, "I must refuse the experiment of initiating disorder and governmental collision."

The chief justice of Ohio concluded his unhappy decision with an attempt, "most uncharacteristic of judges," to imagine himself in the place of the defendants before him.[10] After first repeating his fidelity to the law, Swan admitted that "if a weary frightened slave should appeal to me to protect him from his pursuers, it is possible I might momentarily forget my allegiance to the law and constitution, and give him a covert from those who were upon his track." Even so, Swan continued, he would be willing to accept the price of following his conscience:

> And if I did it, and were prosecuted, condemned and imprisoned, and brought by my counsel before this tribunal on a habeas corpus, and were then permitted to pronounce judgment in my own case, I trust I should have the moral courage to say, before God

and the country, as I am now compelled to say, under the solemn duties of a judge, bound by my official oath to sustain the supremacy of the constitution and the law: "THE PRISONER MUST BE REMANDED."[11]

The rescuers could take little solace in the opinions of the two dissenting justices, especially because the prosecutors moved immediately to press their advantage. Court had scarcely adjourned when District Attorney Belden declared that the defendants' presence in Columbus, as arranged by Sheriff Wightman, had amounted to a "constructive escape from jail." Accordingly, he announced that each man would have six days added to his sentence to "compensate for the time they had been at large" on their way to and from court.

Fifteen Oberlin rescuers were still incarcerated, including Bushnell and Langston.[12] Having already spent more than six weeks in jail, the thirteen defendants who remained to be tried had little hope of either acquittal or reversal of the inevitable convictions. Their spirits sometimes flagged, but they were continually cheered by encouraging words from their friends and supporters, as well as by the belief that their sacrifices continued to bolster the antislavery movement.

Although they had been rebuffed by Ohio's highest court, they still had some recourse in the local courts of Lorain County. In early May the four slave hunters—Jennings, Mitchell, Davis, and Lowe—had been indicted for unlawfully arresting and imprisoning "one John Price, the said John Price then and there being a free black person." Immediately after Langston's sentencing, all four were arrested by the Lorain County sheriff, spending eight days in jail before they were released on bail. Their trial was set for July 6, which was about ten days before the prosecutions of the rescuers were set to resume.

If the slave hunters' trials proceeded on schedule, there was every likelihood that they would be in jail and therefore unavailable to testify in Judge Willson's court. Of course, the charge against them was specious. John Price had been a slave when they arrested him, not a free black man. The law of Ohio, however, presumed that every man was free, and with Price safely in

Canada, the slave hunters had no way of proving otherwise. Although Jennings and Mitchell had known Price as a slave in Kentucky, as criminal defendants they would not be permitted to testify at their own trials. Thus, in an exquisite turnabout, they faced almost certain conviction if they were brought before a jury in abolitionist Lorain County.

George Belden was beside himself. Having won his case at every level thus far, he now faced frustration at the hands of a mere county court of common pleas. Along with Marshal Johnson, Belden traveled to Washington, D.C., to consult with his superiors. The federal officials decided that their best approach would be to invoke the highest authority in the land, so they obtained writs of habeas corpus from Justice John McLean of the U.S. Supreme Court. McLean had started his political career as a Democrat, but he later became a Free-Soiler and then a Republican, as his antislavery views pushed him away from the Pierce and Buchanan administrations. Because McLean had dissented vigorously in the Dred Scott case, Belden might have believed that the justice's signature would carry extra weight in Lorain County. If so, he was about to be disappointed.

Writs in hand, Belden returned to Ohio, where he made a disastrous strategic mistake. The U.S. attorney convinced all four of his key witnesses to surrender themselves to Lorain County Sheriff Herman Burr so that Belden could immediately free them, and thus squelch their impending trial, by serving his federal writs. Belden and his four indicted witnesses arrived in Elyria on July 2, just four days before the kidnapping trial was set to begin.

Sheriff Burr, however, refused to cooperate with Belden's plan. He slipped out of town at night, thus thwarting service of the federal writs. Now the alleged kidnappers found themselves in the worst of all possible worlds. Relying on Belden's assurances, they had placed themselves within the jurisdiction of Lorain County, only to discover that the federal prosecutor could not deliver on his promise to secure their release. With their trial about to begin, and "the penitentiary in prospect," they complained bitterly that Belden had betrayed their trust. Jennings and Mitchell, who could have stayed safely in Kentucky, demanded that Belden enter some sort of compromise with the rescuers' attorneys. Belden, however, was "inexorable." Having sworn to punish the Oberliners, he was determined to do it, "cost what it might."

Jennings and Mitchell, however, were unwilling to be pawns in a power struggle. Rather than spend time in prison while waiting for the jurisdictional dispute to be resolved, they engaged separate counsel, former congressman Richard Stanton of Kentucky, to act on their behalves. Stanton arrived in Elyria on July 5 and immediately opened three-party negotiations with Albert Riddle (who represented the rescuers) and attorney D. K. Cartter (a former Republican congressman who had been retained to conduct the Lorain County prosecution). By this time the Kentuckians were "in great terror at the prospect of facing the music," leading attorney Cartter later to mock their fearful trembling. "You could ha' wa-a-a-shed your ha-a-a-nds in the sweat o' their faces," he said.

The obvious deal was quickly reached. The Lorain County prosecutions would be dropped if Belden would dismiss all of the remaining charges against the rescuers. The U.S. attorney at first refused to be a party to such coercion, but he eventually realized that he had no choice. Attorney Richard Stanton informed Belden that none of the essential Kentucky witnesses (including slave owner John Bacon and clerk Robert Cochran) would ever return to Cleveland to testify. Belden had been outlasted by the defense, and his plan for conducting sequential trials had simply fallen apart. After some additional wrangling over the precise terms, including the resolution of several objections by Judge Willson, all of the charges were dismissed, and the rescuers were discharged from custody. They had spent eighty-three days in jail.

Jacob Shipherd, one of the imprisoned rescuers and the first chronicler of their story, was overjoyed to be released. "So ended *The First Siege of Oberlin*," he exulted.

The Oberlin Rescuers were free and unrepentant. Before even leaving jail, they passed a set of resolutions condemning the Fugitive Slave Act and declaring that their "hatred and opposition to that unjust and unconstitutional law [was] more intense than ever before."

> We will hereafter, as we have heretofore, help the panting fugitive
> to escape from those who would enslave him, whatever may be the
> authority under which they may act.

The rescuers had worn down the federal government and emerged from jail with their principles intact, but not everyone in Ohio rejoiced at "this signal triumph of the *Higher Lawites.*" The proslavery *Cleveland Plain Dealer* railed against the reciprocal dismissals as an injustice against the Kentuckians who had been jailed "on a false charge of kidnapping."

> Finding no law in Lorain but the higher law, and seeing the determination of the sheriff, judge, and jury to send them to the penitentiary any way, for no crime under any human law, but on a charge trumped up on purpose to drive them out of the country . . . they proposed to exchange nolles, and the district attorney consented to it. So the government has been beaten at last with law, justice and fact all on its side, and Oberlin with its rebellious Higher Law creed is triumphant.

John Mercer Langston would never have conceded that the kidnapping charges were false (although they were, in fact, trumped up), but he otherwise found himself in uncharacteristic agreement with the *Plain Dealer,* at least as to the result of the cases. "The counter indictments . . . against the Kentucky kidnappers," he said, "ended the most stupendous, unjustifiable and outrageous proceeding ever presented and prosecuted against any American citizens." The rescuers were freed.

"At last the Higher Law was triumphant."[13]

⟲ EPILOGUE ⟲

HARPERS FERRY AND BEYOND

The trials of the Oberlin rescuers attracted national attention in the spring and summer of 1859, but they were soon overshadowed by events. Before the end of the year, John Brown staged his attack at Harpers Ferry, only to be captured and hanged for murder and treason. Brown's execution was inevitable from the moment of he was taken prisoner, but the Virginia authorities still proceeded with the formality of a trial. That trial provided Brown with the opportunity to deliver his defiant final speech, invoking the higher law as a justification for all he had done.

John Brown's career as an abolitionist was closely tied to the struggle on behalf of fugitive slaves. Even as a child, he was aware of his father's hatred of slavery, and as a teenager he joined his father as an active worker "for the Underground Railroad, ready at all times to hide fugitives and help them on their way north."[1] For more than thirty years, later with the help of his many sons, John Brown would continue to transport runaways to Canada or to help them find safe havens in Ohio or New York. Gradually over that time he developed a militant ideology that justified not only escape but also armed resistance to slave hunters.

In January 1851 Brown founded the short-lived League of Gileadites, a paramilitary organization dedicated to resisting the Fugitive Slave Act. He was "convinced that God sent the new law to warn whites to shed their racism and blacks to prepare for the armed battle" against slavery, and he insisted that his followers take up weapons "and be ready to use them at all times." Brown managed to attract forty-four blacks, many of them fugitives, to the first meeting of the Gileadites, where he instructed them to attack slave catchers on sight, killing them if necessary: "Let the first blow be the signal for all to engage; and when engaged do not do your work by halves, but make clean work with your enemies." Although the Gileadites never did engage in battle, Brown's opening address to his would-be troops stands out as the first time in American history that a white person proposed "preemptive armed warfare . . . against proslavery foes."[2]

John Brown did not have the opportunity to participate in any of the famous fugitive rescues. His key financial backers, however, the so-called Secret Six, were all deeply involved in rescue efforts. Three of the six—Theodore Parker, Thomas Wentworth Higginson, and Gerrit Smith—were charged with violations of the Fugitive Slave Act, although none was ever convicted. The other three—Samuel Gridley Howe, Franklin Sanborn, and George Luther Stearns—were also active in the Sims and Burns cases, although they managed to avoid arrest. Their remorse over the failure to free either Sims or Burns almost certainly made them more receptive to Brown's extraordinary proposal to invade the South in order to free slaves by force.

In December 1858 Brown embarked on his first rescue, crossing from Kansas into Missouri, where he and his men raided the homes of three slave owners and liberated eleven slaves, including men, women, and children. Thus began a thousand-mile journey through Kansas, Nebraska, Iowa, Illinois, Indiana, and Michigan, as Brown escorted the former slaves to freedom while also using the opportunity to raise funds for his future plans. Even though Missouri Governor Robert Stewart and President James Buchanan had offered rewards for his arrest, Brown and his band traveled openly, virtually daring the authorities to apprehend him. Brown made good on his boast that he would "not be taken," eventually reaching Detroit, where he placed his black friends—now numbering twelve, as a child had been born en route—on a ferry to Ontario.

Brown headed next to Ohio, arriving in Cleveland in late March 1859, just as Simeon Bushnell's trial was about to begin. As before, Brown made little effort to hide from the authorities, meeting with Congressman Joshua Giddings and other supporters. He even presented a public lecture at which he praised the Oberlin rescuers and compared their efforts to his own exploits in Missouri, where he had "forcibly taken slaves from bondage."[3] Brown also attended Bushnell's trial on at least one occasion. Along with his collaborator John Kagi, Brown visited Charles Langston and several of the other rescuers in jail, attempting to recruit them for his rapidly developing plan to raid Harpers Ferry. Preoccupied with their own defense, none of the rescuers accepted Brown's invitation to join his command.

Brown remained in Cleveland for two weeks. He stayed long enough to see Simeon Bushnell convicted, but he departed before Charles Langston's dramatic speech at sentencing. Still, it is known that Brown continued to monitor the Oberlin case, as he stayed in touch with John Kagi, who was both covering the trials for the New York *Tribune* and secretly continuing the attempt to gather recruits. Charles Langston repeatedly rejected the request to join the underground army, but he supplied Kagi with the names of several other black men from Oberlin as likely enlistees. By midsummer Langston had been released from jail and Kagi headed east to meet with Brown, still uncertain about the results of his efforts.

Kagi might have been discouraged, but Brown did not give up easily. He had clearly been impressed by the rescuers' militant resolve, and especially by the reports of Charles Langston's memorable speech, and in late August 1859 he sent another envoy to Oberlin. John Mercer Langston was busy at work in his study when a stranger named "John Thomas" called upon him and requested a meeting. Langston was conferring with a client, so he asked Thomas to return after lunch. When the appointed hour arrived, the cautious white man revealed what Langston had suspected all along. "My name is not Thomas," he said. "It is John Brown, Jr., and I have called to see you upon matters strictly secret and confidential." The younger Brown explained that his father was imminently planning to strike "a blow which shall shake and destroy American slavery itself."

> On this whole subject I desire to talk freely with you, and secure your services at least to the extent of aiding us with your knowledge and advice in securing one or more men.[4]

Langston complied with the white man's request, supplying him with the names of Lewis Sheridan Leary and John Copeland, two black men who had come to Oberlin from North Carolina. Copeland had been a leader in the rescue of John Price and was among the indictees, although he fled the state to avoid arrest and returned only after the charges had been dismissed. Leary had also participated in the rescue, though for some reason he was not among the thirty-seven men indicted by the grand jury.

Leary and Copeland soon joined Langston and Brown for an extended discussion of the proposed raid. Although the younger Brown did not know the precise details of his father's plan, he provided Langston, Leary, and Copeland with "a full statement of the purposes" and nature of the attack. In the course of that afternoon, both Leary and Copeland agreed to accompany Brown. Decades later John Mercer Langston would recall Leary's moving words when he agreed to join Brown's troops. "I am ready to die! I only ask that when I have given my life to free others, my own wife and dear little daughter shall never know want."[5]

John Brown's attack on Harpers Ferry was a disaster almost from the very beginning. On Sunday night, October 16, 1859, Brown and his troop of eighteen men entered the sleeping town and quickly took control of a federal arsenal. Shots were fired in the encounter, however, killing a black railroad worker and alerting the town that a raid was under way. By midmorning Monday, Brown and his men were surrounded by local militia whose constant fire killed many of the raiders, including Lewis Leary. (Leary's final request would be fulfilled. Charles Langston married Leary's widow and raised Leary's daughter, Loise. Loise herself had a son, whom she named after her stepfather. That child was Langston Hughes—poet, playwright, and central figure in the Harlem Renaissance of the 1920s.)[6]

Late Monday, October 17, a detachment of federal Marines arrived under the command of Robert E. Lee, and Brown's fate was sealed. At dawn on Tuesday, only five of Brown's men remained standing—several had fled and the others were dead or gravely wounded. When Brown refused a demand to surrender, a squad of Lee's troops stormed the armory. Brown was taken alive along with Oberliner John Copeland and three other survivors.

Brown was turned over to Virginia authorities for prosecution. He was soon indicted on counts of murder, inciting servile rebellion, and treason against the State of Virginia. All three crimes carried the death penalty, making the charge of treason against Virginia both incongruous and unnecessary. Virginia Governor Henry Wise, however, had decided to use the prosecution as a means to assail the entire abolitionist movement. Thus, the indictment not only recounted the specific events at Harpers Ferry, but also went on to blame the raid on the "counsel of other evil and traitorous persons."[7]

John Brown, too, understood the potential political impact of his trial. Refusing secret offers to organize his rescue, he explained that "I cannot now better serve the cause I love so much than to die for it; and in my death I may do more than in my life." Then Brown set about orchestrating the events leading up to his own execution, using the courtroom as a platform from which he could explain and justify his armed assault on slavery.

In the days immediately following the raid, Brown had been disowned by leaders of the abolitionist movement, including his financial supporters, nearly all of whom were fearful of being tarred by association. Republican newspapers referred to Brown as a "solitary madman," a "lawless brigand," and worse. The reaction of Ohio Governor Salmon Chase was typical. "How rash— how mad—how criminal then to stir up insurrection."[8] When he was given an opportunity to address the court, however, Brown's deeply emotional speech succeeded in stirring northern consciences and, astonishingly, turning the reviled leader of a suicidal raid into an abolitionist hero.

The trial itself was held in nearby Charles Town, beginning just ten days after the raid. The evidence against Brown was overwhelming, with numerous witnesses testifying to the killings committed by his men. At first the defendant was represented by two Virginia lawyers who had been appointed by the court. Despite their conscientious efforts, Brown soon dismissed them in favor of two more politically sympathetic attorneys who had arrived midtrial from Cleveland and Washington, D.C. Those lawyers did their best to present a defense, knowing that there was no hope for Brown to avoid the noose.[9]

Following a day of pretrial motions and four days of testimony, it took the jury only forty-five minutes to return a verdict of guilty on Monday, October 31. The judge set sentencing for the following Wednesday morning.

The defendant appeared almost serene when court reconvened. Visibly exhausted from the trial, neither Brown's lawyers nor the prosecutors asked to address the court, so certain were they of the impending death sentence. As biographer David Reynolds observed, "No one suspected that this would be a day of victory for John Brown."[10] The trial judge certainly did not anticipate what was coming when the defendant was asked "whether he had anything to say why sentence should not be pronounced upon him."

Brown arose and delivered "a trenchant appeal to a higher law."[11] In terms that recalled Charles Langston's speech at his own far less severe sentencing, Brown said, "It is unjust that I should suffer such a penalty," even if it is provided for by statute. "This Court," he continued, "acknowledges, too, as I suppose, the validity of God's law." That higher law teaches, he said, "to remember them that are in bonds." Brown therefore had neither apology nor regret, because "I endeavored to act up to that instruction."

I believe that to have interfered as I have done, as I have always freely admitted I have done, in behalf of His despised poor, I did no wrong, but right. Now if it is deemed necessary that I should forfeit my life for the furtherance of the ends of justice, and mingle my blood further with the blood of my children and with the blood of millions in this slave country whose rights are disregarded by wicked, cruel and unjust enactments, I say, let it be done.[12]

The effect of Brown's speech was stunning, drawing convulsive reactions on both sides of the Mason-Dixon Line. In the North, significant public opinion swung behind Brown, who was suddenly seen as an abolitionist martyr. One antislavery newspaper warned that the execution of Brown would lead to the end of slavery more surely than "if he had succeeded in running off a few hundred slaves." Henry David Thoreau, Ralph Waldo Emerson, and Wendell Phillips all gave speeches lauding Brown. Phillips declared that Brown "has twice as much right to hang Governor Wise, as Governor Wise has to hang him."[13] Oberliner Charles Langston was more outspoken than most. He praised Brown as a "noble old hero" whose "aims and ends were lofty, noble, generous, benevolent, humane and Godlike."[14]

More than anything else, a phrase of Emerson's captured and intensified reaction to Brown's transformative speech, describing him as

that new saint, than whom none purer or more brave was ever led by love of men into conflict and death,—the new saint awaiting his martyrdom, and who, if he shall suffer, will make the gallows glorious like the cross.[15]

Emerson's invocation of the "gallows glorious" sped across the country "like a ricocheting bullet." Abolitionists and even some moderates in the North were heartened, but Southerners were enraged, using the occasion to demonize not only Brown but also every political figure associated with the antislavery movement. Jefferson Davis, then a senator from Mississippi, called for his colleague William Seward to be hanged for the crime of encouraging Brown's raid and inciting "slaves to murder helpless women and children." It was Seward who had first articulated the claims of higher law, which in turn made him responsible for Brown's invasion of the South, "and that invasion, and the facts connected with it, show Mr. Seward to be a traitor, and deserving of the gallows."[16]

John Brown was duly hanged in Charles Town, Virginia, on December 2, 1859. Due to persistent rumors of an abolitionist rescue plot, Virginia's Governor Wise had ordered extraordinary security for the event, marshaling more than 1,500 troops from seven regular and militia regiments. No civilians were allowed anywhere near the gallows, and howitzers were placed at either end of the scaffold as an extra precaution. According to Major J. T. L. Preston of the Virginia Military Institute, it was "the greatest array of disciplined forces ever seen in Virginia." Preston hoped that the execution might signal the end of radicalism on both sides. "So perish all such enemies of Virginia," he shouted after the trapdoor swung open. "All such enemies of the Union!"[17] Others in attendance would come to hold far different ideas. John Wilkes Booth had temporarily attached himself to a company of the Richmond Grays assigned to guard the execution—having abandoned a play in midproduction—and he was stationed only a few yards from the gallows. In his later career as a Confederate sympathizer, Booth would exaggerate his role in the hanging, going so far as to intimate that he had taken part in Brown's capture at Harpers Ferry.[18]

After nearly a decade of mistrust and recrimination over the conflict between slave catching and higher law, many in the North and South now found themselves even more fundamentally at odds. As Northerners increasingly hailed Brown as a hero, panicky Southerners execrated him as the devil himself. If the occasional rescue of fugitives in Pennsylvania, Massachusetts, and Ohio had endangered the Union, the lionization of John Brown threatened to shatter any hope of reconciliation. As one South Carolina editor put it, "The day of compromise is passed [and] there is no peace for the South in the Union."[19]

As much as John Brown's trial and oratory infuriated slave owners and exhilarated abolitionists, it put the fear of radicalism in the mainstream Republican Party as southern fire-eaters did all they could to connect Brown's insurrection to Republicanism. Hundreds of pikes had been recovered when Brown was captured—he had intended to distribute them among liberated slaves—and many of the frightening weapons were soon distributed to southern governors, with a warning that the pikes constituted "impressive evidence of the fanatical hatred borne by the dominant northern party to the institutions & people of the Southern states." Fifteen of the pikes were displayed in the Washington, D.C., office of Alabama Senator Clement Clay, again as a reminder that they stood for the "unscrupulous & atrocious means resorted to for the attainment of the objects sought" by the Republicans.[20]

The charges were untrue, of course, but that made them no less compelling. As the critical election year of 1860 began, every prominent Republican had to be wary of guilt by association. Perhaps most affected was the Republicans' presidential front-runner, William Seward, whose invocation of "higher law" and "irrepressible conflict" had made him a prime target for the sort of wild accusations that could cripple a campaign. Salmon Chase, the party's other leading contender and the champion of "natural rights," was also closely associated with antislavery radicalism and was considered by many to be unelectable.

As the Republicans' nominating convention approached—to be held that May in Chicago's recently erected Wigwam—many local party leaders began looking for a more centrist alternative to Seward or Chase. Abraham Lincoln was the logical choice. His antislavery credentials were solid but not extreme. Lincoln was firmly opposed to the expansion of slavery into the territories and he had delivered scathing critiques of the *Dred Scott* decision, but he always rooted his antislavery views in constitutional doctrine, rather than appeal to Seward's vision of higher law or Chase's philosophy of natural rights. He was also from the crucial swing state of Illinois and it was therefore thought that he might appeal to moderate voters in other border states such as Indiana, New Jersey, and Pennsylvania.

Although he was well aware of the importance of the fugitive slave issue to northern abolitionists, Lincoln had staked out a strategically moderate position on enforcement of the Fugitive Slave Act.[21] He did not endorse resistance to the law, much less threaten to "trample" it, as had Seward and Chase. In fact, Lincoln conceded its constitutionality and, in his failed 1858 Senate campaign against Stephen Douglas, he allowed that Southerners were entitled to "legislation for reclaiming their fugitives." In 1859, in the aftermath of the Oberlin Rescue, Lincoln had cautioned Chase against turning the fugitive issue into a national campaign plank: "The introduction of a proposition for repeal of the Fugitive Slave Law into the next Republican national convention will explode the convention and the party."[22]

His careful triangulation on the Fugitive Slave Act did not endear Lincoln to abolitionists—Wendell Phillips famously called him a "Slave-Hound from Illinois"—but it was Lincoln who was in better touch with the national electorate. The Republicans' "limited antislavery coalition" was much closer to Free-Soilism than to abolitionism. That tended to "marginalize the fugitive slave issue" as the party attempted to broaden its membership and enlarge its support.[23] In March 1860 even the prosecutor in a fugitive rescue case invoked Lincoln's views, calling him "the highest authority [of] the best section of his party" and praising his "great moral heroism to announce that he was in favor of 'an efficient fugitive slave law.'"[24]

Lincoln won the Republican nomination on the third ballot. Seward had indeed been thought "too radical on slavery." The more temperate (if not less zealously abolition-minded) Chase had disastrously failed to secure the united support of his own state's delegation, in part because Ohio Republicans were divided over issues related to the Oberlin Rescue.[25] The Republican Party's national platform forthrightly affirmed the provocative principle that "all men are created equal" and expressed "abhorrence [at] all schemes for disunion." It condemned "the new dogma that the Constitution of its own force carries slavery into any or all of the territories of the United States," and it asserted that "the normal condition of all the territory of the United States is that of freedom." But it made no mention of the Fugitive Slave Act.

The silence of the Republican platform made no impression on southern slaves, who continued to run away to the North as they always had. More fugitives were apprehended by slave catchers in 1860 than in all but three of the other ten years since passage of the Fugitive Slave Act. Fortunately for Lincoln, however, there was only one rescue and there were no controversial trials between his nomination in May and his victory in November.[26] At least in the northern states—which were the only states where the Republicans campaigned—the Fugitive Slave Act was not an overriding issue in the election.

The fugitive slave problem still boiled in the South, however, as the advocates of disunion were unmoved by Lincoln's apparent moderation on the question. Throughout the "secession winter" of 1860–1861, the "fugitive slave issue remained one of the irreducible elements in the crisis of the Union," and repeated efforts were made to keep the nation intact by sacrificing the freedom of runaway slaves.[27] In his annual message to Congress on December 3,

1860, outgoing President Buchanan proposed an "explanatory amendment" to the Constitution that would "recognize the right of the master to have his slave who has escaped from one State to another restored and 'delivered up' to him." Buchanan's amendment would also have affirmed the "validity of the fugitive-slave law enacted for this purpose" while declaring "that all State laws impairing or defeating this right are violations of the Constitution, and are consequently null and void."[28]

The Republican Party also sought to placate the secessionists by giving them "complete satisfaction" in "the matter of fugitive slaves." Various resolutions called for repeal of the northern states' personal liberty laws and even the imposition of penalties against states that interfered with recapture and rendition.[29] When the 36th Congress reconvened following the election, special committees in both houses recommended strengthening the Fugitive Slave Act. Lincoln himself authorized a proposal resolving that "the fugitive slave clause of the Constitution ought to be enforced by a law of Congress, with efficient provisions for that object," though he specified that it should include "the usual safeguards to liberty, securing freemen against being surrendered as slaves."[30]

The provision of safeguards to liberty was apparently "much too much for southern radicals," who proceeded to lead their states out of the Union.[31] By the time Abraham Lincoln was inaugurated in March 1861, seven states had voted in favor of secession, with four more to follow later that spring after the firing on Fort Sumter.

The outbreak of the Civil War, however, did not resolve the fugitive slave problem, even though the Confederate states had become—by the logic of their own declarations—a "hostile foreign country" that was not entitled to invoke the remedies of the U.S. Constitution.[32] Four slave states—Missouri, Kentucky, Maryland, and Delaware—did not secede. President Lincoln was determined to retain the loyalty of the border states at almost any cost, believing that military victory would be impossible without them. "I hope to have God on our side," he is reputed to have said, "but I must have Kentucky."

Accordingly, Attorney General Edward Bates ordered the U.S. marshal in Missouri to continue to enforce the Fugitive Slave Act in July 1861. The current "insurrectionary disorders," Bates said, did not change the "legal status" of the state or its residents, and refusal to execute the Fugitive Slave Act would therefore constitute an "official misdemeanor."[33]

Lincoln's generals faced a more difficult situation in the theaters of battle, as thousands of slaves—known as "contrabands"—fled from rebel masters and sought refuge with the Union forces. Army policy toward these runaways was inconsistent in the early years of the war; some commanding officers sheltered them, while others refused "to receive such fugitives into their lines." That problem was eventually resolved by the Confiscation Acts (which forfeited the rights of rebel slave owners) and then, of course, by the Emancipation Proclamation of 1863.[34]

Lincoln's government continued to enforce the Fugitive Slave Act in the border states, as well as in the District of Columbia. By the summer of 1863, with the Emancipation Proclamation in force, the Fugitive Slave Act had "lost its usefulness" to the Union and it fell more or less into desuetude. It would be another year, however, until Congress voted to repeal the odious law, acting pursuant to bills sponsored by the old abolitionist heroes Thaddeus Stevens (in the House) and Charles Sumner (in the Senate).[35]

President Lincoln signed the bill of repeal on June 28, 1864. The Civil War would not end for nearly another full year, but the U.S. government had finally rid itself of the bitter burden of slave catching.

As a cornerstone of the Compromise of 1850, the Fugitive Slave Act had been enacted in the hope of bringing about a national reconciliation. Instead it only deepened sectional division by thrusting the problems of slavery deeply into the North, while convincing Southerners that they would never obtain willing cooperation in the free states. Successive proslavery federal administrations—under presidents Fillmore, Pierce, and Buchanan—managed more or less to enforce the law, but they failed to make it respectable. Over nine years of captures, rescues, renditions, and trials, adherence to the higher law was transformed from an abstract principle into a vigorous political movement. In the spring of 1850, when Senator William Seward first observed that there was a "higher law than the Constitution," he might have expected his words to echo in the streets and legislative chambers, but he would not have predicted that they would also be heard one day—and even taken seriously—in courtrooms.

The higher law hovered unacknowledged over the Christiana trial in 1851. In Philadelphia and beyond, Castner Hanway's supporters loudly praised "freedom's battle" against slave catchers and justified the killing of Edward Gorsuch. But during the trial in Independence Hall, the defense attorneys were careful to profess their undivided allegiance to the Constitution and the Fugitive Slave Act, going so far as to concede the legitimacy of slave hunting. There was little doubt that the defendant and his attorneys believed, as Hanway had announced before his arrest, that fugitive slaves had "a right to defend themselves," but no lawyer would have dared suggest as much before the bench.

Boston was an abolitionist stronghold in 1854, where the higher law was preached from pulpits and proclaimed loudly at meetings and in lecture halls. In the courtroom, however, it remained a doctrine that dared not speak its name. Richard Henry Dana and his colleagues intimated, suggested, and implied that the federal law should be bent and reinterpreted in order to avoid the evil demands of the Fugitive Slave Act, but they never argued that it should simply be abrogated. Their jurisprudence distinguished sharply between human rights that derived from natural law, and legal rights that depended upon the standard conventions of statutes, cases, and writs. Only the latter had purchase in the judicial courts of Massachusetts.

Finally in 1859, following the most tumultuous and divisive decade in the nation's short history, the higher law was openly proposed as a defense to criminal charges. Attorney Albert Riddle declared himself a votary of the higher law, and his colleague Rufus Spalding called upon a federal judge to defy the U.S. Supreme Court. But most outspoken was the black defendant, Charles Langston, who risked additional jail time by announcing his intention to continue rescuing fugitives who had managed to reach Ohio's free soil "by the exercise of their own God-given powers." Langston fully expected that his eventual sentence would be lengthened when he informed the court that he endorsed the forcible defense of human rights "which God gave us that we need not be slaves." The defendant might have been the most surprised person in the courtroom when the stern Judge Hiram Willson instead reduced this sentence, almost apologizing to Langston for the necessary enforcement of the law.

It would be too much to claim that resistance to the Fugitive Slave Act made the Civil War inevitable, or that John Brown took his cue from abolitionist lawyers and their clients, or even that Lincoln secured the Republican nomination by intentionally distancing himself from the radical defense of fugitive slaves. But it is fair to say that the emergence of higher law—whether expressed in court, in the streets, or on the gallows—helped to create an unbridgeable gap between the free states and the slave power. And that process was placed powerfully in motion by the courage of escaping slaves who, as Charles Langston put it, exercised their rights to "liberty under the laws of God."

NOTES

Introduction

1. John H. Franklin and Loren Schweninger, *Runaway Slaves: Rebels on the Plantation* (New York: Oxford University Press, 2000), 279, 293; Stanley W. Campbell, *The Slave Catchers: Enforcement of the Fugitive Slave Law, 1850–1860* (New York: W. W. Norton & Co., 1968), 6–7.

2. Campbell, *Slave Catchers*, 136n77.

3. Don E. Fehrenbacher, *The Slaveholding Republic: An Account of the United States Government's Relations to Slavery* (New York: Oxford University Press, 2001), 251.

4. William Freehling, *The Road to Disunion*, vol. 1, *Secessionists at Bay, 1776–1854* (New York: Oxford University Press, 1991), 536.

1. Slavery and the Constitution

1. Jonathan Elliot, ed., *The Debates in the Several State Conventions on the Adoption of the Federal Constitution*, Proceedings of the Commissioners to Remedy Defects of the Federal Government, September 14, 1786, 5 vols., 2nd ed. (Philadelphia: J. B. Lippincott & Co.), 1:118, quoted in Max Farrand, *The Framing of the Constitution of the United States* (New Haven, CT: Yale University Press, 1913), 9–10.

2. Max Farrand, ed., *Records of the Federal Convention of 1787*, 3 vols. (New Haven, CT: Yale University Press, 1911), 1:486.

3. Joseph J. Ellis, *Founding Brothers: The Revolutionary Generation* (New York: Vintage Books, 2002), 102.

4. Farrand, *Records*, 2:9–2:10.

5. Joseph J. Ellis, *American Creation: Triumphs and Tragedies at the Founding of the Republic* (New York: Alfred A. Knopf, 2007), 10.

6. Samuel Johnson, *Taxation Not Tyranny; An Answer to the Resolutions and Address of the American Congress*, 4th ed. (London, 1775), 89.

7. Abigail Adams, *Letters of Mrs. Adams, the Wife of John Adams*, ed. Charles F. Adams, 2 vols. (Boston: Charles C. Little & James Brown, 1840), 1:24.

8. George Washington to Robert Morris, April 12, 1786, *George Washington Papers*, Series 2: Letterbooks, 1754–1799, Library of Congress.

9. Farrand, *Records*, 2:364, 2:371.

10. Paul Finkelman, *Slavery and the Founders: Race and Liberty in the Age of Jefferson*, 2nd ed. (New York: M. E. Sharpe, 2001), x.

11. Christopher Collier and James L. Collier, *Decision in Philadelphia: The Constitutional Convention of 1787* (New York: Ballantine Books, 1987), 30. Ellis, *Founding Brothers*, 102.

12. David O. Stewart, *The Summer of 1787: The Men Who Invented the Constitution* (New York: Simon & Schuster, 2007), 68.

13. Farrand, *Records*, 1:593.

14. Ibid., 2:221–2:222.

15. Finkelman, *Slavery and the Founders*, 12.

16. Farrand, *Records*, 1:566.

17. Mark A. Graber, *Dred Scott and the Problem of Constitutional Evil* (New York: Cambridge University Press, 2006), 101. Jack N. Rakove, *Original Meanings: Politics and Ideas in the Making of the Constitution* (New York: Vintage Books, 1997), 93. Madison later referred to the framers' "scruples against admitting the term 'slaves' into the Instrument." Farrand, *Records*, 3:436.

18. Farrand, *Records*, 3:254.

19. Ibid., 2:443.

20. Finkelman, *Slavery and the Founders*, 32. It is interesting to speculate on Butler's use of "he or she" in his initial proposal, given that the female pronoun does not appear anywhere in the Constitution as ratified. Perhaps he was thinking that some female slaves were particularly likely to run away, or perhaps he simply wanted to be especially inclusive when it came to reclaiming human property. In any event, Butler's wording was later tweaked, and "she" was removed from the Fugitive Slave Clause in the final document.

21. Ibid., 32. Some delegates believed that the term "legally held to service or labor" implied "the idea that slavery was legal in a moral view." Thus, the word "legally" was removed before the final vote. Jack N. Rakove, *The Annotated U.S. Constitution and Declaration of Independence* (Cambridge, MA: Belknap Press of Harvard University Press, 2009), 202; Edward J. Larson and Michael P. Winship, *The Constitutional Convention: A Narrative History from the Notes of James Madison* (New York: Modern Library, 2005), 151).

22. Don E. Fehrenbacher, *The Slaveholding Republic: An Account of the United States Government's Relations to Slavery* (New York: Oxford University Press, 2001), 206. Rhode Island and Connecticut had similar provisions in their own gradual emancipation statutes enacted in 1784. Finkelman, *Slavery and the Founders*, 219n4.

23. Simon Schama, *Rough Crossings: Britain, the Slaves and the American Revolution* (New York: HarperCollins, 2006), 7.

24. *Somerset v. Stewart*, 98 E.R. 499, 510 (K.B. 1772). See also Steven M. Wise, *Though the Heavens May Fall: The Landmark Trial That Led to the End of Human Slavery* (Cambridge, MA: Da Capo Press, 2005), 182.

25. Ira Berlin, *Many Thousands Gone: The First Two Centuries of Slavery in North America* (Cambridge, MA: Belknap Press of Harvard University Press, 1998), 237.

26. Simon Schama, *Rough Crossings*, 18; Steven Wise, *Though the Heavens May Fall*, 200.

27. Jonathan Elliot, ed. *The Debates in the Several State Conventions on the Adoption of the Federal Constitution*, the Debates in the Convention of the Commonwealth of Virginia, on the Adoption of the Federal Constitution, June 17, 1788, 5 vols., 2nd ed. (Philadelphia: J. B. Lippincott & Co.), 3:453.

28. Akhil Amar, *America's Constitution: A Biography* (New York: Random House, 2005), 21.

29. Finkelman, *Slavery and the Founders*, 42–43.

30. Farrand, *Records*, 1:206.

31. Fehrenbacher, *Slaveholding Republic*, 208. Both before and after the adoption of the Constitution, many southern states required private citizens—especially slave

owners—to participate in local "slave patrols" that "served as the eyes and ears of the white community." Lacy K. Ford, *Deliver Us from Evil: The Slavery Question in the Old South* (New York: Oxford University Press, 2009), 58, 89, 495. The patrols often recaptured runaways, but they did not typically have any extraterritorial reach.

32. Thomas D. Morris, *Southern Slavery and the Law, 1619–1860* (Chapel Hill: University of North Carolina Press, 1996), 341.

33. Thomas Mifflin to Beverley Randolph, June 4, 1791, *American State Papers: Miscellaneous,* 1:40. Finkelman, "The Kidnapping of John Davis and the Adoption of the Fugitive Slave Act of 1793," *Journal of Southern History* 56, no. 397 (1990).

34. James Innes to Beverley Randolph, undated, Palmer and McRae, eds., *Calendar of Virginia State Papers and Other Manuscripts,* 11 vols. (Richmond: R. F. Walker, 1893), 5:327.

35. Fugitive Slave Act of February 12, 1793, ch. 7, § 3, 1 Stat. 302, 304–305 (repealed 1864).

36. Finkelman, *Slavery and the Founders,* 81; Finkelman, "The Kidnapping of John Davis and the Adoption of the Fugitive Slave Act of 1793."

2. The Missouri Equilibrium

1. David Brion Davis, *Inhuman Bondage: The Rise and Fall of Slavery in the New World* (New York: Oxford University Press, 2006), 262.

2. Mark A. Graber, *Dred Scott and the Problem of Constitutional Evil* (New York: Cambridge University Press, 2006), 5.

3. Don E. Fehrenbacher, *The Dred Scott Case: Its Significance in American Law and Politics* (New York: Oxford University Press, 2001), 100.

4. John H. Franklin and Loren Schweninger, *Runaway Slaves: Rebels on the Plantation* (New York: Oxford University Press, 2000), 192.

5. Don E. Fehrenbacher, *The Slaveholding Republic: An Account of the United States Government's Relations to Slavery* (New York: Oxford University Press, 2001), 217–218.

6. *Wright v. Deacon,* 5 Sergeant & Rawle 62, 63 (Pennsylvania Superior Court, 1819).

7. Robert M. Cover, *Justice Accused: Antislavery and the Judicial Process* (New Haven, CT: Yale University Press, 1975), 150.

8. Salmon P. Chase, *Speech of Salmon P. Chase, in the case of the Colored Woman, Matilda: Who was Brought Before the Court of Common Pleas of Hamilton County, Ohio, by Writ of Habeas Corpus, March 11, 1837* (Cincinnati: Pugh & Dodd, 1837).

9. John Niven, *Salmon P. Chase: A Biography* (New York: Oxford University Press, 1995), 78.

10. Fergus M. Bordewich, *Bound for Canaan: The Underground Railroad and the War for the Soul of America* (New York: HarperCollins, 2005), 133.

11. Unless otherwise noted, quotations from the *Van Zandt* case are taken from Mark S. Weiner, *Black Trials: Citizenship from the Beginnings of Slavery to the End of Caste* (New York: Alfred A. Knopf, 2004).

12. Cover, *Justice Accused,* 173.

13. "Argument of Mr. Hanbly, of York (Pa.) in the Case of Edward Prigg, Plaintiff in Error, vs. The Commonwealth of Pennsylvania, Defendant in Error: in the Supreme Court of the United States" (Baltimore: Lucas & Deaver, 1842), 8, reproduced in Paul Finkelman,

ed., *Slavery, Race, and the American Legal System 1700–1872, Series II, Fugitive Slaves and the American Courts: The Pamphlet Literature,* 4 vols. (New York: Garland Publishing, 1988), 1:128.

14. "Argument of Mr. Hanbly, of York (Pa.) in the Case of Edward Prigg, Plaintiff in Error, vs. The Commonwealth of Pennsylvania, Defendant in Error: in the Supreme Court of the United States (Baltimore: Lucas & Deaver, 1842), 9, reproduced in *Slavery, Race, and the American Legal System 1700–1872,* 1:129.

15. Fehrenbacher, *Slaveholding Republic,* 219. Paul Finkelman, "John McLean: Moderate Abolitionist and Supreme Court Politician," *Vanderbilt Law Review* 62 (2009): 545.

16. R. Kent Newmyer, *Supreme Court Justice Joseph Story* (Chapel Hill: University of North Carolina Press, 1985), 373

17. *Prigg v. Pennsylvania,* 41 U.S. 539, 625 (1842). In all, the court produced seven separate opinions in *Prigg,* with only Justice McLean dissenting on the ground that the Fugitive Slave Clause did not prohibit free states from requiring jury trials and other procedural safeguards for alleged runaways. *Prigg,* 658.

18. Fehrenbacher, *Dred Scott Case,* 44.

19. Chief Justice Taney concurred in Story's conclusion that state laws could not interfere with a master's right to recapture an alleged slave. Unlike Story, however, Taney also opined that each state had a duty "to protect and support the owner, when he is endeavoring to obtain possession of his property found within their respective territories." *Prigg,* 627. Taney's more expansive view of free-state obligations to assist slave owners was later codified in the Fugitive Slave Act of 1850. Years later, Story's son William would claim that the *Prigg* opinion was in fact a "triumph of freedom" because it established that state legislatures were "prohibited from interfering even to assist in giving effect to the [fugitive slave] clause in the Constitution." Story's biographer disputes that characterization, pointing out that Story's theory of exclusivism was at best a "two-edged sword" that "cut for slavery in the hands of slaveholders." Newmyer, *Supreme Court Justice Joseph Story,* 374–375.

20. On the reaction to Story's theory of federal exclusivity, see Weiner, *Black Trials,* 142; Paul Finkelman, "Story Telling on the Supreme Court: *Prigg v. Pennsylvania* and Justice Joseph Story's Judicial Nationalism," *Supreme Court Review* (1994): 247; Paul Finkelman, "*Prigg v. Pennsylvania* and Northern State Courts: Anti-Slavery Use of a Pro-Slavery Decision," *Civil War History* 25, no. 1 (March 1979) 5–35. Thomas D. Morris, *Free Men All: The Personal Liberty Laws of the North, 1780–1861* (Baltimore: Johns Hopkins University Press, 1999), 130.

21. Cover, *Justice Accused,* 171.

22. "Legal Injustice," *The Liberator,* November 4, 1842.

23. Ibid.

24. Finkelman, "Northern State Courts," 23; Morris, *Free Men,* 111.

25. The exceptions were Illinois, Indiana, and Minnesota. Stanley W. Campbell, *The Slave Catchers: Enforcement of the Fugitive Slave Law, 1850–1860* (New York: W. W. Norton & Co., 1968), 88.

26. *Acts of the General Assembly of Virginia,* 1849–1850 (Richmond: William F. Ritchie, 1850), 250, quoted in Campbell, *Slave Catchers,* 14.

27. Niven, *Salmon P. Chase*, 83.

28. Salmon P. Chase, *Reclamation of Fugitives from Service: An Argument for the Defendant, Submitted to the Supreme Court of the United States at the December Term, 1846, in the Case of Wharton Jones v. John Van Zandt* (Cincinnati, Ohio: R. P. Donogh & Co., 1847), 54.

29. Chase, *Reclamation of Fugitives*, 93

30. *Jones v. Van Zandt*, 46 U.S. 215, 231 (1847).

3. The Compromise of 1850

1. Edward W. Emerson and Waldo E. Forbes, eds., *Journals of Ralph Waldo Emerson*, 10 vols. (Boston, 1909–14), 7:206; also quoted in James McPherson, *Battle Cry of Freedom: The Civil War Era* (New York: Oxford University Press, 2003), 51.

2. Quoted in McPherson, *Battle Cry*, 56.

3. Kenneth M. Stampp, *The Peculiar Institution: Slavery in the Ante-Bellum South* (New York: Vintage Books, 1989), 211.

4. Fergus M. Bordewich, *Bound for Canaan: The Underground Railroad and the War for the Soul of America* (New York: HarperCollins, 2005), 289. It was a crime throughout the South to persuade, entice, or "inveigle" a slave to run away, with potential sentences ranging from two to twenty years' imprisonment. Thomas D. Morris, *Southern Slavery and the Law* (Chapel Hill: University of North Carolina Press, 1996), 345.

5. Bordewich, *Bound for Canaan*, 291.

6. William Freehling, *The Road to Disunion, vol. 1: Secessionists at Bay, 1776–1854* (New York: Oxford University Press, 1991), 480. David M. Potter, *The Impending Crisis: 1848–1861*, completed and edited by Don E. Fehrenbacher (New York: Harper & Row, 1976), 89.

7. Don E. Fehrenbacher, *The Dred Scott Case: Its Significance in American Law and Politics* (New York: Oxford University Press, 2001), 157–159.

8. *Congressional Globe*, "Seventh of March," Speech of Daniel Webster, 31st Cong., 1st sess., March 7, 1850.

9. Robert V. Remini, *Daniel Webster: The Man and His Time* (New York: W. W. Norton & Co., 1997), 676.

10. *Congressional Globe*, "Freedom in the New Territories," Speech of William H. Seward, 31st Cong., 1st sess., March 11, 1850.

11. Fugitive Slave Act of September 18, 1850, ch. 60, § 6, 9 Stat. 462, 463 (repealed 1864).

12. As Daniel Webster put it, the fugitive would only be "remitted for an inquiry into his rights and the proper adjudication of them." Daniel Webster, *The Writings and Speeches of Daniel Webster* (Boston: Little, Brown & Co., 1903), 12:229.

13. Charles S. Sumner, Rep. No. 38–25 (1864).

14. Quoted in Thomas D. Morris, *Free Men All: The Personal Liberty Laws of the North, 1780–1861* (Baltimore: Johns Hopkins University Press, 1999), 132. At one point in Senate debate, Kentucky's Henry Clay offered an amendment that would have provided fugitives a limited right to jury trial following return to a slaveholding state. Even that slight bit of due process was deemed excessive by southern senators, and the amendment was roundly defeated.

15. Potter, *Impending Crisis,* 130–131. Don E. Fehrenbacher, *The Slaveholding Republic: An Account of the United States Government's Relations to Slavery* (New York: Oxford University Press, 2001), 232. McPherson, *Battle Cry,* 77.

16. *Congressional Globe,* 31st Cong., 1st sess., August 19, 1850, Appendix, 1583; also quoted in Freehling, *The Road to Disunion, vol. 1: Secessionists At Bay,* 501.

17. Allan Nevins, *The Emergence of Lincoln, vol. 2: Prologue to Civil War, 1859–1861* (New York: Scribner, 1950), 489, quoted in McPherson, *Battle Cry,* 79. Fehrenbacher, *Slaveholding Republic,* 233.

18. Thomas D. Morris, *Southern Slavery and the Law* (Chapel Hill: University of North Carolina Press, 1996), 341.

19. In *State v. Mann,* 13 N.C. 263 (1829), the North Carolina Supreme Court held that a master could not be charged with a crime for shooting and wounding a slave. Justice Thomas Ruffin explained that the nature of slavery required that the "power of the master must be absolute, to render the submission of the slave perfect," and that "the slave, to remain a slave, must be made sensible, that there is no appeal from his master."

20. Frederick Douglass, *My Bondage and My Freedom,* ed. John David Smith (New York: Penguin Books, 2003), 265–267. Douglass was brave, but he was also pragmatic. In 1845 he left Boston for England to avoid recapture, and he later allowed British supporters to purchase his manumission so he could have freedom of movement upon his return to the North.

21. John Hope Franklin and Loren Schweninger, *Runaway Slaves: Rebels on the Plantation* (New York: Oxford University Press, 1999), 274–279.

22. Samuel Cartwright, "Diseases and Peculiarities of the Negro Race," *De Bowe's Review of the Southern and Western States* 11 (1851): 331–333, quoted in John H. Franklin and Loren Schweninger, *Runaway Slaves,* 274–275; quoted in William Freehling, *The Road to Disunion, vol. 2: Secessionists Triumphant, 1854–1861* (New York: Oxford University Press, 2007), 41.

23. William Craft, *Running a Thousand Miles for Freedom: The Escape of William and Ellen Craft from Slavery,* R. J. M. Blackett, ed. (Baton Rouge: LSU Press, 1999), 33–39, 57.

24. Lawrence Lader, *The Bold Brahmins: New England's War Against Slavery 1831–1863* (New York: E. P. Dutton & Co., 1961), 141, quoted in McPherson, *Battle Cry,* 82.

4. But We Have No Country

1. Stanley W. Campbell, *The Slave Catchers: Enforcement of the Fugitive Slave Law, 1850–1860* (New York: W. W. Norton & Co., 1968), 116n8. American Foreign and Anti-Slavery Society, *The Fugitive Slave Bill; Its History and Unconstitutionality; With an Account of the Seizure and Enslavement of James Hamlet, and His Subsequent Restoration to Liberty* (New York: William Harned, 1850), reproduced in Paul Finkelman, ed., *Slavery, Race, and the American Legal System 1700–1872, Series II, Fugitive Slaves and the American Courts: The Pamphlet Literature,* 4 vols. (New York: Garland Publishing, 1988), 1:535.

2. Philip S. Foner, *History of Black Americans, vol. 3: From the Compromise of 1850 to the End of the Civil War* (Westport, CT: Greenwood Press, 1983), 17; Ella Forbes, *But We*

Have No Country: The 1851 Christiana, Pennsylvania Resistance (Cherry Hill, NJ: Africana Homestead Legacy Publishers, 1998), 111.

3. "Hear a Colored Man," *The Liberator,* November 1, 1850 (emphasis original).

4. Foner, *History of Black Americans, vol. 3,* 20–28; American Foreign and Anti-Slavery Society, *The Fugitive Slave Bill; Its History and Unconstitutionality; With an Account of the Seizure and Enslavement of James Hamlet, and His Subsequent Restoration to Liberty* (New York: William Harned, 1850), appendix 35, reproduced in Finkelman, ed., *Slavery, Race, and the American Legal System 1700–1872, Series II, Fugitive Slaves and the American Courts: The Pamphlet Literature,* 4 vols. (New York: Garland Publishing, 1988), 1:571.

5. The fullest contemporary account of the Christiana resistance and the ensuing trial is Thomas P. Slaughter, *Bloody Dawn: The Christiana Riot and Racial Violence in the Antebellum North* (New York: Oxford University Press, 1994). Many of the facts surrounding the "riot" are taken from Slaughter's book; other sources are also noted.

6. James J. Robbins, *Report of the Trial of Castner Hanway for Treason, in the Resistance of the Execution of the Fugitive Slave Law of September, 1850* (Philadelphia: King & Baird, 1852), 196.

7. Frederick Douglass, *My Bondage and My Freedom,* ed. John David Smith (New York: Penguin Books, 2003), xx; Frederick Douglass, *Three Addresses on the Relations Subsisting between the White and Colored People of the United States* (Washington, DC: Gibson Bros., 1886), 11; Foner, *History of Black Americans,* 3:28.

8. Frederick Douglass, *Narrative of the Life of Frederick Douglass, An American Slave, Written by Himself,* ed. John R. Blassingame, John R. McKivigan, and Peter P. Hinks (New Haven, CT: Yale University Press, 2001), 70.

9. William Parker, "The Freedman's Story: In Two Parts. Part I," *Atlantic Monthly* 17 (February 1866): 159.

10. Ibid., 162.

11. Slaughter, *Bloody Dawn,* 11–14.

12. Ibid., 14.

13. William M. Padgett to Edward Gorsuch, 28 August 1851, quoted in W. U. Hensel, *The Christiana Riot and the Treason Trials of 1851: An Historical Sketch,* repr. ed. (Lancaster, PA: New Era Printing Company, 1911; New York: Negro Universities Press, 1969), 24. Citations are to the Negro Universities Press edition.

14. Slaughter, *Bloody Dawn,* 44.

15. Jonathan Katz, *Resistance at Christiana: The Fugitive Slave Rebellion, Christiana, Pennsylvania, September 11, 1851, A Documentary Account* (New York: Thomas Y. Crowell Co., 1974), 74–75.

16. William Parker, "The Freedman's Story: In Two Parts. Part II." *Atlantic Monthly* 17 (March 1866): 282.

17. Robbins, *Report of the Trial,* 57.

18. Parker, "Freedman's Story. Part II," 283.

19. R. C. Smedley, *History of the Underground Railroad in Chester and the Neighboring Counties of Pennsylvania* (Philadelphia, 1883), 115.

20. Douglass, *My Bondage,* 140 (italics in the original).

21. Parker, "Freedman's Story, Part II," 283.
22. Ibid.
23. Hensel, *Christiana Riot*, 30.
24. Parker, "The Freedman's Story, Part II," 285.
25. Slaughter, *Bloody Dawn*, 63.
26. Robbins, *Report of the Trial*, 59.
27. Parker, "The Freedman's Story, Part II," 286.
28. Ibid., 287–288.
29. Hensel, *Christiana Riot*, 32.
30. Robbins, *Report of the Trial*, 81.
31. Parker, "The Freedman's Story, Part II," 287.
32. "National Free Soil Convention, Speech of Frederick Douglass at the Mass Convention at Pittsburg," *Frederick Douglass' Paper (North Star)*, August 20, 1852.
33. Frederick Douglass, *The Life and Times of Frederick Douglass: In His Own Words* (Hartford, CT: Park Publishing Co., 1881; facsimile edition, New York: Kensington Publishing Corp., 2002), 288–289.
34. Slaughter, *Bloody Dawn*, 86; Hensel, *Christiana Riot*, 40–41. Quoted in Katz, *Resistance at Christiana*, 123.
35. Hensel, *Christiana Riot*, 40.

5. A Traitorous Combination

1. James J. Robbins, *Report of the Trial of Castner Hanway for Treason, in the Resistance of the Execution of the Fugitive Slave Law of September, 1850* (Philadelphia: King & Baird, 1852), 93.
2. David R. Forbes, *A True Story of the Christiana Riot* (Quarryville, PA: Sun Printing House, 1898), 23, 27.
3. Jonathan Katz, *Resistance at Christiana: The Fugitive Slave Rebellion, Christiana, Pennsylvania, September 11, 1851, A Documentary Account* (New York: Thomas Y. Crowell Co., 1974), 133.
4. Paul Finkelman, *The Treason Trial of Castner Hanway*, in *American Political Trials*, rev. ed., ed. Michael R. Belknap (Westport, CT: Greenwood Press, 1994), 84. Thomas P. Slaughter, *Bloody Dawn: The Cristiana Riot and Racial Violence in the Antebellum North* (New York: Oxford University Press, 1994), 97–101.
5. Governor E. Louis Lowe to His Excellency, the President of the United States, 15 September 1851, *Letterbooks of Governor and Council, Unit 4, 1845–1854*, Maryland State Archives, 253–255, also quoted in Slaughter, *Bloody Dawn*, 105.
6. Daniel Webster, *Speech of Hon. Daniel Webster, to the Young Men of Albany, May 28, 1851* (Washington, DC: Gideon & Co. Printers, 1851), 14.
7. Francis Wharton, *A Treatise on the Criminal Law of the United States; Comprising a Digest of the Penal Statutes of the General Government and of Massachusetts, New York, Pennsylvania, and Virginia; with the Decisions on Cases Arising Upon Those Statutes; Together with the English and American Authorities upon Criminal Law in General*, 1st ed. (Philadelphia: James Kay, Jun. & Bro., 1846), 580.
8. Webster, *Young Men of Albany*, 14–15.

9. Gary Collison, "'This Flagitious Offense': Daniel Webster and the Shadrach Rescue Cases, 1851–1852," *New England Quarterly* 68, no. 4 (1995): 609–625; Daniel Webster, "Speech at Syracuse," in *The Writings and Speeches of Daniel Webster*, 18 vols., national ed. (Boston: Little, Brown & Co., 1903), 13:419.

10. W. S. Derrick to the Governor of Maryland, 16 September 1851, *Letterbooks of Governor and Council, Unit 4*, 256, also quoted in Slaughter, *Bloody Dawn*, 106.

11. Finkelman, *Treason Trial*, 84.

12. *A Full and Correct Report of the Christiana Tragedy in the County of Lancaster, Pa., Sept. 26, 1851* (Lancaster: J. H. Pearsol, 1851), 7, reprinted in Paul Finkelman, ed., *Slavery, Race, and the American Legal System 1700–1872, Series II, Fugitive Slaves and the American Courts: The Pamphlet Literature*, 4 vols. (New York: Garland Publishing, 1988), 2:57. See also Forbes, *True Story*, 29.

13. *Full and Correct Report*, 11, reprinted in Finkelman, *Fugitive Slaves*, 2:61.

14. Forbes, *True Story*, 32.

15. *Full and Correct Report*, 8, reprinted in Finkelman, *Fugitive Slaves*, 2:58.

16. Quoted in W. U. Hensel, *The Christiana Riot and the Treason Trials of 1851: An Historical Sketch*, repr. ed. (Lancaster, PA: New Era Printing Company, 1911; New York: Negro Universities Press, 1969), 48–49.

17. Forbes, *True Story*, 39.

18. Ibid., 36.

19. Quoted in Hensel, *Christiana Riot*, 55, 46.

20. Ibid., 57. Ibid., 57–58.

21. Robbins, *Report of the Trial*, 268; *A History of the Trial of Castner Hanway and Others, for Treason, at Philadelphia in November, 1851. With an Introduction Upon the History of the Slave Question by A Member of the Philadelphia Bar* (Philadelphia: Uriah Hunt & Sons, 1852), 46.

22. Robbins, *Report of the Trial*, 268–269.

23. Forbes, *True Story*, 36.

24. Finkelman, *Treason Trial*, 85–86. Hensel, *Christiana Riot*, 62. Quoted in Slaughter, *Bloody Dawn*, 115–116.

25. Slaughter, *Bloody Dawn*, 117. Wharton had been prominent at least since 1846, when he first published *A Treatise on the Criminal Law of the United States*. Wharton's 1852 second edition discussed the Christiana case at some length, praising the "lucid exactness" of Judge Kane's grand jury charge and Justice Robert Grier's instructions to the trial jury. Wharton did not disclose that he had consulted with the prosecution in the case. *A Treatise on the Criminal Law of the United States*, 2nd ed. (1852), 777.

26. *History of the Trial of Castner Hanway*, 42–43.

27. Finkelman, *Treason Trial*, 86.

28. Quoted in Slaughter, *Bloody Dawn*, 108.

29. Ibid., 108.

30. Ibid., 108.

31. *Report of Attorney General Brent to his Excellency, Gov. Lowe, In Relation to the Christiana Treason Trials, in the Circuit Court of the United States, held at Philadelphia* (Annapolis, MD: Thomas E. Martin, 1852), 3, reprinted in Finkelman, *Fugitive Slaves*, 2:187.

32. *History of the Trial of Castner Hanway,* 50.

33. Quoted in Slaughter, *Bloody Dawn,* 115.

34. *History of the Trial of Castner Hanway,* 49.

35. Ella Forbes, *But We Have No Country: The 1851 Christiana, Pennsylvania Resistance* (Cherry Hill, NJ: Africana Homestead Legacy Publishers, 1998), 93. Slaughter, *Bloody Dawn,* 93.

36. "To the government that destroys us, we owe no allegiance." "Freedom's Battle at Christiana," *Frederick Douglass' Paper (North Star),* September 25, 1851.

37. Ibid.

38. Katz, *Resistance,* 170.

6. Prosecution at Independence Hall

1. *A History of the Trial of Castner Hanway and Others, for Treason, at Philadelphia in November, 1851. With an Introduction Upon the History of the Slave Question by A Member of the Philadelphia Bar* (Philadelphia: Uriah Hunt & Sons, 1852), 52.

2. Unless otherwise noted, all quotations from the trial record are taken from James J. Robbins, *Report of the Trial of Castner Hanway for Treason, in the Resistance of the Execution of the Fugitive Slave Law of September, 1850* (Philadelphia: King & Baird, 1852).

3. John Williams Wallace, *Cases in the Circuit Court of the United States, for the Third Circuit,* vol. 2 (Philadelphia: T. & J. W. Johnson, 1854), 134–135.

4. Jonathan Katz, *Resistance at Christiana: The Fugitive Slave Rebellion, Christiana, Pennsylvania, September 11, 1851, A Documentary Account* (New York: Thomas Y. Crowell Co., 1974), 180.

5. Daniel Webster, "Speech at Syracuse," in *The Writings and Speeches of Daniel Webster,* 18 vols., national ed. (Boston: Little, Brown & Co., 1903), 13:420.

6. Jermain W. Loguen, *The Rev. J. W. Loguen, as a Slave and as a Freeman: A Narrative of Real Life* (Syracuse: J. G. K. Truair & Co., 1859), 401.

7. Fergus M. Bordewich, *Bound for Canaan: The Underground Railroad and the War for the Soul of America* (New York: HarperCollins, 2005), 338; Earl E. Sperry, *The Jerry Rescue, October 1, 1851,* ed. Franklin H. Chase (Syracuse: Onondaga Historical Association, 1924).

8. Octavius Brooks Frothingham, *Gerrit Smith: A Biography* (New York: G. P. Putnam's Sons, 1878), 118–119.

9. Quoted in Thomas P. Slaughter, *Bloody Dawn: The Christiana Riot and Racial Violence in the Antebellum North* (New York: Oxford University Press, 1994), 124.

10. *History of the Trial of Castner Hanway,* 56.

11. *Report of Attorney General Brent to His Excellency, Gov. Lowe, In Relation to the Christiana Treason Trials, in the Circuit Court of the United States, held at Philadelphia* (Annapolis, MD: Thomas E. Martin, 1852), 4–5, reprinted in Paul Finkelman, ed., *Slavery, Race, and the American Legal System 1700–1872, Series II, Fugitive Slaves and the American Courts: The Pamphlet Literature,* 4 vols. (New York: Garland Publishing, 1988), 2:188–2:189.

12. *History of the Trial of Castner Hanway,* 59.

13. *Report of Attorney General Brent,* 4–5, reprinted in Finkelman, *Fugitive Slaves,* 2: 188–2:189.

14. Katz, *Resistance,* 192.

15. Robbins, *Report of the Trial,* 100–101. This segment of the examination is somewhat truncated, with a number of questions and answers omitted. For the sake of readability, ellipses were used only where several separate answers were combined.

16. Quoted in Slaughter, *Bloody Dawn,* 124.

17. Charles Richardson, *A New Dictionary of the English Language* (Philadelphia: E. H. Butler & Co., 1851), s.v. "care"; Joseph E. Worcester, *A Pronouncing, Explanatory, and Synonymous Dictionary of the English Language* (Boston: Hickling, Swan & Brown, 1856), s.v. "care."

18. *History of the Trial of Castner Hanway,* 61.

7. Sir—Did You Hear It?

1. Unless otherwise noted, all quotations from the trial record are taken from James J. Robbins, *Report of the Trial of Castner Hanway for Treason, in the Resistance of the Execution of the Fugitive Slave Law of September, 1850* (Philadelphia: King & Baird, 1852).

2. *Report of Attorney General Brent to his Excellency, Gov. Lowe, In Relation to the Christiana Treason Trials, in the Circuit Court of the United States, held at Philadelphia* (Annapolis, MD: Thomas E. Martin, 1852), 5, reprinted in Paul Finkelman, ed., *Slavery, Race, and the American Legal System 1700–1872, Series II, Fugitive Slaves and the American Courts: The Pamphlet Literature,* 4 vols. (New York: Garland Publishing, 1988), 2:189.

3. Jonathan Katz, *Resistance at Christiana: The Fugitive Slave Rebellion, Christiana, Pennsylvania, September 11, 1851, A Documentary Account* (New York: Thomas Y. Crowell Co., 1974), 218.

4. *Report of Attorney General Brent,* 17, reprinted in *Finkelman, Fugitive Slaves,* 201.

5. Quoted in Katz, *Resistance at Christiana,* 239–240; quoted in William Cheek and Aimee Lee Cheek, *John Mercer Langston and the Fight for Black Freedom, 1829–65* (Urbana and Chicago: University of Illinois Press, 1996), 188.

6. *Historical Papers and Addresses of the Lancaster County Historical Society, vol. 15: The Christiana Riot and the Slavery Question Prior to That Event and Subsequently* (Lancaster, PA: New Era Printing Co., 1911), 94.

7. Michael W. Kauffman, *American Brutus: John Wilkes Booth and the Lincoln Conspiracies* (New York: Random House, 2004), 88.

8. Quoted in Ella Forbes, *But We Have No Country: The 1851 Christiana, Pennsylvania Resistance* (Cherry Hill, NJ: Africana Homestead Legacy Publishers, 1998), 135. Frederick Douglass, *The Life and Times of Frederick Douglass: In His Own Words,* fac. ed. (Hartford, CT: Park Publishing Co., 1881; New York: Kensington Publishing Corp., 2002), 288.

9. Quoted in Thomas P. Slaughter, *Bloody Dawn: The Christiana Riot and Racial Violence in the Antebellum North* (New York: Oxford University Press, 1994), 135.

8. Athens of America

1. *Commonwealth v. Jennison* (Mass. 1783) (unreported), quoted in Robert M. Cover, *Justice Accused: Antislavery and the Judicial Process* (New Haven, CT: Yale University Press, 1975), 48.

2. *Commonwealth v. Aves*, 18 Pick. 193, 223 (Mass. 1836).

3. Ella Forbes, *But We Have No Country: The 1851 Christiana, Pennsylvania Resistance* (Cherry Hill, NJ: Africana Homestead Legacy Publishers, 1998), 128. Gary Collison, *Shadrach Minkins: From Fugitive Slave to Citizen* (Cambridge, MA: Harvard University Press, 1998), 80, 82.

4. William Craft, *Running a Thousand Miles for Freedom: The Escape of William and Ellen Craft from Slavery*, R. J. M. Blackett, ed. (Baton Rouge: LSU Press, 1999) 60–62.

5. Collison, *Shadrach Minkins*, 99. Forbes, *No Country*, 106. Blackett, *Thousand Miles*, 62.

6. Quoted in Robert V. Remini, *Daniel Webster: The Man and His Time* (New York: W. W. Norton & Co., 1997), 695–696. Quoted in Forbes, *No Country*, 105.

7. Quoted in David M. Potter, *The Impending Crisis: 1848–1861*, completed and ed. Don E. Fehrenbacher (New York: Harper & Row, 1976), 121. Millard Fillmore, "The President's Message (State of the Union Address)," *National Anti-Slavery Standard*, December 5, 1850.

8. Quoted in Collison, *Shadrach Minkins*, 99. Charles Francis Adams, *Richard Henry Dana: A Biography*, 2 vols. (Boston: Houghton, Mifflin & Co., 1891), 1:179.

9. Blackett, *Thousand Miles*, 45.

10. Quoted in Collison, *Shadrach Minkins*, 118. Events surrounding the Shadrach Rescue are largely taken from Collison's book; other sources are also noted.

11. Ibid., 113.

12. J. Clay Smith Jr., *Emancipation: The Making of the Black Lawyer, 1844–1944* (Philadelphia: University of Pennsylvania Press, 1993), 96.

13. Benjamin R. Curtis, *A Memoir of Benjamin Robbins Curtis, LL.D.: With Some of His Professional and Miscellaneous Writings*, ed. Benjamin R. Curtis, 2 vols. (Boston: Little, Brown & Co., 1879), 1:136.

14. "A High Handed Act—Rescue of an Alleged Fugitive Slave from Custody," *Boston Daily Atlas*, February 17, 1851.

15. Adams, *Richard Henry Dana*, 1:182; Robert F. Lucid, ed., *The Journal of Richard Henry Dana, Jr.*, 3 vols. (Cambridge, MA: Belknap Press of Harvard University Press, 1968), 2:412.

16. Austin Bearse, *Reminiscences of Fugitive-Slave Law Days in Boston* (Boston: Warren Richardson, 1880), 17, 19. Quoted in Collison, *Shadrach Minkins*, 135.

17. Quoted in Don E. Fehrenbacher, *The Slaveholding Republic: An Account of the United States Government's Relations to Slavery* (New York: Oxford University Press, 2001), 247. Quoted in Fergus M. Bordewich, *Bound for Canaan: The Underground Railroad and the War for the Soul of America* (New York: HarperCollins, 2005), 321. Quoted in Collison, *Shadrach Minkins*, 140; Bearse, *Reminiscences*, 19.

18. Lucid, *Journal*, 2:430.

19. Gary Collison, " 'This Flagitious Offense': Daniel Webster and the Shadrach Rescue Cases, 1851–1852," *New England Quarterly* 68, no. 4 (1995): 616.

20. Quoted in Smith, *Emancipation*, 96.
21. James Oliver Horton and Louis E. Horton, *Black Bostonians: Family Life and Community Struggle in the Antebellum North*, rev. ed. (New York: Holmes & Meier, 1999), 61.
22. *U.S. v. Morris*, 26 F. Cas. 1323, 1323 (C.C.D. Mass. 1851) (No. 15815). Lucid, *Journal*, 2:466.
23. *U.S. v. Morris*, 26 F. Cas. 1323.
24. Quoted in Collison, *Shadrach Minkins*, 111. *U.S. v. Morris*, 26 F. Cas. 1329.
25. *U.S. v. Morris*, 26 F. Cas. 1329–1331.
26. Quoted in Stuart Streichler, *Justice Curtis in the Civil War Era: At the Crossroads of American Constitutionalism* (Charlottesville: University of Virginia Press, 2005), 56.
27. Collison, *Shadrach Minkins*, 194.
28. Cover, *Justice Accused*, 194. *U.S. v. Morris*, 26 F. Cas. 1333.
29. *U.S. v. Charles Davis: Report of the Proceedings at the Examination of Charles G. Davis, Esq. on a Charge of Aiding and Abetting in the Rescue of a Fugitive Slave* (Boston: White & Potter, 1851), 27–28, reprinted in Paul Finkelman, ed., *Slavery, Race, and the American Legal System 1700–1872, Series II, Fugitive Slaves and the American Courts: The Pamphlet Literature*, 4 vols. (New York: Garland Publishing, 1988), 1:599–1:600.
30. Adams, *Richard Henry Dana*, 1:183; Lucid, *Journal*, 2:412.
31. Stanley W. Campbell, *The Slave Catchers: Enforcement of the Fugitive Slave Law, 1850–1860* (New York: W. W. Norton & Co., 1968), 151. Quoted in Collison, *Shadrach Minkins*, 193.
32. Adams, *Richard Henry Dana*, 1:179.
33. Ibid., 1:127.
34. Leonard Levy, "Sims's Case: The Fugitive Slave Law in Boston," *Journal of Negro History* 35, no. 1 (1950): 42.
35. Quoted in Levy, "Sims's Case," 44.
36. Bearse, *Reminiscences*, 22.
37. Ibid., 23.
38. Ibid., 23. Quoted in Levy, "Sims's Case," 53.
39. "Court Calendar," *Boston Daily Atlas*, April 7, 1851. *Trial of Thomas Sims on an Issue of Personal Liberty, on the Claim of James Potter, of Georgia, Against Him, as an Alleged Fugitive from Service: Arguments of Robert Rantoul, Jr. and Charles G. Loring, with the Decision of George T. Curtis: Boston, April 7–11, 1851*, 46, reprinted in Finkelman, *Fugitive Slaves*, 1:662.
40. "Court Calendar," *Boston Daily Atlas*, April 7, 1851.
41. Thomas Wentworth Higginson, *Cheerful Yesterdays*, repr. ed. (Boston: Houghton, Mifflin & Co., 1899; New York: Arno Press, 1968), 141.
42. Lucid, *Journal*, 2:411–2:412, 2:420.
43. *In Re Sims*, 7 Cush., 285, 290 (Mass. 1851).
44. Ibid., 310.
45. Quoted in Albert J. Von Frank, *The Trials of Anthony Burns: Freedom and Slavery in Emerson's Boston* (Cambridge, MA: Harvard University Press, 1999), 28. Quoted in Levy, "Sims's Case," 61. Lucid, *Journal*, 2:420.
46. *In Re Sims*, 7 Cush., 308.
47. *Trial of Thomas Sims*, 7, reprinted in Finkelman, *Fugitive Slaves*, 1:623.

48. Ibid., 23, reprinted in Finkelman, *Fugitive Slaves,* 1:639.

49. "Court Calendar," *Boston Daily Atlas,* April 10, 1851.

50. Higginson, *Cheerful Yesterdays,* 140, 143.

51. Ibid., 143.

52. *Trial of Thomas Sims,* 43, reprinted in Finkelman, *Fugitive Slaves,* 1:659.

53. Quoted in Fehrenbacher, *Slaveholding Republic,* 243.

54. *Trial of Thomas Sims,* 47, reprinted in Finkelman, *Fugitive Slaves,* 1:663.

55. Theodore Parker, *The Trial of Theodore Parker for the Misdemeanor of a Speech in Faneeuil Hall against Kidnapping,* repr. ed. (Boston, 1855; Freeport, NY: Books for Libraries Press, 1971), 151.

56. Levy, "Sims's Case," 69.

57. Quoted in Henry Steele Commager, *Theodore Parker: Yankee Crusader,* 2nd ed. (Boston: Beacon Press, 1960), 223.

58. Quoted in Remini, *Daniel Webster,* 696.

59. Quoted in Bearse, *Reminiscences,* 25.

9. Kidnapping Again!

1. Stanley W. Campbell, *The Slave Catchers: Enforcement of the Fugitive Slave Law, 1850–1860* (New York: W. W. Norton & Co., 1968), 207.

2. James McPherson, *Battle Cry of Freedom: The Civil War Era* (New York: Oxford University Press, 2003), 88.

3. Quoted in McPherson, *Battle Cry,* 122.

4. Quoted in David M. Potter, *The Impending Crisis: 1848–1861,* completed and ed. Don E. Fehrenbacher (New York: Harper & Row, 1976), 159.

5. Potter, *Impending Crisis,* 163.

6. Charles Francis Adams, *Richard Henry Dana: A Biography,* 2 vols. (Boston: Houghton, Mifflin & Co., 1891), 1:253–1:254. Samuel Shapiro, "The Rendition of Anthony Burns," *Journal of Negro History* 44, no. 1 (1959): 35.

7. The fullest account of the Anthony Burns case is found in Albert J. Von Frank, *The Trials of Anthony Burns: Freedom and Slavery in Emerson's Boston* (Cambridge, MA: Harvard University Press, 1999). Many of the facts surrounding the Burns case are taken from Von Frank's book; other sources are also noted.

8. Charles E. Stevens, *Anthony Burns: A History,* repr. ed. (Boston: John P. Jewett & Co., 1856; Williamstown, MA: Corner House Publishers, 1973), 180.

9. Quoted in Stevens, *Anthony Burns,* 252.

10. Stevens, *Anthony Burns,* 17.

11. Ibid., 18–19.

12. Robert F. Lucid, ed., *The Journal of Richard Henry Dana, Jr.,* 3 vols. (Cambridge, MA: Belknap Press of Harvard University Press, 1968), 2:625.

13. Ibid., 2:625.

14. Stevens, *Anthony Burns,* 22; Lucid, *Journal,* 2:625.

15. Stevens, *Anthony Burns,* 25.

16. "The Case of Anthony Burns." *Monthly Law Reporter* 17, no. 4 (August 1854).

17. *The Boston Slave Riot, and Trial of Anthony Burns. Containing the Report of the Faneuil Hall Meeting, The Murder of Batchelder, Theodore Parker's Lesson for the Day, Speeches of Council on Both Sides, Corrected by Themselves, Verbatim Report of Judge Loring's Decision, And a Detailed Account of the Embarkation,* repr. ed. (Boston: Fetridge & Co., 1854; Northbrook, IL: Metro Books, 1972), 20.

18. *Boston Slave Riot,* 7.

19. "The Case of Anthony Burns." *Monthly Law Reporter* 17, no. 4 (August 1854); Stevens, *Anthony Burns,* 25–26; Lucid, *Journal,* 2:626; Richard Henry Dana, *Remarks of Richard H. Dana, Jr. Esq. before the Committee on Federal Relations, on the Proposed Removal of Edward G. Loring, Esq. from the Office of Judge of Probate, March 5, 1855* (Boston: Alfred Mudge & Son, 1855), 16, reprinted in Paul Finkelman, ed., *Slavery, Race, and the American Legal System 1700–1872, Series II, Fugitive Slaves and the American Courts: The Pamphlet Literature,* 4 vols. (New York: Garland Publishing, 1988), 3:60.

20. Dana, *Remarks,* 16–17, reprinted in Finkelman, *Fugitive Slaves,* 3:60–3:61.

21. Lucid, *Journal,* 2:626.

22. Ibid.

23. Von Frank, *Trials of Anthony Burns,* 11.

24. Lucid, *Journal,* 2:626.

25. Ibid., 2:626–2:627.

26. Wendell Phillips, *Argument of Wendell Phillips, Esq. before the Committee on Federal Relations (of the Massachusetts Legislature,) in Support of the Petition for the Removal of Edward Greely Loring from the Office of Judge of Probate, February 20, 1855* (Boston: J. B. Yerrinton & Son, 1855), 29–30, reprinted in Finkelman, *Fugitive Slaves,* 3:29–3:30.

27. Lucid, *Journal,* 627. Quoted in Von Frank, *Trials of Anthony Burns,* 2:18; Dana, *Remarks,* 18, reprinted in Finkelman, *Fugitive Slaves,* 3:62.

28. Reproduced in Von Frank, *Trials of Anthony Burns,* 10.

29. Austin Bearse, *Reminiscences of Fugitive-Slave Law Days in Boston* (Boston: Warren Richardson, 1880), 16.

30. Anna Mary Wells, *Dear Preceptor: The Life and Times of Thomas Wentworth Higginson* (Boston: Houghton Mifflin Co., 1963), 67. Quoted in Von Frank, *Trials of Anthony Burns,* 27. Thomas Wentworth Higginson, *Cheerful Yesterdays,* repr. ed. (Boston: Houghton Mifflin & Co., 1899; New York: Arno Press, 1968), 147; Von Frank, *Trials of Anthony Burns,* 20.

31. Higginson, *Cheerful Yesterdays,* 149.

32. Ibid., 149–150.

33. Lucid, *Journal,* 2:627–2:628.

34. *Boston Slave Riot,* 7.

35. Ibid., 8.

36. Stevens, *Anthony Burns,* 38. *Boston Slave Riot,* 9. Stevens, *Anthony Burns,* 294–295.

37. *Boston Slave Riot,* 9.

38. Stevens, *Anthony Burns,* 41.

39. Higginson, *Cheerful Yesterdays,* 152. Lucid, *Journal,* 2:630.

40. Higginson, *Cheerful Yesterdays,* 152–153.

41. Wells, *Dear Preceptor,* 88; Stevens, *Anthony Burns,* 44.

42. Stevens, *Anthony Burns,* 47.

43. Quoted in Von Frank, *Trials of Anthony Burns,* 72.

44. Von Frank, *Trials of Anthony Burns,* 72–73.

45. Lucid, *Journal,* 629, 631.

10. The Height of Cruelty

1. Charles E. Stevens, *Anthony Burns: A History,* repr. ed. (Boston: J. P. Jewitt & Co., 1856; Williamstown, MA: Corner House Publishers, 1973), 82–83; *The Boston Slave Riot, and Trial of Anthony Burns. Containing the Report of the Faneuil Hall Meeting, The Murder of Bachelder, Theodore Parker's Lesson for the Day, Speeches of Council on Both Sides, Corrected by Themselves, Verbatim Report of Judge Loring's Decision, And a Detailed Account of the Embarkation,* repr. ed. (Boston: Fetridge & Co., 1854; Northbrook, IL: Metro Books, 1972), 26–27.

2. Stevens, *Anthony Burns,* 83.

3. *Boston Slave Riot,* 24.

4. Ibid., 25.

5. Ibid., 25–26.

6. Ibid., 26.

7. Robert F. Lucid, ed., *The Journal of Richard Henry Dana, Jr.,* 3 vols. (Cambridge, MA: Belknap Press of Harvard University Press, 1968), 2:629.

8. Stevens, *Anthony Burns,* 63.

9. Ibid., 70.

10. *Boston Slave Riot,* 31.

11. Ibid., 33.

12. Richard Henry Dana, *Remarks of Richard H. Dana, Jr. Esq. before the Committee on Federal Relations, on the Proposed Removal of Edward G. Loring, Esq. from the Office of Judge of Probate, March 5, 1855* (Boston: Alfred Mudge & Son, 1855), 19, reprinted in Paul Finkelman, ed., *Slavery, Race, and the American Legal System 1700–1872, Series II, Fugitive Slaves and the American Courts: The Pamphlet Literature,* 4 vols. (New York: Garland Publishing, 1988), 3:63.

13. *Boston Slave Riot,* 38. Stevens, *Anthony Burns,* 83.

14. *Boston Slave Riot,* 38.

15. Stevens, *Anthony Burns,* 84. *Boston Slave Riot,* 39, 44.

16. Jane H. Pease and William H. Pease, *The Fugitive Slave Law and Anthony Burns: A Problem in Law Enforcement,* ed. Harold M. Hyman (Philadelphia: J. B. Lippincott Co., 1975), 41. Lucid, *Journal,* 414.

17. *Boston Slave Riot,* 44–45.

18. Ibid., 45.

19. Ibid.

20. "The Case of Anthony Burns." *Monthly Law Reporter* 17, no. 4 (August 1854): 186.

21. Ibid.

22. Paul Finkelman, "Legal Ethics and Fugitive Slaves: The Anthony Burns Case, Judge Loring, and Abolitionist Attorneys," *Cardozo Law Review* 17, no. 6 (1996): 1812.

23. "The Case of Anthony Burns," 186.

24. *Boston Slave Riot*, 46.

25. Albert J. Von Frank, *The Trials of Anthony Burns: Freedom and Slavery in Emerson's Boston* (Cambridge, MA: Harvard University Press, 1999), 133. *Boston Slave Riot*, 46.

26. *Boston Slave Riot*, 46.

27. Ibid., 46.

28. Ibid., 47.

29. Ibid., 48.

30. Ibid., 51–52.

31. Ibid., 50.

32. Ibid., 49.

33. Ibid.

34. Ibid., 56.

35. Worthington Ford. "Trial of Anthony Burns," *Proceedings of the Massachusetts Historical Society* 44 (January 1911): 332.

36. *Boston Slave Riot*, 56.

37. Stevens, *Anthony Burns*, 95. *Boston Slave Riot*, 56–57.

38. *Boston Slave Riot*, 58.

39. Ibid., 59–60.

40. Ibid.

41. Ibid., 59.

42. "The Case of Anthony Burns," 194; *Boston Slave Riot*, 61.

43. *Boston Slave Riot*, 62.

44. "The Case of Anthony Burns." *Boston Slave Riot*, 62. William I. Bowditch, *The Rendition of Anthony Burns* (Boston: Robert F. Wallcut, 1854), 29, reprinted in Finkelman, *Fugitive Slaves*, 2:457.

45. Lucid, *Journal*, 631; Charles Francis Adams, *Richard Henry Dana: A Biography*, 2 vols. (Boston: Houghton, Mifflin Co., 1891), 2:138.

46. Except as noted, all excerpts from Dana's argument are taken from *Boston Slave Riot*, 62–72.

47. Lucid, *Journal*, 2:632.

48. *Boston Slave Riot*, 72. Except as noted, all excerpts from Thomas's argument are taken from *Boston Slave Riot*, 72–76.

11. Judge Loring's Predicament

1. Robert F. Lucid, ed., *The Journal of Richard Henry Dana, Jr.*, 3 vols. (Cambridge, MA: Belknap Press of Harvard University Press, 1968), 2:632.

2. Albert J. Von Frank, *The Trials of Anthony Burns: Freedom and Slavery in Emerson's Boston* (Cambridge, MA: Harvard University Press, 1999), 193.

3. Richard Henry Dana, *Remarks of Richard H. Dana, Jr. Esq. before the Committee on Federal Relations, on the Proposed Removal of Edward G. Loring, Esq. from the Office of Judge of Probate, March 5, 1855* (Boston: Alfred Mudge & Son, 1855), 24, reprinted in Paul Finkelman, ed., *Slavery, Race, and the American Legal System 1700–1872, Series II,*

Fugitive Slaves and the American Courts: The Pamphlet Literature, 4 vols. (New York: Garland Publishing, 1988), 3:68.

4. Charles E. Stevens, *Anthony Burns: A History,* repr. ed. (Boston: J. P. Jewett & Co., 1856; Williamstown, MA: Corner House Publishers, 1973), 114. Smith to Edmands, 31 May 1854, reproduced in Stevens, *Anthony Burns,* 266. Quoted in Von Frank, *Trials of Anthony Burns,* 198.

5. *The Boston Slave Riot, and Trial of Anthony Burns. Containing the Report of the Faneuil Hall Meeting, The Murder of Batchelder, Theodore Parker's Lesson for the Day, Speeches of Council on Both Sides, Corrected by Themselves, Verbatim Report of Judge Loring's Decision, And a Detailed Account of the Embarkation,* repr. ed. (Boston: Fetridge & Co., 1854; Northbrook, IL: Metro Books, 1972), 76.

6. Stevens, *Anthony Burns,* 113.

7. All quotations from Loring's decision are found in *Boston Slave Riot,* 80–82.

8. Loring was far from the first American jurist to express concern over the severity of bondage while strictly enforcing the law of slavery. In 1830, for example, Justice Thomas Ruffin of the North Carolina Supreme Court held that a slave owner (or the lessee of a hired slave) could not be prosecuted for shooting and wounding a slave. "The slave, to remain a slave, must be made sensible that there is no appeal from his master," he wrote. "The power of the master must be absolute to render the submission of the slave perfect." In closing his opinion, Ruffin then added, "I most freely confess my sense of the harshness of this proposition; I feel it as deeply as any man can; and as a principle of moral right, every person in his retirement must repudiate it." Compassion apparently had its place "in retirement," but not on the bench. *State v. Mann,* 13 N.C. 263 (1830). See Mark Tushnet, *Slave Law in the American South:* State v. Mann *in History and Literature* (Lawrence: University Press of Kansas, 2003), 20–37; Mark Tushnet, *The American Law of Slavery, 1810–1860: Considerations of Humanity and Interest* (Princeton, NJ: Princeton University Press, 1981) 54–65.

9. "The Case of Anthony Burns." *Monthly Law Reporter* 17, no. 4 (August 1854); Stevens, *Anthony Burns,* 263.

10. Stevens, *Anthony Burns,* 270–274.

11. Lucid, *Journal,* 2:633.

12. Ibid., 2:634. Stevens, *Anthony Burns,* 145.

13. Stevens, *Anthony Burns,* 143.

14. Lucid, *Journal,* 2:636.

15. *Boston Slave Riot,* 85; Samuel Shapiro, "The Rendition of Anthony Burns," *Journal of Negro History* 44, no. 1 (1959): 45. Richard Winsor, "How John Price Was Rescued," *Oberlin Jubilee, 1833–1883,* ed. W. G. Ballantine (Oberlin, OH: E. J. Goodrich, 1883), 254.

16. Von Frank, *Trials of Anthony Burns,* 213. Shapiro, "Rendition," 49. Amos Lawrence to Giles Richards, 1 June 1854, quoted in Jane H. Pease and William H. Pease, *The Fugitive Slave Law and Anthony Burns: A Problem in Law Enforcement,* ed. Harold M. Hyman (Philadelphia: J. B. Lippincott Co., 1975), 43.

17. *Boston Slave Riot,* 16.

18. Quoted in Von Frank, *Trials of Anthony Burns,* 93.

19. E. R. Hoar, *Charge to the Grand Jury, at the July Term of the Municipal Court, in Boston, 1854* (Boston: Little, Brown & Co., 1854), 8, reprinted in Finkelman, *Fugitive Slaves,* 2:476.

20. David R. Maginnes, "The Case of the Court House Rioters in the Rendition of the Fugitive Slave Anthony Burns, 1854," *Journal of Negro History* 56, no. 1 (1971): 37.

21. Maginnes, "Court House Rioters," 37.

22. Claude M. Fuess, *The Life of Caleb Cushing,* 2 vols. (New York: Harcourt, Brace & Co., 1923), 2:212. David R. Maginnes, "The Point of Honor: The Rendition of the Fugitive Slave Anthony Burns, Boston, 1854" (PhD diss., Columbia University, 1973), 256.

23. Benjamin Robbins Curtis, *A Memoir of Benjamin Robbins Curtis, LL.D, With Some of His Professional and Miscellaneous Writings,* ed. Benjamin R. Curtis, 2 vols. (Boston: Little, Brown & Co., 1879), 2:207, 2:210, 2:211.

24. "Conclusion of the Burns Riot Trials—The Indictments Quashed," *Boston Daily Atlas,* April 13, 1855.

25. Henry Steele Commager, *Theodore Parker: Yankee Crusader,* 2nd ed. (Boston: Beacon Press, 1960), 245.

26. Quoted in Maginnes, "Court House Rioters," 40–41.

27. Ibid., 40.

28. Von Frank, *Trials of Anthony Burns,* 294. Theodore Parker, *The Trial of Theodore Parker for the Misdemeanor of a Speech in Faneuil Hall Against Kidnapping,* repr. ed. (Boston, 1855; Freeport, NY: Books for Libraries Press, 1971), 68.

29. Commager, *Yankee Crusader,* 247. Parker, *Theodore Parker,* 67–69.

30. Quoted in Paul Finkelman, "Legal Ethics and Fugitive Slaves: The Anthony Burns Case, Judge Loring, and Abolitionist Attorneys." *Cardozo Law Review* 17, no. 6 (1996): 1833.

31. Stevens, *Anthony Burns,* 222.

32. Ibid., 228. See also Finkelman, "Legal Ethics," 1846–1852.

33. Stevens, *Anthony Burns,* 224.

34. Robert M. Cover, *Justice Accused: Antislavery and the Judicial Process* (New Haven, CT: Yale University Press, 1975), 179.

35. House No. 63, February 9, 1855, "Remonstrance of Edward G. Loring," 4–5, reprinted in Finkelman, *Fugitive Slaves,* 3:158–3:159.

36. Wendell Phillips, *Argument of Wendell Phillips, Esq. before the Committee on Federal Relations (of the Massachusetts Legislature,) in Support of the Petition for the Removal of Edward Greely Loring from the Office of Judge of Probate, February 20, 1855* (Boston: J. B. Yerrinton & Son, 1855), 6, reprinted in Finkelman, *Fugitive Slaves,* 3:6.

37. Phillips, *Argument,* 38–39, reprinted in Finkelman, *Fugitive Slaves,* 3:38–3:39.

38. Dana, *Remarks,* 2–23, reprinted in Finkelman, *Fugitive Slaves,* 3:46–3:67.

39. Stevens, *Anthony Burns,* 241.

40. House No. 302, May 10, 1855, "To the Speaker of the House . . . on E. G. Loring. Statement of Gov. Henry Gardner," 10, reprinted in Finkelman, *Fugitive Slaves,* 3:254.

41. Stevens, *Anthony Burns,* 190.

42. Von Frank, *Trials of Anthony Burns,* 235.

43. Stevens, *Anthony Burns,* 207.

44. "Anthony Burns in New York," *The Liberator,* March 9, 1855.
45. Stevens, *Anthony Burns,* 215. Maginnes, "Point of Honor," 20.
46. Lucid, *Journal,* 2:673–2:674.

12. Freedom on the Western Reserve

1. The fullest account of John Price's escape—as well as his later rescue and the subsequent trials—is found in Nat Brandt, *The Town That Started the Civil War* (Syracuse, NY: Syracuse University Press, 1990). Most of the facts of Price's life are taken from Brandt's book; other sources are also noted.
2. The slave owner, John Bacon of Kentucky, was no known relation to the slave catcher John Bacon of Georgia, who apprehended Thomas Sims in Boston.
3. Robert Samuel Fletcher, *A History of Oberlin College: From Its Foundation Through the Civil War,* 2 vols. (Oberlin, OH: Oberlin College, 1943), 1:401–1:402. William Cheek and Aimee Lee Cheek, *John Mercer Langston and the Fight for Black Freedom, 1829–65* (Urbana and Chicago: University of Illinois Press, 1989), 296. John M. Langston, *From the Virginia Plantation to the National Capitol,* repr. ed. (Hartford, CT: American Publishing Co., 1894; North Stratford, NH: Ayer Co. Publishers, 2002), 168.
4. Fletcher, *History of Oberlin College,* 1:402. Quoted in Brandt, *The Town That Started the Civil War,* 42.
5. James McPherson, *Battle Cry of Freedom: The Civil War Era* (New York: Oxford University Press, 2003), 164.
6. The violence was not one-sided, as both factions engaged in running warfare sporadically through the years 1854–1858. Most notoriously, John Brown and his men massacred five proslavery settlers near Pottawatomie Creek in Kansas in 1856, an act that was itself in retaliation for the sack of Lawrence a few days earlier. Brown's raiders also killed a slaveholder during an 1858 expedition into Missouri, during which they liberated eleven slaves.
7. *Scott v. Sandford,* 63 U.S. 393, 451 (1857). According to legal historian Mark Graber, Taney's "conclusion that slavery could not be banned in the territories . . . was constitutionally as plausible as the contrary views" of his critics. Mark A. Graber, *Dred Scott and the Problem of Constitutional Evil* (New York: Cambridge University Press, 2006), 4, 66.
8. Don E. Fehrenbacher, *The Dred Scott Case: Its Significance in American Law and Politics* (New York: Oxford University Press, 2001), 452, 562. Roy P. Basler, ed., *The Collected Works of Abraham Lincoln,* 9 vols. (Piscataway, NJ: Rutgers University Press, 1953), 2:467. Fehrenbacher, *Dred Scott Case* at 562.
9. William C. Cochran, *The Western Reserve and the Fugitive Slave Law: A Prelude to the Civil War* (Cleveland: Western Reserve Historical Society, 1920), 121.
10. Ibid., 123–125.
11. Jacob R. Shipherd, comp., *History of the Oberlin-Wellington Rescue,* rep. ed. (Boston: J. P. Jewett & Co., 1859; New York: Negro Universities Press, 1969), 77. Cochran, *Western Reserve,* 125.
12. Shipherd, *Oberlin-Wellington Rescue,* 16, 99.
13. Ibid., 120.
14. Ibid., 35.

15. Roland M. Baumann, *The 1858 Oberlin-Wellington Rescue: A Reappraisal* (Oberlin, OH: Oberlin College, 2003), 28.

16. Cheek and Cheek, *John Mercer Langston,* 14, 19. The Quarles-Langston relationship was unusual, but not unheard of. For the depressing story of a female slave's sexual exploitation, see Melton A. McLaurin, *Celia, a Slave: A True Story of Violence and Retribution in Antebellum Missouri* (Athens: University of Georgia Press, 1991). For a discussion and explanation of the affectionate relationship between Thomas Jefferson and Sally Hemings, see Annette Gordon-Reed, *The Hemingses of Monticello: An American Family* (New York: W. W. Norton & Co., 2008).

17. Frederick J. Blue, *No Taint of Compromise: Crusaders in Antislavery Politics* (Baton Rouge: Louisiana State University Press, 2006), 67–68.

18. Unless otherwise noted, the events of the Margaret Garner case are taken primarily from Steven Weisenburger, *Modern Medea: A Family Story of Slavery and Child-Murder from the Old South* (New York: Hill & Wang, 1998).

19. Pendery did, however, allow Margaret to testify in separate proceedings over Gaines's claim for the rendition of her surviving children. As historian Steven Weisenburger notes, that may have been the "only time after passage of the 1850 law that an alleged fugitive slave was allowed to speak before a U.S. court." Weisenburger, *Modern Medea,* 164.

20. Unless otherwise noted, events of the rescue and the subsequent legal proceedings are taken from Shipherd, *Oberlin-Wellington Rescue.*

21. John Mercer Langston, "The Oberlin Wellington Rescue," *Anglo-African Magazine* 1 (July 1859): 210; Cheek and Cheek, *John Mercer Langston,* 319.

13. The Son Betrays and the Father Indicts

1. John M. Langston, *From the Virginia Plantation to the National Capitol,* repr. ed. (Hartford, CT: American Publishing Co., 1894; North Stratford, NH: Ayer Co. Publishers, 2002), 185–186.

2. Unless otherwise noted, events of the rescue and the subsequent legal proceedings are taken from Jacob R. Shipherd, comp., *History of the Oberlin-Wellington Rescue,* repr. ed. (Boston: J. P. Jewett & Co., 1859; New York: Negro Universities Press, 1969) (all emphases and spellings original).

3. Quoted in Thomas D. Morris, *Free Men All: The Personal Liberty Laws of the North, 1780–1861* (Baltimore: Johns Hopkins University Press, 1999), 155.

4. Langston, *Virginia Plantation,* 186.

5. H. E. Peck, "The Slave-Rescue Case in Ohio," *The Liberator,* January 28, 1859.

6. David Van Tassel and John Grabowski, eds., *The Encyclopedia of Cleveland History* (Bloomington and Indianapolis: Indiana University Press, 1987), 833; *Annals of the Early Settler's Association of Cuyahoga County* 3, no. 1 (Cleveland: Williams Publishing Co., 1892), 3:495; Nat Brandt, *The Town That Started the Civil War* (Syracuse, NY: Syracuse University Press, 1990), 145.

7. Langston, *Virginia Plantation,* 187–188.

8. William N. Brigance, *Jeremiah Sullivan Black: A Defender of the Constitution and the Ten Commandments* (Philadelphia: University of Pennsylvania Press, 1934) 58–60.

9. William C. Cochran, *The Western Reserve and the Fugitive Slave Law: A Prelude to the Civil War* (Cleveland: Western Reserve Historical Society, 1920), 146.

10. Although there had been thirty-seven indictments in the case, a number of the rescuers were never arrested or served with process and did not appear in court.

11. Quoted in Cochran, *Western Reserve*, 140–141.

12. It was only in 1864 that Congress guaranteed there "shall be no exclusion of any witness on account of color" in U.S. courts. Act of July 2, 1864, ch. 210, §3, 13 Stat. 344, 351. Prior to that time, federal judges had discretion to exclude African-American and Native American witnesses, as was done universally in the slave states and intermittently in the free states. S. REP. NO. 38–25 (1864). Interestingly, the federal version of the interested party rule was abolished (for civil cases only) in the same act.

13. *Daily National Democrat*, April 16, 1859, quoted in Brandt, *The Town That Started the Civil War*, 161.

14. Votaries of the Higher Law

1. Unless otherwise noted, events of the rescue and the subsequent legal proceedings are taken from Jacob R. Shipherd, comp., *History of the Oberlin-Wellington Rescue*, repr. ed. (Boston: J. P. Jewett & Co., 1859; New York: Negro Universities Press, 1969)(all emphases and spellings original).

2. "The Oberlin-Wellington Rescue Case," *Oberlin Evangelist*, April 27, 1859, retrieved online at www.oberlin.edu/external/EOG/OberlinWellington_Rescue/Oberlin Evangelist/ArticleList.html, also quoted in Nat Brandt, *The Town That Started the Civil War* (Syracuse, NY: Syracuse University Press, 1990), 161.

3. Quoted in Brandt, *The Town That Started the Civil War*, 162.

4. The "Fillmore Whigs" might very well have been the last two such men in the United States. The Whig party had thoroughly collapsed by 1859, and Fillmore had been out of office for more than six years (in 1856 he had run for president as a Know-Nothing).

5. Quoted in Brandt, *The Town That Started the Civil War*, 169.

6. John M. Langston, *From the Virginia Plantation to the National Capitol*, repr. ed. (Hartford, CT: American Publishing Co., 1894; North Stratford, NH: Ayer Co. Publishers, 2002), 189–190.

7. The Mortara case evidently had a powerful impact on American abolitionists. The papal kidnapping was also invoked by defense attorney Edwin Larned in March 1860 at the Chicago trial of Joseph Stout on the charge of rescuing a fugitive from slave catchers. Comparing Edgardo to a fugitive slave, Larned argued that "every Jew could see beneath the arrest of this Jewish boy a principle of despotic power, which, if unrebuked and unrestrained, might overthrow the rights of conscience and destroy the liberty of every other Jew. Such will ever be the sentiments which will animate a people who prize their liberties and expect to retain them." "Argument of E. C. Larned, Esq., on the Trial of Joseph Stout," in *In Memory of Edwin Channing Larned* (Chicago: A. C. McClurg and Co., 1886), 103. Larned's argument might have come in response to prosecutor A. W. Arrington's earlier appeal to anti-Semitism (in the related trial of John Hossack for the same rescue), in which he tied the defendant to the "awful ceremonies of the synagogue." *Report of the Trial of John Hossack, Indicted for Rescuing a Fugitive*

Slave from the U.S. Deputy Marshal, at Ottawa, October 20th, 1859 (Chicago: Press and Tribune Steam Book and Printing Office, 1860), 218; reproduced in Paul Finkelman, ed., *Slavery, Race, and the American Legal System 1700–1872, Series II, Fugitive Slaves and the American Courts: The Pamphlet Literature,* 4 vols. (New York: Garland Publishing, 1988), 4:384.

15. An Irrepressible Conflict

1. Unless otherwise noted, events of the rescue and the subsequent legal proceedings are taken from Jacob R. Shipherd, comp., *History of the Oberlin-Wellington Rescue,* repr. ed. (Boston: J. P. Jewett & Co., 1859; New York: Negro Universities Press, 1969)(all emphases and spellings original).
2. John Mercer Langston, "The Oberlin Wellington Rescue," *Anglo-African Magazine* 1 (July 1859): 211; William Cheek and Aimee Lee Cheek, *John Mercer Langston and the Fight for Black Freedom, 1829–65* (Urbana and Chicago: University of Illinois Press, 1989), 332. Immediately after Simeon Bushnell's sentencing, the court heard extended arguments over scheduling the remaining trials. Charles Langston's sentencing was therefore held over until the following day.
3. Quoted in Nat Brandt, *The Town That Started the Civil War* (Syracuse, NY: Syracuse University Press, 1990), 202.
4. The story of Joshua Glover's arrest and rescue is taken largely from H. Robert Baker, *The Rescue of Joshua Glover: A Fugitive Slave, the Constitution, and the Coming of the Civil War* (Athens: Ohio University Press, 2006); other sources are also noted.
5. *Ableman v. Booth,* 62 U.S. 506, 508 (1859).
6. Robert M. Cover, *Justice Accused: Antislavery and the Judicial Process* (New Haven, CT: Yale University Press, 1975), 186.
7. William N. Brigance, *Jeremiah Sullivan Black: A Defender of the Constitution and the Ten Commandments* (Philadelphia: University of Pennsylvania Press, 1934), 59.
8. *Ableman,* 62 U.S. 515–16.
9. Federal marshals made repeated attempts to imprison Booth beginning in April 1860, but they were thwarted by the violent resistance of his supporters. He was finally taken into custody in October and subsequently pardoned by President Buchanan in March 1861. Baker, *Joshua Glover,* 168.
10. Cover, *Justice Accused,* 255.
11. *Ex Parte Bushnell,* 9 Ohio St. 77, 198 (Ohio 1859) (emphasis and punctuation original).
12. All of the Wellingtonians had been released by the end of May. Most had accepted plea bargains—as part of Belden's effort to separate them from the Oberliners—in which they renounced the defense and the defense lawyers. A few, such as elderly Matthew Gillet, had rejected Belden's terms and refused to plead guilty, leading the prosecutor simply to dismiss the charges against them.
13. John M. Langston, *From the Virginia Plantation to the National Capitol,* repr. ed. (Hartford, CT: American Publishing Co., 1894; North Stratford, NH: Ayer Co. Publishers, 2002), 190.

Epilogue

1. David S. Reynolds, *John Brown, Abolitionist: The Man Who Killed Slavery, Sparked the Civil War, and Seeded Civil Rights* (New York: Alfred A. Knopf, 2005), 37.

2. Ibid., 121–122.

3. "The Harper's Ferry Outbreak," *New York Herald,* Morning Edition, October 21, 1859, 1.

4. John M. Langston, *From the Virginia Plantation to the National Capitol,* repr. ed. (Hartford, CT: American Publishing Co., 1894; North Stratford, NH: Ayer Co. Publishers, 2002), 191.

5. Ibid., 192. Writing more than thirty years after the fact, John Mercer Langston's memory may have been inaccurate, or he might have been exaggerating somewhat for emphasis. Leary's wife was pregnant when he left Oberlin to join John Brown, and the child was not born until after the Harpers Ferry raid. Whatever hopes Leary expressed for the security of his wife and child, he could not have known that the baby would be a girl. Arnold Rampersad, *The Life of Langston Hughes, Vol. I: 1902–1941: I, Too, Sing America* (New York: Oxford University Press, 2002), 6; see also William Cheek and Aimee Lee Cheek, *John Mercer Langston and the Fight for Black Freedom, 1829–65* (Urbana and Chicago: University of Illinois Press, 1989), 354.

6. Langston Hughes, *The Big Sea* (New York: Hill & Wang, 1940), 12.

7. John D. Lawson, ed., *American State Trials: A Collection of the Important and Interesting Criminal Trials Which Have Taken Place in the United States, from the Beginning of Our Government to the Present Day,* 17 vols. (St Louis: F. H. Thomas Law Book Co., 1916), 6:724n28. In 1859, Harpers Ferry was in Virginia; today it is in West Virginia.

8. Quoted in Stephen B. Oates, *To Purge This Land with Blood: A Biography of John Brown* (New York: Harper & Row, 1970), 311.

9. For a full account of the legal proceedings, from indictment to verdict, see Brian McGinty, *John Brown's Trial* (Cambridge, MA: Harvard University Press, 2009).

10. Reynolds, *John Brown,* 353.

11. Ibid., 355.

12. Lawson, *American State Trials,* 6:801.

13. Quoted in Jules Abels, *Man On Fire: John Brown and the Cause of Liberty* (New York: Macmillan Co., 1971), 314. Quoted in Oates, *To Purge This Land,* 318.

14. Charles Langston, "A Card," *Cleveland Plain Dealer,* November 18, 1859. Langston also ridiculed Joshua Giddings, Gerrit Smith, and other abolitionists who were "so hasty in denying all connections with [Brown] or sympathy with his ends and aims," opining that they feared for their political futures. In contrast, Langston pointed out that he had "no political prospects and therefore no political fears," which therefore allowed him to freely express "the very deepest sympathy with the Immortal John Brown in his heroic and daring efforts to free the slaves."

15. Quoted in Reynolds, *John Brown,* 366.

16. Reynolds, *John Brown,* 367, 359. Robert E. McGlone, *John Brown's War against Slavery* (New York: Cambridge University Press, 2009), 317.

17. Brian McGinty, *John Brown's Trial* (Cambridge, MA: Harvard University Press, 2009), 258.

18. Michael W. Kauffman, *American Brutus: John Wilkes Booth and the Lincoln Conspiracies* (New York: Random House, 2004), 110.

19. Quoted in Oates, *To Purge This Land*, 320.

20. Reynolds, *John Brown*, 422.

21. Lincoln's friend and law partner, William Herndon, corresponded for years with Theodore Parker, including a series of letters following Parker's indictment for the failed Anthony Burns rescue attempt. Joseph Fort Newton, *Lincoln and Herndon* (Cedar Rapids, IA: Torch Press, 1910), 82–87; David Herbert Donald, *Lincoln's Herndon: A Biography* (New York: Alfred A. Knopf, 1948), 54–55.

22. Doris Kearns Goodwin, *Team of Rivals: The Political Genius of Abraham Lincoln* (New York: Simon & Schuster, 2005), 167. Roy P. Basler, ed., *The Collected Works of Abraham Lincoln,* 9 vols. (Piscataway, NJ: Rutgers University Press, 1953), 3:386.

23. James Brewer Stewart, *Holy Warriors: The Abolitionists and American Slavery* (New York: Hill & Wang, 1976), 184. Seymour Drescher, *Abolition: A History of Slavery and Antislavery* (New York: Cambridge University Press, 2009), 327. Don Fehrenbacher, *The Slaveholding Republic* (New York: Oxford University Press, 2001), 245.

24. *Report of the Trial of John Hossack, Indicted for Rescuing a Fugitive Slave from the U.S. Deputy Marshal, at Ottawa, October 20th, 1859* (Chicago: Press and Tribune Steam Book and Printing Office, 1860), 218, reproduced in Paul Finkelman, ed., *Slavery, Race, and the American Legal System 1700–1872, Series II, Fugitive Slaves and the American Courts: The Pamphlet Literature,* 4 vols. (New York: Garland Publishing, 1988), 4:384.

25. Goodwin, *Team of Rivals*, 241–243. The 1859 Ohio Republican convention had denied renomination to Chief Justice Joseph Swan following his denial of habeas corpus to Langston and Bushnell, thus splitting the party into factions that remained at odds the following year.

26. Stanley W. Campbell, *The Slave Catchers: Enforcement of the Fugitive Slave Law, 1850–1860* (New York: W. W. Norton & Co., 1968), 206–207.

27. Fehrenbacher, *Slaveholding Republic,* 248.

28. James Buchanan, "Fourth Annual Message," in James D. Richardson, *A Compilation of the Messages and Papers of the Presidents,* 20 vols. (New York: Bureau of National Literature, 1897), 7:3169.

29. David M. Potter, *Lincoln and His Party in the Secession Crisis* (New Haven, CT: Yale University Press, 1942), 100. Fehrenbacher, *Slaveholding Republic,* 248. Thomas D. Morris, *Free Men All: The Personal Liberty Laws of the North, 1780–1861* (Baltimore: Johns Hopkins University Press, 1999), 204.

30. Quoted in Potter, *Lincoln and His Party,* 167–168.

31. Morris, *Free Men All,* 206.

32. Walter A. McDougall, *Throes of Democracy: The American Civil War Era, 1829–1877* (New York: HarperCollins, 2008), 395.

33. Campbell, *Slavecatchers,* 192.

34. Ibid., 190–192.

35. Ibid., 194.

ACKNOWLEDGMENTS

Everyone writing about the history of law and slavery owes a debt of gratitude to Paul Finkelman, whose scholarship has addressed almost every aspect of the field. In particular, I have benefited greatly from his collection, *Fugitive Slaves and American Courts: The Pamphlet Literature,* which reproduced many of the most important primary source materials for this book. Paul also encouraged me as I pursued this project, and he generously provided answers to questions that might otherwise have taken me countless hours to discover on my own.

There have been many excellent books about individual fugitive cases. I have especially relied on the following: Thomas Slaughter, *Bloody Dawn: The Christiana Riot and Racial Violence in the Antebellum North;* Jonathan Katz, *Resistance at Christiana: The Fugitive Slave Rebellion;* Ella Forbes, *But We Have No Country: The 1851 Christiana, Pennsylvania Resistance;* Garry Collison, *Shadrach Minkins: From Fugitive Slave to Citizen;* Albert Von Frank, *The Trials of Anthony Burns: Freedom and Slavery in Emerson's Boston;* Nat Brandt, *The Town that Started the Civil War;* Steven Weisenburger, *Modern Medea: A Family Story of Slavery and Child-Murder from the Old South.*

Three Northwestern University graduate students provided invaluable assistance: Timothy Barouch (communication studies) and Stefanie Bator (history) helped me sharpen and shorten the manuscript, and Jeane Lasser (law) tracked down endless citations and sources. For helpful comments on the many iterations of the manuscript, I am also grateful to Steven Calabresi, Robert Clarke, Bob Yovovich, Stephen Presser, Malick Ghachem, James Schulz, Jeffrey Berkson, Mark Dworkin, Walter Stahr, John McGinnis, Kurt Mitenbuler, Andrew Connor, Arnold Kanter, Ralph Levin, and two anonymous reviewers for the Harvard University Press. For editorial and research assistance, I want to thank Ann Nelson, Marcia Lehr, Erika Nunez, Cynthia Douglas, Pegeen Bassett, Michael Feinberg, Lynn Kincaid, Kathleen Drummy, Antoinette Smith, Michael Haggett, and Peter Neumer.

It would take several pages to fully express my gratitude to Kathleen McDermott of the Harvard University Press, and even that would probably be inadequate. This book would not have been possible without her encouragement, patience, and support, which made a crucial difference at every stage of the process. Many thanks are also due to Ike Williams and Hope Denekamp of the Kneerim & Williams literary agency, who helped guide my progress from start to finish.

I am, as always, grateful for research support from the Spray Trust Fund of the Northwestern University School of Law, and for the encouragement of Dean David Van Zandt.

One of the great joys of late middle age is that my children are now well-educated adults. They have been graciously willing to read excerpts or bat around ideas, and to give me the benefit of their critical thinking (which was tempered, although never displaced, by tolerant affection). Thank you, Natan and Sarah. Thanks also to my nephew Ari, who is always interested in the arc of a good story.

As everyone who knows her immediately recognizes, my wife, Linda Lipton, is brilliant and inspiring. She took time from her own demanding and important work to help me with the manuscript, adding focus and precision to almost every chapter (and especially to the Introduction). I wish I could convince her to wear gardening gloves, but other than that she is perfect.

INDEX

Index

11-30-10